Jews in Germany after the Holocaust

Cambridge Cultural Social Studies

Titles in the series
ILANA FRIEDRICH SILBER, *Virtuosity, charisma, and social order*
LINDA NICHOLSON AND STEVEN SEIDMAN (eds.), *Social postmodernism*
WILLIAM BOGARD, *The simulation of surveillance*
SUZANNE R. KIRSCHNER, *The religious and Romantic origins of psychoanalysis*
PAUL LICHTERMAN, *The search for political community*
ROGER FRIEDLAND AND RICHARD HECHT, *To rule Jerusalem*
KENNETH H. TUCKER, *French revolutionary syndicalism and the public sphere*
ERIK RINGMAR, *Identity, interest and action*
ALBERTO MELUCCI, *The playing self*
ALBERTO MELUCCI, *Challenging codes*
SARAH M. CORSE, *Nationalism and literature*
DARNELL M. HUNT, *Screening the Los Angeles "riots"*
LYNETTE P. SPILLMAN, *Nation and commemoration*
MICHAEL MULKAY, *The embryo research debate*
CHANDRA MUKERJI, *Territorial ambitions and the gardens of Versailles*

What is it like to be Jewish and to be born and raised in
Germany after the Holocaust? Based on remarkably
candid interviews with nearly one hundred German
Jews, Lynn Rapaport's book reveals a rare understanding of how the memory of the Holocaust shapes
Jews' everyday lives. As their views of non-Jewish
Germans, of themselves, their political integration into
German society, and their friendships and relationships
with Germans are subtly uncovered, the obstacles to
readjustment when sociocultural memory is still present
are better understood. This is also a book about Jewish
identity in the midst of modernity. It shows how the
boundaries of ethnicity are not marked by how religious
Jews are, or their absorption of traditional culture, but
by the moral distinctions rooted in Holocaust memory
that Jews draw between themselves and other Germans.

Jews in Germany after the Holocaust

Memory, identity and Jewish–German relations

Lynn Rapaport
Pomona College

PUBLISHED BY THE PRESS SYNDICATE OF THE UNIVERSITY OF CAMBRIDGE
The Pitt Building, Trumpington Street, Cambridge CB2 1RP, United Kingdom

CAMBRIDGE UNIVERSITY PRESS
The Edinburgh Building, Cambridge CB2 2RU, United Kingdom
40 West 20th Street, New York, NY 10011–4211, USA
10 Stamford Road, Oakleigh, Melbourne 3166, Australia

© Lynn Rapaport 1997

First published 1997

Printed in the United Kingdom at the University Press, Cambridge

Typeset in Times 10/12½ pt

A catalogue record for this book is available from the British Library

Library of Congress cataloguing in publication data

Rapaport, Lynn.
Jews in Germany after the Holocaust: memory, identiry,
and Jewish–German relations / Lynn Rapaport.
    p.   cm. – (Cambridge cultural social studies)
Includes bibliographical references and index.
ISBN 0 521 58219 9. – ISBN 0 521 58809 X (pbk.)
1. Jews – Germany – History – 1945–
2. Holocaust survivors – Germany.
3. Holocaust, Jewish (1939–1945) – Germany – Influence.
4. Jews – Germany – Identity.
5. Germany – Ethnic relations.
I. Title.   II. Series.
DS135.G332R37 1997
943′.004924 – dc20   96-41211 CIP

ISBN 0 521 58219 9 hardback
ISBN 0 521 58809 X paperback

CE

For my mother Ryvka, in memory and with love

Contents

Acknowledgments   *page* x

Setting the stage: the Jewish community of Frankfurt and the
voices of its members   1

1 Holocaust memory and Jewish identity   13
2 Living in the land of the murderers? How Jews who live in
   Germany view Germans   39
3 Here in Germany I am a Jew: identity images and the criteria
   for group membership   83
4 I have German citizenship but I wouldn't call myself a German:
   ethnic group loyalty and the lack of national affiliation   125
5 My friends are not typical Germans: the character of
   Jewish–German friendships   162
6 Interethnic intimacy: the character of Jewish–German sex, love,
   and intermarriage   205
7 Theoretical implications and future research   252

   Appendix   263
   Notes   269
   Select bibliography   294
   Index   318

Acknowledgments

What a thrill to write the acknowledgments for this book, and what a challenge to try to thank all those who have helped me in big and small ways. Unfortunately, because of space limitations and obligations of confidentiality, I can only acknowledge a few people by name, and apologize to those not mentioned. Foremost, I am greatly indebted to the interviewees who generously shared their lives with me and showed me their courage and pain. In Germany, Wilfred Kaib, Dieter Klein, Ernst Maug, and Stefan Szajak facilitated my research in very practical ways.

I was fortunate to be guided at different stages of this work by two great sociologists, Herbert Gans and Jeffrey Alexander. As my dissertation advisor, Herbert Gans taught me to be a careful fieldworker, to be true to my data, and most importantly, to be an independent and critical thinker. Jeffrey Alexander nurtured this project from a dissertation to a book – his enthusiasm was encouraging and his concrete suggestions inspiring, as he helped me frame my argument more deeply in cultural studies. I will always be grateful to both of them.

Several other colleagues read most, if not all, of earlier drafts of this work, including Anny Bakalian, Jonathan Cole, Lily Gardner Feldman, Saul Friedlander, Eric Hirsch, Terese Lyons, Charles Meier, Peter Marcuse, Jeffrey Peck, Monika Richarz, Gunther Roth, Ernestine Schlant, and Allan Silver. I thank them for their comments and constructive suggestions, and apologize for any remaining unrealized. Thanks also to Rebecca Boehling, Gayle Hamilton, Robert Herman, Greg Hoertz, Jackson Janes, Christain Joppke, Anna Karpathakis, Philip Kasinitz, Robert Markens, Manfred Stassen, and George Steinmetz. Some of them listened patiently while I thought out loud. Others showed much appreciated support at important times. Jurgen Froehlich double-checked my German, and Maxine Rude and Yad Vashem

Archives generously supplied the photos used to create the cover. A special thanks to Sheila Pinkel, a real trooper, for creating the final photograph for the cover, and to my colleague and pal, Lynn Mulkey, for trying to keep me sane (though not always successfully) during the project's final stages. I am also especially thankful to Christian Klingenberg and to my father, Mayer Rapaport, who, in their own ways, helped inspire the idea for this book, and to my mother, Ryvka Rapaport, whose memory motivated me to pursue it.

I received generous support from a number of institutions including the Graduate School of Arts and Sciences of Columbia University, Pomona College, the German Academic Exchange Service (DAAD), the Fredrich Ebert Foundation, the American Association of University Women, and the Robert Bosch Foundation. The final draft of this book was written at the American Institute for Contemporary German Studies at Johns Hopkins University, which provided an ideal setting for informal discussions of work in progress, and a Bosch seminar that brought several prominent scholars to the institute to read and critique my work.

At Cambridge University Press, this book benefited from the expert advice of the series editor, Catherine Max, and the careful attention of the copyeditor, Sheila Kane.

Finally, my husband, Stephen V. Marks, deserves a medal of honor! He has read the entire manuscript more times than I had the right to ask. It was my good fortune to have married another academic who was also a computer guru, a great in-house editor, and Mr. Organized! His skills, and, most importantly, his love, have been invaluable.

Setting the stage: the Jewish community of Frankfurt and the voices of its members

"What is past is not dead; it is not even past."
(Christa Wolf, *Patterns of Childhood*. Trans. U. Molinaro and
H. Rappolt. New York: Farrar, Strauss, and Giroux, 1980)

The ghetto in the city

Large modern skyscrapers explode from Frankfurt's main streets, testimony to its postwar recovery. Old churches huddle in its alleyways, serving as landmarks to its history. The city is bustling as electric trolley cars transport city dwellers to and from school and work. The streets are congested with automobiles, and cyclists monopolize stone-paved paths on the sidewalks. Shoppers stroll down Frankfurt's main boulevards, while others sit in outdoor cafes smoking, drinking, or just enjoying the day's weather. Frankfurt has all the characteristics of modern city life, general bustle and commotion.

The city is a thriving industrial and commercial center situated about 330 feet above sea level on the banks of the Main river in the state of Hesse. Its location, north of the Upper Rhine Lowlands and about 19 miles east of the confluence of the Rhine and Main rivers at Mainz, makes it a crossroads for land and water traffic. The Frankfurt Rhine-Main airport, the third largest in Europe, is on its doorstep, its harbor is a center for domestic shipping, and the West German railroads converge at its train station. Two main freeways, the Hamburg–Basel highway and the Cologne–Nuremberg highway, intersect just 6 miles to the southwest.

With rapid postwar reconstruction, Frankfurt has become a modern international metropolis. It is Germany's financial capital, the seat of the Bundesbank – the German equivalent of the Federal Reserve – and home to several hundred credit institutions, branches, subsidiaries, or offices of major domestic, continental, and foreign banks. It has become a center for international trade fairs, including exhibitions for furs, books, automobiles, and textiles.

The city is the largest in the state of Hesse, with a total population in 1994 of 652,412. It is populated with more immigrants than other German cities, and has a large American presence, including the United States military, other government agencies, and American business organizations. Excluding the US military, about 24 percent of Frankfurt's inhabitants are foreigners, more than in other German cities. Most are workers from Mediterranean countries – Turks, Yugoslavs, Italians, Greeks, and Spaniards.

A person visiting Frankfurt today would hardly notice a Jewish presence, but 5,715 persons are registered with the authorities as Jews.[1] These persons constitute the membership of the Frankfurt Jewish *Gemeinde* (community).[2] Jews are known to have been present in Frankfurt as early as the twelfth century. During the Middle Ages, Frankfurt was home to one of the largest Jewish ghettos in central Europe. The Börneplatz, a square just east of the old town center, harbors traces of this community's momentous past. There lies what is left of an old Jewish cemetery, the stone gates that once led to the *Judengasse* (the old Jewish ghetto), and a plaque to commemorate the site of an old Jewish synagogue that reads in English and in German: "Here stood the Börneplatz Synagogue that was destroyed by Nazi criminals on the 9th day of November, 1938."[3] Next to the cemetery in the *Judengasse* museum, are ruins of five old homes, two Mikvahs,[4] and the original wall that surrounded the ghetto.[5]

Today the Jewish community has moved away from the Börneplatz. It is dispersed throughout Frankfurt to various locations, but most of its institutions lie to the west of the old Jewish ghetto. The symbol of the community's existence, its main synagogue, lies in the Westend. The Westend is a mainly middle-class neighborhood filled with well-kept, freshly painted townhouses of various architectural eras. The synagogue is situated a few blocks north of the Bochenheimer Landstrasse, a one-time promenade. Just to its east is Frankfurt's famous botanical garden, the Palmengarten, that sits on the edge of the green pastures of Frankfurt's renowned Grüneburg Park.

The Westend Synagogue, an early-twentieth-century shrine, is a grand presence, as its 1,200 seats occupy over half of the block. It is the only synagogue in Frankfurt to survive the Nazi conflagration, and is the site where official commemorative services are usually held. During the high holidays, the synagogue becomes noticeably alive. As Jews take off from work, dress up, fast, and come there to pray, the German police, for security reasons, cordon off the surrounding side-streets.

A few blocks to the south of the main synagogue on a street called Westend, about 500 yards from where Max Horkheimer once lived, lies the headquarters of the Jewish *Gemeinde*. The *Gemeinde* center is a multiple-story complex of two modern white-stone and glass buildings, with a parking lot in between. The building facing Westend Street houses a kindergarten and the bureaucratic offices that attend to the financial and legal business of the community. During the day two German police vans remain parked in the driveway.

Around the corner on a street called Savignystrasse lies the other building. High above its entrance a giant metal Menorah stands grandly. To the left of the Menorah is a Torah (the Jewish tablet of law) carved out of white stone. The Torah is fractured to symbolize the break that exists in Jewish–German relations in the aftermath of the Holocaust.

Most visible community activity takes place within the *Gemeinde* center's walls. Jewish clubs hold their weekly meetings in it, and the youth center is headquartered there. Lectures, slide-shows, and parties take place there, and classes are given regularly ranging from elementary Hebrew to ballet. A restaurant serves kosher and Israeli-style dishes, and Sabbath meals can be ordered in advance. There is a ballroom, a gymnasium, and a grade-school, and there is talk of creating a Jewish *Gymnasium* (high school). It is also the site where Jewish students often congregate. They have a Jewish students' organization, and meetings and activities are held at least once a week. About fifteen students are regulars.

The buildings at first glance appear quite ordinary: modern office buildings on a commonplace, tree-lined residential street. But a closer look suggests a fortified secret lodge equipped with an elaborate security system, including bullet-proof glass, and electric security doors, features not often seen in Frankfurt on ordinary buildings.[6] A security guard is posted in an office at the entrance hall and to enter the building one must be prepared to show identification.

The Jews who make up the Frankfurt community come from all age groups and all walks of life. Some are remnants of the original pre-war community, and some are their descendants. Others are newcomers who have settled there after being liberated from concentration camps, and some are their descendants. Some were strangers to Germany. Others had lived there before the war, and returned thereafter to claim pensions and to die in peace.

Their waking hours are spent predominantly within the company of Germans, as they work, go to school, shop, pursue recreational activities, and attend to the daily business of living. Yet the Jews of Frankfurt will say that they live in an invisible ghetto. It is invisible because there are no physical barriers such as ghetto gates or walls to effectively block their contact with the city or to impede them from developing social relationships with Germans. Nonetheless, Frankfurt's Jews will say that they experience walls or barriers between themselves and the Germans in whose midst they live.

To see this ghetto, one must be aware of the culture of the community and of the institutions and organizations that constitute its social fabric. The central theme around which community life is organized can be summarized as an edict like "One Shall Keep One's Distance From The Germans." The institutions and organizations of the community contribute to this isolationist stance as they function to make the community self-sufficient. It is in this way that the Jews of Frankfurt and their institutions form a social and cultural ghetto. The ghetto is physically dispersed throughout Frankfurt, and its members are actively engaged in the dynamic life of this bustling city. Yet the Jews of this community are cemented together and isolated from the rest of the German population as they experience their problems and pursue common efforts and goals.

Voices of the present that call out to the past

Samuel: The decisive one

Samuel talks openly and excitedly. He is alert, and moves quickly. He is tall and lean, with straight jet black hair and light blue eyes. He shows me into his law office. We are there after hours. Samuel is a professional man – an attorney with a solid income that makes him, according to German standards, upper middle class. He wears a *Mogen David* (Star of David) around his neck, a Jewish emblem that was given to him by his mother. "It's an emotional choice to wear it," he says. He is Jewish, and never wants to hide that fact. He believes that most people can tell that he is Jewish when they see him, but says that he is always surprised to find out that most of the time they don't know. Nevertheless, it is important for him that people know he is Jewish. It defines in a primordial manner who he is.

Samuel was born in 1948 in Freiburg, a city in the German state of Baden-Württemberg. His family moved to Constance after he was born. "Many Jews gathered in Constance at that time, because they thought it was going to be annexed by Switzerland," he explains. In 1961 his family moved to the United States, and settled in the orthodox Jewish community of Williamsburg, in the heart of Brooklyn, New York. They wanted him to learn more about Judaism. He and his family became immersed in the orthodox Jewish religious community life there, but it was too confining for his father's tastes. Neither of his parents liked it there, or in the United States for that matter. At that time his father was forty-five-years old and found a job in a metal factory. "It wasn't a question of money or of social status," Samuel explains, "they just didn't like it there." They couldn't adjust, and came back to Germany because they already knew the language, had friends there, and had networks and connections. After they came back to Germany, they said in retrospect that they should have stayed in the US. They had reservations about immigrating to Israel, because they knew that Samuel would have to go into the army. They came back to the place that they knew. "I don't think the moral question ever entered their mind," says Samuel.

Both of Samuel's parents are from Poland and survived the war in concentration camps. His mother was in Bergen-Belsen. She saw her mother and sister go through the selection process. Her mother was placed on one side, and her two sisters on another. Her siblings wanted to go with her mother, and she saw them being taken away. "She has a guilt complex as to why she didn't go with the others who were killed," Samuel says. He tells me that his parents hate the Germans. "How can you not? My mother's family was wiped out completely. Of course they hate them, and they have no social intercourse with Germans." But they hate the Poles even more. "Compared to the Poles, the Germans were angels," he says. Samuel has a more rational attitude toward Germans. Sometimes he hates them, just like his parents, but mostly for different reasons. "Being an attorney, I know what goes on in Germany," he remarks. "Not much has changed in this country. I think German democracy rests on 250,000 American soldiers. All of Europe keeps a close watch on Germany. On the outside, that's the only thing that keeps Germany democratic. On the inside, not much has changed."

Like his parents, Samuel is very active in Jewish community life in Germany, where he belongs to many social clubs, and has many Jewish friends. He has a steady Jewish girlfriend whom he eventually wants to marry. There are many wealthy women that he could have married here in Frankfurt, he tells me, but that's not what he is looking for. He's looking for the warmth of a Jewish home. We are interrupted momentarily by a knock on the door. It is Samuel's girlfriend Rachel, a tall, thin and lovely young woman with dark brown hair and sparkling emerald green eyes. He introduces me to Rachel, and tells her that he will phone her later when he is through with the interview. As she leaves, he asks me rhetorically whether any German woman could possibly compete in attractiveness with a Jewish woman who looks like Rachel. "German women don't look like that," he tells me with a wink.

David: the tranquil one

The doorbell rings uncannily at exactly 7.30 p.m. I walk to the door to greet David, a twenty-eight-year-old economist, who has offered to come to my apartment in Frankfurt for the interview. David is a young, athletic, and well-groomed man with straight, light-brown hair and big, round brown eyes. He is wearing tight stone-washed blue jeans, and an open-collared Oxford shirt, which makes him look younger than he actually is. He has boyish good-looks, and impeccable manners. His smile is warm and friendly. He is an elegant man, charming and well-bred.

He tells me that he doesn't have many problems living in Germany, although he did contemplate moving to the United States about two years ago, after he returned from living eight months in New York, where he studied urban economics at the New School for Social Research. He enjoyed living in New York. It was the first time he had left Frankfurt for an extended period. "Sometimes I have to say it felt good not to feel like a stranger," he says. "You have more than 2 million Jews in New York. It's more normal to be a Jew in New York. I enjoyed being something normal."

Nonetheless, he tells me that he has a pretty normal relationship with Germans. He can live comfortably in Germany and rarely feels disappointed. He doesn't rule out that the Holocaust could occur again, but he reminds me that the Holocaust did not occur only in Germany. Other countries throughout the world were involved: America implemented immigration quotas on Jews and Switzerland closed its borders to frantic persecuted refugees.

He thinks that other Jews have more problems living in Germany than he does because they isolate themselves as a group from Germans. He explains

When you isolate yourself, automatically you are unhappy. Then others dislike you because you are not content, and then you live here as this strange person. Then you start feeling hate. Maybe hate is too strong a word, but I think that there are two possibilities. Either you assimilate, and this doesn't mean that you give up your Jewishness, but that you are willing to accept aspects of another culture, or you leave... I don't believe you can be happy living in a country that you hate where you isolate yourself from the other citizens.

David's interest in Jewish culture began when he was twelve years old. Prior to preparation for his Bar-Mitzvah, he knew very little about Judaism. He identifies with Jewishness because of his heritage, but he emphasizes that he is not a religious man. "I would never forget where I come from," he says. "Of course, I try to defend everything that Israel does, and what the Jewish people are doing. I know about my Jewish heritage and my Jewish tradition."

David has many good Jewish friends, and many good German friends. He deals with Germans quite differently from the way his parents do. His parents have very little contact with Germans, and don't accept most of his German friends. "There is only one German friend that I have that my mother accepts," he remarks. "She says of him [the friend], 'He is one who would have hidden you just in case...' That's what they think. That's the dimension." He says that he is one of the few Jewish people in Germany who has a very healthy mixture of Jewish and non-Jewish friends.

The problems he encounters living his life in Germany come most directly from his parents. In particular, he can never bring home a non-Jewish girlfriend. If he did, his parents would disown him. As Holocaust survivors from Poland, he says, naturally they are distrustful of Germans. They already disowned him once in his past when he had a serious long-term relationship with a German woman. They cut off his allowance, and continually urged him to break off the relationship. It created problems in his relationship with his girlfriend, because she had difficulty accepting that his parents were so painfully prejudiced against her. Nonetheless, he could imagine marrying a non-Jewish woman, even if it meant becoming alienated from his parents. That she might be German in addition to being a non-Jew, though, would clearly magnify the pain. "I don't know whether they would forgive me if one day I married a non-Jewish girl," he says, but he doesn't exclude the possibility. "I can't live on an island, or off on another planet here in the middle of Germany. I can't orient myself that way," he explains.

He contemplates the possibility of one day marrying a German woman. He doesn't feel very comfortable making stark categorical distinctions between Jews and Germans. The significant criterion for him is the quality of the person, regardless of their national origin or religious affiliation. "Of course I would have problems with a girl who comes from the bushlands, who is uneducated, illiterate, and hygienically underdeveloped," he says. "But as long as they come from my cultural circle it's really irrelevant to me if the person is Jewish, non-Jewish, American, or German."

David believes he lives a fairly normal life as a Jew in Germany. Other Jews, he speculates, have more problems because they orient themselves toward the wishes of their parents, and conduct their lives according to their parents' demands. This does not mean, however, that he is any less a Jew. On the contrary, he strongly identifies with his Jewishness, and will always try to pass on the tradition to his children, even if it is not within the context of a domestic partnership with a Jewish woman. His children, he believes, should have the opportunity to decide for themselves whether they wish to be Jews or Germans. "I see a future for Jews here in Germany," he says. "I know people who aren't coming to terms with this conflict. I can understand those people who move to America or to Israel. It's a personal decision, and it depends a lot on how one was brought up. But me? I have a pretty normal relationship to Germans."

Betty: the conflicted one

On a summer's day on a lazy Sunday afternoon, I meet with Betty, a thirty-two-year-old Jewish woman who was born and raised in Frankfurt. With one sweep of her hand she adjusts her dark wavy hair, so that it falls more naturally along the contours of her delicate but beautiful ivory skinned face. She is intelligent, warm, friendly, and eager to describe to me the intimate details of her life. She holds a master's degree in psychology, and works full-time as a practicing psychotherapist. She tells me that it was not a coincidence that she went into this health-care profession. She believes that living in Germany has made her reflect upon and try to analyze a lot of issues. We begin to talk about her family background.

Betty's father was born in Kiev, Russia, in 1919. His medical studies came to an abrupt halt when the war erupted, and he was forced to enlist in the Russian army. After the war he became a military engineer, and for a short time held a professorship at the University of Warsaw. Neither he nor his family suffered terribly at the hands of Hitler. His family suffered more under Stalin's rule, she says.

Betty's mother was born in 1925 in a small Jewish shtetl near Warsaw. She first was transferred to the Warsaw ghetto, and while there fought with the partisans. Later, she was transported to Auschwitz. As the train made a stop while *en route* to the concentration camp, a member of the Gestapo let her off. He kicked her out, she explains. Her mother was a beautiful woman, only thirteen years of age at the time. Perhaps she was "making eyes" at him. Betty speculates it was her beauty that eventually saved her.

Betty's mother then fled to Russia on false papers that stated she was married to a Russian man. Betty does not know how her mother spent the rest of the war years. Her mother barely speaks about it, only in bits and pieces. Betty tells me that her parents met at a party in Poland after the war. Her mother was then working as a diplomatic journalist at the Russian embassy in Warsaw. They fell in love, but were unable to marry, because her papers stated that she already had a husband in Russia. They made aliyah to Israel where they were eventually able to straighten out the papers and tie the knot.[7]

Her mother did not adjust well to life in Israel. Betty explains that her mother had created a very comfortable life for herself in Poland working for the diplomatic corps, and the conditions in Israel at the time were very harsh. The country was very rugged, and the hot humid climate exacerbated her skin problems until she became seriously physically ill. After four years in Israel, her parents decided to return to Germany because they had a cousin there, with the intention of eventually immigrating to the United States.

Betty doesn't know why her parents never emigrated. More than forty years after they came to Germany, her parents still talk of leaving. Betty has a younger sister who is studying in Paris. Her sister, she says, was not happy in Germany, and never plans to return. Betty also wishes to leave someday. She dreams of moving to California, perhaps San Diego or Los Angeles.

Betty grew up in a non-religious home. Her family never celebrated any of the Jewish holidays, and her parents do not go to the synagogue. Her father comes from a family of staunch communists, and has an aversion toward religion. Her mother is not religious either. All of her mother's family perished during the war, and because of that her mother no longer believes in God. Nevertheless, Betty states adamantly that she still received a very Jewish upbringing. She tells me that she is a proud Jew, being educated in Jewish history and literature. She acquired this pride from her father, who often read to her from the Bible. The pride is not based on the religious doctrine, but on the strength of Jewish heritage, its history.

She has been married for less than two years to a thirty-five-year-old German man named Klaus, who is Catholic. They have one child, a two-year-old boy. She feels guilty that she married a German man, even though her parents accept him wholeheartedly. She says her parents love him because "he is a good human being." He's not "typically German": he is different – warm and loving. Yet she continues to feel conflicted.

As she speaks, tears roll from her eyes. She wanted to marry a Jew. Her first husband was a Jewish man, someone she grew up with and knew well her entire life. Their parents knew each other, and had been close friends. She dated him for several years, and finally married because it was "easy." It seemed the right thing to do. The marriage fell apart after only four years. She outgrew him and realized that she was no longer in love.

With her second husband, it was love at first sight. She didn't mean to fall in love with a German man. It wasn't her fault. It was just something that happened, something over which she felt she had no control. She tries to explain to me why she feels conflicted. She describes the following incident. A while back, she had left her child at her mother-in-law's house for the day. That afternoon the movie *Sophie's Choice* was on television, and she decided to watch it. She began to identify with the main character, "Sophie," a Jew with two children living out the war in Auschwitz, who is forced to chose which of her children to save, and which to hand over to the Nazis to die. Betty then remembered how she herself had given her child to her mother-in-law. At that moment she didn't see her mother-in-law as a close family member, but as a German, a Nazi. She kept repeating to me that she had given her child to a German woman. She questioned her actions – how could she hand over her child to a German woman? It made her sad, and she started to cry.

She says her husband sees the pain she goes through at such times, and it makes him also feel sad. Her parents tell her that she cannot blame her husband for Germany's crimes of the past, because in essence he cannot change who he is. She could have chosen not to marry him, but, since she did, her parents tell her it is unfair of her to make him feel bad. She is still affected by this conflict, and during the interview she continued to cry.

Samuel, David, and Betty live in a world that is still haunted by the shocking events that occurred before any of them was born. None of them personally experienced Nazi persecution. The war caught their parents in diverse ways, in varying places, and at different stages of their lives. This drama of the past plays out differently in each of their lives, and they have each made different choices regarding how they will live effectively as Jews in Germany.

This book is about the role the collective memory of the Holocaust plays in shaping the lives of people like Samuel, David, and Betty, who grew up Jewish in post-World War II Germany. The choices that they have made in their lives regarding how to relate and interact with

Germans, are inescapably connected to the fact that they are all Jewish. Samuel grew up in a Jewish milieu, although his parents shunned the ultra-Orthodox tradition. His parents were incarcerated in concentration camps during the war, and like his parents he has inherited a distrust of Germans. David's parents are similarly of Eastern European origin, and also survived concentration camps. His parents distrust the Germans, and have gone so far as to have stopped supporting him when he was seriously romantically involved with a German woman. Yet David believes that he is more tolerant of Germans than his parents, and could imagine marrying a German woman one day. He feels content living in Germany. Betty grew up in a non-religious home, and her parents were not incarcerated in concentration camps. Her parents accept with open arms her spouse as a member of their family, yet it is she who married a German man, and who feels out of sorts.

The lives of people like Betty, David, and Samuel are nuanced, multi-faceted, and complex. There are no simple explanations for the types of choices they have made in their lives regarding whether to remain in Germany or emigrate, and to what extent they should have friendships or romantic entanglements with Germans. There are also no obvious explanations for the different ways in which the legacy of the Holocaust has impacted their lives. The overly emphasized assertion that all Jews whose parents survived concentration camps hate Germans today and wish to maintain their distance from them does not appear to be true. David is a typical illustration to the contrary – a man with tolerance and openness toward Germans. It is also incorrect to state that all Jews with tolerant parents who survived the war "relatively unharmed" (in comparison to other Jews) perceive no obstacles living with and among Germans. Betty's story is an example that refutes such a claim. Nor is it the case that all Jews whose parents were assimilated German Jews before the war have raised offspring who feel comfortable and integrated in Germany, or that all Jews whose parents were of other national origins have nourished children who feel less at ease in German society today. My data do not reveal such neatly correlated patterns.

What becomes apparent from these brief glimpses of a few very diverse people, and what shows through more generally, is that the legacy of the Holocaust has informed their experience of everyday life in Germany from its inception. The memory of the Holocaust impacts how Jews define themselves as a unique ethnic entity, how they draw boundaries between themselves and Germans, how they assess desirable and undesirable character traits in themselves and in Germans, and generally how classification systems are dramatized within Jewish culture in today's

Germany. It is this metaphor of the Holocaust, the lens through which Jews perceive and interpret everyday life in Germany, the tool they use to construct Jewish ethnic identity, the idiom which affects the tone of Jewish–German relationships, that I wish to explore in this book.

1

Holocaust memory and Jewish identity

Being a child of survivors, born just after the Holocaust in a German Displaced Person's Camp, I have always felt that I imbibed the Holocaust experience with my mother's milk. My parents' lives during the Holocaust is the substance of my dreams. What they experienced directly and consciously, I have experienced in indirect, attenuated form. Not only direct survivors of the Holocaust like my parents, nor just children of survivors like myself, but every Jew alive has internalized the Holocaust. We all live in a post-Holocaust world, a world in which the mass industrialized death of the Jews as a people is not an unimaginable nightmare but an accomplished fact.

(Miriam Greenspan, "Responses to the Holocaust," in Roger S. Gottlieb, *Thinking the Unthinkable*, Nahwah, NJ: Paulist Press, 1990)

This book tells the story of Jews who were born and raised in Germany in the aftermath of the Holocaust. It represents my attempt to grasp how they relate to Germans today, and how they construct their Jewish identity. This is a case study that pays close attention to a particular experience, based on the assumption that it will reveal patterns and designs that pervade other group experiences. The story I tell of how Jews construct their ethnicity can be seen as a sociological inquiry into the general pattern of ethnic identity construction.

Jews in Germany are not religious, have a high intermarriage rate, and outwardly display few ethnic symbols. By conventional standards, they would be considered members of a relatively weak ethnic subgroup. However, the way in which these Jews interact with Germans and construct their identity has profound implications for some of the most important issues in contemporary society, and for social science debates about the persistence and nature of ethnicity and interethnic relations in the face of modernization. For example, what is an ethnic group? How is ethnicity defined? What is the impact of the Holocaust on contemporary Jewish thought and on relations between Jews and Germans in the post-Holocaust world? How do increasingly non-religious Jews define themselves in relation to non-Jews in contemporary life? The answers that I will offer to these questions will be unusual ones, at least from the standpoint of contemporary social science debates. I will argue, for example, that ethnic groups are in many ways defined through the symbolic processes that their own members employ, not necessarily by economic or political interests or even by traditional cultural criteria. I will also argue that the Holocaust plays a central role in contemporary Jewish life in Germany, indeed, that it is the defining element on which ethnicity is based. Finally, I will suggest that we can better understand Jews' struggles for self-preservation in the modern and sometimes anti-Semitic world by adopting a cultural framework grounded in semiotics and the late-Durkheimian tradition to analyze Jewish identity and interethnic relations.

Defining ethnicity and understanding interethnic relations

Social scientists have long been concerned with the nature of ethnicity as a significant source of both group solidarity and intergroup cleavage in modern society. Discussion of these issues has largely been framed in terms of structuralist analyses that have viewed ethnicity as arising from the conscious efforts of individuals and groups to mobilize ethnic symbols in order to obtain access to social, political, and economic resources.[1] Many of these studies have focused on ethnicity as a group identity based on the collective perception of injustice. They have documented hostility and violence against ethnic groups, ethnic stratification, and the struggles of these groups for power and equality. Theories have emerged regarding discrimination manifested in dual labor markets, intercolonial relationships, and Marxist models of ethnic behavior.[2] In these models, ethnicity is viewed as power. The implication is that, as discrimination lessens and groups adapt to their host societies, symbols of ethnic distinction will disappear. Groups will assimilate culturally and structurally, and as Milton Gordon, Peter Blau, and others have argued, the degree of assimilation will be related on some level to how integrated these groups are within society.[3] If ethnicity still persists in spite of assimilation, it might be symbolic, a sentimental last grasp at an identity no longer relevant in people's everyday lives.[4]

But what happens when an ethnic group appears assimilated into the host society's cultural system, yet maintains a distinct sense of peoplehood that is not merely symbolic, but *is* relevant in their everyday lives, and is even an impediment to their integration in the host society? I will show that by any structural account Jews in Germany would be considered assimilated. German is their native tongue. They were educated in German schools, dress as Germans, eat German food, hold German citizenship, have a high rate of intermarriage, are not religious, and exhibit few of the standard indicators of Jewishness. However, inwardly their members draw subjective boundaries between themselves and Germans to maintain a distinct sense of peoplehood. Structuralist approaches would overlook crucial aspects of Jewish ethnicity and Jewish–German relations today because of how they define ethnicity and treat its core concepts, identity and culture. For instance, rather than asking people what ethnicity means to them, structuralist approaches predefine the way groups frame their identities by relying on crude categories and simple measures such as language, cultural traits, intermarriage, and the like.[5] By doing so, they ignore the role of other criteria, such as moral distinctions, in the creation of ethnic boundaries. These models impose *a priori* categories in the structuring of research questions about "ethnic consciousness" by using census data or surveys in which large numbers of people are asked relatively highly structured questions about ethnic practices, from which identity scales or models of accommodation are constructed.[6] While such data may be useful for discerning general trends in institutional membership, specific practices, and opinions, they shed little light on the processes by which groups distinguish themselves from others as coherent ethnic entities, and can thus misrepresent the nature of interethnic relations.

Given the use of these prespecified indicators of ethnic identity in the sociological literature, it is not surprising to discover that we know very little about how people construct their ethnic identities and interethnic relations. Sociologists argue that ethnicity is based on a shared cultural tradition, yet they study what they think ethnicity looks like instead of studying what ethnicity means to its members. No one has ever asked in a systematic way, for example, how Jews define their own ethnicity, what it means to them, what goes on in their heads as they create distinctions between themselves and non-Jews.

A more subjective approach to the issue is warranted: only through in-depth interviews can we begin to discern the process by which groups create ethnic distinctions, and gauge the character of interethnic relations. Thus, this book is based on an analysis of 83 semidirected interviews that I conducted in 1984 (and reinterviews with a subsample in 1994) with a stratified sample of Jews who were born and raised in

Germany after the Second World War (see the Appendix for methodological details).[7] The sample was drawn to include equal numbers of Jews whose parents had diverse survival experiences. Some survived concentration camps, some were in hiding, and others spent the war years in exile. I cast a wide net to include all types of second-generation Jews: those integrated and alienated from the Gemeinde, intellectuals and non-intellectuals, upper class and working class, more educated and less educated, more religiously oriented and less religiously oriented, single persons, some married to Jews, and some intermarried with Germans. I focus on second-generation Jews because they represent the future of Jewish life in Germany. Moreover, as I will argue below, their culture illuminates important theoretical issues about collective memory and ethnic identity, and their role in interpersonal relationships.

As sociologists have been documenting for years, both race and ethnicity are social constructions, based on the distinctions between "us" and "them." This study complements the subjective approaches to ethnicity that have focused on ethnic boundaries as determinants of identity. Most notable in this tradition is Fredrik Barth, who argued that it is at the boundaries of ethnic groups that ethnicity becomes meaningful, and that cultural content is less important, because groups become aware of their identity as they engage with one another.[8] However, very few studies have explored the mental maps by which groups perceive themselves as different in comparison to others. This study fills that gap. One of its contributions is to link the role of these mental maps to the construction of ethnic boundaries – the lines people draw when they categorize themselves and others. But it also shows that cultural content is indeed an important feature in this construction, contrary to the Barthian conclusion. By cultural content I do not mean the standard indicators of ethnicity, such as language, rituals, and traditions, but rather the cultural categories through which groups perceive themselves and others. Thus, this study explores the structures of thought through which ethnicity is constituted by focusing on the nature of the criteria that people use to define and distinguish themselves as a people different from others. I scrutinize the traits and values Jews mobilize to define themselves as superior or inferior to, or different from, Germans, as well as the resources from which they create these lines of distinction, and the significance of these boundaries for interethnic relationships.

I suggest that ethnicity is about a symbolic community, in which people create an imaginary "us" in contrast to imaginary "thems," and these distinctions largely shape their lives. This symbolic community encompasses a subjective dimension, an inner world based on mutual understanding and shared ideas. Thus, my approach is interpretive, suggesting that people do not just react to political and economic forces in a mechanical manner, but rather experience life, and while doing so try to find meaning.

By drawing from semiotics, and focusing on symbolic classifications organized around binary oppositions, we can study the inner world, the meaning that ethnicity has for Jews or for any ethnic group. In *Primitive Classification*, Emile Durkheim and Marcel Mauss argued that human beings name and classify things and people, creating labels through contrast and inclusion, and thus they articulated the relationship between classification and social organization.[9] Drawing on this logic, I show the utility of exploring the structured categories by which groups interpret their world, organize their actions, and behave interethnically. As Pierre Bourdieu suggested in *Distinction*, the principle of organization for all forms of social life is the logic of distinction.[10]

One contribution of this book is to break down the concept of "ethnic identity" to illustrate that the term contains many discrete meanings gathered under a common label and assigned a common status. From a microscopic view, a community's identity may be regarded as an aggregate collection of its members' many, often competing, identities, because a community's identity cannot exist outside those of its people, who create the distinctions between themselves and others. However, the meanings that ethnicity holds for people need not only be personal ones: they can be held collectively as a cultural system. These cultural systems are structured as common generalized interrelated categories of meaning. From an aerial view, these patterns of meanings form an ethnic boundary, which persists as long as these meanings are defended by in-group members.

How are distinctions formed? Perceptions take concrete forms as symbols and typifications, which operate on the basis of belief systems, all of which are firmly rooted in culture. Drawing on Durkheim's distinction between the sacred and the profane, Mary Douglas suggests that notions of "purity" and "impurity" are at the heart of cultural distinctions, and function to protect the integrity of belief systems. That is, what is considered dirty or impure is "matter out of its place" that upsets the classification system. By exploring the perceptions that groups have of themselves and others, and how they categorize themselves as "pure" and others as "contaminated," we can discover some of the characteristics that groups employ to create lines of distinction around themselves as unique ethnic entities.

As Anthony Giddens reminds us, meanings are recursive: they are not drawn out of a vacuum, but rather are deeply embedded within a society's culture and cut from its cultural cloth.[11] These meanings are constructed and transmitted to the group through socialization, and individuals modify and accommodate these meanings to conform to their own system of interpretation. In this book, I show how Judaism has become meaningful to Jews who live in Germany today, by illustrating that Jew–German constitutes a binary cultural code that protects and solidifies a sense of community. I also show how Jews employ their ethnic identity in everyday life by illustrating how this binary code supplies the structured categories of pure and impure into which every Jew and German is made to fit. These categories do not develop merely as generalizations or inductions from structural or institutional factors that frame individual and collective behavior. Rather, Jews create meaning systems, via analogy and metaphor, from the cultural resources they have at their disposal, primarily the collective memory of the Holocaust and the structural situation of being Jewish and living in Germany.

The most important contribution of this study is to enrich our grasp of the role of collective memory in the construction of ethnic identity and to analyze its consequences for interethnic relations. I show how the past remains in the present, and frames the way Jews make distinctions between themselves as morally pure and Germans as morally impure, by illustrating how it provides the cultural categories through which Jews interpret the raw data they receive on others. Jews perceive Germans through the lens of Holocaust experience and make frequent criticisms of what they consider to be "typical Germans," anti-Semites, and other such categories. Rather than being manifestations of parochial prejudices and stereotypes, these criticisms are more specific examples of the social process of maintaining ethnic distinctiveness. I also show how the interplay between collective memory and institutional and demographic factors impact Jews' perceptions of "feeling different," and how this impedes Jews from calling themselves "German Jews." Thus, this book provides a more nuanced understanding of contemporary Jewish life in Germany.

I also show how the Jew–German binary cultural code frames the development of Jewish–German relationships, and ultimately impedes Jewish–German readjustment. I argue that the Holocaust is a barrier that stands in the way of Jewish–German love and friendship. Given the opposite ways Jews perceive themselves and Germans, Jews distrust Germans and are hesitant to reveal their own Jewishness. I show how the cultural categories through which Jews distinguish themselves from Germans, and how their distrust of Germans and hesitancy to reveal their Jewishness impact on all of their interethnic relationships. This focus on the perceptions and moral criteria that Jews use to distinguish themselves from Germans, and to determine which Germans are "safe" for personal or professional intercourse, contribute to a more complex understanding of the state of Jewish–German relations. Although policies and diplomatic relations between Germany and Jewish Diaspora communities deal with readjustment on an official level, or statements by Jewish functionaries and German public officials can mark some extent of readjustment at the public level, readjustment must ultimately take place on the private or interpersonal level to be effective and meaningful.

The implications of these findings cast doubt on the structuralist models of ethnic mobilization that give primacy to socioeconomic or political resources over other types of resources in framing interethnic relations. While these models take a mechanistic view of human behavior, looking at external political and economic forces as stimuli that motivate social life, they greatly underestimate the importance of culture, meaning, and interpretation in people's self-definitions of ethnic identity and behavior. While a host society can define a group as different in order to exclude it from social and material resources, a group can also define itself as different by drawing boundaries to maintain integration, solidarity, community, and identity. The larger social processes are not only economic or political, but can also be cultural. As Erving Goffman and other symbolic interactionists have demonstrated, social life ultimately takes place on the interactive level. Yet the interactive or interpersonal level exists within a larger social and cultural context, and understanding the cultural processes of distinction, and the meanings employed in these processes, sheds light on the complexity and nuances of interethnic relations. These cultural processes can be traditions, memories, or ideologies that help shape the belief systems within which interpersonal interactions occur, and the mental blueprints through which groups organize and assess themselves and others. While sociologists have privileged structure in determining behavior, my findings suggest that Jews draw on macrocultural repertoires to define who they are, and to determine how to behave.

The Holocaust in collective memory

People and ethnic groups live within patterns of meaning they create in response to traditions. In the self-definition of ethnic groups, members' roots and cultural heritage are important standard elements. Myths of creation, stories of the lives of religious and national heroes and villains, and the like, are preserved, recovered, and embellished to help determine group identities and group solidarities. Yet no one has explored how these "roots" in collective memory shape interethnic relations. Socio-logical studies have ignored collective memory as both a conceptual tool and a focus of study in the self-definition of ethnic groups and interethnic relations.

Another contribution of this study is to show how collective memory is important for thinking about collective identities and interethnic rela-tions, particularly over time. I show how collective memory is a systemic element of culture. It functions as a metaphor, the cultural cloth from which patterns of meanings are drawn. I suggest that this function is of considerable importance, especially in places where political dramas have occurred. Understanding collective memory may help us better under-stand fears and prejudices that groups may hold that lack any reasonable basis in contemporary reality. It may help us understand the difficulties in interethnic readjustment at the interpersonal level, when groups may be holding onto concrete conflicts at the ideological level.

As Sigmund Freud discovered, traumatic events often live on as memories in the minds of those who experienced them.[12] From philoso-phical discussions in antiquity to more recent psychoanalytical accounts of forgetting – "repression" and "amnesia" – memory has been studied predominantly as an individual mental faculty, and failures of memory have been viewed as central to the life history and psychological make-up of a person.[13] The psychological literature on the memory of the Holocaust focuses predominantly on the long-term psychological con-sequences of persecution on its victims. Some psychologists have de-scribed a "survivor syndrome," a neuropsychic sequelae with varied manifestations.[14] The Holocaust trauma has been shown to transfer to the second and third generation, although psychologists do not know how, to what extent, or why.[15] Is it conscious and intentional? Is the actual Holocaust imagery of torture, escape, confinement, or starvation transferred, or only parents' emotional pain? Do children absorb the trauma through overexposure to it, or via the protective cover of silence?

Psychologists usually ignore memory as a collective phenomenon, and treat it, in the words of Plato, as individual "impressions sealed in wax." At best, they acknowledge the influence of social factors that affect memory, but fail to recognize that memory can be held collectively when people gather and remind themselves of events or conditions they once experienced.

The sociological perspective is very different. George Herbert Mead said that the past is not something that emerges out of thin air; it is a picture that people imagine. In the process of that imagining, the past becomes "real" as an interval of time discrete from the present and future.[16] That is, pasts are invented and endowed with meaning. Interpretations of events and images of the past are continually renegotiated and recreated. Job applicants continually rewrite their biographies. Organizations often selectively construct landmarks and memorials to give prominence to a cause or event. Governments often use history as a backdrop for establishing public policy. As Eric Hobsbawm and Terence Ranger argue in *The Invention of Tradition*, societies invent pasts, memories, and traditions at specific points in time for concrete purposes.[17] Rituals, memorials, and myths of origin can be constructed to solidify group alliances, and to create and maintain national, ethnic, and group identities.

Although the Holocaust was not a uniform experience for all caught up in it, and personal memories are as varied as life histories would be for any diverse population, personal and collective memories of the Holocaust are inextricably linked: both are shaped by groups and institutions that legitimate history.[18] How exactly can Holocaust memory exist for a generation that has not personally lived through the experience? Several factors need to be present for an event to be remembered collectively.[19] First, collective memories have their roots in group experience. Thus, for the memory of an historic event to be formed and maintained, there need to be people who witnessed the event and deem it worthy of remembrance. In the case of the Holocaust several factors contribute to its remembrance. There are survivors still alive who continue to bear witness to it. Moreover, since the Holocaust occurred within the bounds of a world war, in which a multitude of countries participated or were affected, many participants were touched by it one way or another, at the individual, social, institutional, or governmental levels.

For an event to be remembered there also needs to be some sort of community somewhere that can continue to commemorate the event, even if the original community no longer exists. In Germany today, the postwar generation as well as Jewish institutions and organizations have inherited this legacy. So have nations and their governments who wish to commemorate their war heroes, victims, and soldiers who fell in battle. Furthermore, the event must be carved into the public memory of a community or society. The image of the Holocaust must be dominant in the public sphere. It could appear in the mass or print media, or be symbolically displayed in official commemorative ceremonies, war memorials, or museums. The media play a role in creating and sustaining a public memory, for example, through popular films such as *Schindler's List*, *Sophie's Choice*, *Shoah*, and *Europa, Europa*, or popular books like Hannah Arendt's *Eichmann in Jerusalem*, Art Spiegelman's *Maus*, *The Diary of Anne Frank*, or Jerzy Kosinsky's *The Painted Bird*. The visibility or notoriety of people who experienced the persecution, such as Nobel laureate Elie Wiesel, official commemoration ceremonies, the emergence of Holocaust museums, and the rallying cry used by Jews everywhere – "We Will Never Forget" – are all factors that add to the likelihood that an account of the past will not be forgotten, and will be bequeathed to the following generation. We can see pieces of the Holocaust preserved in public monuments, documents, written texts, photographs, diaries, films, videos, cultural artifacts, moments of silence, memorial gardens, Jahrzeit candles, and the like. Additionally, public memory of the Holocaust and its written history are channeled through personal remembrances. Thus, an individual's personal memory of the Holocaust is bounded by memory that has been socially produced or mediated, whether by people who experienced it, by historians, or by the print and mass media.[20]

Since constructing memories and writing histories are selective processes, determining what deserves remembering and what should be forgotten is a political question. Different segments of a society may have different or even opposing versions of the Holocaust that are consistent with their political agendas. Holocaust memory is diverse, intentional, and at times, even accidental. While Israel may focus on the Holocaust as a Jewish catastrophe, Poland and Germany may have completely different emphases. Segments of every society can create the narrative they wish to tell about the Holocaust by authorizing historians, architects, sculptors, government agencies, statisticians, psychoanalysts, museum curators, artifact collectors, and the like to chronicle and interpret events. They narrate and remember this event according to the juxtaposition of the artifacts, and the rituals performed as part of a commemorative cycle. Just as each nation may interpret the Holocaust differently, so do individuals and groups.[21]

Jews in particular are admonished to remember their past.[22] They must remember the destruction of the Temple, the scattering to the Diaspora, the exodus from Egypt every Passover, the genocidal plots of Haman at the time of Purim, and the destruction of 6 million Jews. Among Holocaust survivors the imperative to remember and to communicate to others what was experienced during the Holocaust is one strategy for coping with the trauma. As Primo Levi, the Italian chemist, writes in *Survival in Auschwitz*, "The need to tell our story to 'the rest,' to make 'the rest' participate in it, had taken on for us, before our liberation and after, the character of an immediate and violent impulse, to the point of competing with our other elementary needs."[23] Remembering the Holocaust is also a means of memorializing those who perished. "We have an obligation to the dead," writes Nobel Peace Prize laureate Elie Wiesel. "Their memory must be kept alive... Indeed, to have survived only in order to forget would be blasphemy, a second catastrophe. To forget the dead would be to have them die a second time."[24] The advancing age and decreasing life expectancy of Holocaust survivors makes the imperative to remember all the more compelling.

As sociologist Maurice Halbwachs reminds us, certain locations in space and time awaken memories.[25] Nowhere else is the trauma of the Holocaust so awakened as in Germany. The Final Solution is an issue that continues to haunt Germans who lived through it, and the postwar generation of Germans who inherited this historical burden. The *Historikerstreit* (historians' debate) about the origins of the Second World War, the controversy surrounding US President Ronald Reagan's visit to the Bitburg cemetery, Germany's emphasis on race and blood ties in its struggle for defining national identity, and the rise of hate crimes perpetuated on foreigners by neo-Nazis, skinheads, and the radical right in the aftermath of reunification and economic recession, provide chilling evidence that the past cannot so easily be swept aside. As Charles Meier discusses in *The Unmasterable Past*, how the Holocaust is ultimately dealt with in the context of German history – whether it is viewed as a unique, and thus non-comparable event, or as the consequence of a sequence of historical circumstances – is as much at the heart of discussions on German national identity and consciousness, as it is an issue for Jews.[26]

For Jews, the experience of being physically on German ground provides a unique social context that reawakens the past. The memory of the Holocaust reverberates into their present. For example, in his autobiographical search for his roots, *When Memory Comes*, historian Saul Friedlander confesses how the past trespassed temporal boundaries and violated for him the moment of the present the first time he set foot in Germany, in 1962, to interview a naval official in Hitler's Reich:

When I reached Mannheim the peaceful, unshadowed landscape that slipped by on both sides of the road suddenly began to look different to me. I would not call it anxiety or panic, but a strange feeling of desolation: this Autobahn was shutting me up in Germany forever; on every hand were Germans, nothing but

Germans. I felt caught in a blind trap. In the ponderous cars going past me, the faces seemed to be suddenly bloated with a rancid, reddish grease; on the shoulder of the road the signs – in German! – represented so many cold injunctions, issued by an all-powerful, destructive, police-state bureaucracy... If our reactions may sometimes seem strange, let there be no mistake about it: behind the harmless surface of words and things, we know that at any and every moment abysses await us. It was only at this time in my life, when I was around thirty, that I realized how much the past molded my vision of things, how much the essential appeared to me through a particular prism that could never be eliminated... A great number of us go through life this way, insensible to a whole range of shades and tones, though, despite everything, the eye still manages to penetrate, in certain situations, far beyond the neutral, aseptic, normal meanings that reality presents.[27]

Holocaust memory can be manipulated politically to legitimize or empower individual or group action. It functions as a type of ideology, a set of beliefs or knowledge that endow action with meaning and provide direction to human behavior. Memories are a part of a group's culture, the fabric from which a group's language, values, norms, and rituals are drawn. I show how the memory of the Holocaust provides a moral framework through which second-generation Jews experience their daily reality.

What is really at issue here is determining the different meanings that Holocaust memory generates for the lines of distinction Jews draw between themselves and Germans, and the role these meanings play in their interpersonal relations. I show how second-generation Jews in Germany draw on Holocaust memory as the ultimate tool for constructing identity and community. They form a community of memory that does not forget its past. They draw on collective memory in daily interactions as they raise and erase group boundaries. The Holocaust provides the framework for representing the past, understanding the present, and envisioning the future. It is their ultimate metaphor, a part of their roots, the source from which the meanings they bestow to daily life are constituted.

Jewish ethnicity and identity

It is difficult today to agree on a precise definition of the term Jew and of Jewish self-identity, because being Jewish in the modern world has a wide range of meanings attached to it. Identity formation in general is an ongoing social process subject to many socializing agents and environmental influences. Identity is shaped at the personal level, as well as at the collective level, by group, state, and social institutions. One's identity is woven from the fibers of one's family background, gender, education, occupation, social class, peers, religion, political orientation, national consciousness, and culture. All these influences arise within the framework of personal life experiences, and societal and world events. In secular, pluralistic Western societies where religious practice has waned, Jewish ethnic and cultural behaviors have become salient characteristics in shaping Jewish identity. For the purposes of this book, I use the definitions proposed by Eisenstadt and Sartre as my working definition of a Jew, namely, that one is a Jew if one considers oneself to be one, and is considered by others as such.[28]

Conventional studies dealing specifically with Jewish ethnicity have focused on "how Jewish" the Jews in the Diaspora are, in light of the extent of their assimilation into a host society's secular culture. The principle debate has been waged between two general perspectives – assimilationist and transformationalist. Assimilationists have measured "Jewishness" in normative terms, that is, according to the degree to which Jews manifest religious observance, formal training in religion and Jewish history, membership in and financial support of religious and ethnic institutions, positive identification with the state of Israel, family configurations, intermarriage with non-Jews, and attitudinal conformity to the ideologies of Jewish ethnic, religious, and national institutions.[29] Some observers in this camp, specifically those focusing on Jewish vitality in American society, envision the majority of Jews assimilating into secular society, with only a small minority holding on to cultural and religious traditions.[30] On the other hand, transformationalists emphasize a persistence of Jewish commitment, though the manner in which this commitment is expressed may be transformed.[31] Rather than focusing on dimensions that constitute specifically Jewish behavior, transformationalists emphasize Jewish cohesion and characterize any manifestation of solidarity as legitimate proof of its vitality. Transformationalists suggest that rather than being grounded in institutions or networks of interaction, ethnicity has become transformed into a voluntary affiliation based on personal concerns for identity, an awareness of one's origins, notions of a common past, and pride in the group's cultural heritage, history, and people. In lieu of institutions and social networks, the use of ethnic symbols satisfies the primordial need for affiliation, and enables its members to distinguish themselves from a homogenized host society. Symbols also offer a sense of commonality and continuity. In other words, ethnicity becomes transformed into symbols that people can identify with, but it plays a very limited role in their daily lives.

Some of the difficulties in defining Jewishness today are based, like the models that define ethnicity in general, on approaches that predefine what Jewishness looks like. However, using the cultural framework outlined above, one can allow Jews themselves to define their Jewishness, and to highlight the indicators that they most value as they distinguish themselves from others. By charting the cultural categories through which Jews perceive themselves and others, and by locating the cultural traditions out of which these categories are drawn, we can begin to understand how Jews remain Jewish, and how their Jewishness may be very relevant in their lives, despite an absence of traditional ethnic symbols or rituals. This study shows that Jews in Germany are secular, know little about their Jewish heritage, and organizationally lack resources for a vibrant Jewish life. They are also economically and socially privileged, vote in local and national elections, have achieved high occupational status and economic integration. I show that Jews date Germans, have sexual relationships with Germans, and marry Germans. Yet these Jews are still very Jewish. They are Jewish because of the boundaries they draw between themselves and Germans. These boundaries are not drawn primarily around cultural or religious distinction, but around differences in personality traits and shared values.

While transformationalists argue that networks or interactions are not as significant, my findings suggest the contrary. I argue that Jewishness is constructed in daily interactions as Jews raise and erase lines of distinctions between themselves and others – when Jews wonder whether Germans are anti-Semitic, when Jews see a police officer or some reminder of the Nazi past, when they participate at a demonstration or read about a neo-Nazi incident, or when they wonder how someone will react to their Jewishness. These boundaries are not drawn merely from ritual behavior, or organizational activity, although I do show how these factors contribute to a sense of solidarity. Yet, I argue that Jewish ethnicity is created and recreated thousands of times daily by the mental distinctions Jews make between themselves and others in the course of everyday life.

By adopting the cultural approach outlined above, I suggest that we may be able to explain how increasingly secular Jews continue to "feel Jewish" even though they publicly display no outward symbols of Jewish identity. While religion has become increasingly less important to many Jews around the world, the maintenance of distinctions between Jews and non-Jews may be the defining feature of Jewish consciousness. The task is to determine the basis upon which ethnic boundaries are drawn, and their role for interethnic relations. Thus, in summary, this study shows how the collective memory of the Holocaust forms the basis from which Jews draw distinctions between themselves and Germans. I explore this issue from several angles. The remainder of this chapter describes the most pertinent aspects of the postwar historical context of Jewish–German relations. Chapters 2 through 4 deal with the construction of Jewish ethnic identity. Chapter 2 considers the manner in which Jews view Germans, and argues that the Holocaust, as a metaphor for contemporary life, is central to the cultural codes that Jews have established within their cultural framework. It articulates some of the cultural categories that Jews use when defining what the term "German" means to them. Chapter 3 deals with the manner in which Jews view themselves. It shows that the means by which Jews create their identity includes a classification system that focuses on what distinguishes them from their non-Jewish German environment. Jews transform negative identity symbols such as "victim" or "rare freak" to more positive ones, such as "holder of superior morals" or "rare entity." Chapter 4 shows how these identity symbols affect their social and political integration into the broader German society. Chapters 5 and 6 address the consequences of this Jewish identity for interethnic relations. Chapter 5 addresses interethnic relations at the level of friendships, and Chapter 6 at the level of love, marriage, and interethnic intimacy. The last chapter discusses the broader theoretical implications of the study.

From past to present: the challenge of reestablishing Jewish communities since the Second World War and the presence of holocaust memory

While Jews have faced discrimination in Germany since their first documented appearance on German soil since the twelfth century, in the process of modernization many middle-class Jews sought to identify with the German language and culture. German and European identification with liberalism and the Enlightenment values of tolerance, reason, and cosmopolitanism, along with historic Jewish struggles for political rights and assimilation, helped forge a German–Jewish identity that enabled new modes of Jewish self-expression, collective organization, and experience, and profoundly influenced German and Jewish intellectual traditions.[32] Jewish assimilation into German society had reached its zenith by the early twentieth century. Today such identification is impossible. In their encounter with modernity, the Jews experienced the Holocaust.

When Hitler came to power in 1933 the Jewish population in Frankfurt totaled about 30,000. In the years to follow, it dwindled significantly.

Many Jews fled Frankfurt; some committed suicide,[33] and others were deported to work and concentration camps.[34] By the end of the war, the Jewish population in Frankfurt had virtually disappeared.

Reconstructing Jewish life after the Second World War

After the war, Jewish communities were reestablished throughout Germany to facilitate aid.[35] Many Jewish international relief organizations sent care packages with food and clothing, and Jews were officially classified as "victims of fascism" entitling them to special rations and other privileges.[36] The communities were reestablished predominantly by Jews who survived the war due to their estrangement from Judaism. In Frankfurt, typical of the other larger Jewish communities throughout Germany, of the 600 Jews who reestablished the Frankfurt community, almost all had Aryan spouses and baptized children and about half were half-Jews (offspring of mixed marriages)[37] who had converted to Christianity before the war, but "became" Jewish because of the 1935 Nuremberg racial laws,[38] in which Judaism was defined by blood as opposed to religious practice. Many were given a special privileged status protecting them from harsh persecution,[39] however, and only late in the war were sent to Theresienstadt, a concentration camp established to serve as a "model Jewish settlement" suitable for Red Cross inspection.[40]

Between 1945 and 1952 the Allied Forces in the occupied zones of West Germany and the United Nations Relief and Rehabilitation Agency set up camps throughout Germany for Displaced Persons (DPs). Displaced persons were Jews who had been liberated from concentration camps or had returned from the Soviet Union. They were primarily from Eastern Europe and had no surviving relatives. They were unable to recover their property, which had been either destroyed or expropriated, and facing the prospect of new waves of anti-Semitism in their home countries, most eventually emigrated to Israel, the United States, Canada, and South America. Some remained in Germany – those who were ill, had hospitalized family members, had been denied visas to their preferred countries, or while waiting for visas, had become economically integrated into German society (either legitimately via retail or illegitimately through black-market trading of care package items). They, along with the remnants of the German–Jewish population, formed the basis of the new Jewish communities.

During the decade between 1948 and 1958, the Jewish population in Frankfurt increased by 65 percent – from 1,470 in 1948 to 2,258 by 1958.[41] This increase was due primarily to an influx of new immigrants;

some who were strangers to Germany, others who had returned after not integrating successfully into other countries, and others who came from other Jewish communities in Germany. The return movement of German-Jews was the strongest between 1956 and 1959, when the West German government began paying DM 6,000 in immediate assistance to returning Jews who had fled or were deported from Germany between January 30, 1933 and May 9, 1945, with preferential treatment in restitution cases for claimants over 65.[42] These Jews returned for various reasons. Some returned because they had not been fully assimilated into their countries of exile. Others came because they were tied to Germany by language or culture, or wished to participate in its redemocratization. Many also returned for economic reasons – to claim pensions, to resume positions that they had held prior to the war, or to start or expand their business pursuits. The 1950s were also characterized by a pattern of return migrations from Israel of both German Jews and DPs who had formerly pledged aliyah.

By the early 1960s, Frankfurt's Jewish population had grown to over 4,000, primarily due to an influx of Jews from Poland, Hungary, Romania and Czechoslovakia. Some were fleeing postwar persecution accompanying a resurgence of anti-Semitism in their home countries.[43] Others came for economic reasons. During the 1970s, Jews came primarily from the Soviet Union and Iran. Many left their countries with visas for Israel, and for economic reasons remained in West Germany along the way.

From the 1970s until the late 1980s, Frankfurt's Jewish population stabilized at close to 5,000. But it was a transient community: a continual influx of Jews into Frankfurt since the end of the war was offset by a simultaneous decline due to the high death rate of an overly aged population. In addition, there has been a common belief in the community, as well as amongst Jews worldwide, that it is wrong for Jews to live in Germany.[44] Thus, there has been a continual exodus of Jews from Frankfurt and from Germany since its postwar reconstruction. Of those Jews who have remained, some reported that they were "sitting on packed suitcases" until accumulating enough resources to emigrate elsewhere. Some Frankfurters have been sitting on their suitcases for close to fifty years.

Since the late 1980s, Germany's Jewish population has increased due to an extensive Russian immigration. About 1,000 Russians have immigrated to Frankfurt, and 22,000 to Germany overall.[45] Reflecting on the changes in the community since the mid-1980s, Stefan Szajak, the director of the Frankfurt Jewish Gemeinde, said: "The Jews have stopped lying to themselves, and now accept that they are going to continue to live in Germany." Indeed, since the early 1990s, the population structure in Frankfurt has become younger, meaning that half of all members were born after 1948, and about a fourth belong to the third generation. For the first time since the Holocaust, there are three generations of Jews, and the third generation are growing up with grandparents, aunts, and uncles.

Even with the increasing youthfulness of its population, and the increase in its numbers due to Russian emigrants, the communities are still sorely pressed to respond to the needs of their members. The communities are not organized according to Orthodox, Conservative, or Reform affiliations as in the United States. Instead, membership is based on where one lives, and to withdraw one must declare resignation before a municipal court.[46] Germany has about 50,000 Jews dispersed in 64 Jewish communities, and Frankfurt is the second largest.[47] Local communities within a state (*Land*) are represented by a state committee (*Landesverband*), and eleven such committees meet nationally to discuss and report rights, interests, and issues concerning the communities within their jurisdictions. The *Zentralrat* is the national umbrella organization. Jews are obligated by law to pay an 8 percent surcharge, which is deducted automatically from their paychecks by tax authorities, and forwarded to their Jewish community.[48] Religious communities, their functionaries and property are exempt from civil taxation and protected under criminal legislation against libel and defamation.

Stefan Szajak claims that the numbers are too small to encourage a vibrant Jewish life, and the Jewish functionaries, intellectuals, elderly, and youth are all struggling with how to define a new direction and secure a future for Jews in Germany. Although most Jews are secular, the intermarriage rate is about 60 percent, and the communities lack many facilities that the prewar communities had. The Frankfurt community offers only Orthodox religious services. Julius Carlebach, the director of the *Hochschule für Jüdische Studien* in Heidelberg, sums up the dilemma: "The main problem of Jews in Germany is that they want to be Jews, but not Jewish."[49]

Germany's struggle with its Nazi past and the Jewish response

In August 1945, the Allied Military Government began a program of denazification to punish and reeducate Germans, and to remold the country into a faithful democratic ally. It outlawed National Socialist parties and other parties that had undemocratic and anti-Semitic Weimarian currents. The task was to eradicate Nazism from public administration, media, judiciary, education, and other influential public spheres of life.[50] But with the increasing sovereignty of the German state, and the transfer of the denazification process from Allied to German hands, by the early 1950s there was a brief reemergence and reorganization of groups and parties that fostered nationalistic, anti-democratic, and neo-Nazi ideology. The prosecution of Nazi war criminals was also deficient. Between 1945 and 1955 scholars have documented a progressive trend toward leniency, coinciding with the transfer of control of the denazification process. In many trials there was little relationship between crime and punishment. Major offenders often received lighter sentences than minor offenders, and when people involved in arbitrary killings in concentration camps came to trial the tendency was to hold defendants accountable only for complicity in murder or as accessories to manslaughter. In the last 50 years the Special Office of Investigation into Nazi Crimes in Ludwigsburg initiated 106,178 investigations of Nazi war crimes, of which only 6,494 resulted in convictions and 5,570 remain unresolved, the remainder possibly were dismissed.

In addition, numerous former Nazis and even some criminals continued to hold important civil service jobs and government posts. In May 1951 the West German government passed a law to reemploy pre-1945 government officials and former career officers and soldiers, and to provide pensions to them as well as to their widows and orphans. It was required that 20 percent of the employees of all official agencies and public law corporations be such reemployed persons, many of whom had been active participants in Hitler's terror policies.

Jewish–German relations have rested on initiatives of reparation and restitution. The West German government has supported the rebuilding of the Jewish communities, and has given much financial aid to Israel. The Week of Brotherhood is celebrated in all major German cities. Universities have opened Jewish studies programs, and organizational awards are continuously given to prominent Jews and non-Jews who have actively fought or continue to fight anti-Semitism. Stones and tablets commemorating the persecution of Jews, and the sites of former destroyed synagogues, are brought out in historical memory, and major cities sponsor all-expense-paid return visits by former Jewish residents. Synagogues have been reconstructed, and museums hold exhibitions detailing the rise of anti-Semitism, focusing on its impact on family life and its detrimental effect on the Jewish population. Streets have been renamed for Anne Frank, Albert Einstein, and Ben-Gurion, and teachers take schoolchildren on field trips to concentration camps. Newspapers frequently debate whether to give press coverage to neo-Nazi groups and incidents, not knowing if the publicity will encourage or deter crime.

In spite of the public attempts at Jewish–German readjustment, scholars have documented Germany's inability to confront its genocidal past, by demonstrating its absence in literature, film, and the writing of German history. While anti-fascist war themes have been abundant in postwar German political culture, an outright confrontation with the Holocaust has not.[51]

However, television has played an essential role in focusing public attention on two events that rendered the Holocaust a painful reality – the Eichmann trial in Jerusalem in 1961, and the Auschwitz trial in Frankfurt from December 1963 to August 1965. The mid-1960s witnessed a period of strong identification with Israel for both Germans and Jews. In the aftermath of these trials, and the Israeli–Arab Six Day War, a West-German philo-Semitism emerged that equated Israelis and Jews with strength and respect. Germans' pro-Israeli sentiments facilitated an appeasement of their collective responsibility for Germany's past. For Jews, Israel represented a displaced focus of identity, and since the reopening of Zionist youth organizations in Germany 1959, the communities encouraged migration to Israel.

By the late 1960s there was a growing awareness that most older Germans knew about the atrocities committed against the Jews, and should share in the guilt. Nevertheless, Alexander and Margarete Mitscherlich psychoanalyzed postwar German society and documented an "inability to mourn" in their highly successful 1967 book of that title.[52] Simultaneously, a new generation of German youth came of age; some of whom had participated in the 1968 student riots, were critical of the dark years under Hitler, acknowledged their parents' generation's war guilt, and felt uneasy inheriting that guilt. Hajo Funke spoke for many in this movement:

We did not want to inherit our parent's guilt... We reproached our parents' generation for being too cowardly to stand up to their history and confess. In the process I ascertained their inability to mourn through my own inability to mourn for them. It was for me, as for many of my generation, a necessary reaction to the unmitigated guilt of the war generation and to the ten years of silence. But still, and especially in our angry distancing of ourselves from them, we were unfortunately also their children.[53]

For most Germans, however, the 1970s were characterized by a fascination with Hitler. Triggered by Albert Speer's best-selling memoirs, *Erinnerungen*, an avalanche of books began to appear on Hitler's personality, writings, and speeches. This literature culminated in a cultural trend in which purportedly respectable historians minimized Hitler's role in German atrocities.[54] This somewhat nostalgic attraction to the past surfaced in the media from quiz shows to cinema and pornography. For instance, Joachim Fest's successful documentary film, *Hitler, eine Karriere,* focused on Hitler's popularity among the masses and hardly mentioned the persecution of the Jews.[55] Flea markets and second-hand stores experienced an increased demand for Nazi relics. Prices for original editions of Hitler's *Mein Kampf* soared, as did prices for the Stars of David that Jews were forced to wear during the Nazi regime. It even became trendy for teenagers to wear Nazi emblems as fashion statements.

During this decade, several empirical studies documented the ignorance among German youth about Jews, anti-Semitism, the Holocaust, and German history in general. Most notable was Dieter Bossmann's *Was ich über Adolf Hitler gehört habe* (What I heard about Adolf Hitler). Bossman published the results of a survey of what schoolchildren in Germany knew about Hitler and the Third Reich. Some of the responses were: "He (Hitler) called those who opposed him Nazis. He stuck the Nazis in Gas Chambers," one thirteen-year-old said. "He (Hitler) let the Jews out through the chimney. The Jews were allowed to rot in the gas chamber. Some were allowed to play games. Russians were allowed to play soccer, and the Jews were allowed to play leap frog in the mine fields," a fifteen-year-old said. "He (Hitler) had a friend, and he was Jewish. The Jew lent him money, and Hitler wanted more and more money. But, the Jew said, no, no more money. So Hitler began to hate him and let all Jews be gassed and killed," a sixteen-year-old said.

Since the reestablishment of the Jewish communities, its official leaders had promoted a pro-Zionist agenda, and had worked peacefully with the German government. The West German government cooperated with the *Zentralrat* to promote goodwill through educational and cultural programs. Several institutions dealing with Jewish life were established: the *Gesellschaft für Christliche-Jüdische Zusammenarbeit* in 1948, the *Deutsch-Israelische Gesellschaft* in 1955, the *Institut für die Geschichte der deutschen Juden* (in Hamburg) in 1963, the *Hochschule für jüdische Studien* in 1979. Yet Jewish officials were careful not to publicly confront Germany's past. While the official leaders protested anti-Semitism, they carefully maintained a low profile in Germany's public life, and drew little attention to old wounds. For instance, Doris Kuschner shows that officials who were responsible for designating commemorative stones and epitaphs of Jewish victims of persecution were tentative about publicly criticizing Germany, out of fear of upsetting Jewish–German relations, even while they sympathized with the Jewish population for the horrors of the past. Indeed, in the Cologne synagogue an epitaph on a tablet asks in German that visitors "Pass by in silent thought on six million innocently murdered brothers and sisters." The request in Hebrew is different: "Let us reflect on the six million pure and holy souls of our brothers, the sons of Israel, who were killed, slaughtered, burned, butchered, buried alive, and exterminated in cruel and unnatural manners, and let us unite with them so that the soil will never be able to cover their blood."[56] Alphons Silbermann, a sociologist in Cologne researching the extent of latent anti-Semitism in the Federal Republic of Germany, has publicly criticized the *Zentralrat* for manifesting a policy of appeasement *vis-à-vis* the German government. When Silbermann published the results of various research projects indicating that latent anti-Semitism in the Federal Republic of Germany was widespread in about 50 percent of the general German population, the *Zentralrat* refuted Silbermann's claims.[57] In another incident, in 1978, Hans Filbinger, a former Nazi judge during the Third Reich, was pressured to resign from his post as Christian Democratic Union minister president of Baden-Württemberg, when it was revealed that he was responsible for condemning to death a soldier who had expressed anti-Hitler sentiments after the war had ended. Werner Nachmann, then president of the *Zentralrat*, defended Hans Filbinger, and his defense was accepted by the German public as the official position of all Jews living in Germany.

These incidents became catalysts for a few second-generation Jews to become informal leaders in the community, and incited Henryk Broder and Michael Lang to gather different experiences of Jewish life in *Fremd im eigenen Land* (Strangers in their Own Land).[58] Besides openly criticizing the official leadership of the Jewish *Gemeinden*, a few second-generation Jews became publicly critical of the German population. In 1980, Leah Fleischmann, a schoolteacher now living in Israel, showed how the past is still present through her autobiographical depiction, *Dies ist nicht mein Land* (This is Not My Country), of growing up Jewish in post-Holocaust Germany.

In Frankfurt a small grassroots movement emerged among intellectuals, predominantly on the Left, who were disgruntled by their inability to discuss Germany's past and its influence on Jewish–German relations within the *Gemeinde*. They founded the *Jüdische Gruppe* (Jewish Group) as an alternative forum to scrutinize Israeli militarism, Jewish community politics, the German government, the new German Left, Jewish–German relations, anti-Semitism, Zionism, and the difficulties of growing up

Jewish in post-Holocaust Germany. Aware of the significance of the past in the present, one founding member critiques the Gemeinde as follows:

They don't want to open discussions and to deal with their past. They react very formally. Once in a while they publish an article that argues against anti-Semitism, but in a sense in which anti-Semitism doesn't exist anymore in Germany. Like neo-Nazis, who I don't think play such an important role here. And whenever somebody goes to the Jewish cemetery and does rumble-tumble there, they write something. But these are not the real problematic things in the issue. They fear any kind of interference in public life. They are not really dealing with their own identities, and with their identity as a community.

Within years, similar groups of young critical Jewish leftists emerged throughout Germany.[59] The criticism of these second-generation Jewish intellectuals was particularly poignant regarding the Israeli-Palestinian conflict, when, during the 1982 Israeli invasion of Lebanon, West Germans began equating Israelis with Nazis. Although the *Jüdische Gruppe* no longer exists in its original form in Frankfurt, its founding members have established a journal, *Babylon*, that expresses their views.

More recent developments in Jewish and German struggles over memory

At the time of my interviews, Jews were in the process of becoming more self-consciously Jewish, and more publicly confronting Germany's Nazi past. The leftist intellectuals and community functionaries were beginning to cooperate more publicly in presenting a unified stance against anti-Semitism and battles over Holocaust interpretation. For instance, Ronald Reagan's visit to the Bitburg Cemetery resulted in organized protests by official *Gemeinden* and community members. Moreover, in the fall of 1984, debates were raging regarding a public protest over the plans of the Main Opera House in Frankfurt to perform Rainer W. Fassbinder's play *Der Müll, die Stadt, und der Tod* (Garbage, the City, and Death). Frankfurt's Jews began to protest the play's performance because of its anti-Semitic undercurrent and its stereotyped leading character, a "scrupulous Jewish capitalist." The protest culminated on opening night, October 31, 1985, as Frankfurt's Jews occupied the stage, blocked rehearsals, and turned the event into a discussion about anti-Semitism and the Holocaust. After several months of controversy, the theater finally withdrew the play.

It was not accidental that in the following year several of Frankfurt's intellectuals and leftwing political activists started to work for the preservation of the remnants of the Jewish ghetto of Frankfurt. During construction work on a central public administration building these remnants had surfaced again. (They had been determinedly buried under a main traffic throughway in 1954, during the first reconstruction of the bombed city after 1945.) Finally, after the site was occupied by protesters in August 1987, the city council decided to incorporate the remnants into the administration building by using glass walls to create a museum-like display. About the same time, the *Historikerstreit*, or conflict among German historians, began to take shape in the West German academic community. The main question was how to contextualize the Holocaust within the framework of German or world history.[60]

How to deal with the memory of the Holocaust continues to be a complicated issue for Germans and for Jews. For instance, when the president of the West German parliament, Phillip Jenniger, in a speech in 1988 to commemorate the fiftieth anniversary of Kristallnacht (the night the Nazis destroyed the Jewish synagogues in Germany), tried to stimulate the recollection of the Holocaust, the speech was so controversial that it led to his immediate resignation. On November 9, 1989, the Berlin wall came down. Trying to define German identity became even more complicated, as two countries separated by different political orientations and a different relationship to their past were trying to merge into one. Discussions emerged regarding who was a "German," and how much responsibility the former East Germany bore for restitution and indemnification. The discourse was complicated by the increase in immigration by asylum seekers, mainly from Eastern European countries. The radical right-wing backlash to immigration and the economic recession in the early 1990s, as expressed in an increase of neo-Nazi and anti-foreigner attacks, was accompanied by an increase of desecration of Jewish cemeteries and memorials. Yet the most significant difference from pre-war anti-Semitism, and especially Nazism, is that today Jews are not the chief targets, or even important subjects of concern, of extreme right-wing or nationalist parties or movements. The focus today is on hostility to the foreigner – the person who looks and acts differently and who Germans think occupies or competes for scarce jobs. To be sure, the rise of nationalist sentiments and rallying cries such as "Germany for Germans" makes Jews ill at ease, as do violent attacks on foreigners, because such attacks, or anti-foreigner attitudes, are never far removed from other expressions of extreme nationalism. Such sentiments and acts of violence create a climate of disillusionment and bitterness for ethnic minorities, and those who feel different, which continues to raise the specter of the Nazi past.

While the number of right-wing extremist groups has increased in recent years, their total membership has declined. However, the isolated violent attacks on foreigners and Jews have escalated and become politicized, particularly in the aftermath of German reunification. For example, the Federal Ministry of the Interior estimated 2,584 extremist right-wing motivated acts of violence in 1992, a rise of about 22 percent from the previous decade. Besides the increase in the number of attacks, they were also more brutal and violent. The attacks were responsible for seventeen deaths, of which seven victims were foreigners. The attacks were met with a sharp public outcry, and protests symbolizing acts of solidarity with the victims. Indeed, about 90 percent of the German population opposes violence against foreigners and Jews. In the last several years, the number of attacks has declined. Yet the failure of German politicians to respond quickly and curb such violence tends to reopen wounds and raise questions about the relationship between Jews and Germans, and about Germany's historical failure to stop such incidents half a century ago.

Official public opinion regarding the causes and extent of anti-Semitism in postwar Germany is mixed. Some argue that there is no anti-Semitism in Germany, only a few anti-Semites. Others contend that the "rowdies" are just expressing the latent sentiments of society at large, thus justifying the need for a thorough self-examination and cleansing. While many demand ostracism and severe punishment for swastika daubers and terrorists, others criticize such measures as illegitimate means by which the public at large can alleviate its unresolved guilt feelings. The German government has taken some steps to battle anti-Semitism, neo-Nazism and right-wing extremist attacks, and there is protective legislation against anti-Semitic outbursts. This is accompanied by a general taboo, experienced by the majority of the population, against overtly expressing anti-Semitic sentiments.[61]

A series of social-scientific studies have tried throughout the past fifty years to determine the causes and extent of postwar latent anti-Semitism in a population that, for the most part, experiences a Germany free of Jews.[62] The newsmagazine *Der Spiegel* published the results of a 1992 public opinion poll on German attitudes toward Jews. The results indicated that about 15 percent of the German population held explicitly anti-Semitic attitudes; 60 percent felt that anti-Semitism would remain at its present level, and 18 percent thought it would increase. A 1994 public opinion poll by the EMNID Institute found that 30 percent of the German population felt that Jews had too much influence in the world, and 22 percent would not want Jews as neighbors. Recently, a 1996 poll by the Forsa Institute indicated that 43 percent of the German population would like to put closure on the memory of the Holocaust, and 75 percent felt that Germany no longer had any special political, cultural, or financial responsibility toward Jews because of the past.

"Auschwitz," wrote Henryk Broder in an article in *Der Spiegel*, "grows stronger in the Jewish consciousness the farther it recedes in time."[63] Indeed, reflecting on the changes within the Frankfurt *Gemeinde* since the mid-1980s, Stefan Szajak, and others I interviewed in 1994, suggest that the memory and interpretation of the Holocaust has become a political weapon around which Jews more openly mobilize. In the past decade state-sponsored Holocaust memorials, Jewish museums, research institutions and Jewish studies programs have sprung up throughout Germany. Jews are compelled now more than ever before to keep the memory alive, and to protest in Germany over its interpretation.

Conclusion

The Jewish community that was gradually reconstructed in the wake of the Holocaust was markedly different from its prewar predecessor. The enduring question of whether Jews should remain in Germany, the diverse backgrounds of the reconstituted Jewish population, and the state of Jewish–German relations in the postwar era, provide the context in which the second generation came of age.

The notion of normalizing relations between Jews and Germans in the aftermath of the Holocaust has been problematic. The inadequate denazification process, the persistence of postwar anti-Semitism, and variable attempts in Germany to come to terms with the past have impacted the social and political relations between Jews and Germans. Jews in contemporary Germany are still struggling to find their place in German society, but their struggles today are with the trauma of the Holocaust, and with the people of the nation responsible for its occurrence. How do Jews perceive Germans and living in Germany? Chapter 2 addresses this question.

2

Living in the land of the murderers? How Jews who live in Germany view Germans

...it is the past's function to haunt us ... the world we live in at any moment is the world of the past...
Hannah Arendt ("Home to Roost." *The New York Review of Books*, June 26, 1975)

The past is still present

Elisabeth, a thirty-five-year-old woman, with olive skin and clear dark eyes, sits back on a white leather sofa in the luxurious living room of her home. She becomes somber and reflective as she describes to me her family background. Her parents, from Poland, are Jews. Her father survived three brutal years in a concentration camp, where his parents, brothers, and sisters perished. Her mother concealed her Jewish identity, and lied to officials by telling them she was Christian. They believed her. She spent the war years as a foreign laborer in a work camp in Germany. Her parents met after the war in a refugee camp outside of Frankfurt. In 1948 they were married, and a year later Elisabeth was born. With the exception of a few years she spent in England studying, Elisabeth has lived in Germany her entire life. She described to me her feelings toward Germans as she was growing up:

I had a very paranoid feeling as a child. I hated to live here. I wanted to leave. I thought I couldn't even talk to Germans, couldn't look at them or even touch them. That was a big problem for me. I think that somehow it had been delegated from my parents. Maybe they sort of delegated all of this feeling of hatred and fear onto their children... Psychologically, I lived in the world of the war. It was sort of clear to me that this wasn't the case, but psychologically, you know, it was like living twenty years earlier.

39

This chapter explores the manner in which second-generation Jews like Elisabeth view Germans. I explore the various categories Jews use to assess the moral status of Germans. I compare the different meanings that my respondents use to differentiate different types of Germans, and I discuss the role played by collective memory in assessing Germans' moral status. In this sense, I am exploring the internal logic of ethnic cultural construction by focusing on the manner in which Jews have defined Germans as an out-group. I will focus on their belief system, by exploring the cultural meanings and the symbolic codes and classifications that underlie these definitions. These symbolic codes, in my view, provide a window into understanding the manner in which groups interpret their everyday reality. They also represent the markers of the symbolic boundaries that Jews have created to distinguish themselves from Germans as an ethnic entity.

The Holocaust as a lens through which to interpret experience

George Herbert Mead and Maurice Halbwachs have written on the importance of the past as conceptualized in memory.[1] They have sought to explain how our memories of past experiences, both individual and collective, can condition the manner in which we perceive and interpret our everyday life. Specific events, people, and situations in one's past will shape the way one views, and ultimately experiences, the world. Following their ideas, the manner in which the past provides a mold out of which the present is contoured can be understood and revealed as Jews provide illustrations for how the collective memory of the Holocaust shapes their interpretations of everyday life.

In the doctors' rest area of the eye clinic of a large hospital in Wiesbaden, a city about 20 miles from the heart of Frankfurt, I spoke with Judith. At age twenty-eight, she is a physician, a licensed ophthalmologist. She has lived in Frankfurt her entire life, and resides with her mother in a small two-bedroom apartment. She is dressed in a white doctor's smock, has thick glasses, and a slightly hefty build. She speaks calmly and thoughtfully as she describes to me what it was like to grow up Jewish in Germany after the war. She speaks of how she thinks the memory of the Holocaust affected her:

Very often I interpret things that the other person didn't even mean. It's because I'm so sensitive. I'll give you an example. My brother has two daughters, and they go to the Jewish school. At Christmas they were here with me, and we went to a store. Someone said to one of them, "What are you getting for Christmas?"

The girls said, "We're not getting anything for Christmas, we're Jewish." I would never have said anything like that. My stomach turned. The girls said so straightforwardly, "We're Jewish, we're not getting anything for Christmas." And the butcher said, "Yes, good, you're Jewish." I don't know what he thought. Perhaps he thought he couldn't give us any pork, or something like that. That was my sensitivity. And my stomach turned. Why did she say that?

Judith describes the dilemma she felt by having her identity as a Jew revealed by her nieces to a German butcher. She questions the legitimacy of her emotions, and of her reactions to the revelation, and concludes that she is reacting in an overly sensitive manner. She recognizes that her discomfort has sprung from a past that has impaired her vision of the present, and suggests the near impossibility that she can achieve a more neutral reading of this situation. She illuminates the presence of two voices, each seeking independent expression, that are engaged in a dialectical discourse. One voice speaks to her of her discomfort of having her Jewishness so unexpectedly revealed, while the other doubts the legitimacy of her interpretation of the situation as mediated through the prism of the past.

Julius, another respondent, has worked as a schoolteacher his entire life. His parents were German Jews who were fortunate enough to flee to Palestine before the outbreak of the war. At war's end, when Julius was a small child, his parents returned eagerly to Germany, to help rebuild democracy. He speaks about his work as a schoolteacher. He loves children, and loves working with them. The flow of conversation stops momentarily. Julius is wide-eyed and intense, as he is reminded of the impact the Holocaust has had on his life as a Jew in Germany. He reports to me the following example as an illustration: "I think I react much more sensitively to everything. When children say things at school, there are sayings that if one does something to the point of exhaustion – 'until a cold gassing' or 'to the end' – others can say this very carelessly. But, for me, it means something else, because I immediately have a picture in my mind of what a cold gassing is." Certain colloquial expressions in the German language evoke instantly for Julius images and meanings that might go unnoticed by others. Julius interprets and reacts to situations in everyday life through the lens of Holocaust imagery.

Like many other Jews living in Germany, those of the second generation believe that they are more sensitive than others to their surroundings. They notice words, behaviors, phrases, songs, symbols, buildings, hair-cuts, clothes, and the like, that speak to them of the Holocaust. They see older Germans, people in uniforms, swastikas as graffiti,

Second World War museum exhibits, commuter trains, SS reunions, the presence of neo-Nazi groups, and neo-Nazi trials as reference points. As Maurice Halbwachs argued, reference points are markers that form a linkage to the past by bringing it to life in the present. Although more than fifty years have passed, the collective memory of the Holocaust provides a cognitive backdrop for the everyday experience of Jews in Germany. The memory of the Holocaust "blows like a wind from my past into my present," is how one respondent described it. "The fact that you are in the place where it happened makes it a constant presence without having to think of details," explains another.

Because of the collective memory of the Holocaust, Jews overinterpret remarks and symbols. Monika, a child of Polish Jews who survived the war in concentration camps, explains why:

After the war, you don't react to this personal anti-Semitic remark or writing of a certain person, but you answer against the whole concentration camp system. And it takes on a meaning that this one remark doesn't have, yet it still has it... You could say, "Ah this little nothing, he can say what he wants." It's useless anyway to discuss anti-Semitic prejudices, because you can't enlighten prejudiced persons with arguments. On the one hand, you have the feeling that you don't want to exaggerate this little stupid remark. On the other hand, you sort of have this whole history in the background. You fight a fight that has nothing to do with this little remark. And still, on this background, it has something to do with it. So, every little thing becomes a tremendous problem.

Second-generation Jews often use the terms "interpretation," "sensitivity," and "meaning" in their accounts, as they reflect on how the past influences their present-day experience. They interpret certain remarks and symbols as threatening. Judith is reacting to the unanticipated disclosure of her Jewish identity. Julius is reacting to a slang expression that apparently makes Holocaust allusions. Monika illustrates the difficulties of responding to an anti-Semitic remark. These incidents triggered for the respondents certain emotions – feelings of anxiety, sensitivity, and of the need to defend oneself. Objectively, there was no real danger. Their lives were not really threatened. But danger existed in the perceptions that they manufactured in their minds, or, in the words of William I. Thomas, in "their definition of the situation." It is in this sense that the danger was real for my interviewees.

Perceptions, as well as memory, are constructed and selective. Never do two people examine or describe in the same way or with the same words a particular situation, occasion, interaction, object, relationship, or event. As Max Weber pointed out in his concept of *verstehen* (to understand), we experience the world subjectively.[2] For example, two people viewing a twentieth-century lithograph will inevitably be attuned to different aspects of its composition; one may emphasize the color tones, another the form and structure, one may view it in terms of other lithographs by the same artist or artists within the same aesthetic genre, another as a unique exemplar, and so on. The same is true regarding images of the past.

However, regardless of individual contingency, the framework of culture acts as a filter – organizing, clarifying, and classifying social phenomena – and thus enables human beings to communicate and share the assessments necessary for constructing and experiencing commonality in their ways of life. Through the framework of culture, Jews make sense of their experience of living in Germany, and communicate to each other the understandings implicit in their social world. The collective creation and use of symbols pervades these cultural frames, allowing Jews a shared sense of order and comprehension through which to interpret events, objects, nature, and human action. In order to better understand their relationship to Germans, it is essential to uncover what these symbols are, and to analyze their meanings, as they frame their outlook and perceptions, and ultimately determine the manner in which Jews come to experience their life in Germany.

The symbolic meanings of the term "German"

The "German" is a symbol with specific meanings in Jewish culture. Symbols can come in the form of objects, gestures, sounds, or images, but they are always related to some empirical item of experience that they are trying to represent. Symbols may carry different meanings for different groups of people, depending upon the experience to which they are related. As Victor Turner points out, symbols also function not only as a set of cognitive classifications, but also as a means to rouse and channel powerful emotions.[3]

In the context of the symbolic systems of primitive religions, the sociologist Emile Durkheim reminds us that "one must know how to go underneath the symbol to the reality which it represents and which gives it its meaning."[4] Following Durkheim, if we explore in greater depth the underlying meaning for Jews of "German," we can begin to recognize what it means symbolically in terms of an ideology, a system of beliefs, constructed around a cultural system that differentiates between purity and pollution. That is, in both in-depth interviews and casual conversations, respondents described Germans in terms that included both manifest and latent moral conceptualizations. These conceptualizations reveal basic symbolic statements of values and concerns that are deeply embedded within Jewish culture.

Jews have constructed an ideological system of German totemic resources that possesses components of a classical pollution-taboo system. Anything German is a cultural symbol that emerges as dangerous, destructive, and dirty, but that can serve multiple functions and address varied realities. The memory of the Holocaust has followed the German through time, like a ball and chain around his or her leg. In the eyes of Jews, Germans cannot liberate themselves from history; wherever the German goes, and whatever the German does, he or she is always dragging along these memories. The cultural reservoir associated with anything German has been poisoned. It is not the German as a human being, but rather the symbolic associations of the concept "the German" that have become contaminated. It is the German as an archetype, a composite of individuals and an embodiment of a philosophy that exists within the myths Jews create about themselves and German society, that has become polluted. Gertrud, a housewife with two children, who is married to a Jewish man and has lived in Germany her entire life, illustrates this distinction.

Q: When you see older people do you ever wonder where they were during the war?

A: Not often. But sometimes I think maybe he murdered my grandmother. Perhaps he is the one who gassed my grandmother. But not often. It's not the person, rather the age – being German and old. The person himself, I can't say that I hate him. The person who I see in front of me is really only a picture. It's a perception, a thought, an image.

In most societies the meanings of symbols associated with concepts or objects are not shared by everyone at all times. As Gertrud's statement above illustrates, she does not often think of the role older people played during the war, only sometimes. The concept of "the German" takes on divergent meanings in different social contexts, producing ultimately differing consequences and understandings in relation to intergroup dynamics.

Myths are positive phenomena that can serve their believers well. The various polluted categories of "the German" function as contaminated properties from which Jews should maintain distance. By transforming Germans into the antithesis of archetypal Jews, Jews can affirm the differences of identities and identification between themselves and

Germans. By articulating the characteristics that go into the construction of these polluted categories, Jews are drawing symbolic, moral boundaries that enable them to maintain their ethnicity by distinguishing themselves as a unique ethnic group in Germany.

Alternative meanings of Germany and Germans

Although most Jews perceive Germany as a democratic society, Jews describe Germans in terms of polluted categories. The moral standards Jews use to create labels of Germans as Nazis, murderers, anti-Semites (including philo-Semites), and xenophobes are shaped around personality traits conceptualized as the "authoritarian personality." The binary opposition of Jew and German carries descriptions, evaluations, and prescriptions that are imputed via the metaphor of the Holocaust. This metaphor supplies the structured categories of "pure" and "impure" into which almost every Jew and every German is made to fit.

The new Germany – a democratic society

Most Jews in the study firmly believed that Germany today is a parliamentary democracy, concerned with social welfare and equality. Ignatz Bubis, the current head of the *Zentralrat*, expressed the official Jewish position that democracy has taken a firm and unconditional hold in Germany – that the terroristic violence and ideological opportunism of National Socialism has been aborted in favor of modern liberal and democratic institutions.[5] In his view, the birth of the new German state, the Federal Republic of Germany, has more in common with early Weimar and previous democratic traditions than with the totalitarianism and terror of the Third Reich.

Like Alexis de Tocqueville, who judged the extent of American democracy in 1835 against the backdrop of the memory of European feudalism, the Jewish discourse on German democracy since the establishment of the Federal Republic of Germany employs Nazi Germany as a comparative framework from which to assess Germany's progress in reestablishing democracy. A parliamentary governmental system is contrasted with a totalitarian regime, and respect for individual rights is contrasted with the earlier ability of the government to mobilize masses by means of propaganda and terror.

In contrast to the state-imposed genocide of the Third Reich, the core value within the constitution of the Federal Republic of Germany, the Basic Law, is human dignity. Article 1 of the Basic Law, declares: "The dignity of man is inviolable. To respect and protect it is the duty of all state authority." Respondents believed that the Federal Republic of Germany had undergone profound changes, but that a number of historic events have left deep scars on Germany's postwar generation. The Allied military government's process of denazification to transform a new German state into a stable democracy, and the process of dismembering Germany into Allied occupied zones, and ultimately into two distinct countries, with families being torn apart, were among the facts mentioned. Some second-generation Jews stated that because the postwar generation of Germans was forever reminded of the atrocities of the war, and had inherited the responsibility to somehow confront the lessons of the past, they were not prone to the appeal of totalitarian propaganda or sentiments. There was widespread feeling among the interviewees that Germany today was not the same country as the one that started the Second World War. Herbert, a master's candidate in business administration whom I interviewed in my office at the Goethe University in the heart of the Westend section of Frankfurt, was typical of many: "I think democracy in Germany has stabilized since World War II. I think there was a certain shock, and I think this shock helped stabilize the democracy for such a long time – well, for Germany it's a long time. I think a lot of younger Germans are aware of what populism and mass movements mean." Similar sentiments were expressed by Monika, who spoke to us earlier in this chapter. Monika pointed out that many values deeply embedded in today's German culture and society are different from those of Nazi Germany: "I think that a lot of things have changed since the Weimar Republic, and because of the Holocaust. I really think that Germany has a democratic society, and that the parliamentary system really works. People are so interested in individualistic issues, and in their own lives, that I don't think that a party that wants to impose a totalitarian ideology would be very successful here."

In contrast to the deeply established value of individualism within American culture which, according to Robert Bellah and his colleagues in *Habits of the Heart*, inhibits Americans from working toward the collective good, Monika views individualism within German society as a protective and preventive mechanism against destructive collective behavior.[6] The notion of Germans "working cooperatively toward a common goal" brings back references to an earlier period. As historians have pointed out, the Holocaust was not a result of random violence or terror carried out by misfits or a radical fringe group within society. On the contrary, it was official government policy that was implemented through political processes and modern technological capabilities that functioned so successfully precisely because of the cooperation from practically every sector of society. Attorneys and legal experts wrote legislation and decrees that made genocide legal. Artists helped imagine and create effective German propaganda. Teachers and writers taught and contributed to the promotion of anti-Semitic ideology. Physicians conducted medical experiments and scientists tested theories on "Jewish" guinea pigs. Business owners benefited from cheap labor. Others profited from the demand for destructive technology and products such as crematoria, the toxic gas Zyklon B, and so on. Without the active or passive cooperation of German society, the hundreds of thousands of citizens who carried out their regular jobs, like train conductors, or those who were in charge of coordinating efficient train schedules that transported people to death camps and brought empty trains back from the camps into circulation, the systematic annihilation of two-thirds of the world's Jewish population would not have been possible.

For Monika, German collective behavior, or working toward a common goal, is not a collective "good." It is a tendency that must be carefully monitored, because it is associated with the behavioral pattern of caving in to social pressures. A significant aspect of the German character, second-generation Jews say, is a tendency toward conformity; Germans go along with the crowd, trying desperately to fit in, doing what others do, being followers rather than leaders. Alexander, a real estate agent, put it this way: "I think you can influence the Germans pretty easily. Just tell them what to do. Tell them to be capitalists, and they will be the best capitalists. Tell them to be communists, and they will be the best communists. Just tell them what to do, and they will do it perfectly." In this context individualism serves an important function: it provides a check on German collective behavior. If Germans can now think or act independently and in their own interests, rather than in the interests of the "collectivity," they will be more difficult to mobilize, and less likely to actively participate and cooperate in a destructive venture.

The characterization of Germany as a democratic state on a more general level also serves a functional purpose for many of the respondents. In the political sense it allows Jews a categorical classification that they find inclusive, enabling them on some level to be integrated into German society. It allows Jews to continue to live in Germany with the hope that they will be relatively secure, and their civil rights protected. For example, Georg, a thirty-five-year-old dentist with a warm, friendly disposition, believes he is well integrated into German society:

I'm pretty much of a *goy* [Yiddish slang for a non-Jew]. Yes, with a lot of *goyish* behavior. German and *goy* is the same thing. That means being straight, being a good citizen of the state, paying taxes, not trying to avoid things that others avoid. Trying to do things that others have to do, and being very conscious of them, of all of the things you must do, and so on... Being very polite. That's a very typical German attitude. Being superficial, and not looking for conflicts.

While Georg and others described Germany as a democratic society, they also felt ambivalent because the past was still with them. For example, when I asked Georg whether he thought of the Germans as his people, he made clear his opposition to such a categorization: "No, I'm different. I feel I'm more warm hearted than they are. I'm much more dependent on contact than they are. They are straight, polite, and I'm not. They lie a lot, and I'm not like that."

Curiously, Georg referred to himself as a *goy*, and referred to Germans as *goys*, yet did not make the logical connection of referring to himself as a German. Identity slippage could occur between Jew and *goy*, and between German and *goy*, but the boundaries separating Jew from German were rigidly maintained.

Georg, Monika, and others referred to Germany as a stabilized democracy, but went on to question the extent to which it has exorcized its Nazi past. The term democracy was used by respondents to describe political or social processes, but the undemocratic aspects of German society were best seen in their descriptions of the personality traits of the Germans. They seemed to imply that while the social and political institutions of the German state have been dramatically transformed, some of the German people have not. When Georg compared Germans to himself, he described them as dishonest, emotionally cold, and less interested in contact with others. Monika would have agreed:

I think there are a lot of people who have never really coped with their past. Maybe most of the people. There's a kind of unspoken guilt feeling that emerges in this whole debate, aggressiveness against people who want to bring up the topic of the Holocaust again. A lot of people still have their racist and anti-Semitic ideas, but they are expressed differently today than during the time of the Weimar Republic or National Socialism.

Yet Monika hesitates to make blanket generalizations. She notes:

A lot of things have changed... I see, let's say, in the Social Democratic party, and the Green party, or the student movement, or what is left of it, and even in groups like the Punks, there's an anti-authoritarian tendency that I think is becoming rather strong, and it would take a much more differentiated analysis to see which parts of society have really changed. But I think there is a change. I absolutely don't believe that everything is like it used to be.

Authoritarian personality traits

Germany was generally viewed by my respondents as a complex package of contradictory elements consisting of both democratic and authoritarian tendencies. The political structure and its institutions appeared to function as a democracy, yet its national character, the sentiments and values held by the population at large, were viewed with suspicion and disdain. Even if its extensive social welfare system is often associated with compassion and concern for others, it was not a frequently mentioned theme in discussions of Germans or of the German state. Instead, Jews focused on particular personality traits that defined Germans as having a polluted moral status.

Personality is, in some sense, a complement to culture: if culture refers to all aspects of a society that all its members share and pass on to the next generation, personality refers to the unique combination of traits that differentiate individuals within a culture.[7] Jews mobilized personality traits as a standard from which to evaluate how to draw ethnic boundaries. History was the key to demonstrating that Jews did not share the same personality traits as Germans and were therefore culturally different. To substantiate that Jews and Germans have little in common, Jews tended to focus on the ideology of National Socialism, and the traits associated with the type of personality that allowed the Holocaust to occur. For instance, Monika mentioned that the "authoritarian personality" continued to be a central characteristic of the German population.

There are a lot of dimensions of the authoritarian character that are still very alive in Germany. There's a tendency for a lot of people not to want to take responsibility in their jobs. In the whole system of civil servants, which is a problem that is very related to National Socialism, people don't want to take responsibility for what they do. They tend to give the responsibility to the person in a higher position. And that's something that I think is extremely unpleasant and terrible. Civil courage doesn't exist here very much, and people are very hesitant to formulate their own opinions. Especially anything that's connected with taking individual responsibility, which was one of the big problems in National Socialism and in running the totalitarian state.

In the foreward to Theodore Adorno, et al., *The Authoritarian Personality*, Max Horkheimer questions how one can explain "the willingness of great masses of people to tolerate the mass extermination of their fellow citizens."[8] In the study presented in this book, Theodor Adorno and his colleagues create and test a prejudice scale that identifies personality traits associated with ethnocentrism, anti-Semitism, fascism, and paranoia. Adorno and his colleagues argue that the authoritarian personality posits the qualities of conventionalism (rigid adherence to conventional middle-class values), authoritarian submission (uncritical attitude toward idealized moral authority of the in-group), authoritarian aggression (tendency to look for, and to condemn, reject, and punish people who violate conventional values), anti-intraception (opposition to the subjective, the imaginative, the tender-minded), superstition and stereotype (the belief in mystical determinants of the individual's fate, and the disposition to think in rigid categories), power and "toughness" (preoccupation with dominance-submission, strong-weak, or leader-follower dimensions), destructiveness and cynicism (generalized hostility, vilification of the human), projectivity (the disposition to believe that wild and dangerous things go on in the world), and exaggerated concern with sexual matters."[9]

Many of these character traits are central to the Jewish discourse on the meaning of being German, and the establishment of Germans as an out-group. With the exception of the characteristics of projectivity, superstition, and exaggerated concern with sexual matters, my interviewees, when describing Germans, alluded to all of the other characteristics described by Adorno and his colleagues.

The unquestioning obedience to authority, or, in Adorno's terms, authoritarian submission, was a central cultural trait associated with being German. For instance, to Monika, it was signaled by a lack of civic courage, and an inability to think for oneself. Georg focused on the character trait of conventionalism – conforming behavior, doing what "others do," and always being aware of how others are acting. That is, Germans lacked a philosophy of "live and let live." Germans were seen as being uncomfortable with those who violated conventional values and behavior. Germans were compulsive conformists exhibiting anxiety at the appearance of any social deviation. A joke I heard about the difference between American and German national character focused on German conventionalism as the distinguishing characteristic feature – that Americans have a tendency to "mind their own business," while Germans often mind the business of one another. Harry, a thirty-five-year-old businessman, married with two small children, echoed this view. He has lived in Germany his entire life, and employs a number of Germans in his garment factory. Harry provides the following description of the German mentality:

I feel good with Italians. I don't know why... The Swiss, I don't like them, but that's personal. That's a mentality. They have this German mentality that I particularly dislike... I mean, if I park my car badly, someone will come up to me and tell me that I'm parking my car badly. I know that I've parked my car badly, but in Germany the people will tell you that you've parked your car badly. I think that's what I don't like about it. In England, nobody would do that. I don't know how it is in the States. Probably nobody cares. But it's their particularities over here that I don't like, and I don't feel warm toward.

In general, in the eyes of Jews, the archetypal German with an authoritarian personality is incapable of following humanitarian philosophical ideals like morality, love, wisdom, and freedom. Authoritarians are not seekers of truth and reason, but followers of dogma and petty power. Germans with such personalities are not viewed as humane, noble, or tolerant, but rather as comical and villainous, drawn to dogma. They oppose tolerance, particularly the tolerance of the Enlightenment, which was born of compassion and pragmatism. They exhibit a reverence toward orders, bureaucracy, and authority. They live a life that finds favor in the eyes of their superiors, filled with form, but lacking content. The form, however, is significant, because it governs and influences action in life. The form is of deed and act, over thought and sentiment.

Germans are seen as both enjoying using authority and accepting it from others who are higher in status. The consequence is an unquestioning acceptance of the commands a person receives and passes on and an acceptance of a system which permits the communication of orders. If the orders are unreasonable, there is no readily available means to challenge them.

The authoritarian personality attributed to Germans is a composite archetype of individuals and an embodiment of a philosophy – a synthesis of National Socialist ideology and the philosophies of modern anti-Semitism and racism. One with such a personality tends to distort reality by viewing the world and its people in black-and-white terms. The authoritarian has an intolerance for ambiguity, and fails to appreciate the subtleties of complex situations. Such a German does not make fine distinctions with respect to those things he or she does not believe in, even in the face of new evidence. A person with such personality traits tends to be emotionally deficient and to repress feelings of fear and aggression toward authority figures by displacing such feelings onto others meeker than oneself.

In the eyes of Jews, authoritarian personality characteristics embodied in Germans are reflected in a German opposition to humanity, morality, and ethics. By such a characterization, Jews can seek to demonstrate the lack of appeal of German culture, its lack of sympathy toward Jews, foreigners, or anyone different, and find differences between themselves and Germans. (Respondents' descriptions of Jewish personality traits is discussed in Chapter 3.) By characterizing the German as different in *Geist* – spirit and soul – Jews can create and mark the symbolic boundaries of their classification system.

German thoroughness and technological sophistication

Although many Jews stated that the state of Germany was no more or less hostile toward them than were other countries around the world, some Jews drew further moral boundaries in the types of criteria they employed to distinguish Germans from other Europeans. Germans were singled out as being morally more deficient than other non-Jews. Aggression was perceived as a component of German nature that becomes dangerous when misguided. Germans had the capabilities to be more destructive than other Europeans because their aggression could be amplified on the basis of two additional characteristics – German thoroughness and technological sophistication. While other countries might have anti-democratic or anti-Semitic tendencies, these two characteristics set apart the German people because they amplified the destructive potential of racial hatred. With an acceptable outlet for aggression, such as killing during wartime, Germans would be able to discharge fully their destructive energy. Hermann, a tall and youthful forty-year-old physician, with a long bearded face, points out the tendency toward the "vilification of the human being," in Adorno's terms, as it is embodied in the German character: "The mentality of racism is international. In Germany, it's of an entirely different type, a German type. If they do anything, they do it thoroughly. The French have great problems with the Jews, and so do the British. They hate them, and try to enslave them. But to gas them individually? That is typically German." Viktor, a thirty-three-year-old mathematician, who speaks perfect English with a heavy British accent, makes a similar point:

I think the main difference between Germans and some other Europeans does not lie in the fact that they were anti-Semites, and that they killed Jews, but I think it's really a quantitative and technological difference. Nobody has ever really gone so far technologically speaking in trying to erase a whole group of people from the map. To that extent, I think the Germans are quite unique. It's rather fitting with their character of being, perhaps, a little more profound in what they do, in both the good and bad things. And this is a particularly bad instance of where they were trying to be thorough.

Viktor is referring to the physical side of technology, those technological and industrial aspects of modernity that brought about a reorientation of notions of time and efficiency. Rapid innovation, like the manufacturing of large-scale death factories, and the toxic gas Zyklon B, coupled with excellent management and strategic planning, allowed Germans to best utilize their technological capabilities to achieve their goals, as heinous as they might have been.

Theodor, a twenty-five-year-old sociology student, suggests that now Germans may question some of their strategic decisions. Acknowledging that their genocidal behavior has become difficult to justify is, for Theodor, a symbol of the change that has occurred in the German postwar period.

I don't see the Germans as any different than the French or English. They have made only one mistake. They are more thorough. What happened here could have happened in France, except the French aren't such perfectionists. It's not a German phenomenon. They haven't changed. Maybe they changed in that they see it was a mistake to have killed Jews. Maybe they should have just made them work.

German thoroughness is reflected in that Germans are "very serious, and very heavy," explains Gertrud, a housewife. "Always so scientific, and always talking and talking. Everything is a problem which must be analyzed and evaluated." In similar fashion, the historian Lucy Dawidowicz demonstrates that part of the Nazi ideology was to pose Germany's national goals and interests as issues, questions, and solutions. That is, the issue became a search for more *Lebensraum* (living space), which framed the eventual policy discussions as questions and solutions. How to eliminate the Jews to create more living space became known as *die Judenfrage*, or Jewish question, and the answer was addressed by the actual program of genocide known as the *Endlösung*, or Final Solution.[10]

Theodor, Viktor, Hermann, and others refer to an underlying aggressiveness that lies dormant in the German character, and is activated by different criteria and circumstances. Like Freud's assumptions of human nature that people are instinctively aggressive, in the eyes of Jews, Germans are instinctively aggressive and this aggression becomes maladaptive when carried to the extreme. Due to Germany's capable organizational skills, human and physical resources, and how Germans utilize their culture and structure, Germans are able to maximize and utilize destructive instincts better than other peoples. The result is that "a Frenchman will be patriotic, a German a fascist," as Georg, the dentist points out. Yet, Helena, a twenty-seven-year-old mother and part-time flight attendant for El Al, the Israeli airline, takes issue with the notion of Germans as being exceptionally violent, but questions Germany's democracy by focusing on German conventionalism as itself an anti-democratic tendency to quickly exchange one set of values for another.

You'll always find anti-Semitism in Germany, but probably more so in England, because there are more Jews there. For me, it's not a matter of how violent it is for the Jews, because they [Germans] really aren't that violent. But I would accept it more in England than in Germany, because the Germans, they are the last who should be neo-Nazis after the war. I don't trust the German mentality. I think Germans can be very extreme. They could change their opinion from today to tomorrow. They don't have a sense of democracy.

The polluting categories of being German

Nazis and Murderers

The concept of a "German" in itself has significant symbolic value. This concept can be more clearly understood by looking at the categories that Jews mobilize to describe Germans. Several polluting categories may be used when speaking about the German or the German people. To begin with, the term "German" is often used synonymously with the expression "Nazi." Even though Nazi is a name for a member of a political party that no longer exists, and the Nazi party today is outlawed in Germany, as are neo-Nazi organizations, my respondents exhibited no concrete consensus or consistency in delineating the two terms, particularly in casual comments. Esther, a thirty-year-old law student put it succinctly, when she stated that "the Germans are the main reason for the Jewish Holocaust." Betty, the woman described in the Prologue, explains these views with more certainty: "The Holocaust happened and was carried through in this country where I live. Certainly, I see Nazis in many people, and because of that I am more careful and distrustful of the people here."

Betty superimposes the images of Nazis onto many people she encounters. Esther, however, makes no clear distinctions between Germans as a population, the National Socialist political leadership, and different types of responsibility incurred by different organizations, groups, and individuals. The expression "Nazi," however, was not to be confused with the term neo-Nazi. Jews did make distinctions between Germans and neo-Nazis. Neo-Nazis were seen as a radical fringe group, severely alienated and disturbed young punks, but not politically significant. Nevertheless, they must be taken seriously and their behavior must be monitored, as Jews must continually look out for their own safety.

Given that about a third of the respondents had at least one parent who was a Holocaust survivor, I was not surprised by the view of German as Nazi. Growing up in Los Angeles, myself a child of Holocaust survivors, I was aware of the reverberation of these images of Germans within Jewish communities, particularly for those families with Holocaust survivor roots. What did surprise me, however, was that this conceptualization appeared across my interviews, being just as prevalent among second-generation Jews whose parents were not incarcerated in work or concentration camps. For example, the conceptualization was often used randomly by second-generation Jews, even if their parents were of German–Jewish origin, or had been in exile or living outside Germany during the war.

Retrospective analyses of Nazi concentration camps provide evidence that many "normal," mentally stable, and untroubled individuals engaged in persecuting Jewish people and other so-called "undesirables" because they believed that the German war effort required such extreme action. Indeed, in *Nazi Doctors* Robert Lifton documents the beliefs and actions of physicians conducting unethical experiments in the face of the Hippocratic Oath of Medicine. In *Hitler's Willing Executioners* Daniel Goldhagen shows how ordinary Germans were willing to murder Jews, even though they could have refused without sanctions.[11] This behavior can be understood in terms of a more widespread human tendency. Research carried out in other settings, particularly in the United States, has shown that ordinary individuals, even people who may be highly respected in their communities, might engage in interpersonal cruelty if they perceive that the situation warrants such behavior. As Stanley Milgram's classic study *Obedience to Authority* illustrates, people will administer painful shocks to others as part of their role as teacher, if they feel that a visible authority figure will take the blame for any harm done.[12] Likewise, Philip Zimbardo's prison study showed that when assigned the role of prison guard, ordinary people will engage in sadistic behavior toward others who are role-playing as prisoners.[13]

As sociological evidence has indicated, situational factors can have a powerful effect on behavior. Yet social scientist Robert Brislin noted that people usually attribute behavior to personality traits, because these traits are more noticeable than the situational factors which might have elicited the behavior.[14] My interviewees' reflections are consistent with Brislin's observations. Nazis, according to my interviewees, can be spotted by the way they dress, speak, and behave. Nazis are devoted to militarism, bureaucracy, intolerance, oppression, anti-Semitism, and *völkisch* culture. They tend to seek professions in the military, police force, or other social control agencies. Nazis are accused of barbaric and uncivilized moral codes, devoid of civilized culture and *Geist*. One could tell a Nazi by looking for certain characteristics. Nazis are rigid, and enjoy giving orders. Nazis were mean and cruel, and prone to erratic violence. By observing how a German treated children, foreigners, or workers in service occupations like waiters or bus drivers, one could tell if he or she was a Nazi. Nazis were usually old, but this did not exonerate the younger generation. Instead, younger people displaying such characteristics could inherit the polluting label of being "children of Nazis."

Being German is a tribal stigma, a marker of moral self-expression. According to my interviewees, this meaning holds true for Jews who lived through the war and those born after it. It is reflected by the intensity with which Jews associate Germans with their Nazi past. A history professor born after 1945, told me, "I experience this state, at least in the mentality of the people, as a continuous line from the Third Reich." Another respondent, a young journalist whose German–Jewish mother was hidden in France during the war, questions whether Germans can ever be exonerated when she says that "one observes [Germans] as if one looks simultaneously at their guilt."

One symbolic ramification of the representation of German as Nazi is to equate German with murderer. Murderer implies one who slaughters wantonly with premeditated malice. A murderer may be one who kills innocent people, including women and children. Nazis did not murder randomly. Instead, they targeted specific groups of people, Jews in particular. In the eyes of my interviewees, Nazis attempted through premeditated murder to annihilate their families. This motif of equating German with murderer and Jew with victim is revealed forcefully, particularly when respondents talked about why their parents stayed or returned to Germany. Like Esther and Betty, Simon, a twenty-five-year-old law student, whose Polish-born parents survived concentration camps, describes being Jewish and living in Germany by saying, "I still live in the country with the people who actually killed my family." Max, whose mother was in a labor camp in Russia, expressed similar sentiments when referring to her situation. "My mother must live here in the land of the murderers of her parents." This sentiment was reflected not just by second-generation Jews whose parents were Holocaust survivors, but also by those whose family were in exile during the war. Eva, whose parents fled from Germany to Palestine before the war and returned after it ended, echoed this sentiment when she said, "My parents came back here to the ones who wanted to kill them."

Implicit classifications

While Jews explicitly characterized Germans as murderers, implicitly their characterizations revealed three other less denigrating, but nonetheless polluted typifications. That is, German as a social identity concept is multifaceted, and the data reveals four overall general types of characterizations: (1) the explicit derogatory characterization as "murderer"; and the implicit less derogatory characterizations as (2) anti-Semite (including philo-Semite); (3) xenophobe; and (4) "typical German."

Murderer for some Jews refers to Germans known or suspected of being Nazis, particularly in the SS or wartime high official positions. For others, the term is applied universally, irrespective of one's war function or past actions. Another polluting category used by Jews to refer to Germans is anti-Semite. Anti-Semites are thought to be widely distributed among the German population. They are found specifically among the less educated, less wealthy, rural and politically conservative or less politically mobilized masses. Highly educated and wealthy Germans are also thought to be anti-Semitic, but due to good breeding and refined manners are perceived as less likely to display visibly anti-Semitic thoughts and feelings.

Anti-Semites show little reason, differentiate people on the basis of race, and attack their civil rights. The anti-Semite does not evaluate the Jew based on personal, individual characteristics, but rather views the Jew *qua* Jew. The anti-Semite fears the Jew: he or she does not want Jews in the neighborhood, would not support their political candidacy, perceives that Jews exploit the Holocaust for personal gain, and believes that Jews are wealthy and have too much influence in the world.

German anti-Semites, in the eyes of my Jewish interviewees, are also ethnocentric. They are unreflective, show little interest in other cultures, don't benefit from a cross-cultural experience, feel superior to those who differ, and can be blatantly unfair toward them. This provincialism is at the heart of prejudice, argues Alexander, a thirty-year-old real estate broker:

It's in the German nature not to be nice to anyone who is strange, who is here from a different nation... I notice that people are anti-Semitic when I notice that people are narrow-minded, and inflexible, and when they make racist remarks – not against Jews particularly, but that they disregard everything that is foreign.

One sees it clearly when Germans are on vacation. One sees how they stick to their German culture, and don't experience anything new. And these are characteristics that one can find out very quickly – if one is open-minded or narrow minded. And it is usually the tendency of people who are not so open-minded to be anti-Semitic, rather than people who reflect intellectually.

Anti-Semites, according to my interviewees, are distributed across the political spectrum. They are not limited to the extreme political Right, but also come from the far political Left, masked as anti-Zionists. One respondent, who was active in the German Left during college days, explains:

What strikes me from a distance is a very uncomfortable note from the extreme Left. But they don't call it anti-Semitism. They call it anti-Zionism. I sometimes have trouble distinguishing that. I must admit. But I think that this is a bell that rings rather louder than some of the neo-Nazis, who just seem neurotic, and politically not particularly relevant, whereas the other lot are somehow more relevant, for whatever reason. There are probably more of them around.

Philo-Semites, Germans overtly expressing sympathetic sentiments toward Jews, are held as anti-Semites incognito with unresolved guilt feelings or urges to repent. Rather than viewing Jews in negative terms, philo-Semites are uncritical of Jewish behavior, and because of guilty feelings on the part of themselves, their families, or Germans in general, are favorably predisposed to Jews to redress prior civic injustice. Sylvia, a pharmacist, is able to see through such behavior:

There is this kind of philo-Semitism that I don't like, which is nothing more than anti-Semitism turned around. For example, it was very prominent in 1967 during the Six Day War; many German militarists loved Israel. Israelis were such good soldiers, or people suddenly thought that all Jews were great.[15] Or that every Jew is a good person, and especially intelligent. These kinds of statements would be made. There isn't much of a great jump from saying Jews are especially intelligent, and then seeing the consequences; that now they are especially sly, attentive, and they make a lot of money, and exploit the Christian.

Moreover, Sylvia describes anti-Semites and philo-Semites as people who are unable to evaluate a person based on their individual qualities but see them only as members of particular groups. The Jew is liked or disliked because of his or her ethnic status, an embellishment no different than money, clothes, hair, eyes, profession, or social standing. Social scientists have long been aware that certain categories, particularly racial and ethnic ones, can be so central to a person's thinking that they will be employed repeatedly. Gordon Allport, for instance, illustrated how anti-Semitic individuals categorize Jews in ways that, even when challenged with contradictory evidence, are extremely resistant to change.[16] Being seen as an element of a category, of which all members are similar and liked or disliked based on certain social characteristics, is the hallmark of prejudice. Joshua, a psychiatrist, explains: "I would not distinguish between philo-Semitism and anti-Semitism. Because in both situations, I feel as if I am not being recognized, or accepted, or understood as a whole person who is also Jewish, but I am being seen only as a Jew."

Another category, the xenophobic German, is the most widely mobilized label in describing Germans. Jews believe that xenophobic Germans who are prejudiced against Turkish and other guestworker populations – and they feel most Germans hold those prejudices – are disguised anti-Semites currently displacing their prejudices against Jews. Because it is no longer politically acceptable to be prejudiced against Jews, the ethnocentrism that abounds in the German character gets transferred to foreigners.[17] Anna, a forty-year-old physician, offered her thoughts:

I believe there is anti-Semitism in the German population. It's not probable that there shouldn't be, because there has been so much for centuries. I don't believe it's been erased. So, there must be. And there must be also among physicians. And it must be among my generation as well. The best proof, I would say, is that anti-Semitism today is not centered against Jews, but solely directed against Turks. But it's the same thing.

Miriam, a thirty-year-old housewife, argued that the foreigners who bear the brunt of xenophobic attacks function as a buffer for violence directed against Jews. "Even if I'm not personally confronted, I see that there are still people who hate Jews. I know that if there weren't those other foreigners living in Germany, Jews would be attacked."

The "typical German"

Jews' consciousness of Germans has been polluted, and few symbolic resources exist that would allow them to create totems of Germans that are uncontaminating. For example, the only non-denigrating way of referring to a German is to call him or her a "non-typical German." As we will see in Chapters 6 and 7, this category is usually reserved for close German friends and lovers and is a negation of what Jews consider a typical German. Jews avoid contact with typical Germans, as Celia, a thirty-two-year-old soft-spoken and serious pharmacist, whose parents survived concentration camps, describes:

Germans have a different mentality. I don't have much contact with older Germans, but we have a big social circle, and there are a lot of Germans there. Germans and Jews. The people I am together with are open-minded, worldly. One cannot say that they are typical Germans. With typical Germans who are nationalistic, I couldn't have much contact, because it would disturb me.

The typical German is a cultural typification signifying a certain type of mentality – a person who is precise, punctual, stubborn, predictable, not spontaneous, orderly, clean, organized, stupid, serious – lacking humor, obedient and foolish; like Robert Merton's bureaucratic man, blindly following rules and orders solely for their bureaucratic necessity.[18]

In the elegantly furnished living room of her mother's apartment, Suzanna, tells me that her father, an architect, was very active in Jewish community life in Germany, and helped rebuild many of Germany's synagogues. An intelligent and attractive twenty-seven-year-old physician, she followed in her mother's footsteps in the study of medicine. Neither of her parents directly suffered at the hands of the Germans during the war, but they had been interned in labor camps in Russia. She describes an incident she had with a "typical German," as she went to visit her mother at the clinic where she worked.

Many people are very typically German. I once had a very strange experience. I wanted to come and visit my mother at work, and I went to the door and the porter says to me, "You cannot use this door, you must use the back door." So I didn't tell him that I'm the daughter of one of the doctors in the house. So, I asked, "Why?" He said, "Because the law says that between twelve or half past twelve and one o'clock, you have to use the back door according to paragraph such and such." The porter was giving me a whole lesson about the law about backdoors between twelve-thirty and one o'clock. I was so shocked, because I said without people like this, who believe in bureaucracy like this little man does, exact and perfect, unbending, Hitler could never have existed, and could never have done what he had done. And this is absolutely true for the German mentality. This exactness. To be perfect. To do it not 100 percent, but 1,000 percent. In Italy not even one Jew was murdered until Hitler came. There was anti-Semitism, but there was no killing. They [Italians] are much too imperfect for organized killing.

Whereas the German of the Enlightenment was open-minded, worldly, humanitarian, and cosmopolitan, Suzanna describes the typical German personality as the antithesis of these values. The typical German is unimaginative, prone to stereotypical thinking, and has little insight into him or herself. The typical German is also cold and emotionless, lacking warmth or compassion, unable to give and express love – due to being raised on orders and never having learned the process of freely expressing emotion. These traits make the German unattractive to Jews. Suzanna described to me her fondness for Italy and other countries in Mediterranean settings, and finds German men less attractive than men from these countries: "There is something less special about Germans than, for example, Italians. They're not as good looking, they're not as funny, they're not as romantic as Italians." Elisabeth echoes Suzanna's view on German men: "Oh, Germans, they aren't charming enough. They have very little sense of humor. I see German men like I see Swedish or northern men, too cold."

Interviewees described Germans by a negation of traits that are commonly associated with Jewish culture, such as warmth and humor. The typical German was constructed as a pastiche of fragments from Aryan and Prussian characteristics. Some respondents described visual images of the typical German, including, surprisingly, hair and eye color, which played a prominent role in Nazi–Aryan ideology. As one respondent put it, "The typical German is correct, pedantic, has blond hair, blue eyes, and is very accurate, narrow-minded, and uninterested in anything that goes on outside Germany."

The lack of emotional warmth was a major signifier for determining the polluted status of Germans. For instance, Georg, who earlier in the chapter described himself as a *goy* or acting *goyishly*, quickly dissociated himself from being German, when being German was viewed as anti-intraception, in Adorno's terms, the opposite of tender minded. A typical German expresses aversion to emotionalism, but has unconscious inferiority problems centered on feeling emotionally inadequate. A typical German feels little emotional affinity with others, and has little understanding or patience for human sociability.

A comment I heard often is that Germans are more fond of dogs than of children, implying that they do not put a high premium on human life. Attitudes toward children are also partly a result of attitudes toward alternative uses of time and wealth. Children are expensive to raise, and parents must weigh the advantages of having children against the advantages of conspicuous consumption. Germans' preferences (and interests) for dogs over children were viewed as materialistic, self-centered, and uncompromising. Germany was viewed as a wealthy country, where concern over material comfort took precedence over raising a family. This preference for dog over child was even perceived as being institutionalized as if dogs are surrogate children. For instance, it was pointed out to me that dogs are allowed (and often taken instead of children) in restaurants and on buses, and that dogs and children both pay similarly reduced fares on buses.

Regarding the lack of love believed to be ingrained within the German mentality, Rosabeth, a thirty-three-year-old psychoanalyst, hypothesizes it to be a result of a rigid, overdemanding, authoritarian parenting style including harsh punishment, love conditional upon a child's good behavior, and the importance placed on rigid rules. Rosabeth, who works with both Jewish and German patients, offers this interpretation of Germans:

Most of their problems are that their parents didn't love them, and their parents hit them. Really, 90 percent of my clients are all telling me the same stories: "My mother did not love me, my mother did not kiss me." Most were not kissed by their mothers, and girls never kissed their fathers. Can you imagine? I see how my family is, I mean, I can't get away from my father kissing my legs today. He's running after me. It is a completely different relationship that they have. And they are brought up with orders. The girls can stay away for the night with their boyfriends if they want, nobody cares. But they have to be home for lunchtime at 12.00. If they come at 12.15, they are going to be killed by their parents... I have some Jewish clients, and they tell you, "My mother loved me too much, and loves me too much, and I feel guilty if I leave her, because she can't live without me." It's exactly the opposite.

A special language – the Holocaust as metaphor

Each of these characterizations – murderer, anti-Semite, philo-Semite, xenophobe, and typical German – is charged with symbolism. As Durkheim noted, symbols, by definition, have some sort of rational relationship to an empirical item of experience, a thing or concept, that they represent. This set of cognitive classifications can be plotted along a continuum of degrees of perceived prejudice and discrimination. In other words, these conceptualizations reveal a classificatory hierarchy – a hierarchical ordering based on criteria that are meaningful to Jews.

If one takes each of these categories independently, in isolation from the others, one is struck by the generic basis of German attitudes and behavior. This hierarchy encompasses *rationally* motivated behavior at the low end of the scale, to *emotionally* driven behavior, with a specific target, the Jews, on the high end. For example, the typical German bases his or her behavior on rational grounds, following the rules, without targeting any specific group. The typical German is anal-retentive, unemotional, locked into behavior mechanistically, the rules of his or her social roles prescribing and circumscribing his or her everyday actions.

The xenophobe, on the other hand, is emotionally driven. His or her behavior is based on fear, a fear of strangers in general, of which Jews may or may not be targets. The behavior of the anti-Semite and philo-Semite is also emotionally driven. Their behavior is based on hatred, and the target is more focused – the Jews are now singled out. The murderer by his or her actions takes this prejudice to the extreme, discriminating against Jews, and ultimately depriving them of their right to live.

All social categories are variable in meaning. The meanings imputed to certain symbols will not be shared by all members of society at all times, nor by members of a particular group. The term German is no exception. The meanings of German vary depending on the circumstances of interactions between Jews and Germans, and how Jews interpret this interaction in the context in which it occurs.

Nonetheless, there are collective agreements about connotations of the term German that are persistent within Jewish culture. For instance, if one looks at the entire categorization of Germans – murderer, anti-Semite, philo-Semite, xenophobe, and typical German, one notices that they are thematically related. These diverse categories are rooted ideologically in an orientation that merges an image of the German from fifty years ago with one from the present. Despite the dual nature of the orientation, one image is produced, similar to looking through binoculars, but seeing only one view.

For example, we see the past in Suzanna's description of her encounter with a typical German, the porter. It is a past that Suzanna did not experience personally, nor did her parents, but she has knowledge of it collectively, and its potent influence has left its mark on her. She layers her interpretation of the altercation with the porter with images from a previous time frame. She is describing the porter not in the language of a postwar democratized German society, but in a language haunted by cloudy memories. These memories are not hers, of course. They are those of her culture, her community.

Suzanna is shocked by the porter's behavior. His behavior explains to her how Hitler could have "done what he had done." The expression "typical German," is not one that she has created on her own, as language is not a function of the speaker. This is not to suggest that the speaker does not use language to express his or her own thoughts. But as the Swiss linguist Ferdinand de Saussure reminds us, language is shared knowledge that is learned, like other cultural traits that enable individuals to communicate with one another. Suzanna has assimilated this classificatory scheme passively, from her linguistic community. As de

Saussure explains, "language is a product of the faculty of speech and a collection of necessary conventions that have been adopted by a social body to permit individuals to exercise that faculty."[19] In other words, language is collective behavior; it is essentially a social act. It is a fundamental part of culture that comprises a set of symbols and rules, allowing individuals to communicate with each other in a meaningful way. Like culture, it is patterned; it has laws and conventions that shape the patterns by which sounds are used in various combinations to make up units of meaning.[20] That does not mean that language is necessarily static. Rather, it is flexible and constantly changing, because every member of a linguistic community participates in using it, and thus it is influenced by all.[21]

In this way, Suzanna's choice of words reflect both the manner in which she wishes to express her thoughts, and some insight into the repertoire of expressions and thought available to her from her community. That is, Jews form in some sense a "speech community," where they define for their members the appropriate body of linguistic forms – specialized terminology, particular words or phrases, or slang – to be used among themselves when defining Germans.[22] If language mirrors social experience, then the use of special language or words will reflect differences in how people's experiences are cognitively organized. The language Jews use to describe Germans implicitly and explicitly highlights those aspects of Germans that they regard as important.

On the other hand, Rosabeth, the psychoanalyst who described the difference between Jewish and German parental love, and other respondents illuminate for us a complex scheme of cultural categories. Rosabeth describes Jews and Germans in a language characterized by a set of semantic oppositions; a classificatory system that dichotomizes Jews and Germans as binary opposites. In societies marked by class, racial, gender, and similar sharp divisions, language tends to mirror social stratification. For example, accents, dialects, and specialized language are associated not only with geographical regions, but are also characteristic of a particular social class, caste, racial or ethnic group, gender, generation, and occupation.[23] Every functioning group uses a certain language that embodies and highlights matters of interest or significance to its members.[24] The linguist Joseph Vendryes refers to this as a "special language," a language "employed by groups of individuals placed in special circumstances."[25] If language mirrors social experience, then the use of special language or words will reflect differences in how people's experiences are cognitively organized.

As sociologists Suzanne Kessler and Wendy McKenna point out when a dichotomy is established as gender, the classificatory distinction between male and female cognitively exacerbates the differences between the categories, while simultaneously minimizing the similarities.[26] In the same manner, Rosabeth in describing her experience as a psychoanalyst treating Jewish and German patients, heightens the differences between the categorical classifications of Jew and German, while simultaneously diminishing their similarities. Her choice of words also reminds us of references made by Suzanna. They are imbued with metaphors from the Holocaust. She describes the relationship that Germans have with their parents. "They are going to be killed by their parents if they don't follow orders." Weren't the Jews killed if they didn't follow orders? Weren't the Germans threatened if they didn't follow orders? The binary contrast is portrayed regarding emotional displays within the family. Since the institution of the family is central to Jewish culture, it is not to Germans. Germans give precedence to rules and regulations over emotional attachments toward their children. The Jews are loved too much by their parents, the Germans are not loved enough. German behavior also demonstrates a weakening of traditional family values. Rosabeth's phrase regarding German daughters and their parents, "the girls can stay out all night and nobody cares," illustrates a sense of promiscuity, another moral degradation, that results from the German tendency to value following orders over parental love and morality.

Holocaust imagery serves as a source of metaphors for Jewish culture, providing the vocabulary for, and thus enabling, the articulation of their social and moral conceptualizations. Jews' use of this imagery cuts across differences that stem from family background, divergent Holocaust experiences, varieties of psychological trauma, recovery, and adaptation successes, a multitude of parenting styles and types of upbringing and socialization.

What is the importance for Jewish culture of the German as a ritual object? What is the significance of the Holocaust metaphors around which the German is endowed with meaning? As Friedrich Nietzsche reminds us, metaphors form the basis of cultural truths about human relations.[27] Metaphors not only inform a body of thought, but they also shape cultural practice, and organize social life. In the case of Jewish culture in Germany, these metaphors provide a language for conceptualizing the relationship between Jews and Germans, and, on a more general level, the relationship between Jews and non-Jews, or, more commonly, the conceptualization of Jews as the embodiment of otherness.

More importantly, the language of metaphors also depicts the manner in which the human mind has represented conceptual differences and has sought to answer fundamental questions regarding the human condition. In this particular case, the Holocaust metaphors associated with Germany and Germans, and their implications for the set of relationships between Jews and Germans address such fundamental binary oppositions as life and death, good and evil, morality and immorality, chance and circumstance, victim and perpetrator, among others. As the montage of quotations illustrating the cultural categories associated with Germans shows, the Holocaust metaphor is filtered through several layers of mediation in which the past speaks to the present. For Rosabeth, the psychoanalyst, the Holocaust is mediated by psychoanalytical theory in her analysis of Jewish and German parent-child relationships. For Suzanna, who was visiting her mother at the clinic, the imagery is mediated by her interpretation of the encounter with the porter. German identity in the eyes of Jews is multifaceted, fragmented, and continually in flux, but overshadowed by the memory of the Holocaust.

The experience of the Holocaust is certainly of a different period in time and of a distinct social world, but metaphorically Jews make excursions into this world from their present one. The rules of this other world serve as a type of mirror that reflects onto the rules of today; these rules provide guidelines regarding how Jews should live in Germany with Germans here and now. The collective memory of the Holocaust provides the binary scheme that distinguishes Jew from non-Jew.

Making inferences: social perception and appraisal

Most Jews, irrespective of generation, do not perceive all Germans with whom they interact as anti-Semitic or as de facto murderers. Even so, the cultural typification of Germans as murderers prevails, because in the minds of Jews there is uncertainty: Germans whom they see or with whom they come into contact *could* potentially hold anti-Semitic views or might have committed murder. As one second-generation respondent put it, "For me, all are potential murderers – especially those who scream very loudly that they saved all of these Jews."

The obvious reason for such uncertainty is that this type of biographical information is generally not initially visible. Such knowledge is essential in social interaction. When one enters the presence of others, as the sociologist Erving Goffman has pointed out, one commonly seeks to acquire information about the other, or bring into play information already possessed. "Information about the individual helps to define the situation, enabling others to know in advance what he will expect of them and what they may expect of him. Informed in these ways, the others will know how best to act in order to call forth a desired response from him."[28] The information will be about the other's general socio-economic status, conception of self, attitude toward them, competence, trustworthiness, and so on.

In routine encounters in public places, Jews have incomplete and inaccurate biographical information documenting the past actions and identifying the political or social orientation of the Germans with whom they come into contact. Their world view, their social stock of knowledge, their cultural expectations of Germans are not based on accurate biographical data. Instead, they are inundated with collective memories. These memories permeate their impressions and perceptions of Germans. Jews appraise Germans and in the process strive to assess the meanings of these appraisals for their own manifold plans of actions. As Oskar, a social science researcher remarked, "In Germany most old peoples' past you don't really know, and if you do find out about them, you usually can't respect it." Avital, a thirty-eight-year-old school teacher, whose parents returned from exile in Palestine to help rebuild Germany's democracy, describes the dilemma: "If you see an older man, who knows where he was. Maybe he was at the front. Maybe he was a soldier. Maybe he was in the SS. Maybe he killed Jews. But who knows the real differences?... I can't just go up to everyone and say, 'tell me where you were.'" Tanya, a thirty-eight-year-old physician, who is married to a non-Jewish man, states:

Well, actually, I have no hard feelings against my generation, but very often I do wonder when I meet someone about the age of sixty, what his attitude might have been during wartime. And I especially hate people who claim to have saved Jews, because it seems false. But my generation, I don't hold them responsible for anything. And I don't even feel any antagonism against them. It's really different from their parents' generation.

Jews evaluate German character on the basis of inferences. As William I. Thomas pointed out, social interaction functions by individuals making inferences. He writes: "It is also highly important for us to realize that we do not as a matter of fact lead our lives, make our decisions, and reach our goals in everyday life either statistically or scientifically." He gives the following example: "I am, let us say, your guest. You do not know, you cannot determine scientifically, that I will not steal your money or your spoons. But inferentially I will not, and inferentially you have me as a guest."[29] The processes of imputation and attribution form the cornerstone for these inferences.

It is in this sense that Jews do not interact with Germans directly as objects or as persons, but rather with their images of Germans as objects that they have clothed with collective identities and meanings. Through the process of social perception and appraisal, Jewish culture filters these sensory experiences, tidying up and cataloguing masses of stimuli into more organized and refined categories that make them coherent. These stimuli are filtered through a screen of Jewish culture into which is woven certain characteristics and categories that Jews have constructed in their images of Germans, such as, for example, collective responsibility. This system of classification or cultural ordering is preserved in part by means of a taboo that exists, an extreme reluctance to ask older Germans specific information about their past.

The danger of asking older Germans about their Second World War whereabouts

As Mary Douglas reminds us, the pollution beliefs of a culture are related to its moral values. They function to maintain solidarity and order around a society or group's belief system, and to protect these ideas from ambiguity within the moral sphere. Rules upholding pollution beliefs, such as taboos, reinforce cultural solidarity. The taboo between Jews and Germans of talking about the Holocaust, or more specifically, asking older Germans about their whereabouts during the war, prohibits potentially threatening disturbances of their belief system and constructed social order. By such avoidances, social definitions of Germans such as their polluted categories of Nazi, murderer, anti-Semite, and typical German remain clear and intact. The transgressing of a taboo can imply the invoking of some type of danger – as we will now see when Jews ask older Germans what they did in the war – and has consequences for Jewish behavior. The extent to which the danger is real is not the issue. What is important is the pervasive belief that the danger is real.

Maintaining the taboo

Theodor, the young sociology student, observes that to avoid potential conflict with Germans, there are topics that Jews and Germans don't discuss: "I think there's a silent agreement that Germans and Jews don't talk about the Holocaust. You need to know the people very, very well before you can talk about this subject. And even if their parents were not involved in crimes, they could get a bad feeling. When one speaks about it, it can hurt. It's a theme that there is usually stony silence about. Nobody talks about it, and nobody brings it up."

Conflict avoidance results in a collusive arrangement where both Jews and Germans maintain a prohibition about discussing the war whereabouts of their parents. This behavior was experienced by over half of the respondents. That is why one Jewish housewife stated that both Jews and Germans are "playing the same game." According to my interviewees, very few Germans voluntarily attempt to divulge to them accurate biographical accounts documenting their whereabouts and actions during the war, and likewise my interviewees were reluctant to inquire. For instance, Betty, whom we met earlier, says: "I was afraid to ask what people were not able to talk about." For Herbert, the business administration student, as for many other respondents, avoiding the topic is a coping strategy for living in Germany. "If I asked," he says, "then I couldn't live here anymore." Finding out the actual war histories of older Germans with whom they come into contact is for the most part a theme that for many living in Germany has become taboo.

Several factors contribute to the construction and maintenance of this taboo. To begin with, both generations of Jews, first and second, have little or no contact with Germans old enough to have participated in the war. The opportunity structures allowing them to become acquainted with older Germans and to inquire into their backgrounds are limited. According to my respondents, their parents consciously avoid the contact; as for themselves, their personal and professional lives rarely intersect with those of elderly Germans.

Another significant factor is basic distrust in the type of information that might be communicated. Most respondents anticipated that if they did inquire into the war history of Germans, the information they would receive would be disingenuous. Jews believe that Germans deal with them in a devious manner, and that they withhold the disclosure of such information either through concealment or by outright deception. Their views were unlike the American credo that one is "innocent until proven guilty." Rather, their initial assumption is that Germans are collectively responsible for participating in war crimes, unless proven innocent, and because of this the German as a social category is fundamentally immoral or impure.

The revelation of having participated, either actively or passively, in the war crimes of genocide is deeply discrediting. It is indicative of a deviant biographical life line that affects the moral status of the individual. Such information is a stigma, a character blemish, that affects the public image of the individual, and ultimately, his or her social relations. In his classic work *Stigma*, Erving Goffman distinguishes between stigmata that can cause one to be discredited and those that cause one to be discreditable. The former refers to attributes that are immediately known about or visible to others, such as obesity, blindness, and physical abnormalities; the latter refer to attributes that are not immediately apparent to others and can be concealed, such as having a criminal record, being an alcoholic, or being sexually impotent. Curiously, my findings suggest that Jews view German collective responsibility as a discredited attribute, one that is immediately visible because one is German, a type of tribal stigma that is transmitted through lineage and can contaminate equally all members of a family. However, Jews perceive that Germans view their own collective responsibility as a discreditable or potentially stigmatizing attribute that is not readily visible, and that they can attempt to conceal from others.[30] We can see this more clearly by exploring the manner in which Jews perceive the various strategies they believe Germans use to control information, including deception and disidentification, to manage their stigmatized biographical information.

Germans are not viewed as passive, powerless individuals who have no say in their identity management. They are seen as strategists attempting to manage potentially stigmatizing information about themselves. It is as if they have a terrible secret that would blemish their biography, and ultimately their identity. While Jews perceive that Germans see themselves as having this secret and that they attempt to manage information disclosure, Jews stated that they see through such strategies. "I don't believe anyone," says Nathan, in response to our discussion of why he does not ask older Germans about their war whereabouts. I interviewed Nathan, a thirty-year-old banker, at his small second-story apartment, which he shared with his wife, Shoshana. These sentiments were echoed by his wife, who said, "I don't expect a true answer." His beliefs about German manipulation of stigmatized information are based on personal encounters and interactions with Germans. Nathan describes to me the responses he received when he asked Germans about their war whereabouts.

A: Usually when you ask – I've asked a couple of people already – and usually the answer you get is "[we were] in a Russian prison," or, "we didn't know what was going on."
Q: Do you believe them?
A: No. So, what do you do? You live here. So, let them live as well. But I don't believe them.

For Nathan, the information that a German spent the war years in a Russian prison is a form of biographical deception, an explicit distortion of the conditions or circumstances of one's actual participation in the Second World War. Being in a Russian prison equates the German with prisoners, or the perpetrator with the victim; thus it allows one to avoid responsibility for the Holocaust. Yet, the other excuse, the strategy of claiming no knowledge of the atrocities, implies that one was unable to take action against the genocide because of ignorance. It absolves the German of personal responsibility for the Holocaust through a process of self-transformation. This is the transformation of German collective responsibility. The responsibility for the Holocaust is laid on governmental machinery. This implies that ordinary citizens had no direct, indirect, active or passive responsibility for perpetuating the heinous crimes. That is, like other deviant groups with a stigma, such as ex-mental patients or ex-drug addicts, there is a tendency to renegotiate societal conceptualizations of discreditable attributes.[31] For Nathan, these examples illustrate processes of negotiation that older Germans engage in as a bid for acceptance. Yet he takes their explanations in his stride, since he has made a decision to remain in Germany.

Similar skepticism about Germany's collective redemption is expressed by Samuel, the attorney we met earlier: "Older people, Germans. When they find out that you are Jewish, they tend to tell you 'Oh, I had a very good friend who was Jewish, and I saved him.' Or, 'I saved that person.' And, when you put it all together, there were many more saved than killed. So, I just couldn't believe those stories."

Preventive deception – volunteering deceptive information without even being asked – is an information managing strategy that, according to Samuel and other respondents, Germans regularly employ. Rather than being a perpetrator, this German in Samuel's quote was the opposite, a hero – one who defied Nazi perpetration, who resisted, and acted morally by saving Jews. Indeed, John Czaplicka, research associate at Harvard's Center for European Studies, in a public lecture entitled "Revisions in the Commemorative Landscape: Monuments and Memorials in the Successor States to the Third Reich," has illustrated that this notion of heroism and anti-Nazi resistance is formulated in the public commemorative practice, as depicted by architecture in Holocaust commemorative monuments and sites, to illustrate immutable and shared cultural values in Germans' struggle to revise their nation's history and forge a new national identity.[32] Rather than depicting itself in commemorative monuments and memorials in terms of perpetrators, Germany instrumentalizes the history of resistance to revise its national history.

Judith, the ophthalmologist we met earlier in the chapter, has given up asking Germans about their World War II whereabouts. She anticipates information manipulation, and justifies her stance of not making direct inquiries: "No, I never ask. If I would ask someone, I think he might wonder why I am asking what he has done. He might guess that I am Jewish, and then he might not give me a real answer."

The distrust of German biographic information allows Jews to maintain their belief system – the German as Nazi – along with all of its symbolic meanings. Distrust maintains the consistency in the structure of ideas that Jews have formulated to categorize Germans. The distrust also supports the hierarchy of goals and values that guides the community in its dealings with Germans. It is inconceivable for Jews to assume that Germans were in the resistance, or in exile during the war, because such thoughts are threatening to Jewish culture. They cause dissonance and ambiguity in the established belief system. They may even necessitate the radical overhaul of that belief system, a redefinition of their ideology and the redrawing of the boundaries that distinguish them as Jews in contemporary Germany.

Some respondents mentioned that it was unnecessary to inquire into a German's past, because the topic readily surfaces in conversations. In these instances, the German is viewed as having a bad conscience, or feels repentant or ashamed, and perhaps brings up the topic as an act of moral catharsis. The following respondent resented discussing the Holocaust with Germans for this reason. "If somebody feels like talking about the past all the time, I don't feel very affected. I'm also sick and tired of discussing these things. Maybe it's wrong, but I feel like I am being used, like a tool, just for them [Germans] to get relief."

Since honesty and integrity are morally superior characteristics attributed to Jews, Germans are by default assumed to conceal their wartime experiences. Gertrud, the housewife, describes how her curiosity about a German's war past peaks when she hears a pat answer:

Usually when you have a conversation, and they ask, "Where do you come from? Who are your parents? Where have you been?" And, so, I tell them that I am Jewish, and my mother was in Auschwitz. Then they say, "Oh, it was such a horrible time. And we saved so many of our friends. Really, we had them sheltered in our cellars." I know it really isn't possible for so many people to have sheltered Jews, and when they tell me that, I feel they must be covering something up. And I grow very suspicious.

Amalie, a thirty-year-old medical student, who has many German friends, offers a telling illustration of confronting Germans' dishonesty and pat answers regarding their war whereabouts:

I don't need to ask. They tell me automatically. Because when they meet a Jew, they have a bad conscience. And because I am often friends with Christians, I am also invited to their homes, and they ask, and the theme comes up. Then many say they didn't know. I can't believe that. And then I say, "When someone was taken away, there had to be a reason." They cannot answer this, and want to make excuses. Then I say, "Let's stop this and talk about something else." And then they become honest and say, "Okay, I was there. Why did I do this? Why did this happen? Because the people were dumb."

In the course of maintaining their belief system about Germans, some Jews said that it was unnecessary to inquire about a German's war background. They claim that they already knew the answers; Germans were guilty by implication. "I don't have to wonder about them," said Harry, a thirty-five-year-old businessman, with a tone of moral superiority. "I know where they were. They were probably here. I'm sure they were in the SS. I mean, if you walk down the street, you'll see them all. They were all there."

Finally, some Jews stated that they did not inquire into a person's whereabouts during the war, because such knowledge would not affect their behavior toward Germans or their overall well-being. Herbert, the master's student in business administration illustrates this sentiment:

Q: Do you want to know?
A: No, because it won't make a difference. It won't make a difference to me. It won't help me to know that there are millions of cases where everybody knows who that particular person is. And, you see, as a result, nothing comes from it. It doesn't give me any guarantee that it won't happen again.

The danger of inquiring and breaking the taboo

"In the house of the hangman," writes philosopher-sociologist Theodor Adorno, "you don't mention the noose. It stirs up resentment."[33] In general, the Jews I talked with wished to avoid asking older Germans about their war whereabouts for fear of provoking an uncomfortable or confrontational situation. Overall, the norm that guides them is one of conflict-avoidance to prevent the incitement of potential trouble or danger.

Many respondents felt uncomfortable soliciting such interrogatories, anticipating that the nature of their subsequent communication would be jeopardized. Franz Steiner writes that taboos deal with the sociology of danger because they are concerned with "the protection of individuals who are in danger, and with the protection of society from those endangered – and therefore dangerous persons."[34] The danger would be an uncomfortable or awkward situation for the German as well as the Jew. Some respondents avoid broaching the subject of the war or the Holocaust because it reinforces the boundaries between the two groups. The line dividing "us" from "them" becomes clearly marked and, as respondents put it, might "ruin a comfortable relationship," "make it difficult to talk to the person," or "show borders."

A number of respondents considered it important not to broach these topics for they feared that it might create disharmony that could ultimately interfere with their personal lives or professional role obligations. This danger was stressed most strongly when respondents dealt with older Germans in professional relationships. For instance, a physician reported that he considers this issue often when treating older German patients, but never questions them. When I asked why, he said, "Then I'd have to stop being a doctor. If I found out, I would not only not treat him, but I would try to hurt him, and do whatever evil and terrible things that I could toward him." The same anxiety about the potential eruption of resentment and vigilance was expressed by another interviewee, an accountant, whose parents had survived concentration camps. "I don't ask them [older Germans]. Because if they told me they were an SS officer, then should I start to fight, or kill them? I wouldn't do what I actually should do, because I decided to live here. If I lived in Israel or in America and I came here and met such a person, then I could imagine that I would react differently." The knowledge that a German had a tainted war history might create a breach in the pre-established pattern of social relations. In this sense the taboo functions to protect Jews from ambiguity regarding how to behave in encounters with Germans. This is especially important for Jews in the health care profession, who must provide for Germans a service according to a professional code of ethics. Judith, the ophthalmologist, describes the dilemma:

A: I don't have to ask these people where they were during the war, because I deal with the eyes. They don't say it directly to me. We had one who was in the war, and he was a fighter, but he didn't tell stories that he killed anyone, or anything like that.

Q: Do you want to know?

A: No. Actually not. And especially not when they would tell me something like this, that they were soldiers who also killed Jews. Then I don't know if I could treat them... I am a doctor, and I must treat everybody equally. So, then I do it. But if they were to tell me more, I think I would be disturbed, and wouldn't be able to treat them objectively.

If the German is perceived as a moral deviant, the possibility further exists that Jews might provoke feelings of embarrassment for Germans, or for themselves, by transgressing this taboo. One disposition that Jews can hold in response to a deviancy, as Goffman has written, is to treat the person with benevolent social action intended to soften and ameliorate the stigmatized identity.[35] As one respondent affirmed, it was inappropriate to inquire about someone's background, "I don't think it's socially acceptable to ask someone that." Another respondent rationalized that it was not a part of proper business etiquette to probe into such matters: "In business I have to deal with older people. But no, I don't ask them because I think it would be very discourteous. You don't go up to someone and say, 'Where were you during the war?' You just don't do that."

Under certain circumstances the broad distinction between the dangers of the Nazi past, its cruel barbarism and total unpredictability, and the safety of a modern, civilized, and redemocratized German society becomes blurred and ambiguous. In this sense, the taboo serves the latent function of safeguarding Jews against the possible danger of acknowledging that they might be meeting bona fide murderers, especially those who could have killed their family. As Mary Douglas argues, taboos function because a community develops a consensus on the kinds of solidarity that will help its members cope with their environment.[36] Thus, avoidance of this topic is a coping strategy that enables Jews to better deal with their polluted social environment. It allows them to maintain a safety zone around their moral sphere, and reduces the likelihood of contamination by morally flawed values. Such contamination can create a difficult situation:

Q: When you meet older people, do you ever wonder where they were during the war?

A: Yes.

Q: Do you ask?

A: No.

Q: Why not?

A: I think it's because I don't want to provoke aggressive situations. If I have a discussion with an older person, and this subject comes up, I would probably ask. But, if I would wonder, is it possible that this person was a Nazi, then I probably would not ask this question, because I wouldn't want to provoke any aggression.

Transgressing the taboo

The health care profession brought together second-generation Jews with elderly Germans in the greatest frequency: the Jews were employed as physicians or health care workers and elderly Germans came to see them as patients. These interviewees mentioned intriguing methods of transgressing the taboo in the course of performing their occupational roles. As physicians and health care workers are often obligated to obtain background information on their patients, they found it possible to pry into the war histories of elderly Germans while recording their case histories. One Jewish physician whose mother survived Bergen-Belsen explains:

Being an internist, you have to take a long case history. They start talking. It's not unusual for them to mention "Well, during the war I had this or that disease, and I was brought to this or that hospital." And then I start asking them. They are mostly taken aback and ask me, "Why do you ask? What's your special interest?" I ask, "What were you doing there? Were you a mere soldier, or did you have a higher position?"

Another medical intern describes:

A: Sometimes one hears where they were when one talks with them. The information comes out. For example, with patients, one hears it quite often. "Where do you have this scar from?" "Oh, yes, at one time I was one of the biggest, under him, and so on."

Q: Does it affect you?

A: Yes it does. I ask them. Yes, I handle them as I did before, but for me, everyone is the same. I cannot allow myself to treat him any differently, because he is a patient, and nothing else, in that sense. First, most of them are not even on the level intellectually to discuss these things. Most are simple people. One will never change them. They are already too old. It wouldn't make much sense.

For a few Jews, when they do transgress the taboo and unearth information regarding older Germans' war whereabouts, they get distressed. Such information can affect their professional relationship. For example, another physician, Anna, whose mother survived Auschwitz, describes her ambivalence in treating older patients whom she suspects are anti-Semitic:

A: I really feel an aversion towards dealing with those people and towards treating them. I can't help it. One guy, I remember, didn't exactly have something to do with Treblinka, but he had to select people to go to Treblinka. That's what he told me. And he said that there were a bunch of lies written in all of those newspapers about how many were killed, and that it's all lies, it's all propaganda to blame the Germans. You couldn't reason with that guy.

Q: Did you tell him about your mother's experience?

A: No, I didn't. I knew that that guy was so full of shit. I told him there are documents and it has been proven. "It's all lies, it's all lies," he said.

Q: Was your treatment of him different?

A: I didn't want to, but, I had to treat him because I was on duty. I treated him the slightest amount that I had to in order not to endanger him. And then I left. I mean, that was the extreme experience... With the exception of this one man, most of them try to diminish the experience.

Anna knows many "nice, sweet old ladies" and doesn't wonder about their war whereabouts. Yet, if she comes across older patients, generally men, with "crisp and short" dispositions, she wonders if they could have been concentration camp officers.

Cultural symbols and meanings that order experience have significant implications for how groups live and how they relate to other groups and institutions. The taboo in this sense helps maintain the ordering of experience, whereas its transgression operates against the already existing normative order. For instance, Claudia, a speech and hearing therapist, gives an excellent illustration of what can happen when the taboo is transgressed, and the normative regulation of behavior is interrupted. She describes an episode she had when she suddenly found out that the patient she was treating was a former SS officer.

I'm working with people who are over sixty. It happened to me once, when I was working at a hospital at the University clinic here, and I was doing electrode therapy, and I had an old man, about seventy, as a patient. It's kind of typically German that after two sessions, they start to tell you their whole life story. Especially the older people, but not just the older people. I'm working with Germans, with older and younger ones, but I'm very much in contact with Germans because of my work. So, this man started to tell me that he was in the SS. He was sitting there, adoring me, "Mrs. K. this," and "Mrs. K. that," and "whenever you have time," you know. And he started to tell me about where he came from, and then he said, "When I was in the SS..." And I thought, "You are sitting here, Claudia, and your mother was in a concentration camp, and you have a patient, you are curing this patient, and he was in the SS." The first thing I did was to put the electrode on very high. It was kind of an instinct, a reflex, and I mean, I couldn't have killed him with it, but he suffered so much pain, that he started to cry. And I said to him, "You have to keep it this way. You have to keep it this way." And this old, stupid man kept this electrode this way and he was getting shocked for about one minute. His whole head was shivering, and I couldn't stop. Really, I couldn't stop. And then I stopped it, and I said, "Today it had to be like this, uninterrupted." And then I said, "I want to finish the therapy." I didn't tell him I was Jewish. I didn't want to. I knew the moment I said I was Jewish, he would say: "But I wasn't there in the SS. I was there in another place." And I didn't want to have this kind of conversation or discussion, especially with older people. I said I needed to interrupt the therapy. And the next time he came he brought flowers. He sent me flowers three times.

Transgressing the taboo upsets the established pattern of social relations. It generates a social crisis for Claudia. It is as if Claudia, for a moment, has gone back in time to the Second World War. As Victor Turner describes, in times of liminality, the lowly and the mighty reverse social roles. At this juncture the balance of power between Jew and German is inverted. The former SS officer's sense of impotence is linked to Claudia's sense of strength; she alone is capable of providing nurturance or exacting punishment. She is now the one who is in the superior position passing judgment on others. The knowledge that her patient had been in the SS disrupts her professional role as nurturer or healer. Her account is more than a mere story; it represents her search for her identity. This search allows her to rescue her history for the moment. She recasts the passive image of Jews who were frightfully violated, to resisters, fighters, heros, conquerors. Perhaps she is avenging her mother's incarceration. In her account, she is more clever than the SS officer; he is the "stupid one," following her orders, and injuring himself.

Claudia's case was an extreme example of transgressing the taboo. Yet it demonstrates an overall principle. By imputing to Germans terrors greater than Jews experience themselves, Jews seek to build a rationale for separation, resulting in the perception of security and safety. For most Jews though, this rationale exists, even though the thoughts of Germans' war whereabouts lie dormant. The more typical scenario is that certain situations or stimuli trigger such thoughts. As explained by Helena, the young mother and part-time El Al flight attendant: "It always affects me when I see a sixty-year-old person on the street. I want to ask, 'What did you do?' I end up saying it to myself. It's not a conscious question, but an unconscious one. I will think of it if something excites me." For David, whom we met in the Prologue, it is a display of particular behavioral characteristics that will spur his thoughts on this issue:

When I see older people on the street, I never wonder where they were. Only if I meet somebody and we talk. Maybe then. But, if I am walking down the street, no... But maybe when somebody is antipathetic. Or, if I have the feeling that somebody has been an old Nazi, yes... If he's a little aggressive, and acts militaristic. Then maybe.

These sentiments were echoed by Theodor, the young sociology student:

Consciously I don't think about where they were during the war. But certainly, there are situations... I cannot say so specifically, but when older people criticize their children who are playing, and they react so harshly that one has to call the police, then I have the feeling that this person certainly longs for earlier times.

Physical appearance was another characteristic that signaled interviewees to be alert to the possibility that they might be meeting possible Nazis. Gertrud, the housewife, said that she thinks about it when she sees an older German, especially on television, with a typical German face, very tall, fair hair, red face, and cold blue eyes. Harry, who is in the garment business, also pays close attention to attire. As Murray Davis writes, "a particular cut and style of clothing implies that it would be worn only by a particular cut and style of person."[37] Harry, explains:

No, I don't think about it. Only when they remind me of it from their appearance. When, for example, someone comes in and they are wearing a long leather jacket, or boots, and also a hairstyle, short hair. Then I would say that it reminds me a lot of the past, and then it reminds me that he could have been one who killed my family. I don't meet such people. I go out of my way not to meet such people. When I meet these people, then I immediately feel aggression and aversion.

Similarly, several interviewees said that their parents reinforced these attitudes because they often warned them to be wary of Germans. One respondent said that her mother tried to "impregnate" her with the idea that most of the people around her were murderers. Another said that his father constantly told him to "be careful and watch out. These people could be people who killed your grandparents or who were in the SS. They could be anti-Semites who don't know that we are Jewish." This sentiment of potential danger embodied in the German, of which one meaning is equated with Nazi or murderer, is intrinsic to their belief system. Second generation Jews have inherited these views from their parents and their culture. The sentiment of danger is omnipresent.

Conclusion

I have shown in this chapter that Jews have constructed Germans as an out-group. This is part of the process of establishing their own ethnic identity. The collective memory of the Holocaust is at the core of many of their definitions, which are multifaceted and complex. Generalizing about Germans is a specific example of a more common cognitive practice – a mental technique, a pattern of thought, that organizes the perception of social phenomena, and facilitates social interaction. For instance, in modern complex societies one cannot possibly know all of the personal characteristics of others one encounters. Identifying indicators such as ethnicity, gender, age, occupation, and the like, provide a basis upon which generalizations are made. They organize and guide expectations and make predictions about interactive behavior in various social situations.

Cultural typifications differ from common forms of generalizations in that the categorization may go beyond existing evidence. Cultural typifications are collective representations; they are pictures or images, beliefs and disbeliefs, and standard meanings of events or objects one carries in one's head. They are embedded in community culture; members learn them either through primary or secondary socialization, and they are more or less transmitted from one generation to the next. When typifications about another group are negative, they can foster social-distance norms within that culture.

Selective perceptions may vary tremendously from objective reality. For instance, at the time the interviews were conducted, less than a third of the present German population could have been murderers or accomplices to Jewish genocide: over 50 percent of the population was born after the Second World War, over 60 percent either during or following the war, and almost 70 percent after Hitler took power on January 30, 1933 (meaning the eldest cohort was twelve years old when the Nazis surrendered.) The average age of Chancellor Helmut Kohl's cabinet was fifty-five. Most of its members became politically involved after the war. Demographically, less than 30 percent of West Germany's current postwar population is within the proper age cohort to have participated directly or indirectly in the implementation of the systematic extermination of Jews.

Groups and individuals have sensory limitations regarding both the breadth and the acuity of their perceptions. When one perceives stimuli, one's vision is sensitive to only a tiny fraction of the total electromagnetic spectrum, and similar to the other senses of touch, smell, hearing, and taste, one is altogether limited in terms of the distance at which events can be detected and in the acuity of perceiving small objects.[38] When one is referring to the symbolic typifications of another group, the perception is even more selective. Perception is based not only on sensory limitations, but also on other constraints imposed by the perceiver. These constraints may be rooted in past training, experience, learned cultural patterns, the individual's personal history, and so on. These factors contribute to the determination of which subset of incoming stimuli is perceived and which is ignored.

Moreover, the information that is processed is further altered by how the perceiver interprets the data. Groups mediate facts and create and endow meaning to social phenomena; these shared meanings and outlooks are culturally grounded. Different groups hold different perspectives on reality, and group members often share social definitions about the dominant culture, about other groups in society, and about their own social and political situation within that social context. These definitions can be based on and influenced by a multitude of factors: historical circumstances, political and economic conditions, power distributions, cultural heritage including creation myths, foundation legends, sacred history and traditions, and the like. By definition, being a member of a particular group implies sharing a culture. A group member is socialized to be attuned to those aspects of reality that the group has deemed meaningful.

Jews hold shared definitions of Germans. Germans for Jews are an out-group. The Jewish perception of Germans is a selective one. Jews could conceivably focus on any number of various attributes that have come to characterize the German persona – a strong tradition of scholarship, literary, musical, and artistic achievements, political diplomacy, and the like. Jews, however, perceive selectively, paying attention to those aspects of the German persona they believe are most relevant to their own course of action, while disattending other aspects that they judge as inconsequential. Jews' perceptions of Germans are colored by their collective memory of the Holocaust. The most significant distinguishing feature for Jews of the German persona is the extent and breadth of German Second World War war guilt and/or anti-Semitism distributed across the general German population. Through the lens of Jewish experience, Germany is not recorded as a democratized, reconstructed Federal Republic. Instead, one predominant meaning for Jews of living in Germany is to live in the land of the murderers. The term murderer refers to the categorical nature of Germans, not to a particular individual. This categorical nature, and the traits that Jews focus on to devalue Germans enable them to better differentiate themselves from Germans as a distinct ethnic identity.

How Jews have come to define Germans is one part of the process regarding how they eventually define themselves. Now that we have explored that which Jews are not, Chapter 3 turns to their self-definitions, to traits and attributes that constitute what Jews are.

3

Here in Germany I am a Jew: identity images and the criteria for group membership

How difficult it is in this tangle of emotions, fears, prejudices, and racial arrogance to find one's identity, and how impossible it is to discover a satisfactory understanding of all of the complexities of the situation.
(Isaac Deutscher, *The Non-Jewish Jew and Other Essays*. New York and London: Oxford University Press, 1968)

A world of contrasting mentalities

Margret is a medical student who came to Frankfurt at the age of four from Lodz, Poland, where she was born. She is married to a Jewish man who emigrated from Poland in 1966, and they have two small children, one age five and the other age two.

Margret's parents are Polish Jews. Her father was a physician before the war and came from a prominent and wealthy Jewish family. They paid others to hide them during the war, and miraculously the entire family survived. Her mother, however, was not so fortunate: she came from a religious Hassidic family, and spent the war years in a concentration camp in Poland, where almost every member of her family perished.

Margret's parents met after the war in Lodz and were married there. Her mother came to Germany as a tourist in 1959, and brought Margret with her. The marriage was in trouble, and her mother decided not to return to her husband in Poland. Margret's father had a prominent position there, and did not want to immigrate to Germany.

Meanwhile, Margret's uncle, her mother's brother, had opened a clothing store in Frankfurt, where he was becoming quite prosperous. He took Margret and her mother in, and supported them. Upon his death, Margret's mother took over the clothing store, and Margret's parents subsequently divorced.

Margret says that her mother suffers from a fear of persecution. While her mother maintains professional contact with Germans because of her business, she has no German friends. Margret has much more contact than her mother with Germans. "I was raised with Germans, so that I have one friendship circle that is German, and another one that is Jewish." Margret feels more comfortable in Germany than she thinks her mother feels. "I have known the characteristics of the Germans since childhood. And I also know their culture. In part, I grew up with the culture, so I can fit in. If I want to do it or not is another question. But since I live here, I do it, naturally."

Margret does not wear a *Mogen David*. "I needn't. I know that I'm Jewish," she says. "I needn't show it to others." She had religious education for two hours twice a week until she finished her *Abitur* (high school diploma), and knows how to celebrate the Sabbath, but today, because of time constraints, only celebrates the high holidays.

Margret identifies herself first as a Jew, but makes some qualifications. "I wouldn't say that I have a pure Jewish mentality, but I would say that I have a little more of a European mentality. I think this is because I have lived in two European countries [Poland and Germany], and I would never say that I feel German or Polish, but more international." She says Judaism is a religion, but feels its most distinctive aspect is the "Jewish mentality":

A: There are two types. One is an Israeli mentality which is different from a European–Jewish mentality. There are further differences – the Eastern European mentality and the German mentality. There is also an English–Jewish mentality, and an American–Jewish mentality. There are various mentalities that are influenced by the culture. Here in Frankfurt, in the second generation the East European mentality is very strong. It comes from our parents, the majority of whom are from Eastern Europe, from Poland, Russia, and Romania.

Q: And what is this mentality?

A: I would say that it's a certain type of ghetto thinking. It's strongly bound up with religion and this notion that "only what is Jewish is good," and everything else is bad. This is exactly how the Germans thought as well. They don't like people who are different or who think differently from them. This being different disturbs them, and there are always problems, especially between Jews and Germans, when you have a Jew who thinks this way, and he comes into contact with a narrow-minded German.

Margret lives in a social world inhabited by people that she characterizes as having "different mentalities." It is by contrasting herself with others, that she, and many of the Jews I interviewed, come to define themselves. She illustrates the distinct sacred and profane spheres within Jewish culture when she describes the Jewish mentality as "ghetto thinking," with the explicit association between being "good" and being "Jewish." This association reinforces the ethnic boundaries between Jews and others, particularly within Germany, in which the relatively small size of the Jewish population guarantees a high incidence of interactions with Germans. In Chapter 2 we explored the polluting categories and characteristics that Jews used to define Germans as an out-group. They drew moral boundaries based on character traits that they assessed as indicative of an individual's worth. This definitional process was part of the larger process of constructing ethnic boundaries.

The main objective of this chapter is to explore how Jews define themselves as an in-group. I will articulate the characteristics that Jews value as they try to construct ethnic boundaries between themselves and Germans. I will also explore the difficulties that Jews face in defining their Jewishness, and the adaptive strategies they have developed to deal with these difficulties.

The meaning of Judaism for those who identify themselves as Jews

Jewishness as a self-ascribed identity

In modern complex societies, individuals have various group affiliations, such as family, social class, occupation, gender, race, ethnicity, religion, political party, neighborhood, social club, and the like. As Georg Simmel pointed out in *The Web of Group Affiliation*, identities are unique constellations of group affiliations, formed by the intersection of group associations, and often pushed and pulled in different directions simultaneously by competing loyalties toward different group associations.[1] Some social scientists have suggested that because of modernization these multiple group affiliations have diminished group allegiance to any one attachment, and that ethnicity eventually would be undermined by other group loyalties and attachments or by the rise of universalism.[2] Indeed, in *The Ghetto*, one of the earliest studies of Jewish ethnicity within American society, Louis Wirth predicted that the distinctiveness of Jews as an ethnic group would disappear over time, as Jews were able to leave the ghetto and experience cosmopolitan life.[3] This was the predominant view of social scientists studying the processes of ethnic group assimilation, and in the United States, these arguments became known as the "melting pot" theories.

One of the core determinants of Jewish identity is that its members recognize group affiliation and express a positive desire to acknowledge their Jewishness. As Sartre and Eisenstadt have asked, can one really be a Jew if one does not acknowledge one's Jewishness? "I feel my Judaism in the expressions of my face, in my gait, in my facial features," wrote Gustav Landauer, the Jewish–German philosopher, "and all these signs assure me that Judaism is alive in everything that I am and do."[4] Inspired by Martin Buber and his concept of a primal Jewish religiosity or spiritual sensibility, Landauer describes his Jewishness as one that is estranged from the Jewish religion and communal institutions, and independent of doctrine and ritual prescriptions.

How do Jews interpret and represent their Jewishness both to them-selves and to each other? Jewishness is a self-ascribed identity. I asked my respondents the question, "What does it mean to you to be Jewish?" Their responses varied, but most seemed to describe Judaism in Buber-like terms of a primal religiosity or spiritual sensibility that they felt formed the core of their existence. "Everything. Everything and any-thing. I feel really Jewish," said Gertrud, the housewife. "I could not think of myself as being alive without being Jewish," is how Judith, the ophthalmologist we met in Chapter 2, expressed it. "It's my identity. I am nothing else," responded Samuel, the attorney featured in the Prologue. A thirty-five-year-old Jewish social worker mentioned that she experiences her Jewishness in the same primordial manner in which she experiences her femininity.

Thus, while historian Sidney Bolkosky and others have pointed to a particular "Germanization" of certain sectors of the Jewish community before the Holocaust, this does not seem to be the case for the second-generation Jews who live in contemporary Germany. Being Jewish is for Jews in Germany nowadays a crucial marker of their identity. However, defining one's identity is a difficult task, and Kurt, a thirty-two-year-old attorney, struggles with this question. Even though he is estranged from the doctrine and is not religious, he does not question or challenge his Jewishness, and has no intention of abandoning it as a feature of his identity.

Q: What does being Jewish mean to you?

A: Cleverer people than myself have tried to answer this question, and have not managed. I think it's very difficult... Being Jewish is not something that everyone can give a personal definition to. I mean, there has to be some sort of relevance to every kind of definition one gives. I certainly wouldn't seriously consider changing my faith. First, I'm not a believer, so why should I change? I don't even consider getting out. Now, I'm not sure why. But I don't think I would consider it even if I said I didn't believe.

Norbert, a law student, wrestles with the various cultural factors that have been traditionally employed to define his Jewishness:

I feel I am a European Jew, which is a lot different from an Israeli Jew and other kinds of Jews. I don't think Jewishness is a very homogeneous thing. I don't think there is any other religion where somebody could say, I'm an atheist, yet I feel distinctively Jewish. It's unimaginable for a Catholic to say, "I'm a Catholic, but I'm an atheist." It's a straight contradiction. I don't think this is a contradiction for a Jew. One can be a Jew and still be an atheist. There are some traits in me that are distinctly Jewish. The things that I've outlined. Also that I speak Yiddish with my father, but, on the other hand, anything that has to do with religious customs, habits, observances is way beyond that.

Norbert describes different kinds of Jewish identities, as did Margret. Indeed, the Jewish discourse on identity construction and on the basis for cohesion of the Jewish community reveal that identity is multifaceted. But while Norbert and others mentioned different types of traditional "cultural content" of being Jewish – speaking Yiddish, practicing religious rituals, and the like – they believed that one criterion had overriding significance: being born a Jew. Being Jewish was described as an immutable biological and social fact, ascribed at birth like sex or skin color. Walter, a medical intern, sums it up, "I've always felt like a Jew."

The lack of significance of religious devotion for determining Jewish identity

In the words of Emil Fackenheim, the existentialist thinker, a Jew is "anyone who by his descent is subject to Jewish fate"; in other words, one who by fate is urged to faith and subject to the covenant.[5] Religious rituals are highly charged symbolic codes designed to gear the participants to the realm of the sacred. As social activities, they confer status on their leaders, intensify social norms, and contribute to the overall integration of the community by creating bonds of loyalty to group members and leaders. While social scientists have traditionally looked at Jewish ritual behavior and doctrinal beliefs as significant indicators of Jewish authenticity, my data suggest that such a focus is too narrow.

Indeed, only a few of my respondents defined a Jew as being a member of a religious group.

One reason why traditional studies of Jewish ethnicity cannot account for Jewish behavior in present-day Germany is that they assume a uniform definition of doctrinal beliefs. My evidence suggests that Jews have broad conceptualizations of what constitutes Jewish religion, and are not constrained by parochial attitudes toward God, Torah, prayer, ritual, practice, and the rabbi. For example, one respondent, Hermann, declared his link to the religion in primordial terms, "I was born with it. It's my religion," but did not refer to the devotional aspects of the faith. Only two respondents described Judaism exclusively in terms of religious ritual in accordance with traditional Jewish laws. One was a real-estate broker who said that being Jewish meant to him "to behave the way the Jewish religion asks me to behave." The other described how he planned to follow the prescribed cultural codes: "Jewishness is something today that I can say gives meaning to religion. I feel a responsibility to say that I will live my life according to this belief, and this is the reason that I will marry a Jewish girl, and raise Jewish children."

Others, when they did refer to Judaism as a religion, emphasized the boundaries that defined themselves in opposition to other religions. For Suzanna, the physician who had the encounter with the porter, Judaism's beliefs about God distinguish it from other world religions:

The belief in one God. That the Messiah hasn't come yet. I think that's also the basic point that makes us different from Christian or other religions. There the Messiah has come in the form of Jesus or Mohammed, whereas we have the belief in one God. This is the only dogma in Jewish religion, whereas other religions, especially the Christian religions, consist of many dogmas. I look upon Jewish religion more as an orthopraxie, not just an orthodoxy. The orthodogma is the belief in one God, and the orthopraxie is either you do it or you don't.

Finally, while others viewed Judaism as a religion, the cultural criteria they used to attribute Jewish status were blurred. For instance, Walter said, "Principally, it's a religion." When I probed further, however, instead of pointing out the importance of practicing Jewish rituals, he added that "an essentially important aspect of the religion is that it has many struggles, but also lots of pride." Walter does not have a clear notion of what Jewish religion means as a social institution. Like other respondents, Walter does not place significance on religious codes, but confounds the notion of Judaism as a religion with the characteristics of Jews as a people and the historical tradition characterized by lots of "struggles" and "pride."

The sociologists Arnold Dashefsky and Harold M. Shapiro prefer to distinguish between the terms "identity" and "identification," the latter being an attachment to people, the former a core element of self-definition.[6] When the Jews with whom I spoke tried to define their Jewish identity to me, they generally did so in terms of identification (to use Dashefsky and Shapiro's term) – loyalty toward the Jewish people, but not specifically to its religious precepts – a result not unique to Jews in Germany. According to the Council of Jewish Federations' 1990 National Jewish Population Survey, less than 5 percent of Jewish respondents in the United States consider themselves Jews because they are members of religious groups.[7] Other studies on Jewish identity in various Diaspora communities report similar results.

The secondary role of religious institutions

The institutions of the Jewish community, while influenced by societal conditions, clearly impact on Jewish life. Sociologists have long documented that group identification is promoted by a variety of techniques and institutions. Religious rituals, as stated by the French sociologist Emile Durkheim, are the rules of conduct which prescribe how an individual should act in the presence of sacred objects.[8] Religious rituals function to help promote group integration and solidarity, by reaffirming the group as a moral community. Because the Jewish religion is highly ceremonial, legalistic, and ritualistic in orientation, it relies heavily on the existence of a large Jewish population, in which Jews live by the day-by-day and hour-by-hour *mitzvot*, divine commandments that are pleasing to God. "The thrust of Jewish sacramentalism," writes Marshall Sklare, "is to diminish the sacred-secular dichotomy by investing all routines of life with sacred significance." He explains that, "to insure ritual correctness, a 'fence' of supplementary observances and prohibitions is elaborated."[9] Jewish sacramentalism circumscribes an all-encompassing way of life based on the Torah and the vastness and variety of Jewish tradition – including dietary restrictions, specifics regarding dress and clothing, rituals and customs regarding sacred spaces (the home and the homeland) and sacred times (festivals and fasts), and so on.

Jewish religious institutions in Germany operate within the framework of the local communities, but play a limited role in promoting group identification within community life. One reason is that the Jewish *Gemeinden* in Germany do not have support networks and infrastructure to encourage a flourishing religious life. Only twelve rabbis minister to all of Germany in fifty-three functioning synagogues and an additional twenty-two chapels or places of worship.[10] None of the rabbis have been trained in Germany: the educational facilities do not exist. All are imported from Israel or the United States, and most serve more than one community.

One major complaint voiced by Jews living in Germany is that there is a lack of vibrant Jewish religious life there. Stefan Szajak, the director of the Jewish *Gemeinde* in Frankfurt, emphasized that fostering the Jewish religion was the most pressing challenge facing Frankfurt and other *Gemeinden* within Germany in the coming years. In spite of this complaint, however, my field work leads me to conclude that interest on the part of the community in religious worship, liturgy, or sacramentalism is at best lukewarm. The Frankfurt Jewish *Gemeinde*, typical of other *Gemeinden* in Germany, is secular in orientation. The maintenance of religious services benefits only those who wish to use them. In the major centers, services are held on the Sabbath and on the holidays. Sabbath services, however, are poorly attended, while high holiday services attract a larger congregation. For example, Frankfurt's Westend synagogue, built in 1910, and the only synagogue in Frankfurt whose walls survived the Nazi conflagration, seats 1,200. On an ordinary Saturday the building remains virtually empty for Sabbath services. Rabbi Szobel leads the service for a mere 100 persons – 70 men on the ground floor and 30 women in the balcony. Only young people between the ages of twenty and forty are present. The majority of those present are over fifty years of age. The service is orthodox, entirely in Hebrew, and some men are praying. A constant murmur resonates from the women in the balcony; only a handful have open prayer books.

Although Frankfurt has six places of worship, they are full only during the two holiest days of the Jewish calendar, Yom Kippur and Rosh Hashonah.[11] Many of the worshippers are considered "Three-Day Jews," attending synagogue on two days for Rosh Hashonah and one day for Yom Kippur. Over 70 percent of the second-generation Frankfurters in the sample, and over 70 percent of their parents, attend synagogue on these high holidays. Only 3 percent of the second generation, and 20 percent of their parents, attend synagogue on a regular (Sabbath) basis. No second-generation respondents, and only 7.5 percent of their parents, attend synagogue on a daily basis. These findings are consistent with numerous studies that have documented that almost all measures of ritual observance and doctrinal belief, with the exception of observance during the high holidays, decline with distance from the immigrant population.[12]

Religious rituals in the home

In modern industrial societies, Jews can opt out of organized Jewish life, and ignore Jewish institutions, while still maintaining a distinct Jewish culture, and viewing themselves as Jewish. Many researchers have posited that Judaism in the modern era is expressed in a variety of ways, and that the extent of synagogue attendance year-round, or during religious holidays, is not the best indicator of Jewish religiosity. The family is a central Jewish institution, around which the core of Jewish identity is located. Because Judaism has been conceptualized as more of a lifestyle than a religion, another indicator of Jewish heritage and identity is religious ritual practiced in the home. The home, according to sociologist Marshall Sklare, "is a more nearly perfect reflection of individual conviction and desire," because religious practice is conducted by a group of intimates without pressure from religious specialists or organizations.[13]

Following Sklare's ideas, I questioned second-generation Jews in Frankfurt about their religious practices in the home,[14] and found that they are selective regarding Jewish sacramentalism, adhering to rituals and obligations that require the least ongoing obligation or sacrifice. The most popular observances were attending high holiday services and Passover seders, fasting on Yom Kippur, and lighting candles on Chanukah.[15] Among the respondents, 71.2 percent attend a Passover seder, and 50 percent refrain from eating bread during Passover. More than half fast for Yom Kippur, and 57.6 percent light candles for Chanukah. Those rituals that require the most obligation are performed less frequently, including lighting candles and having a special dinner on the Sabbath, buying kosher meat, refraining from eating bacon or ham, and not smoking on the Sabbath. Among my respondents, only 30.3 percent light candles on Friday night, 22.7 percent prepare or go to a special dinner for the Sabbath, 27.3 percent refrain from eating bacon or ham, 12.1 percent purchase kosher meat regularly, and 6.1 percent refrain from smoking on the Sabbath.[16]

These cultural distinctions are bound up with mundane routines of family and collective life that fundamentally help shape a people's identity. But, when Jews do participate in religious ritual, it is as an activity set apart from their everyday routines, something they might engage in for a few hours a week or month.

Additional explanations for the lack of religious devotion

The lack of religious interest and devotion of the community, some second-generation respondents say, can be attributed to the socialization they received from their parents. Many of their parents had grown up devoutly religious in small Jewish stetls in Eastern Europe, and had subsequently acclimated to a more secular Western lifestyle. After surviving persecution because of their Jewishness, their parents have developed a more pragmatic view of the role of religion in their lives. This pragmatic view can be interpreted as questioning the advantages of being Jewish, particularly after experiencing too great a sacrifice because of Jewish affiliation during the Second World War. Consequently, many have chosen to downplay the spiritual element of being Jewish.

The moral questions that philosophers and theologians have raised after the Holocaust are key issues with which several respondents' parents have been struggling. In particular, can one believe in God after the Holocaust? Respondents say that rather than expressing an actual opposition to religious doctrine or spirituality, their parents often feel indifferent. Some do not acknowledge the legitimacy of the Halachic tradition, even though they might have been raised religiously, and might have strongly adhered to the rituals before the war. The inference based on their prior war experience could be that Jews are socially constructed as "sub-human" or "not worthy of life." Being religious, or displaying outwardly that one is a Jew today might be a handicap, particularly in Germany.

That respondents' parents were not especially interested in raising the interviewees religiously may reflect their interest in subordinating religious values to more universal ones. The point was not to downplay the fact that they were Jewish, but to subordinate the religious aspect of being Jewish to a more ethnic one based on the Jewish–German dichotomy rooted in the collective memory of the Holocaust. This is illustrated by Betty, the woman featured in the Prologue as she explains why her mother chose not to raise her religiously:

My mother comes from a very religious family. But she doesn't want to think about God, because if she starts to think about God, she has to think about her past, so she distances herself from it. She thinks we should be brought up like human beings, and nothing else. Before the war she decided that she would not bring up a child who would be Jewish. She was just afraid. I was the first thing that really belonged to her, because after the war she didn't have anybody else, and she was so afraid something might happen to me. So she said, if she's not Jewish nothing can happen to her. If I were a boy we would have had problems, because my father would have wanted me to be circumcised. She told me, "If you had been a boy, I would run away with you in order not to circumcise you, because this is why my brothers were killed." It's not because she hated the religion, but because she was afraid.

Another factor is the lack of an infrastructure in Frankfurt and throughout Germany to support religious life. Frankfurt has only one kosher butcher shop, one kosher restaurant, no kosher bakeries, and no orthodox schools of learning. I was only able to locate one Jewish woman, Leah, who had grown up religious in Frankfurt and still lived there. Most religious Jews have emigrated to Antwerp, Strasburg, Israel, the United States, and other areas, to reside in communities where religious social institutions and support networks exist.

Leah experienced tremendous social isolation as she grew up devoutly Jewish in Germany. "Being religious is always restrictive," she remarked. But, by residing in Germany, her religious lifestyle imposed more stringent limitations because it constricted her circle of possible available contacts and interactions: "You can't mix with the Germans, and you can't even mix with the few Jewish people here, since they are not religious enough." Leah's feeling of isolation was also fed by reactions to her devout religiosity as being deviant. Leah described herself as "the religious black-sheep" of the community, and was aware of her marginal status within it.

The last factor is inadequate leadership within the Jewish *Gemeinde* and religious organizations, which fails to incite religious devotion or tolerate religious pluralism. Indeed, the intellectuals in the community believe that the Jewish functionaries and religious leaders are not in touch with the demands and interests of the general Jewish public. They would like to see more diversity in religious offerings, such as official services held in reform or conservative traditions. Pnina Nave Levinson, for instance, refers to the "insular character" of the communities regarding both liberal and orthodox religious developments.[17] She argues that while religious developments have occurred in other countries, including those with small Jewish populations, there have not been any new seminars or courses for religious instructors in Germany.[18] School psychologist Yizhak Ahren also emphasizes this point: "From a religious perspective ... Germany is a desert, infiltrated by the suffering of Nazism's victims ... Most Jews have gone to Jewish kindergarten, and that's the extent of their Jewish education."[19] Levinson writes, "An insulated character and lack of reflection characterizes both the orthodox and liberal religious traditions in Germany." My respondents agreed with Levinson's observations. When I asked Monika, a Jewish intellectual whom we met in Chapter 2, whether she thought there was a future for Jewish life in Germany she replied, "It's an extremely dried out community." She added, "The only Jewish institution in Frankfurt that is healthy in the sense of income and expenditure is the cemetery and the old age home, and there is absolutely nothing creative here." What is needed, Levinson argues, is a liberal religious education that instills a desire to learn, and provides more options for Jews, including a variety of religious activities derived from conservative, liberal, and Orthodox traditions.

In various communities throughout the years there have been a number of innovative approaches in worship and religious rite. A desire among young people for an understandable service, women wanting to take a more active role in religious life, and the influx of Russian immigrants who have intermarried and have little knowledge of Judaism, have spurred controversies in several communities throughout Germany. For instance, in 1995 when Bea Wyler, a Swiss woman, was chosen to head two Jewish congregations in Lower Saxony, Ignatz Bubis, the head of the *Zentralrat*, publicly stated that he would not attend any service she leads. (Orthodox Jewry does not recognize female rabbis.)

The Jewish functionaries are aware of these difficulties. What is lacking, Stefan Szajak said to me, is not the interest but a critical mass from which a vital Jewish existence can be created. The Jewish functionaries contend that the small Jewish population cannot support religious diversity, and only orthodox religious services are viable and desirable.

In an attempt to remedy this situation, the Academy for Jewish Studies at Heidelberg was opened in October 1979. Initiated by the *Zentralrat*, and funded by German state agencies, it was the first institution of its kind since the Second World War, and was established to train Jewish religious leaders, cantors, educators, and social workers, and to give non-Jews an opportunity to learn about Judaism. The faculty is imported from Israel and the United States, and the Academy has affiliations with the University of Heidelberg and North American and Israeli institutions. While the Academy was established to respond to some of the needs of the Jewish community, it has fallen short in solving its problems. For instance, it had hoped to attract a large Jewish student body, yet of 146 students enrolled, about three-quarters are non-Jewish. Additional Jewish studies programs have opened recently throughout Germany, like the Moses-Mendelsohn Center for European Jewry in Potsdam and the Fritz-Bauer Institute in Frankfurt. These institutes, however, focus on Jewish history and the Holocaust, rather than on the training of rabbis.

Judaism as a tradition: collective consciousness and moral values

Throughout history, Jews have been able to integrate alien ways into their formal cultural behavior, without losing their ancient moorings and severing their ties with the established tradition. They have been flexible in changing important aspects of their culture over time, yet have simultaneously maintained an enduring sense of peoplehood. They have integrated successfully into various societies throughout the world, and to an outside observer may display few visible features that set them apart from non-Jews. Outsiders, however, rarely have access to the inner boundaries within a group's moral sphere and the value orientations that underlie the motivations for individual or group behavior. While Germans may not see distinctions between themselves and Jews, and likewise Jewish cultural features may blend easily into mainstream German society, identity demarcations can occur in the minds of Jews as they compare and contrast themselves with Germans. That is, Jews are able to identify with Jewish culture, whether or not they believe or live according to religious precepts. A more significant factor for the construction and persistence of identity is their cultural system, their values and moral community from which they believe they derive a sense of strength and ultimately delineate the boundaries between themselves and their non-Jewish social environment.

A sense of peoplehood

The evidence suggests that a sense of peoplehood is a predominant basis on which Jews in Germany establish ethnic boundaries. Objective cultural criteria and religiosity play a weaker role in identity formation. As illustrated in Chapter 2, Jews have a variety of distinct images of Germans. Their classifications of themselves are not as concretely articulated. The one exception that is clear to all my respondents is their sense of peoplehood, as a people different from the Germans, with a distinctive history and set of values. In other words, while the boundaries distinguishing Jews from non-Jews are clearly articulated, the features within those ethnic boundaries, the "cultural stuff," in Fredrik Barth's terminology, are muddled and fuzzy. Specifying the specific cultural traits that define what being Jewish means, as Kurt, the attorney, suggested earlier, was a difficult task. Gertrud, the housewife, reports how little she knows of objective cultural criteria to define her Jewishness:

I don't know any religion, philosophy, not too much of history. So, I have a gap, and I would like to fill it. So far, the feeling consists of being together with Jews. I sometimes feel that this gives me a little bit of an identity, and an understanding, too, but still, it's not enough. It's still a very small part of it. It's a big feeling of what it could be, but it's just the tip of the iceberg. That's why I decided to get into it more [Jewish community life].

For Gertrud, the key to defining her Jewishness is the feeling of being together with Jews. This sense of "tribal attachment" comes out strongly, particularly within the larger societal context of living in Germany. Being Jewish in Germany means being a part of the Jewish people as opposed to the German people, a theme which will be developed more completely in Chapter 4.

A real estate executive whose parents survived concentration camps echoes Gertrud's emphasis on peoplehood. For him, it makes no sense to distinguish between ethnic and national identity. He uses both concepts to describe his Jewishness, insofar as they are employed to illustrate alliances with other Jews as opposed to Germans: "I feel Jewish nationally. I define being Jewish as a people, so it's not a religion. If it were only a religion, then I wouldn't consider myself Jewish. Nationally, I feel Jewish, and culturally. I speak Hebrew ... I had Hebrew courses here, and after graduating from high school, I spent half a year on a kibbutz in Israel. So, I speak Hebrew pretty fluently."

Given that Jews constitute such a small number within the general population of Germany, most Jews spend the majority of their time on a daily basis within the company of Germans. Yet this notion of Jewishness has a broader meaning than feelings of community characterized by face-to-face interactions. Much has been written in the literature about Jewish clannishness, but in Germany this sense of tribal attachment extends beyond kinship linkages to include a wider circle. The obligations one feels toward the people within that circle are similar to the obligations one feels to one's family: another Jew is someone one can relate to without pretense, someone one understands immediately, someone to be treated as a family member.

Community in this sense implies a moral community through which Jews derive their identity. Within this community another Jew is viewed as someone special, and feelings of obligation toward one another serve to initiate, fulfill, and re-initiate social life. Jews experience a type of religious transcendence, a sense of extending beyond oneself and feeling a sense of unity with others. As Landauer noted, "Judaism is not an external contingency, but an inalienable inner property which transforms a number of individuals into a single community."[20] Jewish communalism in Germany is strong. This sense of belonging is a type of consciousness of close association resulting in feelings of "we-ness" and emotional bonding, as opposed to "them-ness" and emotional distance. This notion of we-ness is not limited to Jews in Germany. Indeed, Dashevsky and Shapiro in their study of the American Jewish community also found that a "special bond" between people whose only common characteristic was being Jewish appeared again and again in their casual conversations with Jews.[21]

Batia, a school teacher, whose parents fled from Germany to Palestine before Kristallnacht and returned when she was a young child, expressed these sentiments of alignment when she explained what being Jewish meant to her.

Q: What does being Jewish mean to you?
A: It means to belong to a certain people. To feel a little something extra when I am talking to a Jew, even if I don't know him. There is always more there than when talking to another person.

The premium that Jews place on being Jewish is reflected in another respondent's sentimental attachment to other Jews. Ruth, a Jewish lesbian, who was brought up without much Jewish education or tradition, goes so far as to look for ethnic signals to determine if someone else is Jewish. For Ruth and other Jewish interviewees, this special bond occurs among Jews regardless of religious or political orientation, background, education, or personal values. What is important is that one knows that the other is a Jew. Ruth explains, "It's still a kind of emotional bond, yes. For example, if I meet people, I watch for signs that they might be Jewish. I watch for names, jewelry, things that they talk about. If I meet people whom I think are Jewish, or who are Jewish, I have a high amount of sympathy for them... And I make sure that they know I come from a Jewish background."

Jewish values: a social, moral, humanitarian, and biblical responsibility to strive for human betterment

As we saw in the last chapter, Jews perceive Germans as lacking consideration for human life and dignity. Germans do not think for themselves, lack civil courage and the responsibility to fight for injustice. Germans submit to authority, hold rigid values, and have little consideration for the emotional needs of others. The German character is rooted in a tradition of intolerance that enabled a Holocaust to occur. By contrasting Jewish values with those that are inherently German, Jews

can draw strong ethnic boundaries that function to distinguish themselves as a unique ethnic entity.

How do German values and characteristics contrast with the ones Jews
use to describe themselves? Jews are concerned with being sensitive
toward injustice, being responsible for one's behavior, and having a
social, moral, humanitarian, and even biblical responsibility to strive for
human betterment. This is accomplished by behaving with integrity,
having faith in one's convictions in spite of growing opposition, and
having the backbone to stand up for what one believes. When probed
about the meaning of being Jewish, respondents repeatedly mentioned a
prominent historical task "to struggle for humanity" and to have
compassion and respect for others. This implied a special mission to
fulfill, a fight for equality, and justice – justice not just for one's own
people, but also for others. Being Jewish obligates one to perform a
social mission: to change society for the better, to make a difference. This
is suggested by Sylvia, a pharmacist with a two-year-old-child at home:
"[Jewishness is] a responsibility, a way of thinking. I am more responsive
to my Jewish and non-Jewish worlds. It's my task or duty to change
something for the good, and to be sensitive toward injustice, because I
am Jewish."

This burden of responsibility to fight for justice came out even more
prominently among second-generation Jews when they spoke of their
parents' war experiences. Their family tragedies reinforced the notion
that they must be sensitive to injustice and take action against it. Some
type of political action against injustice was regarded as a crucial form of
moral self-expression. The fight is not done for personal or group benefit,
but for the benefit of humankind. As Nathan, the banker, whose grandparents were gassed in concentration camps, describes,

I was born Jewish and I accept that. Today, primarily, I carry a private grief for
my family who perished because they were Jewish. I feel a political responsibility
when I measure Judaism from a thousand year perspective. I accept that I was
born Jewish, and that it's not a variable. I must try to achieve as much justice as
possible for my generation and for future generations. I do this in my personal
life by trying to live consciously and proudly as a Jew. I never negate it. I am
politically active, and I give a third of my time to this.

Jews praise Old Testament ideals. For instance, in Judaism life is
regarded as sacred. "He who destroys one just life among people, it is as
though he destroyed an entire world," says the dictum; it is not only one
life that is destroyed, but also later generations that might have
descended from this person. The Nazis slaughtered more than 6 million

Jews in the Second World War, and in effect slaughtered their possible descendants. In the same manner, the person who saves a life has also saved an entire world. Being sensitive toward injustice, having compassion, respecting human dignity, and treating all people equally are inherent values in the Jewish belief system.

The focus on justice implies a cultural model where individuals take the initiative to question authority when necessary. Jews are to be judged in the eyes of God rather than in the eyes of society, and if society's rules and regulations are not deemed just, it is a Jewish imperative to try to improve them. A Jew cannot displace responsibility for his or her actions onto another individual. A Jew will always be judged by the deed he or she commits, and should therefore act responsibly.

The traditional values within the Old Testament do not require that Jews follow religious precepts of prayer or worship, or believe in God. What is essential is that Jews embody religious values. The religious belief system of Judaism rests primarily on the notion that for faith to be meaningful it must be translated into action. As Congregational Rabbi Morris N. Kertzer writes, "Judaism is primarily concerned with what God wants us to do, not what God wants us to believe. An old rabbinical saying goes, 'The teaching is not essential; the action is.' Another story has it that God says, "It matters less that they believe in me than that they keep my Torah."[22] In essence, while many of my interviewees said that they did not believe in the religion, the values that they did believe in when describing the "Jewish tradition" were in fact religious values as well as universal ones.

The sharing of values among Jews, and their imputation of morally deficient values to Germans, reinforces the mental constructs through which Jews draw ethnic boundaries. According to Durkheim, "a unified system of beliefs and practices exerts a cohesive integrating influence upon the actions and thoughts, both public and private, of its members."[23] Durkheim saw the religious community as a "collective consciousness" – a cognitive representation of a moral consensus of values and ideas that guide one's conduct in society. Peter, a thirty-four-year-old psychiatrist, who lives with his long-term non-Jewish Hungarian girlfriend, directly acknowledged the existence of this moral soul when describing what being Jewish means to him:

Q: What does being Jewish mean to you?
A: The traditional component: I am tolerant toward very religious people. I understand them, because I grew up in such surroundings. I know how the people are, how they act. I tolerate this. I don't value it.

I cannot accept this, but I tolerate it, and to be Jewish for me means to have a traditional consciousness, and not a lifestyle. I'm not sure if a Jewish lifestyle exists. For a religious person, there is a Jewish way of life that clearly has its instructions. In my environment, I'm not a Jew, but in my friendship circle, I'm Jewish.

Sophia, a low-keyed and sensitive young woman, who is studying for a master's degree in sociology, describes the common circumstances Jews face while saying that being Jewish means to her, "to have a common history, a common unluckiness, a common responsibility. Something that probably doesn't exist, but I do think about it – a common consciousness."

It must be pointed out that the Jewish religion, however, does not distinguish between universal values and those that are particularly Jewish. Some of Judaism's values, such as love for humankind, justice, compassion, and respect for the dignity of all people, are values that are held by many other religions and civilizations. When my interviewees defined what being Jewish meant to them, with the exception of love for the Jewish people, they did not express those values that were exclusively Jewish, such as reverence for one God, or the study and love of Torah, but instead stated those values that traditionally have been intertwined and interdependent with universal values. Nonetheless, in their own eyes, their moral soul or notions of morality were linked with exclusively Jewish values – ideas collectively held of what is right or wrong, good or bad, and superior or inferior.

Emergent ethnicity: the role of the Holocaust in determining Jewish identity

For those Jews whose parents suffered during the Holocaust, their association to Judaism was linked directly via their own family history. Diana, a dancer, who lives in Frankfurt with her Jewish husband and two-year-old daughter, explains her perspective:

Judaism was something that was not so much connected to religion or to history, rather to the past of my parents. To the concentration camp experience. And it was a big problem. The problem had a lot to do with the past of my parents, which for me was identical with being Jewish... To me Judaism means to have survived the Holocaust. That is my main connection to Judaism.

This linkage of family history with cultural heritage is at the heart of the Jewish tradition. By associating Jewishness with the memory of the

Holocaust, second-generation Jews create a bridge to the historical group experience. Diana's sentiments were echoed by other second-generation Jews, such as a law student, both of whose parents had survived concentration camps: "I identify strongly [with Judaism] because of what my parents experienced." Nina, a nurse, said that to be Jewish means "first of all to be in connection with this history." Another second-generation Jewish woman associated herself directly with the victims of the Holocaust, as Judaism for her meant not to belong to the second generation, but rather "to belong to the generation of those who suffered." Collective memory can form the basis of one's identity, particularly in societies lacking religious resources. As sociologist Daniel Bell describes from personal experience: "Lacking faith, I myself can only choose fate. For me, therefore, to be a Jew is to be a part of community woven by memory... In the *minyan* of my fellows, I am linked to my own parent. In the *yizkor*, through memory, I am identified as a Jew..."[24]

In *Roots*, Alex Haley argued that the linkage of family history with cultural heritage promotes new modes of identity and community for blacks in America. Following this logic, the key message Jews are searching for is the resilience and survival of the Jewish tradition, as transmitted from family history through generations.[25] Yet family history within the Jewish tradition is a type of tribal history, extending beyond one's nuclear family or kin. For instance, the Holocaust in collective memory can be a criterion for identity for second-generation interviewees even if their parents survived the war relatively "unharmed" (in comparison to other Jews). A Jewish professor, whose German–Jewish parents spent the war years in exile in Switzerland, provides us with an illustration. Because of the Holocaust and the social context in which it emerged, being Jewish in Germany is endowed with meaning.

Q: How has the Holocaust affected your life?
A: For me it means a very difficult trial to manage this problem of guilt, or fear – German guilt and Jewish guilt. The Germans' objective guilt for what they did to the Jews, and the subjective guilt of Jews who are living in Germany: how can you live here? And then especially in these last years, for me, the question of whether there is a continuation of Jewish culture in Germany. Whether we still can or should reestablish something like that, Jewish culture in Germany, and what it would look like.

Another intellectual, a Jewish writer and publisher, whose parents were German Jews who were not incarcerated during the war, acknowledges how Judaism for her means identifying with the history of the Holocaust:

It [being Jewish] means for me, or for my own identity, a form of belonging to an ethnic group that directly or indirectly participated in a certain historical process. It means a relationship to the recent past, but also to Jewish tradition that, in the last few years, has become increasingly important to me, because I wasn't aware of it before. Judaism means for me, also, especially in Germany because of this history, that I will never feel that I totally belong here, but rather I will feel a bit distanced, which will also be expressed as a political consciousness – a distrust of political developments or movements. For example, my sympathy with the Greens exists along with a mistrust for their nationalistic elements.

Specifically, living in Germany provides the context where Jewish identity can be most directly associated with the Holocaust. A Jewish sociology student explains: "I feel very good as a Jew, especially in Germany, when I define Judaism as a historical process, of which I am a part. I think that is emphasized, especially with the background of the history in this country ... As I said earlier, the German reality or German past is still present."

The Holocaust in collective memory has become a substitute for religion, a surrogate that bestows the same sense of unity earlier granted by religion. As such, the memory of the Holocaust assumes a similar role in terms of the fulfillment of cultural needs: it creates a sense of security, belief, conviction, identity, communal unity, and cultural achievement. As one respondent put it, by being Jewish in Germany one pays more attention to "occupying an exceptional position" and less to the content of Judaism as a religion.

Sidney Bolkosky, in *The Distorted Image*, argues that, prior to the Holocaust, many Jews could not accept or believe that they were outsiders shunned by Germans, or, more precisely, by National Socialist Germans. My findings suggest that the sources of Jewish identity and ethnic community integration exist most strongly today in cultural expression that are manifested precisely in feelings of being outsiders in German society. By looking into the past to create an identity in the present, the search for roots is itself a rebellion against assimilation and the possibility of Jewish community extinction within Germany. Lacking other viable sources of ethnic group identity, Jews in Germany may find the collective memory of the Holocaust to be the strongest viable option at their disposal for maintaining themselves as a unique ethnic entity. Indeed, the ever-present memory of the Holocaust has spurred Jews to create new forms of Jewish identity, new forms of heritage, and new ethnic and cultural myths in their search for roots. Part of this process represents an effort on the part of the community to counteract feelings of alienation, to reanimate their values and ethical codes, and to seek comfort and reassurance that they will survive. This effort is even more crucial as Jews try to assemble new conceptualizations of identity out of the torn pieces of old cultural patterns.

The Jew as the Other

The German discourse during the Third Reich on Jews as a racial category, as non-Aryan, and ultimately subhuman, needed to be counter-balanced in order for the Jewish community to survive in the postwar period. After the war, as Germany was going through a structural transformation from being an authoritarian regime to one characterized by democratic principles, the mission for Jews was to create new cultural symbols. They needed new definitions for themselves and Germans that would reflect the postwar reality. The task at hand was to create a new set of identity constructions that empowered Jews. This could be done by inverting National Socialist symbols that ideologically presented and reinforced dichotomies between German *Volksgemeinschaft* and *Judentum* into ones that were more acceptable to Jews. The conceptualizations they invented portrayed Jews as the embodiment of holiness, humanitarianism, morality, fairness, dignity, integrity, and chosenness, who trace their identity as far back as the Covenant. As Germany begins anew to search for its own roots and identity after reunification, it becomes especially significant for Jews as well to search for their own roots.

I have identified multiple layers of meaning that form the basis of the Jewish discourse on the construction of their ethnic identity. Current identity constructions are intertwined with those imposed on Jews from German culture during the National Socialist era. While the classical ideals and beliefs of the Enlightenment enabled nineteenth-century Jews to shed their feelings of otherness and become insiders, or Germans, National Socialist ideology reimposed the distinction of Jew as other, non-Aryan, or sub-human in its attempt to homogenize German society. In the postwar period, this particular remnant of National Socialist ideology has been incorporated into postwar Jewish culture. In their attempts to homogenize Jewish culture, Jews now envision themselves as strangers, foreigners, or outsiders alienated from the mainstream German society.

Because Jews see themselves as strangers in German society, they have a community that is in a liminal stage – neither fully inside nor fully outside of German society. Germany is viewed as a transit station or temporary place of residence and when second-generation Jews were growing up they felt pressure to ponder whether they should remain in Germany or emigrate. As Victor Turner has argued, individuals who share a rite of passage and experience liminality together develop a "communitas," a state of oneness, equality, and total unity that people living outside of the norms and fixed categories of the social system share. Communitas is a transcendent experience, similar to that which occurs through religious ritual. This bonding, however, is not based on formal social ties or group interaction, but rather derives from community culture, the meanings the community draws on to constitute experienced realities. As sociologist Florian Znaniecki writes of communitas, "this consciousness and willingness constitute a social bond uniting these people over and above any social bonds which are due to the existence of regulated social relations and organized social groups."[26] Since the members of the Jewish community experience liminality, they share a common consciousness. This consciousness in turn reinforces their commonality, which contributes to the solidarity of the community. Jews experience a state of communitas insofar as they experience being special, different, set aside from German society.

Central to Jewish culture in Germany is a discourse on Jewish identity as the embodiment of the "other." Or, to what degree have Jews assimilated into German society? Jews in Germany perceive themselves as members of a distinct ethnic minority group, embracing a unique cultural tradition and historical legacy, neither disadvantaged economically nor politically, yet situated socially and culturally on the fringes of the larger and more homogeneous German society. Typical comments I heard include: "I'm just different"; "I feel very alien in Germany"; "I knew I was not mainstream German." As Monika sums it up, being Jewish in Germany "means being a little different from the other people who live here."

Jewish identity in Germany evokes for Jews both positive and negative images that are intrinsic to their belief system. The positive images reflect a status enhancement *vis-à-vis* the German society, and are associated with cultural innovations to reverse previous hierarchies embedded in National Socialist ideology. The negative images represent a status degradation, and are tied more closely to stigmatized identity images. Jews' awareness of these alternative images in their relationships with Germans becomes a crucial factor in their identity negotiations.[27]

I summarize the formal structure by which Jews draw ethnic bound-

Table 3.1 *Perceptions of Feeling Different*

Dimension	Status enhancement	Status degradation
Cultural: rites, rituals, and their institutionalized forms	Wanting to be different	Wanting to be like everyone else
Structural: relative and absolute population size	Valued commodity	Rare freak
Historical: the Holocaust in collective memory	Moral superiority	Stigmatized identity

aries along three general dimensions that I label as cultural, structural, and historical. By the cultural dimension, I mean how objective cultural criteria such as rites and practices, and their institutionalized counterparts – official *Gemeinden*, Jewish institutions, religious and social organizations, and so on – have encouraged a society to function within a larger society, which provides a "safe haven" for Jews in Germany. This parallel society, I argue, encourages separation and effectively diminishes integration and assimilation into German society. By the structural dimension, I refer to the significance of numbers, specifically demographic variables such as population size, and the consequences of the marginal status of being a minority. By the historical dimension, I refer to being Jewish as a liminal status which is tied up with Jewish culture. I also wish to underscore the analytical distinction between objective cultural criteria (rites, rituals, specific institutions), and the collective memory of the Holocaust and the Second World War experience, and how this memory lingers on.

The typology in Table 3.1 summarizes the multiple aspects of the social status of Jewish identity, including contradictory identity constructions that exist alongside one another, as they vary along these cultural, structural, and historical dimensions. These contradictory constructions were reflected in the ambivalence Jews expressed about their ethnicity. Both positive and negative identity images are tied up with history, and counterbalanced by attempts at new identity constructions. These dimensions are not mutually exclusive, and I am using this typology for heuristic purposes. Multiple conceptualizations of "us," or Jews, exist in opposition to multiple conceptualizations, as we saw in the last chapter, of "them," or Germans.

Cultural organization: rites, rituals, communal and social organizations and services

The ethos of community life is characterized by a tangle of contrary tendencies. As mentioned earlier, the Jewish communities were originally reestablished after the Second World War to help facilitate aid and emigration from Germany. On the other hand, the communities have continued to exist within Germany, as immigration has replenished their populations and efforts have been made to maintain ethnic and religious traditions. As we have seen, the Jews themselves were well aware of the conflicts between emigration and maintaining a Jewish presence in Germany.

Given the small size of the Jewish population, the collective memory of the Holocaust, and a distrust of German goodwill, Jews lacked the kind of self-assurance that might come from large numbers or alliances with other immigrant communities. Furthermore, because the community was not religious and lacked the social control mechanisms that are inherent in Jewish sacramentalism, Jewish life in post-Holocaust Germany has been vulnerable. The community tries to navigate a middle course between adaptation and assimilation: it tries to push for integration by mediating between Jews and the wider German society, yet it discourages assimilation by fostering a strong sense of Jewish identity and affiliation, and by creating strong normative prescriptions and parallel institutions to clearly articulate the ethnic boundaries between Jews and Germans.

Although the community is predominantly secular, religious rituals, albeit infrequent, do provide some benefits for the maintenance of Jewish identity and the vitality of the community. Indeed, worshipping on the high holidays serves a dual function. First, attending synagogue and praying communally affirms and strengthens group solidarity for Jews by reinforcing an attachment to the group in a primordial manner. Even though the motivations behind their religious acts are communal – most Jews state that they go to synagogue on the holidays for social as opposed to religious reasons – attending services and performing rituals symbolically asserts their cohesiveness and thus provides an integrating function for the group.

Second, and just as significant, ethnic identities require signs and symbols to give them salience. By not working on Jewish holidays, closing their businesses, dressing up, fasting or eating special foods, Jews are making a public declaration of their Jewishness. Attending synagogue on days that are ordinary days for Germans mobilizes powerful cultural symbols that Jews have different histories, experiences, tastes, values, and lifestyles. This public display of their holiday observances marks them off from the secular world, and reinforces distinctions between "us" and "them," Jew and German. Given the polluted status of Germans, being different in such a way can at times be perceived as a moral enhancement. This was precisely the way that Avital, a school-teacher, viewed these declarations, when she described to me what she liked about being Jewish:

the holidays, even going to the synagogue and meeting people and sitting around to chat – being different from the rest of the world on *Rosh Hashonah* and *Yom Kippur*. The main synagogue is situated in a residential area in the Westend, near here. And, you know, you could see people [Germans] who were working, walking by the synagogue and seeing all of the men dressed in suits and the women dressed in furs. You know, you have such a feeling that you're different from the rest of the world. That was a big pleasure. Being different from the rest of the world.

These public displays of Jewishness are reinforced by security measures intended to protect the Jewish community. Indeed, the Frankfurt *Gemeinde* has been plagued by bomb-threats, and was victim to a bomb attack several years ago. On the High Jewish Holidays the side streets surrounding the synagogue are cordoned off, and incoming traffic is not allowed. The German police patrol the cross-streets on the corners and the Jewish *Gemeinde* employs its own security system as well – under-cover guards, strong Israeli musclemen, who encircle the synagogue and patrol the neighboring streets, checking for the synagogue admission tickets that are distributed for high holiday services, and attempting to detect unfamiliar and unwelcome faces. During such occasions the non-Jewish city is reminded of its Jewish minority, and the differences in their religion, lifestyle, and feelings of personal security.

Moreover, the official Jewish *Gemeinde* in Frankfurt tries to build ethnic solidarity by fostering a sense of Jewish consciousness and of belonging. In addition to events sponsored around the high religious holidays, the *Gemeinde* sponsors activities around the Jewish holidays of Purim,[28] Yom Ha'atzmauth (Israeli Independence Day), and Passover.[29] The community also tries to encourage an active interest in Jewish culture. A steady stream of distinguished speakers are invited every year to lecture about Jewish topics, and various cultural activities, including song and dance troupes, panel discussions, and sight-seeing events are organized.

Jewish institutions help promote Jewish loyalty by providing a social arena where Jews can gather with other Jews. These social organizations provide a context that helps maintain boundaries, reifying distinctions between Jews and Germans by drawing on and accentuating social conflicts and aspirations rooted in social structure and in collective memory. Public debates are held about the relationship of Jewish citizens to the city of Frankfurt – whether to assimilate, or integrate, or how to adapt. The *Gemeinde* also sponsors political discussions on the subject of Jewish youth and their relationship to the Jewish *Gemeinde*, Israel, the non-Jewish world, and Germany.

While critics hypothesize that Jewish culture in Germany is weak, my findings do not support these claims. Through these social gatherings, a Jewish community is created which, if highly diverse in its constituent elements, nonetheless forges social bonds between essentially different Jewish cultures struggling to adapt to German society. For more recent Jewish immigrants to Germany, these activities illustrate the height of successful adaptation to German society, and provide role models of what Jews in Germany might become. Many members of the community are prosperous, integrated participants in the civic life of Germany, yet maintain a strong sense of Jewish pride and ethnic affiliation.

Another task of the community is to regulate Jewish adaptation to German society. There is a fine line between integrating into certain aspects of German life, like the economy, which is acceptable to the Jews, and a complete makeover, which, if undertaken, could lead to rejection by the Jewish community. Marrying a German is considered unethical, and strong community normative regulations and sanctions are imposed when this is done, as will be discussed in Chapter 7. A perception of Jewish vulnerability in an "unfriendly" environment gives impetus to members' use of the *Gemeinde* as a protective shield, or, for some, as a convenience, making them ultimately less dependent on the external German society for social services and primary relationships. The *Gemeinde* functions as a *Gesellschaft*, becoming a society – or, as its critics call it, "an invisible Jewish ghetto" – that fulfills many social services for its members. It is in this manner that established Jewish organizations promote the adaptation of Jews to German society.

In seeking to follow a middle line between adaptation and assimilation, the *Gemeinde* has developed parallel institutions so that its members can avoid seeking contact with German society. Distinctive Jewish social institutions unambiguously establish visible markers of separation between Jews and non-Jews in Germany. For example, the *Gemeinde* offers a variety of social services for its members including aid to refugees, family and child care services, and professional help for the sick and elderly.[30] The *Gemeinde* operates its own old age home, a Jewish cemetery, and a kosher restaurant.[31] Besides services for the elderly, the *Gemeinde* also provides special services geared toward its youth. In 1960 the *Gemeinde* established an educational advisory agency to help its children and youth overcome educational, emotional or psychological problems.[32]

The *Gemeinde* operates its own Jewish kindergarten and grade school, with a greater demand than can be accommodated. A youth center holds activities such as Israeli folk dancing, karate, ballet, theater, courses on Jewish history and religious ritual, movies, games, trips, seminars and retreats. Five *Gemeinde* members – a sociologist, a psychologist, an educational counselor, a speech therapist, and a Jewish studies major – make up a career guidance and counseling group that meets weekly for two hours, assisting the young people with career decisions, educational choices, and job interviewing, and exposing them to professionals for first-hand knowledge of various careers. For older youth, the *Gemeinde's* Jewish students' organization provides a forum for experiencing Judaism politically, socially, and culturally. They actively monitor anti-Semitic incidents and neo-Nazi activities, displaying newspaper clippings about such happenings on their bulletin boards. The student organization has organized a kosher cafeteria – a special students' menu for a luncheon special at the *Gemeinde's* kosher restaurant. A continuous series of parties, lectures, and discussions are planned throughout the year.

Durkheim argued that the most significant problem of modern society was its lack of social integration and integrative sentiments. In modern society each individual is viewed as a separate being, with careful boundaries drawn around the space he or she occupies as a discrete personage. Durkheim hypothesized that the lack of integration and normative regulation accounted for higher rates of suicide, and suggested that what was needed was some form of group cohesion based on shared values. He believed that occupational and other secondary groupings would perform this integrative function.

The Jewish community (both formal and informal) is the secondary grouping through which Jews become integrated into the larger German society. Rather than drawing boundaries around discrete individuals, boundaries are drawn around whole groups of people. Jews are no longer solitary units who navigate German society, but form a *Gemeinschaft* (community), a network of relationships characterized by close enduring ties, frequent face-to-face interactions, and shared values and interests. These *Gemeinschaft* relationships enable Jews to feel a sense of solidarity with other Jews. Social scientists have long been aware that this type of bonding often results in an increased sense of power and confidence: Le

Bon recognized it in crowd behavior, Gamson noticed it in collective mobilization, Marx observed it in social classes, and Durkheim saw it in the moral community. For example, in *Moral Education*, Durkheim writes, "there is something in all common activities that warms the heart and fortifies the will. There is pleasure in saying 'we' rather than 'I,' because anyone in a position to say 'we' feels behind him a support, a force on which he can count, a force that is much more intense than that upon which isolated individuals can rely."[33] When describing what being Jewish meant to them, several respondents discussed the empowerment they experienced from their membership in the Jewish community. One was Helena, the part-time flight attendant whom we encountered in Chapter 2, who said, "being Jewish is a feeling that you belong to a community, and it gives me a kind of strength that I know I belong to this community, and everything that belongs to it."

Jews have a distinctive culture: they have their own institutions, activities, religious rituals, and social organization that signal strong cultural boundaries between themselves and Germans. The positive aspect of drawing cultural boundaries is reflected in comments by Jews who wish to delineate themselves as separate from Germans and feel pride in doing so. Respondents described their separate culture as affording a way in which Jews can be symbolically displayed as "special," being different from Germans. This difference is equated with a positive value, as being something that generates pride and comfort for its members. For example, Joshua, the psychiatrist, tells me that he cannot achieve a sense of comfort in his non-Jewish environment:

[Being Jewish] means the security that I can move within a group of people who are similar to me, and think spiritually like me, and also feel secure. Secure that they speak the same language as me, and have the same problems. And that I can trust them. And that I can tell them things that I would never tell a non-Jew. Intimate things, financial things. I would never talk about that with a non-Jew; because he doesn't belong to my family; to my Jewish friendship circle. My language. I don't mean so much the language I speak. What is the difference between a Jew and a non-Jew? Chutzpah. That's not a word a non-Jew would say. I cannot speak with him about things I'd like to speak about.

In this context, Jews appreciate their separateness, they value the Jewish institutions, the close-knit community, Jewish humor, rituals, the ghetto lifestyle. Consequently, they develop a sort of cultural elitism, encouraging their children to be schooled in the Jewish tradition, and to be proud of their heritage. They downplay the isolationist aspect of their clannishness, and elevate themselves above Germans in terms of being "different in a good way." As Suzanna, who had the confrontation with the porter, explains: "It [being Jewish] means to be something special. I feel that. I think they are more clever. How they stick together is nice. Also, whenever you go to another country, you always have someone to visit."

There are times, however, when their Jewishness is too visible, and Jews say they feel inadequate in comparison to Germans. The negative image associated with "feeling different" is manifested by Jews who perceive themselves as different, but do not wish to have cultural boundaries so dramatically displayed that they feel singled out. They find the ghetto life too isolated, and wish to more easily blend in, to be and feel like everybody else, not to always be on the margins of society. Downplaying their Jewishness is a key to integration, because it is crucial in making other people feel comfortable. Similarity in culture is particularly important in an environment where difference is expressed by exclusion and non-participation. This is precisely the feeling for several respondents with whom I spoke, particularly when they were in primary and secondary school. In this context, being different because one was Jewish was experienced in a negative light.

As mentioned earlier, there is no separation between church and state in Germany. Consequently, religion is a course taught in the public schools. Unlike the American system where students take courses and electives, where each class has a different mixture of students, in German public schools students are assigned to a cohort of about thirty students, and each cohort takes the same sequence of classes throughout the day. For religion, only classes in Catholicism or Protestantism are offered and Jewish students are not required to participate. Many interviewees repeatedly acknowledged that they were singled out as different because they did not participate in Protestant or Catholic religious studies. In these instances, being Jewish and being different was associated with feelings of anxiety and awkwardness. Being accepted by others socially was at times crucial in the formation of their own personal development. Indeed, this was precisely the context in which the historian whom we met earlier in the chapter, explained his negative associations with "feeling different":

There was always a latent insecurity and always a latent feeling that I was different from the others. This feeling was always negative. That was the ambivalence. I didn't want to be like the others because of this history. On the other hand, I wanted to belong to the others in a way that was understood... The others always belonged here.

As Kai Erikson correctly observed, "human life is frequently a tying of ambivalence and tension of contradiction and conflict and these are exactly the elements one hears the least about in most social science descriptions of culture."[34] Indeed, the notion of contradictory forces is the key to understanding how many of my interviewees experienced these cultural boundaries. On the one hand, there were strong tendencies, abetted by Jewish sentiments, to grow involuted as a small unique community. On the other hand, participating in mainstream German society, and noticing how "different" one was, encouraged strong pressures for integration. As Margret, the medical student featured in the beginning of the chapter, aptly summed it up: "It felt like a weight growing up here. But also like a privilege; like not having to be like everyone else."

The importance of numbers: marginality and valued commodities

Social scientists who have been concerned with Jewish continuity and survival in Diaspora societies have focused on the ebb and flow of the size of the Jewish population, especially regarding the number of births, deaths, intermarriages, and conversions. Sociologists have also noted that the dynamics of interethnic relations depend very much on how many groups are present in an ethnically pluralistic society, and the size, power, and relationship among the groups, and between each group and the host society. A forerunner in this area was the work of Georg Simmel on the significance of group size for interactions and social organization.[35] While using Simmel's ideas as a point of departure, the emphasis here is slightly different. Even though the intention is to focus on a structural element – the significance of numbers, namely, population size – the consequences are not for social organization, but for perceived group identity.

Regarding the Jewish community in contemporary Germany, the size of the Jewish population can affect its ability to influence the host society, or to support and maintain Jewish institutions. It can also affect chances for within-group and interethnic friendship and love relationships, and ultimately, the pride or lack thereof in Jews' expression of ethnic group identity.[36] It is not just relative numbers, but also absolute numbers, as sociologist Claude Fischer reminds us, that can help ethnic institutions survive and remain viable in large urban settings.[37]

My evidence suggests both positive and negative identity images associated with numerical minority status for Jews in Germany, as Jews emphasize different consequences of being "tokens", for their own morale, for their interest in emphasizing their group membership and their pride or shame in so doing, and for the subordinate and super-ordinate status it conveys on them within the larger German society.

Tokenism can be experienced in several ways. For instance, in *Men and Women of the Corporation,* Rosabeth Kanter pointed out that the relative rarity of tokens is associated with three perceptual tendencies – visibility, contrast, and assimilation. By visibility, Kanter means that tokens will be more noticeable than dominants. Contrast is equated with a tendency to exaggerate the differences between tokens and dominants; with such a contrast, the dominants become more aware of their commonalities and of their differences from the token. They try to keep the token slightly outside, to offer a boundary for the dominants. By assimilation, Kanter means that the tokens are more easily stereotyped than members of larger groups. The extent of these tendencies cannot be measured in this case, as they deal with the German population's views of Jews, and are beyond the scope of this book. Yet it is important to keep them in mind, as they provide a clue to the perceptions and identity images that second-generation Jews themselves hold as they struggle to create innovative identity images in post-Holocaust Germany.

The premium placed on tokenism was reflected in the fact that many of the Jews I talked with expressed their belief in the value of scarcity. They argued that in Germany "Jews are special." In terms of the economics of supply and demand, one consequence of their dearth in numbers is that some Jews perceive themselves as valued commodities. The identity construction is a positive one for them that elevates their status *vis-à-vis* the general German population.

This tokenism extends to the domain of ethnic group identification, where several Jews mentioned a desire to identify themselves as being Jewish in Germany, and a feeling of pleasure when they did so. Borrowing Kanter's words, one can say that Jews capture a larger "awareness share." Some Jews I talked to mentioned that Germans "take note" when they meet a Jew, and that Jews are perceived as "unique" and "exotic." These characteristics were associated with feel-ings of pride in being so few in number, and with high ethnic group identification. Jews saw themselves as being superior to Germans in the fact that they were "so few in number" along with the cultural meanings they associated with such scarcity.

Tokenism also appears as a positive attribute when Jews contrast feelings of superiority and inferiority in relation to other Jews who live in other Diaspora communities: being so few in number in Germany has made Jews there more likely to confront the importance of being Jewish, rather than taking their Jewishness for granted. Being a token has forced

Jews in Germany to take note of the differences between themselves and non-Jews, and several say this has made them more reflective about their circumstances and situation than they perceive other Jews to be in Israel, the United States, or other large Jewish Diaspora communities. Not being ordinary or a dime a dozen is what makes Jews in Germany, in comparison to Jews in other societies, a valued commodity. This is precisely the position adopted by Juliane, a secretary who has lived in Frankfurt her entire life. She says, "It's different when you live in Israel or in the States, where there are so many Jews, but over here [in Germany] it's special."

Excessive attention as a Jew can also have its drawbacks. Being visibly on the periphery of German society might not be valued as a positive aspect of being Jewish. Such structural boundaries can become a negative force impeding Jewish identification, particularly for those Jews who on some level are attracted to mainstream German society. The attraction might not be based on wanting to be German, but rather on not wanting to be singled out for being different. This is exactly the position the historian experienced, particularly going through the German school system. He describes the negative aspect associated with being overly visible as a Jew:

I had the feeling immediately at school that there was something wrong. I didn't know what, but, it was mostly the behavior of the teachers. The teachers felt very uneasy having me in their class. In a positive and a negative way, they always treated me differently. When I got marks in school, I didn't know if I got those marks because I was Jewish. There was always something disturbing the immediate relationship. There was always something in-between, an invisible wall, but I wanted to be equal to the others. So, I tried to be like the others. I never wanted to be German, but I didn't want to be Jewish. I mean, I wanted to be Jewish, but I didn't want people to see it. Somehow, you can compare it with the feelings of homosexuals. You don't want to be outwardly seen as a homosexual, yet, on the other hand, you don't want to be heterosexual.

Employing the assumption that schooling serves as an agent of cultural transmission, the historian is caught in a pull of contradictory forces that, on the one hand, strive to conform to the German way of life, and on the other hand, try to maintain some sense of ethnic exclusivity. He is aware of the structural barriers to attaining acceptance into majority society, and in this sense perceives his minority status as a negative force. Being singled out as a Jew, and the subsequent exclusion from German society, causes him frustration. Minority group membership becomes a negative force, and in some cases could become so negative that the

result could be Jewish self-hatred, as Sander Gilman has pointed out in
Jewish Self-Hatred.

The importance of the structural factor is linked to its ease in being
signaled, particularly in small enclosed environments such as schools. Its
influence may decrease in situations where more anonymous relationships prevail due to the size of the population. Kanter has illustrated that
by contrast or polarization, dominants become more aware of their
commonalities and of their differences from the token. This leads them
to preserve their commonality, to create a boundary for the dominants
by trying to keep the token slightly "outside" of it. Documenting the
types of boundaries Germans tried to create is beyond the scope of this
book, but what was apparent was that Jews perceived these boundaries
as based on their differences. Nonetheless, the barriers Jews encounter
because of the structural boundaries they experience could result in
feelings of marginality, being certain of one's status in either group. In
The Marginal Man (a term he borrowed from Robert Park), sociologist
Everett Stonequest describes marginal people as experiencing psychological turmoil, and having difficulty adapting to society. He writes, "The
individual who through migration, education, marriage or some other
influence leaves one social group or culture without making a satisfactory
adjustment to another, finds himself on the margin of each but a member
of neither."[38] Second-generation Jews might be caught in the pull of two
cultural worlds, and what occurs each day as they enter the secular
society is an uncomfortable stepping in and out of two societies. Being a
numerical minority, and particularly an ethnic one, can create conflicts
and dilemmas as second-generation Jews try to struggle to balance ethnic
authenticity with societal integration. Indeed, Chaim Schneider, in his
autobiographical reflections describing the trials and tribulations of
growing up Jewish in postwar Germany, describes this dilemma as being
between worlds. Such feelings were often common, as exemplified in the
following statement by Nathan, the banker, in the course of defining
what being Jewish means to him: "I'm not a religious person, so being
Jewish certainly doesn't mean that much for me religiously. I always felt
marginal in school, and that was my identity. Everywhere I went I felt
marginal. I defined it as a political marginality, and also as a personal
marginality."

This negative association of being Jewish can also be linked numerically with being an outlier, an irregularity, an anomaly that one meets
with curiosity and wonderment. In this context the overvisibility is based
on deviance and the negative connotations associated with holding such
a status. The deviance makes the Jew uncomfortable, and the perception

exists that he or she makes others uncomfortable. In her novel *Jöemis Tisch*, second-generation writer Esther Dischereit reveals this association in a discussion about the meaning of Jewishness between a child and his father. The child asks the father what a Jew is. The father says that the Jew is also a human being, an *Auch-Mensch*. Discherheit notices that across the street live Turkish *Auch-Menschen*. She wonders whether there are other *Auch-Menschen*. She asks, "Can't one simply be a Jew?"[39]

This type of tokenism is reflected in the feelings that the historian experienced while being in school. Sensing that he was seen as a token, and was being judged as a representative of his category, a quintessential Jew, he developed a pragmatic view of his social role. He explains how he subsequently modeled his behavior:

A: I was the only Jew in the school. I tried to be exemplary, as if I were an ambassador. So, I would show them how a Jew is, and who a Jew is.
Q: How did you do this?
Q: I tried to be a good pupil. I tried to be better.

The most blatant drawback associated with being Jewish was the result of feeling displayed as showpieces, museum objects, or rare treasures, what I have labeled a "rare freak." In this context the value of scarcity was viewed with resentment, because Jews sensed that Germans attached less importance to them based on their personal characteristics, and tended to be more interested in them due to their novelty. This German reaction to Jews being so few in number violated Jews' sense of personal dignity. Suzanna sums up her anger at being perceived in such a manner:

Neither am I something very rare that sits around in a cage to be observed, nor am I something that you have to keep and touch with glass gloves like the threatened animals. We have an organization here that tries to protect vanishing animals. I'm not one of those animals. Only two weeks ago I heard someone say, "Oh, it's such a pity that there are so few Jews left in Germany. We have to keep them. We have to do everything so that they wouldn't leave Germany now." I felt like a strange animal.

Collective memory: liminality and stigmatized identity

Although it might not be intentional, the evidence suggests that the memory of the Holocaust is instrumentalized in the process of Jewish identity formation and maintenance within the social context of living in Germany. That is, the collective memory of the Holocaust and the fear of recurrent anti-Semitism are critical criteria Jews mobilize to encourage ethnic distinction. The equating of being Jewish with victimization and German with perpetration is a tool aimed at the simple raising and erasing of group boundaries. For Jews in Germany ethnic identities are categories based on cultural distinctions. Membership in the category of victimhood or perpetration constitutes a third type of standard beyond cultural and structural factors as a basis on which ethnic boundaries are often drawn. As we have seen, in its simplest form these categories are symbolized linguistically by means of labels which are mnemonics for one or more typifications that exist in the cultural domain. Jews recognize the combination of traits that refer to or are associated with being German versus being Jewish.

Belonging to the category of Jew or German provides information on ethnic status to the extent that it signals where one stood during the Third Reich and what one's commitments are to the collective memory of the Holocaust and the contemporary issues upon which it touches. Indeed, the Holocaust and the battling of anti-Semitism are prominent themes around which *Gemeinde*-sponsored activities are organized and around which members of the community mobilize. By continually introducing such themes, and sponsoring activities around such themes, the community continues to reinforce the distinctions between Jew and German, and the character traits associated respectively with the metaphor of the Holocaust.

The Jewish *Gemeinde* commemorates Kristallnacht with an annual memorial service held at the Westend Synagogue, also attended by city officials, and dedicated to the memory of those who perished during Hitler's reign. On another occasion in 1984, the *Gemeinde* sponsored a youth-trip to Poland for Jews aged sixteen to thirty-five, visiting Warsaw, and the site of the Warsaw ghetto, as well as Crakow and nearby Auschwitz. A few weeks later a slide-show was presented documenting the trip as participants described their feelings and experiences to *Gemeinde* members who did not attend. During such events, emotions are highly roused, which contribute to raising barriers between Jews and Germans. What was being commemorated besides Jewish vulnerability was German hostility, Jewish estrangement, and obstacles to reconciliation. It is in this manner that these sentiments reinforce accompanying attitudes representing the degree of social distance one should keep between the two groups. Within this context, it is by maintaining social distance from Germans that Jews maintain a key sense of both personal and collective honor.

Even in non-*Gemeinde* sponsored events, the official *Gemeinde* and some of its members make their presence known to the outside society.

For example, during a neo-Nazi trial held in the main court-house in Frankfurt, official representatives of the Jewish *Gemeinde* attended daily to demonstrate their presence and opposition to the youths. On another occasion, when a reunion of SS *Totenkopf* officers was scheduled to take place in Oberaula, a small village outside of Kassel in the state of Hesse, the *Gemeinde* and Hesse's Jewish *Landesverband* demanded that the reunion be stopped. Letters were sent to the mayor of Oberaula, to Hesse's secretary of interior, and to representatives of the various political parties of the ruling factions in Hesse's government. The goal was to remind government officials that almost all of Oberaula's ninety-eight Jews had been murdered in Auschwitz and Theresianstadt, and that its former synagogue had not been rebuilt to remind the villagers of the perished Jewish presence. The Jews sent the message that if the SS were allowed to carry on their festive reunion, the reputation of their village would be ruined. When the reunion was scheduled to take place anyway, the *Gemeinde* readily provided transportation for a bus-load of Jewish protesters who had been brought together by the Jewish Student organization. The Jews marched alongside 5,000 other demonstrators, with a banner reading "Jews Demand No Nazis Here or Anywhere." Buttons with yellow emblems of the Star of David were being distributed and worn mostly by non-Jewish protesters, against a backdrop of onlooking villagers – some sympathetic to the SS reunion, who occasionally hurled insults such as, "We forgot to gas you at Auschwitz."

These types of interactions with Germans, especially within a social context of potential intergroup conflict, generate unspoken understandings between Jews that allow them to play the same ethnic game – to include themselves into one group and draw a boundary that excludes others. In such interactions there is a seemingly natural commonsense understanding, a meeting of the minds and souls, that one is from a community that is different from the Germans, and that such demonstrations of Jewishness indicate common origin, and reinforce boundary maintenance and ethnic group persistence. As Kurt Lewin and others after him have pointed out, anti-Semitism fosters group belonging and Jewish identification, as Jews band together for protection and self-preservation.[40]

The historical dimension that I refer to in the typology illuminates Jewish perceptions of feeling different based on the collective experience and memory of the Holocaust. The implication here is a moral one. It is a binary opposition between the morally legitimate role of victim versus the morally disreputable role of perpetrator. Indeed, in *Dies ist nicht mein Land* (*This is Not My Country*), Lea Fleischmann provides her interpretation of the "we-the-good" versus "they-the-evil" perspective she picked up while growing up Jewish in Germany. She writes, "When I was a child the world contained two kinds of people: Jews and Nazis."[41] Put another way, the moral superiority Jews perceive is one of having been morally "pure" in contrast to being morally "corrupt," since the victim is perceived as the innocent recipient of a heinous act, and the perpetrator as its aggressive initiator. This is suggested by Amalie, the medical student, when she says: "Being a child of a victim, you're always on the good side of the world... You start talking about these topics with Germans and you find yourself always holding the better moral ground." Peter, the psychiatrist, offers a similar explanation when he says to me, "You don't seem to understand that every German wants to have another image of being German. The only difference is that I can have it."

Moral hierarchies can also be expressed in more ambiguous terms. For instance, Judith demonstrates a desire to raise ethnic boundaries by demarcating her thought processes from Germans based on differences in Holocaust experiences: "Now I am in a phase where I like being special. And it gives you the possibility of having a detached point of view to a lot of things because the history is different."

This moral superiority represents an inversion on the part of Jews of previous social roles that defined the Jewish–German relationship during the Third Reich. If Jews were considered sub-human under the National Socialist regime, and social relationships between Jews and Germans were structured according to role relationships that Jews were sub-human and German-Aryans superior, the task for Jews in the postwar era was to create a different set of structural relationships. As Jews grappled with Germany's social transformation, moving from a fascist society to one that adhered to democratic principles, they were uncertain of their place within that society. Germany was in a liminal transition between different social structures, and Jewish identity derived from bonds of communitas – a consciousness through which they define themselves in opposition to Germans, stressing their differences with Germans, as a people apart. According to Turner, during a state of liminality, the lowly and the mighty may reverse social roles. This liminality enabled Jews to create new social categories that guide structural relations with Germans.

These moral relations do not exist in the society, as Jews are not intrinsically more or less moral than Germans. These distinctions are grounded, rather, in the internal logic of their symbolic code, being induced from the analogy of the Holocaust metaphor. Within this analogy, Jews are no longer "lowly," but have been elevated to a higher status. The survival of the victim in the face of persecution and their elevated morality *vis-à-vis* German society is depicted clearly in the typical attitude of Hermann, the physician we met in Chapter 2.

Q: What does being Jewish mean to you?
A: It is a feeling. It has to do with being better, being closer to some mystery. Being vulnerable, being an endangered species. Being gifted in many ways, prepared for a better survival, and equipped with better survival techniques.

The collective memory of the Holocaust as a key factor around which ethnic distinctions are drawn has negative consequences. In this sense, Jews think about their identity in terms that are consistent with identity images thrust upon them in National Socialist ideology. A negative consequence to Jewish perceptions of identity against the backdrop of the Holocaust is one of feeling stigmatized. Being Jewish symbolizes an embarrassing and stigmatized identity that is activated in relationships with Germans. The sociologist Erving Goffman defines a stigma as follows: "An individual who might have been received easily in ordinary social intercourse possesses a trait that can obtrude itself upon attention and turn those of us whom he meets away from him, breaking the claim that his other attributes have on us. He possesses a stigma, an undesired differentness from what we had anticipated."[42]

This stigmatized identity is rooted in the conceptualization of Jew imposed on him or her from the outside. In *Anti-Semite and Jew*, for instance, Jean Paul Sartre argued that there is really no "Jewish problem" in Germany, but rather that the problem of anti-Semitism forced the Jew into a situation in which he permitted his enemy to stamp him with a self-image. The philosopher Jean Amery takes issue with Sartre's notion of "permitted," and argues that Jews had no choice, that the hostility was too strong, and that Jews stood "with their backs to the wall." In reflecting on how he sees his Jewishness, Amery provides us with a good description of the stigmatized identity:

To be a Jew, that meant for me, from this moment on, to be a dead man on leave, someone to be murdered, who only by chance was not yet where he properly belonged; and so it has remained, in many variations, in various degrees of intensity, until today. The death threat, which I felt for the first time with complete clarity while reading the Nuremberg Laws, included what is commonly referred to as the methodic "degradation" of the Jews by the Nazis. Formulated differently: the denial of human dignity sounded the death threat. Daily, for years on end, we could read and hear that we were lazy, evil, ugly, capable only of misdeeds, clever only to the extent that we pulled one over on others. We were incapable of founding a state, but also by no means suited to assimilate with our host nations. By their very presence, our bodies – hairy, fat, and bowlegged – befouled public swimming pools, yes, even park benches. Our hideous faces, depraved and spoilt by protruding ears and hanging noses, were disgusting to our fellow men, fellow citizens of yesterday. We were not worthy of love and thus also not of life. Our sole right, our sole duty was to disappear from the face of the earth.[43]

This shame associated with being Jewish is based on the attribute that Jews have unwittingly inherited this stigmatized identity. Being a victim or the child of a victim is deeply discrediting. Indeed, in Esther Discherheit's *Jöemis Tisch*, when a father responds to a child's question of what a Jew is, the child remarks that he is not a Jew. He associates being Jewish with this stigmatized identity when he says, "I am German. I don't want to be burned like the others."[44] As historian Dan Diner notes, "images, symbols, and language are cultural contents that cannot be abstracted from one's identity. They brandmark the psyche, cause heavily scarred wounds, and heal only conditionally in a process of confrontation as a means to forming a new identity. The helpless confrontation of a child with other cultural contents experienced as alien, inimical, or delimiting leads to profound injuries."[45]

Rather than infusing the community's culture with values that are inherently worthy, Jewishness becomes the embodiment of a social degradation. The Jew is equated with one who is not equal to Germans, but subordinate and in an inferior position based on associations from the Holocaust. Second-generation Jews frequently equated Jewishness with not being totally able. They mobilized the metaphor of being physically impaired, particularly in terms of the reactions they sensed they drew from the German population once their Jewishness was evident. This is precisely how Elisabeth, whom we encountered in Chapter 2, defines her Jewishness:

Do you know the feeling when somebody close in the neighborhood has died and you have to go to somebody who sits shivah, and you don't know how to behave? Now sometimes you make people feel this way if you say that you are Jewish. People don't know how to behave. And it's strange, because it's the same way if somebody is paralyzed, and you don't know how to behave. Should you help him or not?"

Besides the references to the disabled, Elisabeth also employs the metaphor of the Shiva to demonstrate an awkwardness in dealing with such a situation. To "sit shiva" is a mourning rite that is undertaken in times of both individual loss and national calamity. In the same way that she explains that she feels awkward and uncomfortable with how to behave during a shiva, she draws the analogy that Germans do not know the social rules when encountering Jews. Her equating proper behavior toward a Jew with that toward one who has died dramatically reflects the stigmatized identity.

Conclusion

The cultural and historical legacy of a group is a depository from which cultural items are borrowed to serve in identity formation. These items could be themes, events or incidents, symbols, stories, images, memories, and the like. Their most important function is to create a sense of continuity and to provide a rationale for the group's existence, in some sense, an obligation toward one's ancestors to carry the torch forward.

Analyzing the criteria that Jews in Germany use to constitute their identity leads us to question some of the models, methodological approaches, and conceptual tools that are currently available regarding the study of Jewish ethnicity in particular, or ethnic identity in general. While sociologists have often explored the extent to which objective cultural criteria publicly mark differences between groups in general, and how these cultural criteria have been employed as a means to measure how "Jewish" Jews are in particular, one of the goals of this chapter was to identify the criteria that are most salient in the interviewees' own construction of ethnic boundaries and Jewish identity. That is, rather than imposing *a priori* categories from highly structured identity scales on the respondents, I asked them through open-ended interviews to describe in their own words what being Jewish means to them.

We see that for most respondents religious rituals and sacramentalism are not salient aspects of Jewish identity construction. Even if they state that Judaism is a religion, they illustrate in their own descriptions that it is possible to be a "Jewish atheist," and that Judaism is primarily an ethnic identity for them, as opposed to a strictly religious one. This does not imply that Jews did not identify themselves as Jews. Only that ritual observance and doctrinal belief are not significant criteria upon which Jewish ethnicity is based. This has significant implications for debates within the sociology of religion, and highlights the conceptual ambiguities inherent in exhaustive typologies of Jewish or religious identification. For example, schemes that have attempted to measure the extent of Jewish identity have created composite variables or typologies based on a variety of factors: ritual behavior, participation in formal organizations, informal social ties with other Jews, attitudes toward Israel, doctrinal belief, having or seeking knowledge of Judaism, and some measure of charity giving. By assuming *a priori* indicators, these social scientists ignore other factors which may contribute or supersede conventional indicators of Jewish ethnicity.

Jewish communities in the Diaspora vary with their host societies. For each community, different characteristics of Jewish identity might become salient. In studies on Jewish identity in American society, for example, it is interesting to note that very little attention is paid to the role of the Holocaust, or the collective memory of it, in promoting Jewish identity. Sociologists researching and documenting American Jewish identity have focused more on normative aspects of identity, such as extent of religiosity, cultural practices, financial support for Israel, and the like. One reason the Holocaust in collective memory might not appear as a major part of identity construction for Jews in the United States is that this theme might be overlooked by scholars who construct identity scales with *a priori* social categories. If this is the case, then the fact that scholars do not include the Holocaust in collective memory is itself a significant consideration. Another reason might be that the social and historical context of American society does not encourage the Holocaust to emerge as a significant factor in determining Jewish identity. It is clearly beyond the scope of this book to analyze the absence of the memory of the Holocaust in identity construction in the United States. On the other hand, my data strongly confirm that the memory of the Holocaust is a prominent element in the repertoire or ethnic identity kit of Jews who live in Germany today. The social and historical context of Germany provides Jews with a unique social environment from which to define their identity.

The relative salience of the collective memory of the Holocaust as a social force in defining Jewish identity, at least within the context of the interviews, has implications that take issue with materialist and institutional approaches toward group mobilization, which presume that economic resources by definition are more crucial than other factors. For instance, my evidence suggests that we should introduce the notion of collective memory as a viable conceptual tool through which individuals and groups come to define themselves as such. What remains to be done is to focus more microscopically on these issues. No one has yet focused on discovering Jewish identity by allowing Jews to define in their own words the basis of their ethnic affiliation, and exploring the cultural codes through which their identity becomes meaningful. By doing so, we can begin to understand the process by which memory impacts on the mental constructs that Jews mobilize to create ethnicity. Moreover, whereas sociologists tend to assume that there is one ethnic identity that competes with other types of identity for salience within an individual's repertoire of presentation of self in interactive encounters, my data reveal a variety of meanings for Jewish identity, and a multifaceted array of images associated with being Jewish in Germany today. As we have seen, because of the memory of the Holocaust, some of these images are status enhancements with regards to mainstream German society, for example, holding a higher moral position by being the child of a victim rather than a child of a perpetrator, or being exotic. Other images are status degradations *vis-à-vis* interethnic interactions, such as stigmatized identities with the association of the Jew as sub-human, or a rare oddity.

This chapter has shown also that Jews make distinctions between themselves and Germans such as being morally pure as opposed to impure based on the metaphor of the Holocaust. These distinctions function to articulate the boundaries between the ethnic group and the host society. As these boundaries become more muddled, Jews become less and less distinguishable from Germans based on objective cultural criteria. The myths, ideas, and world views in which Jews find themselves diametrically opposed to Germans represent the antithesis of assimilation. In Chapter 4, we will explore further the strategies that Jews have created in their fight against assimilation into mainstream German society, particularly as they struggle to find a proper level of social and political integration.

4

I have German citizenship but I would'nt call myself a German: ethnic group loyalty and the lack of national affiliation

> The cultural features that signal the boundary may change, and the cultural characteristics of the members may likewise be transformed, indeed even the organizational form of the group may change – yet the fact of continuing dichotomization between members and outsiders allows us to specify the nature of continuity, and investigate the changing cultural form and content.
>
> (Fredrik Barth, *Ethnic Groups and Boundaries,* 1969)

Strangers in their own land

Martin is a graduate student who is studying for his doctorate in economics at Goethe University. At six foot one he stands tall and lean with dark brown hair, glasses, and a large friendly smile. He is bright and outgoing, wholesome and down to earth. Martin's parents are both originally from Galicia, which at the time of their upbringing was a part of Poland. His mother grew up in western Galicia, and his father in the eastern part, which is now governed by Russia.

Martin's father came from a very poor family and worked as an unskilled factory laborer before the war. He was born with a deformed leg, and because of it was not drafted into the Polish army. During the war he escaped to the southern part of Russia, where many other Polish Jews fled. "It was better because it was south, and the climate is better than in Siberia," Martin said.

He wasn't interned there at all. In fact, relatively speaking he had a good time. I mean, you live from speculation. You bought something and then you sold it to another village. I would say that his standard of living then was better than in his childhood, because he came from such a poor family background, and during the war he managed quite well.

Martin's grandparents on his father's side were already dead at the start of the Second World War.

Martin's mother was in school when the war broke out. She was rounded up into a ghetto, and subsequently went into hiding. She spent most of the war years being hidden by Polish people. Her father suffered from a stomach disease, and starved to death during the war; her aunts and uncles were also killed. Her parents and siblings were not killed intentionally (a sister had died before the war).

Martin's parents met in a Displaced Persons' camp outside Munich, and married in 1948. They did not want to emigrate to Israel, and instead applied for visas to the United States and Canada. "My mother had a sister who was mentally retarded. She was living with my parents. Because of this they wouldn't give her a visa for the United States. Then my parents tried Uruguay, but somehow that didn't work, so we remained here," Martin said.

Martin says that he knows people who hate Germans. This is not the case with his parents. "Of all the people I know in my father's age group, he's probably one of the few who has little animosity toward Germans. I wouldn't say he likes them, but he doesn't dislike them. I mean, it's a question of getting used to them." He believes his mother feels the same way.

Martin speculates that because his parents were not in concentration camps it is easier for them than for others to live in Germany. During the war, "my father didn't see any Germans," Martin said. "The only Germans he saw were prisoners of war. His attitudes toward Germans are more abstract. He knows as much as I do about the atrocities that the Germans committed, because he never lived through it. It's difficult for me to understand why my parents live here. But I can understand it more in their case than for the people who survived concentration camps. I cannot understand that at all."

Although he would have preferred to have been raised in another country, Martin doesn't feel badly living in Germany. He would move if he were ready to marry and start a family. "If you are Jewish, and you think about raising children, it's pretty complicated here in Germany. First, because of the small number of Jews living here, and second, because of the past."

Martin says he is not religious. He celebrates the high holidays, and goes to synagogue with his father "to do him a favor." He celebrates Passover with his parents, but he eats bread.[1] He doesn't fast on Yom Kippur. The only time he fasted was when he was with relatives in Great Neck, New York, and it was impossible not to do so. He has a strong Jewish identity, but thinks of Jewishness mainly as a peoplehood. He speaks Hebrew fluently, and was Bar Mitzvahed.[2] During his adolescence he was very integrated into the Jewish *Gemeinde*. He was a member of the *Jugend Zentrum*, and attended activities about once or twice a week.

When Martin was younger, 90 percent of his friends were Jewish, whereas now only half are. Martin has lots of German friends, and has had several German girlfriends. He thinks that when people meet him for the first time, they wouldn't necessarily know that he is Jewish. He has rarely experienced any anti-Semitism, but sometimes has experienced philo-Semitism indirectly, insofar as he knows several Germans who enjoy being with Jews.

Martin is a German citizen, but because of the past doesn't consider himself a "German." "If I went to another country and lived there for a long time, I would still consider myself Jewish. But if I had been raised in the States it would be different. Living in Germany, I wouldn't consider myself German because of the past. It's there. I don't know anyone who considers himself to be German." It is only when Martin is in a foreign country that he feels that he is European, but it is still difficult for him to say that he feels German. "Okay, culturally I have a German background. Culturally, sure, I'm German. I was born here, I went to German schools, it's clear. But to choose an identity is a personal and political decision, and I wouldn't consider myself a German."

Martin tells me that German Jews are a "rare species." They are people of his parents' generation who lived in Germany before the war. He doesn't think an integrated German–Jewish identity exists for Jews today. He can identify with Jews in general, but not with Germanized Jews.

Martin is an ideal typical boundary-maintaining gate-keeper. Although he does not feel hatred toward Germans, his parents were not incarcerated during the war, and both he and his parents are used to living in Germany, Martin doesn't identify himself as German. Being born in Germany, Martin blends quite easily into mainstream German society – according to certain objective cultural criteria such as language, mannerisms, education, and lifestyle. Nevertheless, because of the past, Martin feels aligned with Jews.

Like Martin, when discussing the basis of their identity, Jews point less to objective cultural criteria inherent in either German or Jewish tradition than to distinctions rooted in the collective memory of the Holocaust. This chapter explores how the overlap of being both Jewish and German causes difficulties for Jews in their identity construction and maintenance, and how they mobilize various strategies to articulate more clearly ethnic boundary distinctions.

In *The Fine Line*, sociologist Eviatar Zerubavel illustrates the extent to which distinction, classification, categorization, and rigid mental images pervade most aspects of social life. He shows how, for Jews historically, boundary maintenance has been essential for the preservation of their unique ethnicity. Yet, prior to the Holocaust, many Jews living in Germany held dual ethnic status: they could envision that they were both Jewish and German, and aptly referred to themselves as "German Jews." To develop ethnic membership as Jew or German or both – or to oscillate between Jew and German – were viewed by many as positive possibilities. The diagnostic features taken by Jews to define ethnic lines and distinctions did not inevitably create personal disorganization, conflict, neurosis, or marginality for the individuals concerned. Instead, the Enlightenment notion of the universal human being created an avenue through which some Jews felt comfortable and saw advantages in referring to themselves as German Jews. This no longer holds true in the post-Holocaust Jewish community. The Holocaust has changed the cultural and political context of Jewish life in Germany today, and Jews no longer have a strong desire to become Germans.

The relationship of Jews to German land, culture, and people today

Jews in contemporary Germany are not subordinate economically or politically. They are solidly middle class, educated, and integrated occupationally. They also have full social, political, and economic rights under the Basic Law (*Grundgesetz*), of the German constitution. Promulgated on May 22, 1949, its first nineteen articles articulate basic civil rights including equality before the law; freedom of speech, assembly, the press, and worship; freedom from prejudice based on race, sex, religion, or political opinions; and the right of basic conscientious objection to military service.[3] Yet Jews do not wish to become assimilated *per se*; they wish to maintain their unique ethnic identity.

If the state is the chief political instrument for the organization of society in order to promote a particular set of goals, it functions legitimately with the consent of its members, who relate to the system in various ways. Involvement ranges from the most passive and sporadic to the most active and consistent, and is usually dependent on one's position in society and one's attitude toward the state. It includes such behaviors as voting, discussing politics, seeking information and being interested in politics, writing letters to newspaper editors, sending messages of support or protest to political leaders or state officials, joining and supporting a political organization or party, actively working for a party or candidate, protesting or joining in public street demonstrations, and the like.[4]

My field-work revealed that Jews vote in the national and local elections at about the same rate as do Germans. Most felt it necessary to vote, and to keep abreast of the German political climate. No specific patterns were apparent in terms of their political party choices. They supported specific political parties and candidates from whom they felt they would receive something in return. For example, there were Jews who voted for conservative parties such as the Christian Democratic Union (CDU) which they thought would favor their economic interests. Others voted for more left-oriented parties like the Social Democrats (SPD) whose political platforms included maintaining extensive social welfare policies. Some voted for the Greens because they supported their environmental concerns and their platform to reduce nuclear weapons across Germany, and some for the Free Democratic Party (FDP), to increase the likelihood of a more even distribution of party affiliates within the German parliament. Several respondents mentioned that they voted often for smaller political parties in order to prevent one party from becoming too dominant. Some respondents voted for political parties that they thought had a more supportive platform toward Israel.

Yet Jews' lack of allegiance to the German state can be seen most clearly in their attitudes toward carrying out certain functions that would protect the state, for example, military service. Unlike the United States, Germany has a mandatory draft during peacetime. The Obligatory Military Service Law enacted in July 1956 mandates that all males between the ages of eighteen and thirty-five are subject to conscription for military service, which today requires ten months of active duty and additional reserve obligations. Conscientious objectors are required to serve the country for thirteen months in some alternative capacity. To maintain force levels, approximately 180,000 young men are drafted annually. The majority of Jews living in contemporary Germany would not enlist in the German army or be willing to fight in it. One Jewish physician even rejected a medical internship at a military hospital in part because of her revulsion toward the German military. A "gentleman's agreement" exists under which Jews are exempted from obligatory military service, as a concession for families who suffered from persecution or were forced to flee Germany between 1933 and 1945 on racial, religious or political grounds. In fact, the possible elimination of this exemption from military service for the postwar third generation is of concern to Jews in the *Gemeinde*.

Nationalism is generally understood as a type of consciousness, on the part of individuals or groups, of membership in a nation, and a desire to further its strength, liberty, and prosperity.[5] Members of a society are expected to contribute to the integrity and effective functioning of the nation-state, and to the establishment or maintenance of its independence.[6] One task for the nation is to socialize its members in order to internalize its political culture on some level of consciousness. By political culture, I mean a set of role relationships within the political system that has a culture of its own in terms of attitudes, values, and styles of political behavior. One aspect of this political culture is a sense of national consciousness, which includes a sense of loyalty and identification with the state and its inhabitants. The legitimacy of the state, patterns of change and stability, and processes of political integration and disintegration are dependent in part on the properties of political systems, and the relationships forged between political leaders and their constituencies. Political socialization takes place on many levels, as political information, values, and perspectives are transmitted from parents, teachers, the media, local politicians, political parties, and other agents of socialization.

As we saw in Chapter 3, Jews in Germany maintain estrangement through the establishment of separate institutions. Moreover, while they are integrated economically, they generally invest in liquid capital, rather than in industry or the agricultural sector that would tie them to the place where they reside. These characteristics have been considered to be attributes of sojourners, which is how many of my interviewees feel, even though they continue to live in Germany. Second-generation Jews in Germany feel that they are strangers in Germany, in search of a *Heimat* (homeland), and longing for their *Volk* (people). For most of the last half century, as mentioned in Chapter 1, the Jews in Germany have been "sitting on packed suitcases." In fact, as respondents were growing up, emigrating from Germany was a well-defined normative expectation, and the pressure to do so was severe. This is reflected clearly in a comment by Anna, the physician:

Someone was easily an outcast if they voiced the opinion that he or she might stay in Germany. And this group pressure shouldn't be underestimated. I think it's responsible for a lot of misbehavior that occurred among Jewish youngsters here, who didn't have the capability to tolerate this group pressure... We had a constant pressure to think of emigrating. And a constant feeling that one should have a bad conscience living here and enjoying being here. And that was something I suffered from. Not only me, but my friends as well.

Many of the Jews I interviewed were angry or had felt resentment toward their parents at some point in their lives for having remained in Germany and raising them there. Every respondent had childhood friends or siblings who had emigrated from Germany, and they shared the common experience of questioning whether they themselves should remain. The expectation to emigrate to Israel was emphasized in the Zionistic Youth Group, in which about a fifth of my respondents had been active. The normative pattern was that Jews were expected to reach a decision about their future in Germany upon finishing high school, and many second-generation Jews left. Harry, a businessman, explains: "After I made *Abitur* (high school diploma) a great many of my friends left Frankfurt and left Germany. I didn't want to do that. My parents also encouraged me to go to France or England or Israel. My friends always hated Frankfurt. One is in Italy, another in Switzerland, another in the States, and one is in London."

Longing for a Heimat

The concept of *Heimat* (homeland) is central to the ideas of German nationalism, which still survive today. Johann Herder, the "father of German nationalism," believed, as did those who were to follow, that the German search for an identity and homeland required a common language, a common land, a common will for political unity, and a common culture. According to Germans concerned with the issue of nationality afer Herder, there had to be an organic union of all four elements to have a nation.[7] *Heimat* is defined here as an emotional attachment, a national identity or patriotism tied up with one's relationship to one's physical environment. Political scientist Joyce Mushaben has noted that the concept of *Heimat* reflects an interconnection between a national consciousness and one's personal identity.[8] As political scientist Leonard Doob points out, the land on which people live is the initial referent of patriotism.[9]

"Land, people, and culture," according to Doob, "are the basic stimulus patterns or referents of patriotism; it is they that give rise to, and then become the essential components of 'national consciousness' or whatever the psychological ingredients of patriotism are called."[10] Individuals often associate the land with themselves and their welfare, and on some level the country reflects the important values of the society. As Doob writes, "the land remains a concrete reality: here the home is located, here a living is earned, here the web of human relationships exists, here death eventually occurs."[11]

The German concept of *Heimat* refers to birthplace, but in different contexts it can also mean neighborhood, hometown, country of birth, and nationality.[12] For many German-speakers, the word *Heimat* is filled with pure sentiment, as this quotation from a popular almanac in South Tyrol demonstrates:

When we say this dear word *Heimat*, then a warm wave passes over our hearts; in all our loneliness we are not completely alone and in all our sorrow we are not without comfort... *Heimat* is first of all the mother earth who has given birth to our folk and race, who is the holy soil, and who gulps down God's clouds, sun, and storms so that together with their own mysterious strength they prepare the bread and wine which rest on our table and give us strength to lead a good life...[13]

The Holocaust destroyed this emotional attachment to Germany as a homeland for many Germans of the postwar generation. For a long time after the destruction of the Third Reich, and even nowadays, German youth have had difficulties developing a national identity and love for homeland. It is only in recent years, argues Joyce Mushaben, that the concept of *Heimat* has begun to reemerge as a potential source of community and security, manifested in a revived interest in preserving local dialects, the popularity of an early 1980s TV series called *"Heimat,"* and the widespread interest in recent biographies of regional heroes.[14] Mushaben demonstrates that this holds true for both the Federal Republic of Germany and the former German Democratic Republic. She argues that within the former East Germany, for instance, the notion of *Heimat* was instrumentalized by focusing on the history of local daily life, in order to socialize people toward *Sozialistische Vaterslandsliebe* (a socialist love of the fatherland).[15]

The difficulties of feeling sentimentally attached to Germany as a homeland are even more pronounced for the second generation of Jews in the postwar population. The Jews who live in contemporary Germany have difficulty in feeling sentiments of patriotism or German national identity, and particularly in viewing Germany as their *Heimat*. Recall, for example, the titles of popular books by second-generation Jews: *Fremd im eigenen Land* (Strangers in One's Own Land), by Henryk Broder and Michel Lang; *Dies ist nicht mein Land* (This Is Not My

Country), by Lea Fleischmann; and *Zwischen Welten* (Between Worlds) by Richard Chaim Schneider.

As social scientist Herbert Kelman notes, one important aspect of developing a sense of national consciousness and subsequent patriotism is to internalize a notion of the "sacredness" of the nation-state. This is a difficult task for Jews who live in Germany, and some Jews express ambivalent feelings regarding the actual existence of Germany as a nation-state or as a homeland. My respondents often said that Germany simply left them indifferent. This was the most positive manner in which Jews described Germany. For instance, while discussing her ambivalence about living in Germany, Barbara, an attorney, said, "I feel neutral. Neutral means I don't experience it as Germany, or as the country in which I live. Rather, I experience it as the house, the city. I could live just as well in Paris, London, or New York." On the other hand, feeling indifferent toward Germany can be interpreted as a coping mechanism, an attempt to come to terms with living in Germany. This means that Barbara might not really experience Germany as a nation *per se*, but compartmentalize it into separate geographical or physical units.

The most negative sentiment Jews expressed toward Germany as a nation-state was a wish for its death. A number of the Jews I interviewed complained about the burdens they experienced growing up in Germany. They hated older Germans, they disliked younger Germans, felt claustrophobic within the Jewish community, and ultimately craved a more peaceful existence. A Jewish physician said to me, "I wouldn't mind the A-bomb on Germany." A young Jewish writer, who has subsequently emigrated to France, describes her lack of love of the German fatherland when she says, "I think it's tragic that Germany as a political state still exists. I would have been happy if it had become a part of other countries – if the country as a political entity had been destroyed."

Doris Kuschner, in an empirical study of attitudes of Jews (including first generation) toward Germany, found that less than 16 percent could call Germany their home. She also questioned approximately 100 older Jews of German origin who were at least sixteen years old at the onset of the Second World War, and found that 35 percent of them still had a sense of *Heimatsgefühl* (feeling of homeland) toward Germany. A large proportion of these older Jews had converted to Christianity before or after the war, or had Christian relatives. That is, they were more marginal within the Jewish community.[16] The fact that the *Zentralrat* decided to keep the Nazi-imposed "Jews in Germany," rather than the pre-war "Germans of the Jewish Faith," for the name of its organization is another example of this estrangement.

As most second-generation Jews in Germany reject the label *"Heimat"* for Germany, they think of themselves as lacking a homeland. Their lack of connection to Germany is not immediately mitigated by a strong sense of connection to the state of Israel or the Jewish Diaspora. The tenor of social and political norms and the historical circumstances and social conditions of post-Second World War Jewish life in Germany leaves some second-generation Jews feeling uprooted and lost. The liminality Jews experience is characterized by the expression that "no place is home and every place can be home." The alienation from a place called home is suggested by Rosanna, a medical student, who will choose a home through rational deduction. She says of living in Germany, "What I am occupied with now is the problem that I do not belong to somebody or somewhere or some place or culture. Maybe a culture, yes. But if I belong to a place, it would be through a conscious decision, not through emotional development." An even stronger sentiment expressed by Amalie, a medical student, is to find a safe haven to which she could escape if resentments against Jews increased. She discusses the difficulties of living in Germany in the following terms: "The one problem is not to have a home. Israel isn't really my home, so I cannot go back to Israel. I'd like to have a home in southern Europe that I could visit, where I had the possibility to flee to, if it became uncomfortable in Germany." It does not occur to Amalie that Germany could be her homeland, nor does she any longer feel nostalgic ties to her previous home, Israel. "Homelessness remains a Jewish condition," as Anson Rabinbach noted, "despite, and in part because of, Israel. The pariah people has been redefined as the pariah nation, with global consequences."[17]

Not only did the second-generation Jews with whom I spoke not feel an emotional commitment to Germany as a home, but they also lacked trust regarding the extent to which Germany met their needs and interests. It is important to remember that these feelings are reinforced regularly and repeatedly through the Jewish community's schools, agencies, and platforms where discussion is aired. As we saw in Chapter 3, the Jewish *Gemeinde* and its organizations have functioned as a parallel society for their members.

Second-generation Jews seemed to be caught in the middle. Many felt they had no choice in being in Germany. It was their parents' decision, most were born on German soil or arrived as young children. Some resented their parents or felt angry about it at some point in their lives. Yet today, they seem resigned to live with their fate. For instance, Deborah, the secretary, resolved her need to belong somewhere by redefining the emphasis on place or home and focusing more on finding a comfortable situation:

Before, I suffered a lot that I was so torn – Israeli, German. That made me very crazy. I wished that I had only one identity, and not that I was always torn in two directions. And I believe that made me crazy. I wanted it to stop. Perhaps it has to do with age. I know that it is so. It also won't go away. I accepted it – not to feel at home anywhere. In Israel I didn't feel good, and in Germany I didn't feel good. Where could I live and feel good? Because there are people who live here in Germany who do feel good. And the thought that I would never have this made me crazy. It was a wish. A wish to belong somewhere. But now I feel good. I needn't belong anywhere. I feel like I belong to me. It needn't be a country, rather a situation.

With a few exceptions, my respondents almost always had difficulty committing themselves to certain societal roles that express an attachment to the nation-state. If people refer to an interest in the nation, they do so for the most part by voting, or by keeping abreast of the political situation in Germany. For example, they keep abreast of the rise of extremist right-wing parties or organizations, and monitor the political platforms of politicians and parties regarding their commitment to combat anti-Semitism and anti-foreigner sentiments and actions.

Jews, however, have difficulty with German national symbols. Many felt uncomfortable at the sight of reunification – the images of Germans from the former east and west sides sitting on the Berlin Wall gloriously waving the German flag. None of my respondents expressed the sort of patriotism in which they took pride in Germany, in fighting for a German cause, or in expressing sentiments of attachment to national symbols. For instance, Judith, the ophthalmologist, describes her difficulties in becoming more civically engaged:

Q: Are you German?
A: No... I have a German passport. I was raised in [an invisible] Jewish ghetto and because of this Jewish past I could never feel German. Perhaps my children, if I raised them here, perhaps they could make this jump. I can't make it. My mother was in Auschwitz. I can't and I don't want to. Because it doesn't work emotionally to feel German. There are certainly Jews in America who feel both American and Jewish. They would fight for America. They would go into American politics. I don't know which German citizens I should do this for? For me, they are not my fellow countrymen. This is not the country I would fight for.

Jews are no longer willing to shed their blood to fight in battle to prove national loyalty, or even to devote their talents to other national causes. Samuel, the attorney we met in the Prologue, is a case in point:

I think I am the most Jewish person, and also the most German person. I've internalized so much of both cultures... Of course it's a problem. For me, personally, if you cut out the ugly past, for example, what happened to my parents between 1933 and 1945, then I have no problems. I have to cut it out in order to continue living here. I was a strong Zionist. Not so much because I hated the Germans, but for positive reasons. I wanted to be a national person in a national environment. I could never be a citizen of Germany, waving the flag like you can wave the American flag. The German army, that's out of the question. And, I could never become a German public official. My friends have said to me, "Come on. Be a judge." I just couldn't be a civil servant in Germany.

Feeling of Volksgemeinschaft (peoplehood)

The distances or boundaries that impede individuals or groups from feeling a sense of national consciousness are never purely physical. People can live outside of a political territory, yet still feel a sense of allegiance to it, and, likewise, they can live within a nation's political and territorial boundaries, yet still experience national disaffiliation. No political barriers exist for Jewish integration into contemporary German society, most Jews hold German citizenship, and can legitimately claim that they are German; yet only a few Jews I spoke with were able to envisage a Jewish–German symbiosis. One respondent referred to her multiple ethnic statuses with relative ease. "I see myself with two or more identities," she says. "It's not just Israeli or German. It's more than that." Another interviewee, a real estate broker, when asked whether it was a problem to be both Jewish and German said, "No. I think there is something like German–Jewishness. I mean, that's not so unusual in Germany, that it is within one person. I think some of the ideals of the German bourgeoisie are influenced or at least made up by Jews."

These cases were exceptions to the rule. My respondents almost never referred to feeling as if they were a part of the German *Volksgemeinschaft*. They are very aware of their Jewish identity, and how they differ from Germans. This consciousness of ethnic differences extends to their perception of German society as well. Esther, the law student, explains the distinctions: "If I'm talking about Germans, I always mean non-Jews. If the Jews talk about the Germans, then they say the Germans. And if the Germans are talking about the Jews, then they say the Jews."

According to Kelman, one source of sentimental attachment to the state is embedded within a commitment to the basic values of the national culture, as embodied by the concept of *Volk*. The individual may value the special qualities of the people, as they have evolved historically and are culturally defined, their characteristic way of life, their cultural products – such as language, literature, or art, national and religious traditions – and the goals for which the nation has stood historically. One's attachment to the system is based on the fact that one's personal identity is part of the national identity, and the values that the system represents are similar to one's own values.[18]

In the pre-Holocaust era, for many Jews in Germany and Europe, the identification of the German with liberalism and the values of the Enlightenment – notions of the universal human being as the embodiment of reason and civic or social virtue – encouraged trends toward assimilation. These secular Jewish visions of utopia that equated the German with the Jew in the larger context of the universal human being, were even prominent in the writings of Rosa Luxemburg, Leon Trotsky, and Karl Marx. The notion of assimilation, though, involved more than just becoming a member of the state. It also involved a spiritual, psychological, and cultural dimension beyond the physical or material. Becoming a German did not mean merely a deep affiliation with and glorification of the state; it also meant becoming a member of the German *Volk* or *Volksgemeinschaft*.

Because the concept of *Volk* is central to the German discourse on nationalism, it is important to define it more clearly. The word *Volk* in German originally denoted a band of warriors, and later the servants of a prince. Over time, however, it acquired the meaning of the English word "people," both in the sense of the "common people," as distinct from monarchs and aristocrats, and, after the French revolution, of "sovereign people."[19] Becoming a part of the German *Volksgemeinschaft* meant becoming a German in body and soul, becoming a part of the German *Geist* (spirit). Membership in the German *Volksgemeinschaft* was equated, in the words of Bolkosky, with "total assimilation or total acculturation beyond external manifestations to emotion, feeling, and the murky, mystical, even, arcane, realm of spiritual oneness."[20] In the last decades of the nineteenth century, a *völkisch* movement took place, a neo-romantic revolt by the bourgeois youth against German society, in which Germanness connoted an empathy with land through contact with nature, defined as the landscape of the *Volk*.[21] Landscape, however, in the words of George Mosse, came to mean not only "woods and fields but also villages, small towns, and ancient castles. The landscape stood not merely for an escape from hated modernity but also for a past which reminded them of the natural genuineness of their German roots."[22] German youth sought to establish a connection between their own souls and the "genuineness" which the landscape embodied.[23] The strong demand of the German state that Jews prove their loyalty to secure political emancipation also induced many Jews toward an emotional attachment to the German *Volk*.

In Nazi ideology, however, the term *Volk* also came to imply a genetic group, people who shared a certain set of cultural capacities. In their attempts to homogenize German society, the Nazis claimed that the innate set of capacities could be detected in every aspect of the nation's civilization: language, laws, religion, literature, philosophy, art. Any one of these could serve as a measure of the population's ultimate potential.

The rise of Nazism, the abolition of human and civil rights, the physical and emotional abuse in the form of beatings, vandalism, desecrations, and ultimately genocide perpetrated by the National Socialist regime, made it clear to assimilated European Jews that the Enlightenment tradition and its ideals of tolerance, reason, and cosmopolitanism were not shared by the vast majority of Germans. Many assimilated European Jews felt cheated.

While debates on immigration and citizenship that concerned the integration of foreign workers into German society were much in the news at the time I conducted the interviews, they seemed to play hardly any role in respondents' discussions of feeling German. In these debates there has been a call for recognition of a multicultural society. The point was to make the notion of who was considered German more inclusive. In this manner Turks, Greeks, Yugoslavs, and other "guest-workers" or foreigners could be eligible for German citizenship and other national rights. However, defining German in a multicultural sense was only mentioned by a few Jewish intellectuals in our discussions of identity. Moreover, while scholars in the United States have often referred to the present Jewish population as "German Jews," it is interesting to note that when describing their own identity, as mentioned previously, the Jews I spoke with are reluctant to refer to themselves in that way. Jews in Germany have a different frame of reference for understanding what a German Jew is. In general, my respondents downplayed the importance of objective cultural criteria – the fact that they were born in Germany, held German citizenship, spoke the language, and were educated in German schools – in their own and others' identity. Consider Joshua, the psychiatrist: "There are no German Jews. I don't know any German

Jews. I think I identify with these people who came from Israel and lived here for awhile, like myself. I feel closer to them."

Jews for the most part reject the notion of German Jew as an appropriate image to describe their and others' identity because the concept of German Jew represents for them some type of spiritual assimilation, holding ideas of good and evil in common with Germans, and having the same heroes and allegiances, values and concerns. The concept implies a relationship between Jews and Germans that in the aftermath of the Holocaust no longer exists. When Jews did refer to themselves as German Jews, they were less likely to emphasize their German side, and more likely to emphasize their Jewish side. This is exactly the attitude of Viktor, a mathematician. He describes the dilemma:

It's kind of schizophrenic. I'm a loyal citizen, and I identify with it [Germany]. There is no other language that I can speak as well as German. But my people are Jews. Period. There are no German Jews, just Jews. I have a problem with American Jews. I don't know if they are more Jewish or more American. Before the war, you could make a comparison – who is more Jewish, the German or the American. But today, after the war, not any more.

While in the United States, second-generation Jews have little difficulty in saying that they are Americans, "the German Jews are different from all other Jews," says one of my interviewees. "They would never consider themselves Germans." My respondents almost never describe themselves as feeling German, it even sounds anachronistic. Nor do they acknowledge membership in the German *Volksgemeinschaft*, as a body of people. As we saw in Chapter 3, a sense of peoplehood is at the heart of being Jewish, particularly within the social context of living in Germany. Hermann, the physician, put it best, when he said, "I would never call myself a German. Whenever I am asked, I always answer with the restriction 'I am a Jew in Germany.'"

It is no longer possible to posit a *Gemeinsamkeit*, an organic sense of communal unity between Jews and Germans that was based on Enlightenment characterizations of Germans, and that was at the heart of assimilationist sentiments. As Michael Wolffsohn and others correctly observed, "Once upon a time there was a German Jewry, and a German Judaism, but no longer."[24] The concept of German Jew is symbolic of the dangers of the liberal brand of assimilation. German Jewry's highly successful adaptation, and subsequent betrayal, are examples of what could happen to Jews if they disavowed their ethnic heritage and became assimilated participants in the civic life of Germany. Many Jews I spoke with thought that the assimilation implied by the term German Jew was a useless concept in the post-Holocaust era. This is suggested by Theodor, the young sociology student. Even though his father was an assimilated German Jew who fled to the United States to escape Nazi persecution and returned after the war to help rebuild German democracy, Theodor describes his break with the prior tradition:

Q: Do you feel German?

A: It doesn't work. A Jew is first a Jew. He can never feel or be a German. That happened before the Second World War. But not now.

This same difficulty pushes Jews to cling to their Jewish identity with more vigor than they would in an environment without this historical baggage. In this context, a few Jews I talked with looked to America or Israel to give structure and meaning to their identity. When the social context changes, however, and Jews are no longer on German soil, the criteria for defining their Jewish ethnic lines and distinctions begin to blur. In recent decades, sociologists and anthropologists studying ethnicity have recognized that cultural features can be used contextually. By this, I mean that certain objective cultural features such as language, mannerisms, and lifestyle, might be more important in certain situations than in others as indicators of similarity or commonalty. Rather than viewing ethnic boundaries as an all or nothing matter, where groups shed their distinct cultural features through assimilation in the host society, I suggest that cultural features can be manipulated to stress similarity with and membership in, or difference with and non-membership in, the host society.

For example, when my respondents were outside of Germany, they often noticed how German they were or felt. That is, as the social context changed, and their reference group was no longer Germans, Jews became aware of their Germanness, and only within this context could they express some sense of commonality with fellow German citizens. This is suggested by Julius, the school teacher, when asked if he identifies with German culture: "I am a German Jew ... There are things about me that are certainly very German, that I see when I'm in a foreign country. A certain thoroughness." Leah, the orthodox Jew, feels the same way. She replies to the question of whether she feels German:

That depends very much where I am. Because when I'm in Germany, I say, those goddamn Germans. And when I'm in any other place, I think, "Oh Germany, that's wonderful, everything is so good." This is my German upbringing. It's true, because I remember when I lived in London, I always introduced myself as "I'm Leah, I come from Germany." I did it automatically. Afterwards I thought to myself, why did you say I come from Germany? Who needs to know?

Nonetheless, I always said I come from Germany, and here it's quite different again.

While boundaries based on cultural traits might become blurred when Jews are not physically on German soil, within German society, Jews maintain a widely agreed upon system for evaluating Jewish and German identity. The cultural codes are sharply defined and structured around rigid, binary, and hierarchical oppositions. Jews define themselves in opposition to Germans – to their attitudes, morality, mannerisms, hierarchical submission to authority, lack of humor or spontaneity, and so on. In the eyes of Jews, a German is one who must acknowledge responsibility for Hitler and Goebbels as well as for Beethoven and Goethe, and therefore it is important to distance oneself from him or her. Being German implies a very low-ranking moral status. In general, it is being suggested that Germans have low moral character, and that the personality of the typical German is what enabled an Auschwitz to occur.

If respondents refer to "feeling German," they do so for the most part indirectly, by mentioning sharing qualities often attributed to Germans. The majority of Jews, however, do not exalt the German people as their *Volk*, or place primary emphasis on promoting their culture or interests. This ethnic-boundary articulation is illustrated by Suzanna, the physician who had the encounter with the porter:

A: In a certain way, I feel German. In America I felt very German. I felt very European, or German, because they are oblivious to everything that is going on outside of America; but it's easy for me. I've also lived in other countries, such as Italy and Israel. And I speak a lot of other languages, so I am not regarded as a typical German. Also, my parents are not German, so it's easy for me when I'm abroad, and people don't see me as a typical German.

Q: Who are your people?

A: Here in Germany, they are the Jews. If I were in a foreign environment, and was asked who my people were, I would say everything but German. I would never want to become so German and so perfect and so *Jeckisch*, because this is part of the definition that makes the Holocaust possible. I am not like this, I'm different.

Although Suzanna says that she sometimes feels German in other countries, her Germanness is not defined in terms of the same categories in which she and others have defined Germans. She is an "atypical" German, if she is a German at all; a typification, as mentioned earlier, that is reserved for close German friends and lovers, and will be addressed in more detail in the following chapters. Similar findings are reported by Doris Kuschner, who sampled both first and second-generation Jews and noted that only 8.2 percent think of the Germans as their *Volk*. When Kuschner questioned Jews who stemmed from pre-war Germany, she found that only 18 percent continued to feel a part of the German *Volk*. Kuschner also examined whether they were discriminated against during the Third Reich, and found no consistent correlation. In fact, of those who were discriminated against, she found a slightly higher proportion who identified with the German *Volk*. She attributes this to the fact that many of this group had Christian relatives who helped them during the war and might even have saved their lives.[25]

In an essay on the identity of second-generation Jews in Germany since the Holocaust, Micha Brumlik presents three hypotheses regarding why Jews living in Germany today (even if their parents were remnants from the pre-war German–Jewish community) cannot be compared to the idealized nineteenth-century German Jew. First, he argues that the German Jews between the two world wars were quite different from the ideal typification of the assimilated German Jew. As a result of the rise of anti-Semitism, as well as of the Zionistic movement, Jews had already begun to develop a specific type of identity based on strong Zionistic leanings, with a sound Jewish consciousness. The next stage, he argues, happened during their exile. The German-Jews who returned to Germany from exile in Palestine, Latin America, the United States, or Great Britain must have developed a different type of identity based on nostalgia for the past. If this is so, then their children, whether born in Germany or brought there as small children, were faced with the difficulty of how to integrate into the communities that had been reestablished and that had a substantial Eastern-European DP flavor. In this sense, their experiences do not parallel those of the previous generations: the second-generation children of German Jews have little in common with the German Jews who typify the German–Jewish symbiosis of the prewar era.[26]

The history of German Jewry in particular has been made into a story about morality, with scholars debating the proper role and relationship of Jews to the non-Jewish world.[27] To a certain extent, German Jewry has been viewed as the quintessential representative of European Jewry in its encounter with a non-Jewish world that ultimately betrayed it with both ferocity and indifference. The tension between Jewish and secular society is a theme in all the debates on modern Jewish identity and expression.

People internalize the abstract notion of the nation to create an imagined community. The nation, as Benedict Anderson wrote, "is imagined because the members of even the smallest nation will never know most of their fellow members... yet in the minds of each lives the image of their communion."[28] As we have seen earlier, the notion of the German for the Jew today is as the embodiment of the antithesis of Enlightenment values. The Holocaust aborted a Jewish vision and history of German–Jewish symbiosis. The Holocaust shattered the image of the universal human being, which had been such a strong inducement in the nineteenth century for Jewish assimilation into European society in general, and German society in particular. Jews today feel the necessity to further demarcate themselves from the notion of the German as *Volksgemeinschaft* or nation, and in doing so draw implicitly (if not explicitly) upon values and assumptions that are already a part of their descriptions of reality. If we recall, the predominant view that Jews carry of Germans after the Holocaust is that they are contaminated and morally impure. These patterns of thought fracture the social bonds that sentiments of nationalism and ideas of Germanness might otherwise forge. Because of how Jews imagine Germans, and how they imagine themselves, they cannot feel that they are in communion with them.

The obscuring of group boundaries: the offense of being both Jewish and German

As Martin described at the beginning of this chapter, second-generation Jews carry themselves in such a way that to an outside observer they present no obvious features that delineate them from mainstream German society. Like Martin, they speak German fluently and were educated in German schools. Their mannerisms, clothes, eating habits, and lifestyle are quintessentially German. They have become acclimated to the larger host society, and the distinctive traits and customs that might have characterized their Jewishness centuries ago have disappeared. As we have seen in the previous chapter, however, second-generation Jews maintain a separate sense of ethnic identity, based on shared values, a sense of peoplehood, a moral vision, the overshadowing of the collective memory of the Holocaust, and other subjective features. That is, Martin and other Jews like him perceive boundaries between themselves and Germans. In their minds they have something in common with one another that distinguishes them as a group.

As sociologist Michèle Lamont has illustrated in *Money, Morals, and Manners* – a study which compares French and American upper classes to determine how each defines its social strata – boundaries can be used both to patrol inclusion and to mark exclusion. In preceding chapters I have argued that Jews have created symbolic boundaries to define themselves more clearly as a unique ethnic entity in Germany.[29] This symbolic separation, as well as self-segregating activities, are ways in which Jews attempt to keep their ethnic condition uncontaminated.

We might want to ask, what happens when the boundaries between two groups blur or become diffuse, thereby creating ambiguity regarding where one ethnic group ends and the other begins? Or, to put it another way, what is the nature of Jewish loyalties exacted by ethnic belonging, and how do these loyalties affect the manner in which Jews function within the state? Unlike Ignatz Bubis – whose autobiography is titled *Ich bin ein deutscher Staatsbürger jüdischen Glaubens* (I am a German Citizen of Jewish Belief) – Jews with whom I talked did not believe they could be both German and Jewish.[30] When I asked my respondents whether it was problematic to be both Jewish and German, the usual answer was yes. They felt that it was impossible, or extremely problematic, to reconcile these two identities. Only three respondents reported no difficulty with such an overlap, and they corrected me when I used terms such as "German" or "Jew" by stating that they too were Germans.

Boundaries become increasingly more significant when they relate to intimate areas of one's life or substantial aspects of one's identity. My interviewees experienced severe dilemmas because of the complex reality of being born and raised in Germany after the Holocaust, holding German citizenship, having parents or family who suffered during the war, being acculturated into German society, and facing the omnipresence of the German past that contributed to their perception of being German as a potentially polluting attribute. Many lived their lives constantly confronting these issues, either in personal reflection or in psychological therapy. These issues at times affected their personal happiness and psychological well-being, and for almost all constituted a prominent theme in their interpersonal interactions with both other Jews and Germans. As the next section will show, the diffusion of ethnic boundaries was experienced by many Jews as an identity conflict.

Perceptions of being German as polluting: the clash of collective memories

Second-generation Jews with whom I spoke have woven the past, present, and even the future into a coherent framework that mediates their experience of themselves and Germans in everyday life. The collective identity they share is rooted in the memory of the Holocaust. We must keep in mind, however, that both ethnic groups and nations are modern phenomena. They are not inherent attributes of civilization, but rather modern social constructions. An ethnic group's identity is based in part on a common heritage or tradition, in fact or fiction, within a historically and culturally specific context. A nation also constructs a common past, based on ancient origins, myths of creation, sacred history, the construction of traditions, and the like.

Jews not only cast their own parts in life's daily dramas, but also cast Germans in roles suitable to the scenario they have envisioned. The identity that Jews have constructed is a narrative replete with villains, heroes, and martyrs. The binary opposition of their perceptions of Jew as victim and German as perpetrator makes being both Jewish and German a contradiction in terms. It is almost impossible to integrate two oppositional Holocaust narratives – one the tale of victimhood, the other that of perpetration – as many of my respondents made clear.

For example, the young writer who has recently emigrated to Paris stated, "I just realized that there were two different histories going on. Their German history and my Jewish history." Similarly, Joshua, the psychiatrist, observed, "I would never say that I am German, because it would mean identifying with the history of the Germans."

Jews can say they are German so long as "German" remains an abstract conceptual category. Once the category implies sensibilities – feelings or emotions, or sentiments of peoplehood – it inherits the perpetrator heritage associated with German nationality. Even when respondents acknowledge overlap between Jews and Germans culturally or nationally, these attributes become subordinate when moral associations arise. In the words of the historian *qua* intellectual: "I'm Israeli and I have a German passport. Yes, I've been here since I was four years old, so I am German. But, I cannot say that I feel German, because that incorporates all of the guilt."

Jews are experiencing what sociologist Robert K. Merton has called sociological ambivalence – incompatible attitudinal and behavioral expectations assigned to a position (status or status set) in society.[31] Here the position (status) of being both Jewish and German is experienced as mutually incompatible; in the eyes of Jews, one cannot be both a victim and a perpetrator simultaneously. Although the identities are antithetical to one another, they are nevertheless attached, in the words of Dan Diner, in a sort of "negative symbiosis" that provides definition and substance to both.[32] The identity of German cannot exist as perpetrator without the existence of an identity of Jew as victim.

Identity positioning

We have seen that although Jews have incorporated some of Germany's "cultural stuff," for the most part Jews see Jews and Germans as mutually exclusive dichotomous categories. How to position oneself in relation to these categories is a problem encountered frequently by Jews who had a lot of contact with Germans, such as the young writer who emigrated to Paris. She is an attractive twenty-seven-year-old who is working on her doctorate in history. She describes the difficulties she has with her identity:

Q: Can you be both German and Jewish?
A: I am sitting between two chairs. I can never say "I have no problem with the past. I have no problems with Germany. I have no problems having children with a German man."
Q: How do you feel living in Germany?
A: I am torn up inside of me. I am quite assimilated. I have lived with a [German] boyfriend for seven years, and it's a very close relationship, and lots of my friends are German. It's about 50-50. I am sitting between two chairs. I can never be both.

For this respondent, the ethnic boundaries cannot blur, become diffuse, or overlap. Being either Jewish or German precluded being the other. It was no longer possible to say, as Jakob Wasserman once said, "I am a German, I am a Jew, as much and completely the one as the other."[33] Like other interviewees I spoke with, the young writer defines her identity as a choice between being a Jew and being a German.

However, some Jews mentioned that they may oscillate between identifying with their Jewishness or their Germanness depending on their circumstances. Georg, the dentist, perceives his identity as a shifting set of ascribed statuses: one is sometimes Jewish and sometimes German, depending on the situation, and at times may become involved in role conflict or marginality:

Q: Is it problematic to be both Jewish and German?
A: Yes. Because they don't like each other particularly. One day gefilte fish, one day sauerkraut. It's a permanent struggle for priorities. If you work, nine out of ten situations don't ask for your identity or for a decision between the two. So, in all those cases, there's no problem. Now, there are a few situations where you really have to make a decision. Then it's painful. And then I try to decide according to my feelings.

Thus, for Jews in Germany the process of determining where to position themselves is complex and puzzling. The readiness of any respondent to declare his or her Jewishness is counterbalanced with a tendency to acknowledge that at some level he or she may also be German. Given that Jew and German are defined by a different set of values, lifestyles, and traditions, some Jews felt that they could not be total members of one group or the other.

Adaptive strategies: the symbolic construction and embellishment of group boundaries

How does one determine where to mark the boundaries of one ethnic group in order to keep it from merging into the other? As we have seen in previous chapters, there is not a single universal meaning for the social categories "Jew" or "German," but a range of meanings that are mediated by individual idiosyncratic perceptions and experiences. Language allows Jews to express the range of their perceptions, yet at the same time creates a commonality by aggregating these various perceptions. As Anthony Cohen writes, the linguistic repertoire or "speech community" transforms individual variations in meanings into a recognizable "common form" by providing the means for their "expression, interpretation, and containment."[34] The symbolic repertoire of a community "continuously transforms the reality of difference into the appearance of similarity with such efficacy that people can still invest the 'community' with ideological integrity. It unites them in their opposition, both to each other, and to those 'outside.' It thereby constitutes, and gives reality to, the community's boundaries."[35]

As Jews and Germans become more and more alike in outward appearance, it becomes necessary for Jews to reinforce and embellish these symbolic boundaries. Today there are many realms of potential overlap between Jews and Germans. Jews were themselves cognizant of a possible confusion regarding objective referents, or cultural content that might, to an outside observer, blur the uniqueness of their ethnic entity. Notice how Martin describes his acculturation into German society: "I identify very strongly with the Jewish culture, and also with the German culture. I was brought up in Germany. My mother tongue is German. I was educated in German schools, so that all of my cultural heritage to a large extent is German."

It is precisely because of the outward appearance of similarity that Jews go to great lengths to articulate more clearly the symbolic boundaries between themselves and Germans. Most Jews are German citizens and have been exposed to German culture, and boundary demarcation was deemed necessary in both of these realms of potential group overlap, national and cultural. I have identified a number of strategies that Jews used to demarcate the boundaries between themselves and Germans. These strategies included the displacement of national consciousness, manipulating the meaning of the passport, the separation of mind and heart, and redefining key components of the definition of their identity. I will now consider each of these in turn.

The displacement of national consciousness: Israel as a symbol of Jewish nationhood, and identifying with other national minorities

At the conclusion of an interview, a Jewish professor suggested that I focus more on the state of Israel as a symbol of Jewish identity, because he hypothesized "that this is the strongest focus of concern for Jews today, and that this is the focus of their rather weak [Jewish] identity." This man describes himself as an anti-Zionist, which he believes makes him a marginal member of the pro-Israeli Jewish *Gemeinde*, just as it makes him a problematic person within the German Left, because he is uncomfortable with their equating Zionism with Nazism. He says, "I always have to balance myself on this very thin border between anti-Zionism and anti-Semitism, and I always have to struggle on two sides [with the Jewish community and with the German left]."

As Rafael Seligmann and others have pointed out, the central question concerning Jews in contemporary Germany is: how can a Jew live in Germany after Auschwitz? Seligmann observes that "all aspects of Jewish identity in Germany after 1945 are in one way or another a function of this question."[36] The existence of Israel and its legitimation of a Jewish nation (*Jüdisches Volk*) provided a viable alternative for Jews living in Germany: they could focus on Israel as an idol and equate it with Judaism or Jewry, instead of outwardly confronting the difficulties of forging a new Jewish identity in post-Holocaust Germany. While several of my interviewees equated being Jewish with having "a strong feeling for Israel," one respondent speculated that if Israel didn't exist, "I don't know whether Jews could live in Germany or in other places."

One strategy Jews employed to mark more clearly the boundaries between themselves and Germans was to displace their sense of national affiliation on to Israel. That is, rather than acknowledging ties that bind Jews to the German nation, and promoting its interests, they emphasized their attachment to Israel as an object of loyalty and primordial attachment. Several respondents mentioned that they would rather enlist in the Israeli military than be drafted in the German army, and Israel was exalted above Germany in other ways.

The most obvious way to support Israel instead of Germany is in some sense to serve as Israel's covert ambassadors. Indeed, sociologist Doris Kuschner points out that Jews who live in Germany have given more money in proportion to their numbers to support Israel financially than those who live in France and other European countries.[37] Although the Jews in Germany have one of the smallest Jewish populations in Europe, they are one of Israel's largest financial supporters. For example, on June 4, 1967, at the height of the 1967 Israeli–Arab Six Day War, the philanthropic organization Keren Hayesot (Magbit) called an emergency conference to initiate a solidarity drive for Israel. Delegates from all Jewish *Gemeinden* and organizations in West Germany attended and together raised 24 million DM from approximately 19,000 donors. Given a total Jewish population at the time of only 26,000 (with an additional 5,000 non-registered Jews), this was a major accomplishment, and practically every Jewish family was said to have contributed. The per capita donation was DM 1080 ($270), exceeded in Europe only by Jewish communities in Switzerland and Belgium. The Jewish *Gemeinden* in Germany raised the fifth highest donation of all Jewish communities throughout the world.[38] Those in the community claim that philanthropic support of Israel continues to be exceptionally high. Today Israel is almost universally accepted as a major focus of organizational charity by Jews in Germany. Instead of financing the institutions and needs of Germany or their hometowns, their names appear on projects and buildings in Israel.

Much of the Israel-oriented activity in the community is a result of the active work of WIZO, the Women's International Zionist Organization. The chapters in Germany hold WIZO bazaars and the Frankfurt chapter supports the Theodor Heuss Home in Herzelia, which offers aid to Jewish and Arab mothers. Other active philanthropic organizations in Germany supporting Israel are B'nai Brith and Keren Hayesod.

The folklore of Israel has also become a substitute for enjoying national culture. While money is exported from the communities to Israel, Israeli culture is imported. For example, the Frankfurt *Gemeinde* regularly hosts Israeli dance troupes, musicians, singers, and entertainers. The *Gemeinde* also sponsors youth trips to Israel, holds seminars on Israeli related themes, hosts an Israeli film festival once a year, and imports school teachers and rabbis from Israel. As one second-generation critic of the policies of the Jewish *Gemeinde* described it:

They [the Jewish *Gemeinde*] are very Zionistic without being Zionists in the sense that I was a Zionist. They sort of realize they are living here but they behave as if colonized by the state of Israel. Most of the money that comes in goes to Israel. They support a lot of Israeli institutions and the state, and they don't really invest money in educational or cultural life in Germany.

Israel has also became a strong focus of attention for many Jewish young people. Uncertain of the meaning of their own Jewish existence and future within Germany, focusing on the state of Israel and its society became a logical, valid alternative. Indeed, philosopher Martin Löw-Beer has analyzed a selection of newsletters from the *Jugend Zentrum*, and reports a strong focus on topics concerning Israel, particularly during the 1960s.[39] Similarly, in a content analysis of themes appearing in Jewish community newsletters sampled from issues published from 1947 to 1986, sociologist Y. Michal Bodemann reports that there was a strong emphasis on articles dealing specifically with Israel.[40] Several respondents remarked that the Zionist youth group, *Zionistische Jugend Deutschlands* (ZJD), founded in Germany in 1959 in the spirit of attempting to prevent Jewish youth from assimilating into German society, was instrumental in encouraging aliyah to Israel while they were growing up. About a fourth (28.8 percent) of the second generation in the sample had been members of ZJD during their youth. ZJD fostered an educational program whose aim was to encourage immigration to Israel.[41] Membership began at age twelve, and age cohorts were assigned individual leaders who were responsible for carrying out the educational programs of the organization. Activities included seminars, retreats, meetings and intellectual discussions. The goals of ZJD included educating its members about the history of Israel, encouraging respect and understanding for Israeli and Jewish tradition, and teaching Zionism. The educational phases prepare young people to experience Israel directly by pledging aliyah to Israel. "The aliyah is the high point and consequence of all the spiritual, cultural and practical efforts. A Zionistic youth movement that didn't aspire to such consequences doesn't have the right to exist," stated one ZJD leader.[42] The normative behavioral pattern charted for Jews growing up in post-Holocaust Germany was that it was wrong for Jews to live in Germany: Jews should emigrate and Israel is the preferred destination.

The evidence suggests that identifying with Israel is one way in which Jews express and signal their Jewishness. It is also a means by which Jews can maintain their distance from German society. Earlier in this chapter we saw that Jews stress a sense of peoplehood and shared values to define their Jewish identity. In Chapter 3 we saw how the Holocaust as metaphor informed the manner in which Jews categorized and classified

Germans as an out-group. Historian Julius Schoeps hypothesizes that Jews in Germany are fixated on Israel because of survivors' guilt.[43] Historian Dan Diner argues that in some sense it is a logical connection because the state of Israel grew out of the Holocaust.[44] In addition to feeling ambivalent about living in Germany, Jews in Germany have been criticized by Jewish communities worldwide for remaining in Germany. Counteracting these internal and external sources of dissonance, Israel provides an avenue of redemption both as an acceptable totem of identification and as a target of ethnic action. By exchanging Zionism for German nationalism, I argue, Jews can better prevent assimilation.

Moreover, one of the latent functions of displacing their national consciousness onto Israel is that Jews in Germany could rid themselves of one of the most damaging images attached to being Jewish in Germany – being a victim of persecution. By exalting Israel over Germany, Jews can enhance their self-image by leaving behind their old stigmatized roles and the negative identities associated with them. Eva, who was born in Israel, describes the self-transformation in identity images when she says: "Jewish means I identify with weakness, with death, with Holocaust. Israeli is the other. It's strong, soldier, war."

A second strategy of displacement of national consciousness that occurred primarily among a few Jewish intellectuals in the *Gemeinde* was to view themselves as a supranational group – a nation in Diaspora. That is, they did not view themselves as just a distinct ethnic, religious, or cultural group, but rather as a legitimate, separate national minority, having their place within German society beside other competing ethnic minorities. Although this view was not widely expressed among my interviewees, with the increasing debates about German nationalism occurring today, and the influence of Ignatz Bubis' leadership and public declaration of such alliances, it could become more pronounced in the future. One intellectual I interviewed summarized this view best: "For me it's a question of nationality. For me, Jewishness means that I'm not German. That I'm Jewish like other people are Italian, but live in Germany, or are French and live in Germany. It means to belong to the Jewish people."

In short, Jews displaced their national consciousness onto Israel or, in the case of some intellectuals, other ethnic minorities in Germany, to renegotiate (in their own minds) their national affiliations. By doing so they are not directly confronted with a tug-of-war regarding Jewish ethnic ties and German national ones; they can more comfortably maintain a sense of national ties that are consistent with their ethnic attachments.

The variable meaning of the passport

Another strategy that Jews employed was to manipulate the meaning of holding a German passport. As mentioned earlier, the same cultural referents can be used contextually, sometimes to express ethnic differences, and sometimes to express ethnic commonalties. The passport is one such referent amenable to manipulation depending on the situation. Jews who have German passports define the significance of the passport differently from Jews who do not have German passports. Both groups, however, use the passport as a symbol of distance from membership within German society. Those Jews who did not have a German passport viewed the lack of a passport as proof that they were not Germans. This was exactly the attitude of Gertrud, the housewife:

Q: Are you German?
A: No. I don't have a German passport. I have a foreign stateless passport. My parents didn't want a German passport. I have German rights, and eventually I will get a passport, but I don't care which one, except for practical reasons.

Like Gertrud, Sylvia, the pharmacist put it this way:

Q: Are you German?
A: No. I have a Belgium passport. I never wanted to get a German passport.

Amalie, a medical student, said this:

Q: Are you German?
A: I want to say formally that I am a citizen of Germany. I have a German passport.
Q: Do you feel German?
A: No. I also have an Israeli passport. I have two passports. As long as I can remember, I've had two passports.

These Jews put a premium on the passport because to them it is is a national symbol that implies attachment to the state. Some did not want the German passport, nor did their parents, suggesting that if they did hold German citizenship, they might be considered too German. I even heard that pregnant community members travel to the United States in order to give birth to an American citizen. They said that their children were now Americans because they held the American passport.

The same diagnostic feature, the passport, can be used contextually to distance oneself from membership in the country. As a successful businessman states: "I don't want to belong to them. So why should I say that I'm German? I mean, I think when I say I have a German passport it's clear." Other Jews who held a German passport (as did the majority of the respondents in the study) downplayed the significance of the passport as a defining criterion of national identification. Jews acknowledged the instrumental benefits of possessing German citizenship. A German passport entitled the bearer to rights of citizenship and protection by the state, and being German implied these advantages. Yet when I asked respondents whether they felt German, the answer was uniformly "No." The passport was not significant in defining their identity.

An implicit distinction was being made by Jews regarding the meaning of holding a German passport – did Germany imply a nation-state or was it a body of people? While most Jews acknowledge membership in Germany in their legal relationship to the country as a nation–state, they separate themselves from membership in Germany when it is understood as a body of people. This is consistent with our earlier finding discussed in Chapter 2 regarding Jewish views of Germany. Many respondents felt that the country had changed, but questioned the extent to which its people had changed.

We see this in Martin, as well as in other Jews who would typically remark, "My passport is German, but I wouldn't call myself a German." Therefore, according to these respondents, the passport should not be taken as a symbol of national identification. This is explained by Avital, the thirty-eight-year-old school teacher:

I cannot bring it across my lips to say "I am German," and to say that with enthusiasm. For me, it means something different. Regarding why I have a green passport [a German passport], Jews have even asked me this. I am a traitor, because I don't live in Israel, for example. Then, I say, "I am German," and show them the green thing [the passport], but that doesn't mean that I am German. The same word has a completely different meaning. I will always first be Jewish, and then German. Actually, I cannot be a German, only on paper. The word German provides no source of identity for me. It's different when one likes living here, because the streets are clean, or because the food tastes good, or because if one gets sick, every medicine is available. It's an entirely different story. The social, and medical benefits, the security that one has here is more perfect, perhaps, than in America. That is important, to have a good, pleasant and secure life. It doesn't mean that I am German. I take what the Germans also have at their disposal. And that's why I will never be a German.

While sociologists and anthropologists often seek to explore the connotation of a symbol within a particular collectivity, my findings suggest that this connotation can vary, depending upon social context. The meanings of symbols may still be powerful, but they may not necessarily have the same connotations for all members of the same collectivity in different situations or social contexts. They are multi-meaning and their significance is determined by the context in which they are used. What is consistent, however, is that regardless of which passport they hold (German or other), Jews in Germany manipulate the meanings consistently to signal distance from German society.

The separation of mind and heart: the public and private dichotomy

Another way of exploring the demarcation of ethnic boundaries is to consider the distinction between civic and primordial ties. Civic ties refer to the public self, whereas primordial ties deal with the private self. The category of Jew and German can overlap in the public domain, which deals with the "civic self" or "front" (in the sense of Erving Goffman's presentation of self) that they maintain within the public sphere. Yet it is in the private domain that Jews can truly be themselves. The boundaries are drawn between their outer shell and their private inner being. Feelings, sentiments, and sensibilities are all conditions of the heart. This is illustrated by a professor, whose parents were originally from Germany, but spent the war years in exile in Switzerland. He describes his Jewish and German identity as two extremes, and his strategy of dichotomizing rational attitudes from sensibilities:

Q: Is it a problem to be both German and Jewish?
A: Not a real one, because I never had to make a decision between these two poles, because I can separate my feelings from my political and public activities. It's not so difficult for me to accept that my feelings maybe contradict my political or public work. As an intellectual you can live with that. That feelings and rational attitudes contradict.

Many Jews perceive their identities through a metaphor of whole and parts. This respondent is making a fundamental distinction between his mind and his heart. The mind, with its calculating rational actions symbolizes the public self, his civic role in society. The mind is potentially polluting, as its boundaries overlap with actions and behavior that may appear similar to that of Germans. His heart, however, symbolizes the internal, his ethnic self. His heart is the window to his soul; it is where his true loyalty resides. It is the essence of his identity, and therefore enables him to define for himself his own distinctiveness.

This demarcation between mind and heart, or public and private, was also explicit regarding the overlap of cultural referents with Germans. While Jews generally acknowledged that they were Germans to some extent because they share many attributes of the German culture, for some Jews sharing a culture with Germans was also experienced as potentially polluting. The implication again is that if they share common aspects of a culture with Germans, that might mean that they too are German. Some Jews agreed that they had German mannerisms, others stressed that even so it didn't mean that they were German. A few referred to themselves as Jeckes,[45] and many noted, as mentioned earlier, that in foreign countries because of their German language, culture and mannerisms, they felt very German.

My interviewees tried to emphasize the lack of synthesis between Jewish and German cultures. For instance, for assimilated Jews of the pre-Holocaust era, even Goethe was instrumentalized as a symbol of the heroes and ideals of the German Enlightenment. Goethe represented a dominant tradition of tolerance and reason, along with other such German notables as Lessing, Schiller, Kant, Herde, Fichte, Humbolt, and Mommsen.[46] Yet Judith, the ophthalmologist, ignores this Enlightenment tradition, whose values some German Jewish scholars of the previous era tended to liken to those found in the Old Testament:

Q: Do you identify with German culture?
A: I don't identify with it at all. I use it instrumentally because it's the instrument I learned. But I don't identify with it. I don't get tears in my eyes when somebody speaks about Goethe.

A few of my respondents went so far as to draw dichotomies between German and Jewish parts of their personality – the German part symbolizing rational thought, the Jewish part symbolizing emotions and sentiments. For example, this dichotomy is asserted by Betty, the woman we encountered in the Prologue, even though she acknowledges the mutual influences and similarities in Jewish and German traditions:

Q: How about German? Do you feel German?
A: No. No... I have the German culture. I learned it at school. I was a good student. But it's not my culture. It would never make me cry like the Jewish culture can make me cry. I speak Yiddish very well.
Q: Is it a problem to be both Jewish and German?
A: Let's say, I'm Jewish in my heart, in my humor, which is the heart. When I'm sad or when I'm laughing it's Jewish. Let's put it this way. Crying and laughing is Jewish, but thinking I do in German... I think

that the German culture is very influenced by Jewish people, and that Jewish culture was influenced by German people.

Other second-generation Jews tried to distance themselves from German culture by viewing the German language as a mere mechanical tool from which they felt alienated but that they could use instrumentally for communication:[47] This is illustrated by Celia, the pharmacist:

I speak German. I have to say that German is the language I express myself the best in. On the other hand, I don't identify with the German culture... I don't get into contact with it. If I read a German poem, I don't feel anything. If I read a poem in Yiddish or in English, it touches me.

In other cases, however, although the diffusion of ethnic boundaries along either a cultural or national realm was deemed problematic, Jews were resigned to live with their fate. Such was the case of a sociology graduate student:

A: It's like a conflictual identity. When we first immigrated to America, and I was nine-years-old, it was a terrifying experience, because I didn't understand a word that anyone was saying. I kind of shrank and became like a stone. My mother referred to this as the German in me. I was soon known as the German, because this is how they imagined Germans to be – without feelings, without emotions. So, this was kind of like growing up with different parts around me. One which was more like the Jews around me, and another part which was more like the Germans. And they don't go together too well.

Q: Is it a problem being both Jewish and German?

A: Now it's not a problem for me. But growing up, and trying to bring these different identities into one head. Now I don't think it has to be in one head. I mean, it has to be in one head, but it doesn't have to be. There can be tensions and conflicts. There are different parts, so, they don't have to be totally together.

Identity redefinition

I have argued so far that the ethnic identities of second-generation Jews in Germany are based primarily on cultural distinctions. These cultural distinctions are tied to the collective memory of the Holocaust, and are symbolized linguistically by cultural typifications in the Jewish public domain. That is, Jews who live in the community recognize the combinations of traits that refer to or are associated with them and with Germans. This does not mean, however, that all Jews accept the typifications that are current in their community culture, especially when some of these labels are applied to them. Some Jews have rejected these definitions and developed other defensive ones to fit their objectives. In this different method of strategizing, there is no major attempt to demarcate more clearly between Jews as an in-group and Germans as an out-group. Instead, the strategy is one of redefinition. Here Jews manipulate the commonly accepted, culturally generated meanings of the definition of their living situation, namely being Jewish and living in Germany, which is understood, as we saw in Chapter 2, as the land of murderers. In other words, they tried to redefine their personal identities by rejecting the normative conceptions of Jews and Germans held by the community at large. This was achieved in three basic ways: (1) by focusing on Germany as a body of people and redefining what constitutes the German population, and (2) by focusing on themselves and redefining how long they have been in residence in Germany, or (3) by redefining altogether the boundaries of the territory in which they reside.

The first method focuses on redefining what Germany means when understood as a body of people. In other words, it is the German population, the German *Volk*, that is redefined. We have seen earlier in the chapter how Jews have difficulty stating that they are a part of the German *Volk*. A few respondents suggested that they felt that they were a part of the German *Volk* only when Germans were no longer viewed as a homogeneous country filled only with Nazis and murderers. While it did not occur often, a few respondents recast Germany as a pluralistic society, a multi-ethnic conglomerate, in which Jews participate as one of the many types of minorities. This is illustrated by the professor who stated:

Q: Are Germans your people?
A: On a sentimental level I would not say that. I just don't feel it. But on a rational level I'm definitely sure that I belong to the population of this state, the Federal Republic of Germany. So, somehow they are my people as well... It's not to "the Germans," but let's say the population of Germany including immigrant workers, Italians, Turks, and so on. But this is all rational.

Oskar, a social science researcher, described another strategy to redefine the German *Volk*. When we were discussing who his *Volk* were, and how he related to the Germans as people, Oskar rejected the concept of *Volk* and placed in its stead "people in general." He redrew the boundaries around Germans more narrowly, only to enclose those persons within his personal social circle. He explained:

I feel I am more German than Israeli, as a nationality or culture, but I feel unhappy as a German. I can't really say I feel German, when I think about the majority of Germans, so I must distinguish between people and *Volk*. For me, there is no *Volk*, only people. A few people, then, that I seek out... I always tried to have good friendships. That was always important to me. Not to have a group around me, but I need to have a few persons. Very good friends, but not a *Volk*. I have problems with groups. There is not an ideal group that I feel I belong to. Not that there are more Jews who I think would think like I do – that one can be Jewish without a country and needn't be a Zionist. In any case, I would say that I am Jewish. Jews are my people, but in a Diaspora. A people that is everywhere, but doesn't really fit in anywhere.

The second type of redefinition, which occurs more frequently, is to redefine the territorial boundaries within which they live. In this case Jews downplay the fact that they live in the country of Germany, stating instead that they live in "this apartment," "this neighborhood," "this city," "Frankfurt," or "Europe." The implied assumption here is that Germany is still the land of murderers. But Jews draw new territorial boundaries, and thus redefine geographically where they personally reside. The territorial boundaries are either drawn more narrowly or more broadly. The net effect, however, is the same. Jews no longer live in Germany *per se*, but somewhere else – a place, no doubt, without the same haunting and incongruous connotations.

A third type of redefinition was to redefine how long they had been in residence in Germany. Instead of acknowledging that they were natives of Germany – born, reared, and living there all their lives – or even permanent residents, the strategy was to emphasize that they were only visitors in Germany or at best temporary residents. "Sitting on packed suitcases," as discussed earlier, was the most obvious method. I also heard Israeli-born Jews use the expression "I am an Israeli temporarily abroad," even though they may have come to Frankfurt as young children and were permanent residents. Juliane, a secretary, described how she attempted to avoid a feeling of residential permanency by changing situations continuously:

A: I accept the fact that I don't belong here. I live here in this flat and that's that. It makes it easier for me not to look outside.

Q: What happens when you look outside?

A: Well, I've developed tricks not to do it. Changing situations very often. For example, I won't let myself be defined or tied to a certain situation. I feel I avoid everything that would make me settle down. Having relationships and jobs and anything I do. These are my tricks. Yes, my changing jobs to show that I won't give anyone a reason to say, "See, you belong here because you've got a job. You earn money here, why do you want to get away?"

This process of redefinition places importance not only on the normative order for definitions of identity, but also on the role of the individual's subjective perceptions in the definitional process. In these instances Jews did not accept the typifications that were current in the community, and pressed against their limitations, often through judicious manipulation of definitions. In their process of redefinition, these Jews struggled to recast the problematic set of circumstances in the normative order to a more comfortable reality for themselves. They were not stigmatized Jews living in the land of the murderers, as the normative definitions implied. Their process of redefinition was geared to cope with living in the real world, and it was creative and effective.

Conclusion

The picture that emerges from this chapter is that Jews are alienated from mainstream German society, even if they appear to have become habituated to much of German culture. This feeling is compounded when Jews are questioned about their identity, especially when asked to what extent they feel German. All of this suggests that political integration is a complex process. The dictionary definition of political integration is that it is a legal relationship involving allegiance on the part of the individual and protection on the part of the state, and a sense of national consciousness whereby one nation is exalted above all others and primary emphasis is placed on the promotion of its culture and interests as opposed to those of other nations or supranational groups.[48] Political scientists have focused almost exclusively on voting and other behavior indicators of political participation. I have shown that that is only a partial vision. A community's cultural representation of the host society must be taken into account.

A case in point is a survey by Alphons Silbermann and Herbert Sallen, published as *Juden in Westdeutschland* (Jews in West Germany). The authors collected their data from surveys conducted with 377 Jews in 1990, although they acknowledge that their selection process was neither random nor representative. They present data on the political orientation of Jews, and their voting behavior during the last election before the survey. They use voting as an indicator of political integration, and conclude that because Jews vote, and are interested in politics, that they are integrated politically into German society.

My findings call into question the conclusions drawn by Silbermann and Sallen. While voting is one indication of political interest, a broader framework needs to be developed to analyze political integration. This should include issues of commitment to a host society.[49] There exists a wide range of behavior and attitudes, some of which are more inwardly directed than others, that describe an individual's relationship to the state. According to systems theory, individuals and constituencies may provide both "specific" and "diffuse" support to a political system. Specific support occurs when persons feel they are getting back something concrete, on a *quid pro quo* basis, for a particular type of support. For example, a person might decide to vote for a particular political party because that party's platform is committed to lowering taxes. Diffuse support is unconditional support that includes notions of patriotism and national loyalty, and can be summarized by the chants, "My Country, Right or Wrong" and "My Country: Love it or Leave it." Diffuse support is the social cement that keeps the political system together despite hard times or internal strife.[50]

Social scientist Herbert Kelman proposes six different types of involvement that would fall under the category of diffuse support: (1) commitment to cultural values reflective of national identity; (2) commitment to the role of the national linked to group symbols; (3) acceptance of demands based on commitment to the sacredness of the state; (4) commitment to institutions promoting the needs and interests of the population; (5) commitment to social roles mediated by the system; and (6) acceptance of demands based on commitment to law and order (principle of equity).[51]

According to Kelman, "an individual is sentimentally attached to the state when he sees the system as representing him – as being, in some central way, a reflection and extension of himself. For the sentimentally attached, the system is legitimate and deserving of his loyalty because it is the embodiment of a group in which his personal identity is anchored."[52] The first three sources of involvement listed above are a result of this type of commitment. The last three sources of commitment describe instrumental sources of attachment.

For Jews who live in contemporary Germany, my findings show that personal involvement with Germany as a nation-state is rooted in instrumental rather than affective sources of allegiance. They accept the demands of citizenship based on their commitment to law and order, because such commitment to the nation-state is seen as a means to achieve one's own and the groups' goals. Jews, however, are not integrated into German society in the sense of having national consciousness. They do not feel they owe allegiance to the German state emotionally, nor to its people. With a few exceptions, they are not willing to accept the demands of the state based on a commitment to its sacredness, nor to actively support some of its institutions.

The sources of conflict and strain for Jews within contemporary German society are cultural rather than structural. Anti-Semitism has subsided. Nevertheless, Jews are not totally integrated politically or socially into German society. The collective memory of the Holocaust is omnipresent, and manifests itself in part as a system of ideas about the dangers of Germans. This affects the manner in which Jews organize their actions, as culture prescribes to a large extent a group's attitudes and governs its behavior.

The preceding pages are rich in political implications. For example, they help us rethink the ways in which social forces impact upon the political realm. While most social scientists explore the impact of structural conditions (lack of access to economic or political resources) on political participation, my findings suggest that culture *per se* must also be scrutinized in terms of its impact on political behavior. In this study, for example, we may question the impact of collective memory of a state-imposed genocide on the manner in which subsequent generations relate to the state and its people. A number of unanswered questions remain. How can a state generate loyalty from its various constituencies, when these constituencies may be harboring resentments that continue on the ideological level in their collective memories? What does political integration actually mean and how can it be measured adequately? How does the collective memory of the Holocaust affect the cohesiveness of the German state, its legitimation, and the integration of its members? How can a state increase involvement by its constituents from the most passive to the more active? How can a state socialize its members to internalize its political culture on some level of consciousness, particularly when that culture is considered polluted by some of its constituencies? While these questions are beyond the scope of this study, they are particularly relevant for people who define themselves in opposition to the host society, and have difficulty with the political culture of that society, and its national symbols. One must look beyond passive behaviors such as voting, and sporadic activities such as protests, to define one's relationship to the nation-state and its implications for personal and collective identities.

5

My friends are not typical Germans: the character of Jewish–German friendships

Of all the heavenly gifts that mortal men commend,
What trusty treasure in the world can countervail a friend?
(Nicholas Grimald, "Of Friendship," in L. R. Merril, *The Life and Poems of Nicholas Grimald*, New Haven: Yale University Press, 1925)

Cultural forces and barriers to contact

Danielle is an attractive thirty-seven-year-old with a master's degree in sociology. While she is searching for a position appropriate to her level of training, she is currently doing part-time secretarial temp-work.

Danielle's father was born into a fairly distinguished family in Berahovo, a small town near the border between Czechoslovakia and Hungary. Her grandfather died before the war, and her grandmother immigrated to Palestine. In 1941 Danielle's father fled with the rest of his family to Palestine, while one of his brothers stayed in Czechoslovakia. She thinks her uncle was captured by the Germans and interned in a concentration camp, but managed to survive somehow. "It was a huge family. There are maybe three or four cousins left, that's all. The rest were killed by the Germans," Danielle states.

Danielle's mother was born in Freiburg, Germany, but grew up in Berlin. When the war broke out, Danielle's mother was working as a children's nurse in England. "My mother's family, her mother, her father, two other children [her mother's siblings], and all the rest, well, they were all killed. Only my mother and three others survived. They [Danielle's mother's family] were killed in concentration camps."

Danielle's father came to England after the war by accident, and there he met Danielle's mother. They married, and subsequently immigrated to Palestine. Danielle was born in Palestine in 1947; her brother was born a few years later. In 1958, when Danielle was ten years old, her family immigrated to Germany. "There are reasons why they left Israel, there are reasons why they stayed in Germany in spite of the fact that they didn't want to stay in Germany, and there are reasons why they justify staying in Germany," Danielle says. Danielle's parents did not intend to remain in Germany, but wanted to immigrate to Canada. "This was the mistake," Danielle surmises. "They thought they would get the visas here [in Germany]. That's what they say." They went to Berlin to inquire about restitution, since Danielle's mother's family had lived there before the war. They contacted the Jewish *Gemeinde* in Berlin, and Danielle's father was immediately offered a job in Wimbach. They stayed in Wimbach only a short time, and came to Frankfurt "by accident." "A phone call determined that my parents were going to get a flat in Frankfurt, and that's why we didn't move to Berlin," Danielle explains. Danielle kept asking her parents when the family would immigrate to Canada. According to Danielle, her parents kept saying, "Well, maybe we'll see, maybe next year, maybe in two years, maybe we'll move away, maybe we'll have to stay." "You know, just postponing the decision, and not telling the truth."

Danielle was not raised religiously. While she celebrates some Jewish holidays now, she did not while growing up. Her father considers himself Jewish, but is not religious. Danielle describes her mother as having a good German upbringing – not showing that one has problems, being adaptable to every situation, and not demonstrating any difficulties with change. This good German upbringing, coupled with a "bad conscience of still being alive and all the other things," Danielle contends, creates difficulties for her parents being Jewish and living in Germany. These problems, however, were not dealt with openly. "The whole problem was simply denied in our family." Her family declined to express their Jewishness; they celebrated Christmas and withdrew from the Jewish *Gemeinde*. Danielle began confronting these difficulties once she realized she had problems in her friendships with Germans.

Being Jewish for Danielle is connected to the past – "this part of history, where I come from," she explains. Because of the history, "it's very difficult to find the right understanding with a German about these things – not an intellectual understanding, but an emotional willingness to accept what happened. And it is still very difficult." Danielle describes how most Germans relate to her: "This denial of guilt, or responsibility – 'We don't have anything to do with it, not because we don't know, but because we live now, and we are not responsible for what our parents have done.'" Danielle does not believe that Germans can be exonerated:

They are responsible. They carry on. It's in them. It's in their souls, somewhere, and they have their part of guilt and they struggle to deal with what they want to avoid. It's too difficult for them... They also have been brought up to think that you can start from scratch, that you don't have to be concerned with what happened before... This makes it difficult to have relationships with German men and women.

Danielle seeks an emotional understanding with her German friends. That is the criterion she uses to determine whom to befriend. She observes how Germans react to her when she shows certain emotions. Then she knows whom to trust:

This [emotional understanding about the Holocaust and being Jewish] is something I cannot teach anyone. The Germans have to find out for themselves where they stand with this, and the kind of reaction they show towards me. And I do test them, so to speak, for the kind of reaction they have to show. There are all sorts of ways when I start taking about it [being Jewish] and I start to say that I feel different and what is important to me... I know the Germans very well. I know how much I can say and things I cannot talk about with different people. It depends on the level at which I meet these people.

Danielle has Jewish and German friends, but she keeps these circles apart. "My friends are very different. Most of them I cannot mix because they wouldn't go together very well, and this is why it's separated." She feels closer to her Jewish friends, but does have good German friends. One German girlfriend is different, Danielle says, "because she actually is open to these things. Because she is able to suffer, to feel suffering for somebody else, and to feel this."

My interviews with Danielle and others indicate that the Holocaust in collective memory strongly impacts Jews' interpersonal relationships with Germans. In this chapter I explore this cultural conditioning on the level of friendship, and in Chapter 6 I explore Jewish–German love relationships.

From acquaintance to friend

Because the collective memory of the Holocaust plays an important role for Jews in defining both themselves and Germans, it is not surprising that personal relationships between Jews and Germans are strained and confusing. Many of my interviewees stated that their parents' attitudes toward Germans were saturated with feelings of fear, dislike, and distrust. Some said they shared these attitudes, albeit in a more diluted form. Such attitudes are consequential: Jews wanted to know where

Germans stood *vis-à-vis* their country's history. Jews have difficulty tolerating younger Germans who deny any collective responsibility for the past, and, as mentioned in Chapter 2, they have difficulty with Germans whom they perceive are anti-Semitic or philo-Semitic. These issues will be explored in greater depth later in this chapter when I discuss how Jews determine whom to befriend.

The formation of friendship occurs through a process by which acquaintanceship develops into a friendship. Acquaintances are merely people one meets in situations where two or more people join openly in a mutual activity. Parties, business meetings, conferences, a train ride, and other activities draw people into encounters on a regular basis. While encounters are transitory meetings that generate a pool of potential friendship choices, they are the first stage in friendship development, because friendships occur with people one knows. Through attraction and acquiring information, people come to know and evaluate one another.

The visibility of Jewishness, identity markers, and Jewish badges of pride and shame

Ethnic identities, and the criteria that make such identities distinguishable, are likely to be positively or negatively weighted and ranked within the ideology of the wider society. In situations of conflict, how groups are socially defined and evaluated can have powerful or even tragic consequences, as the Holocaust demonstrated. Recall that Jews sometimes view their Jewish identity as a status enhancement, while at other times it is a status degradation. Since this evaluation affects the role that Jewishness plays in interpersonal relationships with Germans, it is useful to discuss in depth the manner in which Jews perceive that their identity is displayed.

Can Germans tell if Jews are Jewish? About half of my respondents believe that clear markers existed – badges of both pride and shame – that automatically disclosed their Jewish identity. Thus, at times they manipulated the disclosure of their Jewishness for desired ends. Many respondents devised strategies to disclose their Jewishness in order to test Germans and filter out those to be avoided. I will discuss these strategies later.

I have identified five distinct factors that Jews believe can reveal their Jewishness to others. Many respondents mentioned physical appearance. Many also mentioned their names. A third factor was Jewish mentality or behavior. Fourth was a special aura about them. The last factor consisted of institutional practices or settings that *ipso facto* signaled Jewish ethnicity.

The alleged physical uniqueness of Jews has long been linked to anti-Semitism. The caricature of the "Jewish type" with a large hooked nose – linking the primitive sense of smell with sexuality and cultural degeneration – can be traced back to the seventeenth century.[1] In Nazi ideology, Jews were seen as members of a different race, the most distant from the Aryan, on the lowest rung on the scale of physical perfection of eighteenth century biological science. These differences were based on observable physical characteristics and physiognomy: "short to middling stature, a long hooked nose, greasy skin, dark complexion, black, often wavy hair, thick lips, flat feet, and a tendency to run to fat in women."[2] The idea of race was linked closely to the image of the unique construction of the Jewish body and psyche.[3] In the words of one German, physician-author Oskar Panizza, Jews were distinguished by their nose, eyebrows, "fleshy and overly creased lips," "violet fatty tongue, bowlegs," and "curly, thick black locks of hair."[4] The Aryan, on the other hand, had "thick lips, Prussian chin, proud nape of the neck, extraordinary stiff posture; legs, which in their innocence were neither knock-kneed nor bowed; ... which stood on aristocratic and simultaneously pan-Germanic feet, and walked about as if descending from Mt. Olympus."[5]

In Nazi ideology notions of racial purity associated Aryanness with the quintessential refinement of beauty and strength. Jews in contrast were sub-human; they were associated with disease, and vermin that warranted exterminated. The Nuremberg Laws decreed that Jews were not only a religious or ethnic group, but a racial category, and Jewish "blood" was a tribal stigma contaminating three generations of descendants. Anti-Semitic and Nazi ideology presented a classification scheme of racial types. Aryan races were further categorized according to head size, facial features, and hair and eye coloring.

In Germany nowadays, skin color and physical features remain imbued with ethnic significance. Individuals are thus limited in their capacity to affirm or deny a particular identity, unless they take extreme measures to modify such cues – to lighten dark skin or darken light skin, modify nose-structure, add folds to eyelids, or change the shape of eyes, lips, mouth, or body, for example. It can be argued that Jews in Germany are physically indistinguishable from German Christians in skin tone, facial features, body type, and dress code. Most Jews are light-skinned Ashkenazim. They are also secularized, and thus are not clad according to the stereotypical Orthodox dress codes. Married women do not wear wigs, nor do they have long-sleeved, below-the-knee dresses. Men are not clothed in modest black-and-white garb, nor do they grow long beards. Jews in Germany do not have to worry about their presentation of self as Orthodox Jews might.

While no empirical evidence has affirmed that Jews are a physically distinguishable race, for many Jews I talked to, physical features were significant indicators of their Jewish ethnicity. Indeed, in *Idols of the Tribe*, Harold Isaacs emphasizes that physical features are such significant ethnic cues that groups have ways of creating differences that do not exist, or accentuating those that do.[6] Similarly, in *Ethnic Options*, Mary Waters reports that people sharing the same ethnicity often believe they share appearances and traits.[7] Living in Germany, many Jews do precisely what Harold Isaacs observes – they create or accentuate physical differences between themselves and Germans to distinguish themselves as a unique ethnic entity. While Nazi ideology excluded Jews from German society because of their "racial categories," Jews signal their own exclusion from contemporary German society by highlighting their distinct racial or physical differences.

While no respondent referred to Jews as a separate race, some Jews suggested that their physical features could easily identify them as being Jewish or certainly not being German.[8] In fact, a third of my respondents felt that they displayed their ethnicity through visible physical characteristics and contrasted the physical features of the "blond and Nordic-looking German" with the "dark and Semitic-appearing Jew." As color, perhaps even more than body type, unquestionably marks identity, skin and hair color were mentioned frequently as visible cues signaling Jewish ethnicity. A history professor described how he stood out as a child, because his hair was dark and "all German children are blond." An attorney who had practiced in Hamburg had a similar feeling: "In northern Germany people don't look like I look." A physician, who has immigrated to the United States, discussed his sister's appearance: "My sister looks different from Germans. She looks more 'Semitic.' She has darker, olive skin and black hair, which is different from other Germans."[9] Several others explained that they had no control over being identified as Jews. For example, the ophthalmologist we met in earlier chapters explains that while she was growing up, "All of them [Germans] were very fair, blond, and I looked different. I definitely look Jewish. I've got long, dark hair."

Consistent with the prominence of facial features in cultural representations of Jews over many centuries, my interviewees often mentioned facial features as significant cues signaling Jewish identity. For instance, Gertrud, the housewife struggles with her physical distinctiveness: "How I look different? I'm not so sure. One of the reasons I presume is my nose... And maybe the color of my hair. Although it's not different from any other German." Peter, the psychiatrist, expresses similar sentiments when he describes how people know he's Jewish: "Yes, they can see it. I have different facial features, and curls and heavier eyebrows. I don't have a German face."

Many Jews did not feel that their looks gave them away, but that their names did. Mystics have approached names as clues to the essence of a person – a guide to his or her inner reality. Psychologists have documented how names are rich in symbolism, creating associations with personality attributes of the carrier such as sensuality, intelligence, and ambition. Names are of symbolic importance within Jewish tradition: carrying the name of a deceased relative is said to keep his or her spirit alive, while carrying the name of a biblical character supposedly creates the potential for psychological identification, as the biblical hero becomes a role model.[10] Several respondents had Hebrew first names or Eastern European surnames. The name might not identify them as Jewish, but they claimed it identified them as not being German. One Jewish family, aware of names as significant markers of identity, changed their child's name from David to Dieter when he was about to enter school. Several respondents reported that directly after the war some Germans gave their children traditionally Jewish names, like Esther or Abraham, out of solidarity with the oppressed.

While parents in the United States have carte blanche in naming their child, children's names in Germany are more strictly regulated. Miriam, a school teacher, explains:

Some people made remarks about my name because my name was so unusual in Germany. You have lists of names that you give to children. Even up to ten or fifteen years ago, they could still go by those Nazi lists of names. Nobody was called Miriam. When my father registered me after the war, the man insisted that the name didn't exist, because it wasn't in the register of names. There was Hildegard, and Brunhilde, Galinda, and these names. Now in the United States there are other people named Miriam. But in Germany it is still a mark of being Jewish.

Presentation of self – dress styles and traditions, body language, use of props and masks, speech patterns – was also seen as providing blatant markers of Jewish identity. Ruth, the sociology graduate student we met in Chapter 4, described how she could tell a Jewish man by the amount of clothes he wears. According to Ruth, Jewish men overdress. During winter they wear more layers of clothing than necessary – tee-shirt, long-sleeve shirt, vest, sweater, jacket, scarf, hat, and gloves. She speculated that overdressing was a childhood habit engrained by their over-protective mothers, who were fearful their children might catch cold. Similarly, talking loudly, talking with one's hands, or using Yiddish or Hebrew words or expressions in conversation, might inadvertently signal Jewish identity.

Although public declarations of Jewishness might be made unintentionally, German co-workers and acquaintances had ample opportunity to guess one's identity. For example, during the Jewish high holidays most Jewish-owned shops are closed, and most Jewish employers and employees do not work. Moreover, mentioning Passover meals, Jewish New Year's dinners, or other Jewish holidays in casual conversation signaled Jewish ethnicity. Claudia, the hearing specialist we encountered in an earlier chapter, describes a typical manner in which her Jewish identity might be disclosed:

For example, I start to work, and then it's Christmas time. And they say, "What do you want for Christmas?" And I say "I don't give any presents because I'm Jewish, and I don't celebrate Christmas." Or, for example, I say I am going to Israel, and I say I have family in Israel. Lots of times it comes up in the course of a discussion about Israel.

Some Jews I talked with believed their identity was communicated mysteriously, through a radiance or ambience that emanated from their mere presence. In this context their identity was revealed involuntarily, in an incomprehensible manner. As Harry the businessman explained, when asked if people can tell that he is Jewish: "I must have something which makes them wonder. Some aura or something."

The importance of these signals of Jewishness is reflected in the manner in which Jews perceive they are being assessed. Indeed, their presentation of self has a strong impact on their assessment of their social prestige. Recall that one image of being Jewish is being special. This socially constructed image is substantiated by the numerical scarcity of Jews, in that most Germans experience a Germany without Jews. Moreover, as argued previously, against the backdrop of the Holocaust Jewish identity is attributed with moral superiority. These images of Jewishness, Jews believe, are the standards of evaluation that Germans use to single them out. The attitude of Oskar, the social science researcher, exemplifies a common reaction to identity disclosure. When asked if people know he is Jewish when they first meet him, Oskar replies, "I think they perceive me somehow as something extraordinary, somehow. Mostly in a positive way, but also in a somehow stunned way."

For these respondents, all one had to do was present oneself – face, name, dress, or persona – to demonstrate Jewish identity. They assumed their self-disclosure of Jewish ethnicity was often non-verbal and unintentional. In other cases, being Jewish was considered less self-evident, unless respondents voluntarily displayed their ethnic allegiance, adorning themselves with religious emblems. Displaying symbols of their identity – wearing a Star of David, an Israeli *chai*, or a *mezuzah*[11] – disclosed their ethnic affiliation unambiguously. Others flatly refused to adorn themselves with Jewish symbols, remarking that their Jewish identity was not in question. They insisted that they prominently displayed their Jewishness on the inside, in their hearts.

Institutional arrangements sometimes cause Jewish identity disclosure. As mentioned earlier, religious instruction is mandatory in German schools, although only courses on Protestantism and Catholicism are offered. Jews are exempt from participating in these courses, and on Sundays, are expected to attend Jewish classes held at the Jewish *Gemeinde*. The conspicuous absence of Jewish students in religious classes immediately flags Jews as different, warranting an explanation.

There are many cases in which being a Jew may be less self-evident – such as during university admission exams, in job interviews, when applying for a driver's license, voting, obtaining an apartment, entering a hospital, and at death – except that in all these cases one's birthplace is noted on all identification documents. If one's birthplace is Israel, one is not just foreign-born, but very likely to be Jewish. Respondents born in Israel said that because of the official recording of their birthplace on identification documents, employers, school administrators, and other officials knew immediately that they were Jewish.

In *Stigma*, Goffman describes how networks, associates, friends, and contacts provide information about one's identity. Socializing with other Jews immediately identified interviewees as being Jewish. A few respondents mentioned certain restaurants and cafes in Frankfurt that have come to be seen by both Germans and Jews as typical Jewish leisure-time hangouts. Frequenting such locales was all that was needed to display Jewish ethnicity. Norbert, the law student who has both Jewish and German friends, explains:

When you grow up here in Frankfurt, and even when you are going out, the Germans know that you are Jewish. When you go out to a discotheque or coffee house, they know who the Jews are. They know one girl who knows the boy, and the boy knows she's her girlfriend. Frankfurt isn't a big city. There are three or four places you go to, and there are Germans and Jews, and they know who is Jewish. It's a kind of special social area – Jewish and non-Jewish. And in this area they know who is Jewish.

Identity can also be revealed at the work-place when Jews associate with other Jews. Of course, for this to happen there must be a critical mass of Jews at one's place of work. For example, Suzanna noted: "At the University clinic there are so many Jewish doctors. When I go to eat, I know all of them. I would go and sit with them. And the physicians who aren't Jewish know precisely who is Jewish simply from the contact of who knows whom."

However, regardless of the salience of the identity markers, the most frequent way that Germans came to know that respondents were Jewish was when respondents told them. While it was deemed unnecessary to reveal their Jewishness in the work-place, it was essential for friendship relationships. Nathan, the banker, explains:

There are a lot of people I don't tell, because I don't think it's important. It depends on the form of the relationship. It's important when I have closer contact to a person. For example, with a business partner, I don't tell them that. . . Otherwise, it is usually that I like someone, and I want them also to like me. Then I will express it.

His sentiments are echoed by the professor:

Q: Is it important for your friends to know that you are Jewish?
A: Yes. If you are friends with someone, you have a right to know who that person is, with all his mistakes, attributes, and so on. But if you meet people on a professional level, as academics, then it's not important. What's important is the kind of science you studied.

The consequences of Jewish identity disclosure: being treated differently because one is Jewish

In *Weltbürgertum und Nationalstaat*, published in 1908, Frederich Meinecke argued that the awakening of national consciousness in Germany was accompanied by the philosophy of individualism. Liberal values included individual freedom, and emancipation would result in the disappearance of Jews *qua* Jews, as Jews would be transformed into citizens or non-Jews. The Holocaust showed how wrong Meinecke was. Many Jews today continue to believe that they are perceived in terms of certain generalizations that Germans hold of them. My respondents perceive that instead of interacting with them as individuals, citizens, or human beings, Germans classify them as occupants of a category – eternal members of Jewry. This conceptualization shapes all their subsequent interactions.

The categories through which Jews perceive that Germans define them parallel those through which Jews define themselves. Just as Jewish identity images can signal both status enhancements and degradations, so do Jews believe that Germans' categorizations of Jews include both positive and negative elements. Whether German perceptions of Jews generate Jewish identity images, or Jews project their own identity images onto their perceptions of Germans, remains an open question. In any case, many second-generation Jews in Germany resent the perceived categorization. Jews wish to be seen as individuals, not as an identifiable group with a clear and separate identity. They feel uneasy about being categorized on the basis of age-old inherited group characteristics, and believe that the process dehumanizes and degrades them. These sentiments are exemplified by Adam, the real-estate broker:

I see that my being Jewish is an issue for other people, because they mention things which show that they have this on their mind in situations where it isn't appropriate... I realize that if people here speak about you, if non-Jewish people raise your name, one of the characteristics that they always mention – be it your car or where you live, or whether you're tall or small, or have black hair or blonde – one thing they mention is this Jewish guy who does this or that. So, this seems to be an important issue for non-Jewish people.

My respondents mentioned experiences in school where teachers or classmates would confuse them with the other Jewish children and call them by the wrong name. Simon, a law student remarked that people always asked him if he knew certain other Jewish persons once they found out that he was Jewish. Juliane, the secretary, recalls that in her high school history class all of her classmates turned around to ask her whether she would mind leaving the room when they were about to discuss the Holocaust.

A rather different perspective comes from Helena, the part-time flight attendant, who describes how her mother's speech, which signals Jewish identity, bothers her in public places:

My mother speaks German, but when we are in the city, she speaks Yiddish very loudly, so that everyone will hear it and notice it. This makes me uncomfortable. I'm uncomfortable because I am so assimilated, and I don't think everyone needs to know this ... When I'm with my mother and she does this, then I think, my

God, they are categorizing us. And they are categorizing me as nothing more than being her daughter. And I am Jewish, but I am a lot more than that. And as long as I feel that I am perceived as both aspects, then that's fine. But to only be seen as being Jewish, I don't want that.

The reluctance on the part of some Jews to disclose their Jewish identity can be interpreted as an attempt to avoid the negative associations attached to being Jewish in contemporary Germany, or to subordinate them to more positive ones. As Lyman and Douglas suggest, identity switching is a common tactic when a particular identity of the actor becomes disadvantageous and another seems to provide better payoffs in the encounter.[12] For Helena, it is important that she be seen as a complete person, that her Jewishness be one quality among others equally important in defining who she is. The shift from a particular identity, that of being Jewish, to a more universal one, such as being human, is tactically wise when Jewishness stigmatizes Helena and other Jews.

In interpersonal interactions, information is communicated non-verbally or unintentionally, as well as verbally and intentionally, through powerful displays of ethnic cues.[13] There are many ways in which Jews signal their Jewishness to Germans, but such disclosures can sometimes have drawbacks, as was the case for the journalist we met in previous chapters:

I don't like it at all when they [Germans] think I'm something special because I'm Jewish. I hate that, because then they don't mean me, but the picture they have of Jews. It's very difficult to clarify what my fantasy is, or my interpretation of the experience, and what the reality is here. I wouldn't say people love me because I'm Jewish, but it's a plus. It makes me feel very bad. In a way, it makes me feel sick. I get the feeling that it is phony. In a certain way I associate it with people who want to have a disabled friend, and the first disabled person that comes along on the street is supposed to be their friend, but only because they want to adorn themselves by knowing someone disabled, or a Jew, or that they are friends with a Jew.

Like her, many Jews fear that the stigmatized identity is what represents the group to outsiders, and resent being treated as a Jew on this basis. It does not matter whether the consequences of this categorization mean fair or unfair treatment. In such situations, Jews do not take a pragmatic view of their Jewishness. They may even discount favors that they might have gained from Germans on the basis of their Jewishness. In such cases, they downplay the Jewish element of their identity, and are likely to show anger, disgust, irritation, anxiety, and sadness.

The stress on categorization is sustained in part by the perceptions that Jews have about Germans. As discussed earlier, Jews go out of their way to distinguish themselves from Germans, and such attitudes are encouraged by the Jewish *Gemeinde* and various Jewish institutions. Jews in Germany are likely to devalue most of their commonalities with Germans, even though in other circumstances these commonalities might have been viewed as excuses for closer ties. For example, sharing a birthplace or living in the same neighborhood are not sufficient signals for trusting a German acquaintance. Jews remain vigilant in maintaining social distance from the Germans, and tend to manipulate that distance only when they are ready to change the terms of the relationship.

The uneasiness or resentment that Jews experience in disclosing their Jewishness is sometimes a result of feeling deprived of social respect, and in some cases opportunities, relative to other citizens in Germany: Jews want to be treated in the same way that Germans treat other "Germans." This becomes problematic because at the same time they wish to remain Jews, but only on their own terms. Thus, Jewish identity is experienced in a complex and paradoxical manner: the special ties of ethnicity sometimes make Jews hesitant to display ethnic signals, and at other times induce Jews to display ethnic signals as a means of provocation.

Because being Jewish can be a social liability, Jews who are inclined to disclose their identity must determine the appropriate time to do so. Almost every Jew I spoke with had experienced ambivalence about disclosing his or her Jewish identity, and had needed to develop norms for appropriately doing so. The following respondent illustrates this dilemma:

Q: Is it important that people know that you are Jewish?
A: Yes, at a certain time in my life it was important. I don't think that I connected it with an instrumental goal, just that I wanted them [Germans] to know whom they are meeting.
Q: Why the change?
A: Because one day, I do not know exactly when, I became suspicious of whether people treated me maybe in a different, positive way because I'm Jewish, and I just wanted to know what it was like to be somebody without this Jewish attribute.
Q: Did you notice a difference?
A: Yes, I think that if people know that I'm Jewish, they are a little bit more cautious, not in a political way, but because there's a bigger distance, somehow there is a certain distance. You are treated as

somebody who is not completely normal, and who deserves special treatment, or something like that.

Q: How does that make you feel?

A: Very bad.

Q: Do you react in any special way?

A: No, because I don't know how to. Therefore I decided not to tell it to everybody immediately, at least not anymore to people I'm in professional contact with. And on the professional level I don't mention it anymore. Only on the personal level if I want to become personal friends with someone ... I mean, in certain situations, yes, for example, if you are sitting in a discussion of something, politics, science, I don't know, and somebody is making, I wouldn't say an anti-Semitic remark, but some stupid, idiotic [remark], like "It's noisy in here like in a Jewish school, *Judenschule*," then I always think, well, what do I do? Now, do I intervene and say, "Hell, what are you saying?" or just let it pass, and in those situations I am embarrassed to say that I am Jewish just because I don't know whether it would make sense to begin a whole debate on something which is actually not the main point, or not important for the whole situation.

Q: What do you usually do?

A: Usually I would only intervene if I'm sure that there's intended anti-Semitism, or unconscious but heavy anti-Semitism.

Q: Has that happened?

A: In political discussions, yes. In discussions when someone was talking about Israel and so on, and said, "This is the same kind of thing that the Nazis did," I would say, "Just a minute." For idioms like "*Judenschule*," I don't react anymore. But it makes me uncomfortable.

For many respondents, situations occur in which revealing their Jewishness can be embarrassing or awkward. Most Jews get confused, and wonder how they should react. Certain professional situations where remarks could be construed as anti-Semitic can be very difficult to handle. The respondent featured above chooses not to display his ethnic identity in professional situations where he deems the intrusion of ethnicity to be inappropriate. In this context, disclosing one's Jewish identity can signal one's difference and can make both Jews and Germans feel uncomfortable.

My interviewees generally believed that Germans began behaving differently toward them once they realized they were Jewish, and that in such situations Germans often communicated ambiguity about what

Jewishness meant to them. Disclosing Jewish identity could mean upsetting the normative behavioral path that had already been charted in the interaction. However, disturbances, whether trivial or serious, are an inevitable intrusion into all social relationships, and Jews and Germans may not always want to maintain the equilibrium in the relationship, or the relationship itself.

How do Jews interpret disrupted relationships? Disclosing Jewish identity violates the norms of conflict avoidance. It creates an atmosphere that Jews perceive as threatening, provocative, challenging, and ambiguous. The same perceptions might be experienced by Germans in such instances. Disclosing Jewish identity is correlated with Germans modifying their behavior in some way – being more cautious in their disclosure of their own identities, opinions, affinities, and prejudices. Conflict does not necessarily occur, but interaction patterns are altered. For example, Norbert, the law student, when asked if he thought his Jewishness affected his interpersonal interactions, replied, "I very often suspected that people omitted topics, once they knew I was Jewish. Or changed topics. They didn't talk about their war experience as they might have, had they not known that I was Jewish."

Uncertainty about identity disclosure is often accompanied by anticipated negative consequences in interactions with Germans. Some respondents suggested that revealing Jewish identity is loaded with Holocaust metaphors. In this sense, identity disclosure might be read by Germans as an underhanded attempt to subordinate them morally, rather than as mere information disclosure in the course of a casual conversation or friendship development. These attitudes are not far-fetched. Indeed, in a 1994 public opinion survey conducted by the American Jewish Committee and the EMNID Institute on "Current German Attitudes Toward Jews and other Minorities," approximately 39 percent of Germans agree either strongly (15 percent) or somewhat (24 percent) that "Jews are exploiting the Holocaust for their own purposes."[14]

For many Jews, disclosing their Jewish identity means causing discomfort because it forces Germans to confront their past and the persecution of Jews. For instance, the following respondent is highly reluctant to disclose her Jewishness unless she deems it absolutely necessary:

Q: Were you ever afraid or embarrassed to say that you were Jewish?
A: Yes, in a certain way I thought they would think that I was less worthy. But that was a long time ago. In school, in the countryside. In school I expected people to say, "Oh, we can't hear this anymore" – that they want to ignore the history. When I say "I'm Jewish," then

the history suddenly comes up. I am always disturbing the nice harmony. Sometimes I feel they have the feeling that I'm aggressive when I say [I am Jewish]. Even today, I have the feeling that I am reserved, holding back the topic of my Jewishness with my non-Jewish friends. I'm always afraid they'll say "Enough, we don't want to hear this anymore." I mean, not with my very close friends.

This respondent anticipates that Germans associate Jewishness with Holocaust, and fears that revealing her Jewishness might be read as her way of initiating a discussion about the past. While the "stigmatized Jew" was an image that she felt predominated in Jewish identity in the past, today she perceives that "moral superiority" is a more salient component in that identity.

For many Jews I talked to, hesitancy in revealing their identity is justified by their experiences, and their assessment of the situation, because many have experienced anti-Semitism and philo-Semitism. Numerous opportunities have opened or closed for them because of such disclosures. Understandably, most Jews in my sample anticipate Germans will treat them differently once they knew that they were Jewish.

Jews perceive that prejudice is a norm in German society. It must be emphasized, however, that prejudice and discrimination are not the same thing. While some Germans might hold prejudiced views toward Jews, that does not necessarily mean that they will translate their biased attitudes into discriminatory behavior. Nevertheless, several informants mentioned that their first serious bouts with philo-Semitism and anti-Semitism occurred when they entered the working world. Julius, the schoolteacher, provides an example:

When I was teaching at a boarding school, I noticed that my being Jewish was perceived positively. That was a new experience, and it came from kids who were ten years younger than me. They said, "Yes, we noticed immediately that you are different." To them it was very positive that I wasn't like the others. And for the first time I could accept this, that there was something good associated with being seen as Jewish, quite different from the manner in which others here are seen. I didn't have pride before. Then I heard again and again that they saw me as being different – more sensitive, softer, not so hard, funnier than the others, not boring. All of a sudden I received so many compliments because I was Jewish. It was really, really strange.

While more respondents stated they experienced philo-Semitism, as opposed to anti-Semitism, and more opportunities were open to them than were closed to them, recall from Chapter 2 that Jews perceive philo-Semitism as a modified version of anti-Semitism. In this context, for some, revealing that one is Jewish might be a handicap, and those who present their ethnic cues risk discrimination. Anti-Semitism socially constructs Jews as less capable, less interesting, less effective, or less deserving in their personal or professional lives, which contributes to a loss of personal integrity and the sense of alienation second-generation Jews feel from mainstream German society.

As social scientists have well documented, social networks affect professional success, "who one knows" may be as much at the heart of professional mobility as "what one knows." Intertwined networks in which "notables" interact frequently and in different contexts are likely to have a stronger impact on mobility and opportunity structures in more tightly-knit societies like Germany than in more loosely bounded ones such as the United States.[15] This is because there is less mobility in Germany: there is a lower rate of geographical mobility, greater family stability, and less anonymity in elite circles. By contrast, scholars have touched upon the uprootedness, transience of relationships, and feelings of alienation that predominate in American society. *The Lonely Crowd* (Riesman), *A Nation of Strangers* (Packard), and *Lonely in America* (Gordon), are a few of the more popular book titles that have been published. The normative American lifestyle is characterized by ceaseless movement: leaving home for college, starting one's family of procreation in one's own home, the restless search to improve one's career, social conditions, and living conditions. This constant mobility creates many discontinuities in friendship and professional relationships. In comparison, German society is much more stable. Distances traveled are shorter, and there is less frequent uprooting. Much value is attached to social connections which play an essential role in getting access to jobs and other valued resources. Being discriminated against both personally and professionally can be very costly. One Jewish physician, who wears a Star of David around his neck, described such an incident:

After school I decided to get a start in medicine and I worked in a hospital in Frankfurt. And there was a physician. He was blond, tall, German, blue eyes. He taught me some things. He seemed to be German. Really German. But he was sometimes nice to me. But once I was in the same elevator with him and he saw my Star of David. And he asked me, "Are you Jewish?" And I said, "Yes." And that was the last word he ever spoke to me.

Instrumentalizing Jewish identity disclosure in interactions

Self-disclosure is "the act of making yourself manifest, showing yourself so others can perceive you" verbally and intentionally by exchanging information about the past, the present, and plans for the future, or non-intentionally, through dispositions, moods, and non-verbal communication.[16] Jews in Germany live in a real world where they encounter people every day, and therefore must deal with ethnic identity and ascription in face-to-face interactions. As described above, about half of my interviewees perceived that their Jewishness was communicated by their physical features alone. For others, their Jewish identity must be communicated intentionally, through verbal or other means. Regardless of whether Jewish ethnic disclosure was intentional or not, my respondents perceived that interactions with Germans were not ethnically neutral, but rather were deeply invested with ethnic overtones.

Much research on the earlier stages of acquaintanceship has focused on the processes by which two people come to define each other, and the reasons why different sorts of information concerning the other are attractive at different times in the growth of the relationship.[17] For instance, social psychologists Valerian Derlega and Janusz Grzelak have suggested five functions of self-disclosure in relationship development – self-expression, increased self-clarification, obtaining social validation by comparing oneself with others, acting as a vehicle for relationship development, and social control via impression management.[18]

I have identified a series of responses Jews have developed toward disclosing their identity in interactions with Germans: there are some situations where Jews overemphasize their Jewishness, others where they behave normally, and certain others where they hide or underemphasize their Jewishness. In many of these instances, disclosing Jewish identity might be associated with a desire for self-expression, increased self-clarification, and obtaining social validation by comparing oneself with others. More typically, however, a Jew emphasizes the role that self-disclosure plays in providing information. Such knowledge is necessary to infer that the other likes or trusts him or her, or validates his or her own beliefs, enabling Jews to gain valuable information about whether the other wishes to continue the encounter or to further develop the relationship.

Negative German responses toward Jewishness are associated with Jew's own perceptions of typical Germans, and their anticipation of German anti-Semitism and xenophobia. One strategy Jews used to minimize anticipated social sanctions and to protect themselves from the possible pain of rejection was to disclose their Jewish identity immediately upon initial encounter. The rationale for this tactic was that if they should be considered undesirable and subsequently rejected, not much would be lost, since not much had been invested. This type of instrumentalization is discussed by Miriam: "Well, I try to communicate this [being Jewish] as soon as possible. Like, my name is already a label. I want to know how they will react to me being Jewish, because this affects whether I am interested in this person or not... Normally from their behavior, I can tell whether the person is sympathetic or not." Moreover, by outwardly disclosing their Jewish identity immediately, some Jews believed that if Germans did feel unfavorably disposed toward them, social etiquette would dictate against their outwardly expressing it. A Jewish secretary who has lived her entire life in Frankfurt puts it best: "For many years I shielded myself, really spitting into everybody's face, 'I'm Jewish, behave!' or 'Don't try to insult me.'" This strategy is echoed by Esther, the law student:

Q: How did people know that you were Jewish?
A: Because I told them. Very often I wanted them to know, because I was always afraid that they might meet me and somehow insult me. Although I have to tell you it never happened. But I really wanted to prevent an incident like this, so I told them.

Revealing that one is Jewish can also be used as a discretionary mechanism for social control, the most obvious purpose being to ward-off anti-Semitic remarks. As Rosanna, the medical student, stated: "Certainly, when someone makes an anti-Semitic remark, I'll stop and say, 'Wait. You don't know with whom you are speaking.'" Similarly, disclosing Jewish ethnicity can be instrumentalized to instill in Germans a sense of collective responsibility. Harry, the businessman, talks about disclosing his Jewishness while discussing sensitive issues like the Holocaust:

I also use it [disclosing Jewish identity]. I use it in discussions about Israel and the Holocaust. For example, I can say, "I am Jewish and in my opinion Germany has a special responsibility toward Israel." I don't use it a lot. But I use it. I wouldn't use it today in the same form, but I would still use it in political struggles. For example, regarding fighting certain tendencies that exist here, if I can use it. But I think that it doesn't help much anymore today to say that I am Jewish. It doesn't have that much of a political effect.

Respondents felt the timing of self disclosure was important if it was to be used to maintain some control over the interaction. Indeed, given Jews' varied perceptions of what their Jewishness means, and their diverse perceptions and experiences of who Germans are, encounters with Germans are laden with difficult realities that both Jews and Germans must negotiate carefully.

Jews who have easily identifiable ethnic signals, as well as those who must more intentionally disclose their ethnicity, signal their Jewishness to Germans in order to observe the response it generates – to find out where the German stands *vis-à-vis* Jews, foreigners, the Holocaust, and similar topics. In this manner, self disclosure is not merely a consequence of the deepening of relationships, but can also be employed as a strategy to determine whom to befriend. Exchanging personal information facilitates a relatively painless assessment of the likely consequences of taking the relationship further, and allows partners to decide on the level of intimacy they wish to maintain in the relationship. As we have seen, Jews can use identity disclosure instrumentally to manipulate Germans' behavior by forcing the issue. Jews can also subsequently control the pace and direction of the development of the relationship. Hannah provides a provocative illustration:

My name is Hannah. My parents consciously chose the name Hannah. It could be a shortened version of Johanna, and it could be Hannah itself. Whereas in Hebrew my name is Chana. Earlier, when I said, "Chana," people would say, "Where are you from? Aha, you aren't German." I liked that. Sometimes, though, I didn't like it... In school, I am called Hannah, although my friends know the truth. But then, I always said Hannah, so that I wouldn't immediately disclose the information, and then I could determine whom I would tell what to. But often I'm asked, "Do you come from France? You have an accent." I've often lied. I've said that I'm German. And when they said, "That's not true," I said, "Yes, yes. I have a German passport. I was born here." It depends, sometimes it's coquettish. But when I find the people dumb or stupid, I don't tell them everything. And then there are always situations where I stress it very much. Depending on the situation, I can play around with it as I wish.

Thus, Hannah sometimes reveals her Jewish ethnicity, and at other times chooses not to. By withholding the disclosure of her Jewish identity, she manages to maintain some sense of control over an uncertain situation. This control serves a protective function: it maintains a certain distance so that depressive feelings can be minimized if the relationship is disrupted or terminated.

Hannah points out that she sometimes copes with encounters with Germans by identifying herself as other than Jew. Like Hannah, other Jews with whom I spoke used their ability to "pass" as a strategy in official situations. Many Jews easily pass as Germans for several reasons: (1) they physically do not look different; (2) they speak perfect German because they were raised in Germany and educated in German schools; (3) given that so few Jews live in Germany, the German population does not expect to meet one. In brief encounters in public places, this is not surprising. While most Jews will say that they are Jewish if asked, Viktor, the mathematician, aptly explains: "Usually people don't ask, because they don't expect you to be Jewish. Because there are so few Jewish people around, they wouldn't even get the idea that you are Jewish."

Many Jews talk openly about their ability to pass, about situations where it is inappropriate to display Jewish ethnicity, or of situations where out of fear, embarrassment, or avoidance of conflict, they wished to pass. Theodor, the sociology student, was typical of many:

Q: Is it important that people know you are Jewish?
A: I don't like people to know that I am Jewish. It depends. Sometimes, I'd rather not, because I don't want to make everything always *kaputt*.

A few interviewees described entire phases in their youth when they passed to maintain German friends. For these Jews, passing provided a certain comfort level that symbolizes social integration, and rewards them for it. Oskar, a social science researcher reflected thus on his childhood friends: "They never asked. But they made jokes about Jews. And probably out of fear of losing my friends, I didn't say, 'I am Jewish, stop that.'"

While only a few Jews recalled instances of actually lying about being Jewish, most experienced situations when they could have, but did not, mention that they were Jewish. Some Jews just did not like or want to feel that they were different from others. Others wanted to minimize the likelihood that Germans would behave differently once they knew that they were Jewish. Most Jews did not want to be treated differently by Germans because they were Jewish, and did not disclose their Jewishness if they felt it would be detrimental to them or the interaction.

A small group of respondents mentioned that it was their parents who stressed that they should be Jewish incognito. A few men were not circumcised because their parents didn't want them to stand out as Jews. Julius, the school teacher, mentioned that his sister wanted to wear a Star-of-David necklace, and his mother said, "Absolutely not." Another respondent, whose parents were German Jews who had emigrated to Palestine during the war, recalled an incident he had with his mother after the family returned to Germany permanently:

When I came from Israel, I had a jacket, a black jacket, and it had breast pockets with a zipper. On this zipper to open these breast pockets, there was a Star of David button. And one of the first things that my mother did was to remove these Stars of David. To this day I still don't know why. Either she didn't want me to be pointed out because it was similar to the Jewish star that Jews had to wear, or she was preparing me for assimilation.

A few respondents mentioned that out of fear of negative sanctions, they did not always reveal their Jewish ethnicity. Given the violence for which neo-Nazis are known, several Jews, understandably, talked about their fear of revealing that they are Jewish to neo-Nazis. Claudia, the hearing specialist, provides us with a typical response: "I wouldn't say it [disclose Jewishness] to someone who is a Nazi, or who wouldn't be sympathetic. I have to talk with him to find out what kind of person he is. It depends on how he reacts." One interviewee who was writing her doctoral thesis on neo-Nazis, had spent much time interviewing her respondents. She said she was afraid to mention that she was Jewish, both because they might no longer cooperate with her and out of fear for her own safety.

A dentist, who works in an area that he thinks has a high concentration of Nazis, describes the sanctions Jews might face, when discussing his hesitancy at revealing his Jewish ethnicity:

Actually I am always afraid to say that I am Jewish. For example, if I would put on a *Mogen David* tomorrow – I have one in my drawer and for a long time I used to wear it, but currently I've hidden it beneath my shirt – I can have experiences in Hannover where I have my practice. It is a Nazi nest. I could experience personal problems. Then I would immediately have to arm myself. So I won't do it. I don't want to jeopardize my security. That is the problem. Social losses, material losses, the risk is there. That's why I don't declare anything. When someone asks me, I don't lie... The question doesn't come up, because you see how integrated I am. I speak perfect German, accent-free, so nobody asks. The question is not "Why don't you declare that you are Jewish," rather, "What risks might you incur if you disclose that you are Jewish and continually show it." Latent fear is always there.

The dentist mentions that the behavioral norm of constantly avoiding Jewish identity disclosure creates for him severe psychological consequences:

I believe I am a coward. That is the effect. That's the point. Because the way I normally am, I would go on the streets and call it out if I liked. Not fearing any kind of consequences. But I do not. And that's the point. That's enough... I never believed, even as a child, that one had to be a hero. The opposite was the real case. My mother told me very early on that to be a living coward is better than a dead hero. So this might have programmed me in a way. But I was also programmed simultaneously to think I was a coward. So I am the living coward, not the dead hero. That's the point. You have only two possibilities.

Explaining Jewish–German friendships

After spending ten years in the United States, the social psychologist Kurt Lewin observed, "compared with Germans, Americans seem to make quicker progress towards friendly relations in the beginning, and with many more persons. Yet the development often stops at a certain point; and the quickly acquired friends will, after years of relatively close relations, say good-by as easily as after a few weeks of acquaintance."[19] While making a clear statement of the superficiality of what Americans refer to as friends, Lewin is also suggesting the seriousness which is implied by the German word *Freund* (friend). Germans invest more deeply of themselves in friendships than Americans do. The bonds are based on strong affective ties that lead Germans to become deeply involved with one another on a level that surpasses American friendship involvement. It is worth exploring in detail whom Jews find attractive and whom they befriend, for it provides additional evidence about the importance of the past in their lives today.

Whom do Jews befriend?

A friendship in its idealized form is characterized by reciprocated affection, loyalty, and admiration.[20] It is a relationship of intimate, enduring contact, characterized by shared activities, a desire to spend time together, mutual fondness, and an acknowledgment, both to one another and to others, that they are friends. As we saw in Chapter 2, because of the backdrop of the Holocaust, Jews hold typifications of Germans and feel distant from them. The community proscribes Jewish social integration into German society, but at the same time reluctantly tolerates Jewish–German friendships. In spite of all this adverse pressure against forming close relations with Germans, Jews do have friendships with them. And Jews feel close to many of their German friends. How is this possible?

The second-generation Jews I spoke with often experienced social barriers when they come into contact with Germans. They experience emotional and mental boundaries that impede their ability to feel connected with Germans. Kurt, the attorney, had views typical of many: "There was a distance derived from the fact that I was Jewish and everybody knew, not in information and details, but sort of projection, feelings, emotions, that there was the Holocaust. There was a wall between me and the other kids in school."

Social relationships between Jews and Germans tend to be more complicated than those amongst Jews, because Jews must determine whether it is legitimate to charge Germans with collective responsibility. No consensus existed on how to deal with this issue, or whether such a thing as collective war responsibility exists. In particular, a number of questions are worth considering. If collective responsibility exists, who is and who should be held responsible? Which Germans are responsible, and what are they responsible for? Are all Germans responsible for all war crimes? Is it legitimate to charge the younger generation for the crimes that their parents or the state might have committed?[21] Jewish views on these questions require a lengthier and more detailed analysis than can be offered here. Nonetheless, a discussion of the responses of some of my interviewees will reveal the complexity of these issues for Jews.

Charging Germans with collective responsibility for Second World War war crimes is not universal. Some Jews do not deem it fair to charge their German friends or Germany's younger generation with their country's crimes. As Anna, the physician puts it: "I do not think, if their parents did something that was not proper and right, that they [younger Germans] are guilty of that." Along the same lines, David, whom we met in the Prologue, says, "This is a new generation. Not all of them, of course, are wonderful... But they are not responsible for what their parents did." Both Anna and David suggest that collective responsibility cannot be inherited by the mere fact that one was born into German society. Being collectively responsible or responsible requires a more active participation in the extermination of the Jews, and cannot be inferred via a tribal stigma or shared history.

As Danielle pointed out at the beginning of this chapter, though, some sensitivity to the past is a precondition for Jews to form a friendship with Germans. In most cases, Jews expect of their German friends a sensitivity toward their present-day struggles, toward the Holocaust, and toward the suffering of their parents and families. Interestingly, it is precisely those Germans who cultivate their own interest in German history, racism, and the war, to whom Jews become attracted. As Juliane, the secretary, explains: "I couldn't really be friends with a person who isn't interested in his own history, and who didn't deal with his past. I think for me that's a precondition."

While Jews maintain conceptualizations of Germans emphasized in the *Gemeinde* and informal community, their friendships are cultivated with Germans who they believe do not fit these typifications. The transition from a *Bekannter* (acquaintance) to a *Freund* (friend) is thus based on Jews setting aside typifications of Germans as murderers, anti-Semites, xenophobes, and typical Germans, and their conceptualizations of younger Germans as being children of such people. It must be emphasized, however, that Jews do not relinquish their stereotypical conceptualizations of Germans as an out-group. In fact, these typifications remain intact. What does occur, however, is that Jews suspend these global judgments with respect to a particular person. They view this friend as a special case, as a particular German rather than a typical one. The cultural criteria that Jews use to describe the attributes of their friends are negations of the criteria they use to describe Germans in general. Their friends are marginal members of German society, the exception rather than the rule, the German in name only.

These relationships are based on the personal qualities of the individuals involved, which means there is a disassociation of all ethnic typifications. The relationship is forged on the intrinsic qualities of the players, their mutual attraction, their idiosyncratic characteristics. This does not mean that ethnic typifications do not play a role in the process of friendship formation. On the contrary, the qualities that become attractive are those that symbolize an antithesis of the typical German.

For instance, as we saw in Chapter 2, typical Germans are thought to be provincial and narrow-minded. These traits are correlated with a lack of interest in the outside world, a rigidity of opinions and views, and little exposure to different cultural experiences, as a result of limited education or circumscribed personal experience. Jews also say that they are alienated from mainstream Germans because of Germans' pragmatic orientation, lack of cultural sophistication, and anti-intellectualism. While German society is viewed as anti-intellectual, anti-cosmopolitan, and parochial, Jews befriend Germans whom they perceive as diametrically opposed to these values – Germans who are more "international," more "open-minded," "university educated," and those who locate themselves "more to the left" of the political spectrum. Finally, Jews define their German friends as more "sensitive," "empathetic," "emotional," and "warm," than the typical German. While typical Germans are thought to be cold and emotionless, Jews befriend Germans who they say are more "able to feel suffering" and more "understanding" than mainstream Germans. Having a German friend means transforming the German aspect of that person into an archetypal Jew. In this way, the reality is remade into a myth.

Many Jews I talked with pointed out the importance of having German friends who are interested in the same issues and concerns as Jews. Theories on friendship development suggest that a similarity of values is one basis for friendship attraction. Jews look for a similarity of values regarding the collective memory of the Holocaust and present-day concerns with race and ethnic relations. Suzanna, the physician we met in earlier chapters, states:

True friends are very few... And they are interested in the same problems that I am: history, German history, racism, nationalism, work-labor. They do this because it's their interest. Not necessarily because they know me. I believe that this is a reason why we are friends. Because we have something in common.

Judging from the tone of the interviews, and because of the backdrop of the Holocaust, as well as the existence (either actual or anticipated) of anti-Semitism within the general German population, Jews place more emphasis on Germans' attitudes toward the past and present-day race relations than they would in dealing with non-Jewish friendship possibilities in environments without such cultural "baggage."

Another variable that plays a significant role in Jewish–German friendship formation is reciprocity. This reciprocity occurs at the ethnic level. That is, respondents pointed out that a precondition for friendship was knowing how Germans feel toward Jews in general, and towards them as Jews in particular. Reciprocity becomes a filtering device; Jews become friends with Germans who like and accept them as Jews. In fact, reciprocity is a must. Jews become friends with Germans who could not possibly be anti-Semitic. Celia, the soft-spoken pharmacist puts it best when she asked rhetorically: "Why should someone who is anti-Semitic want to be my friend?"

The establishment of trust is also an essential ingredient for the development or maintenance of the friendship. The frame of reference Jews use to determine which Germans to trust is, again, anchored in the collective memory of the Holocaust, and the contemporary issues upon which it touches. "It's time, mostly. Caution and time, and seeing how it develops," is how Harry, the businessman, describes the development of trust. Peter, the psychiatrist, explains how he determines which Germans become worthy of his trust: "It's a feeling. A feeling of sympathy and empathy. A feeling of how close one is, and how well one knows another, and I can be wrong about it. I am not always right."

One common solution to determining whom to trust is to observe how Germans react to certain topics and to their past. If Germans are able to define themselves and their interests in contrast to the values of the Third Reich, or those of typical Germans, then they have communicated that they are different. By doing so, they have adopted positions more morally appropriate to their history than those defined in Chapter 2. Concretely this means that Germans have confronted the Holocaust on some level. As Viktor, the mathematician, explains, Jews can easily determine whether this is the case for a particular German:

Q: How do you know whom to trust?

A: Oh, I can tell. Well, I first notice how people react to history. To their history. I don't have to provoke conversations. They come up automatically. In this country if you don't try to avoid it, then you constantly encounter occasions where the topic comes up. So, I don't have any problems in personal relations. I know exactly whom I can trust and whom I cannot. This is not based on comments or remarks or on things that people say. It's just how people behave... You see how people react when they're confronted with topics, and you can tell whether they are dodging it.

A small number of my respondents demanded a greater sense of loyalty from their German friends to prove sincerity. If friendship obligations are unlimited, then a true friend should want to do anything for another, and will in fact do so. For Jews in Germany, a German friend's moral commitment is tested via a fantasy flight into the past through the Holocaust metaphor. Adam, the real estate broker, is one case in point. He determines which Germans to trust by staging scenarios as if they were in the Third Reich: "I look around the people who surround me, and I think, would they back me? And I ask myself, under similar conditions, would they stand beside you? Would they fight with you? Would they take the dishonor with you? Would they still be your friends if something similar happened?" Ruth, the sociology graduate student uses similar criteria in deciding whom to befriend: "One of the major questions you ask, and I think a lot of Jews that I talk to make their friends by asking, 'Is he or she going to hide me when another pogrom comes?'"

Friendship frequencies

While our exploration so far has focused primarily on cultural factors that motivate Jewish–German friendships, it is reasonable to think that structural characteristics also affect friendship choices. The evidence suggests that structural factors influence the potency of cultural factors in a contradictory manner, simultaneously reinforcing and weakening their impact. This section will concentrate on this contradictory impact, and explore some of the difficulties in reconciling Jewish community-wide cultural messages with the valued exchanges and personal growth that can result from crossing ethnic boundaries.

Table 5.1: *Jewish population of Frankfurt by age*

Age	Number
0–3	89
4–6	89
7–15	237
16–20	164
21–30	704
31–40	520
41–50	394
51–60	892
61–70	859
Over 70	658

At the time the interviews were undertaken (1984), Frankfurt was the sixth largest city in West Germany, with a population of 599,634, of which 471,213 were German citizens.[22] Statistical data on the ages of the members of the Jewish community can help us understand how these structural factors have serious repercussions on friendship choice. The total Jewish population in Frankfurt as of September 3, 1984 was 4670, and broke down by age cohort as shown in Table 5.1.

There are over 100 times more Germans in the population of Frankfurt than Jews. Thus, German society provides a larger pool of potential contacts for friendship development for two reasons: there is a systematic difference in each group's ability to provide a *supply* of potential friends for Jews, and to provide everyday *opportunities* for friendship development.

Whereas German society provides a limitless pool of potential acquaintances and friends, in Jewish society, given the small population size, particularly within an age cohort, sooner or later, saturation occurs. It is not surprising that every Jew knows of, has heard of, or has met every other Jew. Interviewees also reported knowing other Jews their age in other Jewish *Gemeinden* throughout Germany. Jewish networks are small, insular, and well-connected. For many respondents, maintaining only Jewish friends was perceived as too confining, and resembled an "invisible Jewish ghetto." Adam sums up a typical sentiment regarding cultivating only Jewish friends: "I didn't want to be stuck in this ghetto." David, whom we met in the Prologue, describes the dilemma: "If you choose to have a lot of Jewish friends and you live in Brooklyn, it's okay. But in Germany, just numerically there are so few Jews, if you choose to stay only with Jews, it's like living in a village of 200 people."

These differences in the opportunity structures for cultivating contacts between Jews and Germans on an everyday basis were most pronounced when my interviewees were growing up. The only ethnic school that existed was a Jewish kindergarten. Jews lived geographically dispersed throughout Frankfurt, and attended primary and secondary schools in their neighborhoods. The Jews I sampled were usually the only Jew in their class, and one of two or three Jews in their school. Therefore, the probability of their encountering other Jews on a daily basis was low. Being thrust into frequent encounters with Germans increases the likelihood that friendly relations will develop, since public propriety dictates that cordial relations be maintained with those one meets in social and occupational roles. Thus, the geographical dispersion of Jews throughout Frankfurt played a central role in Jewish–German friendship formation, particularly at school age. As Anna, the physician, aptly described it, having German friends "was circumstantial just by the fact that all of my classmates were non-Jews, and my social contacts were mainly with these classmates."

Friendships with Germans were associative relations, born out of circumstance and propinquity. They were established at school, the university, the work-place, and political clubs. Over 75 percent of the respondents met their close German friends at school. In contrast, friendships with Jews were formed in the *Gemeinde* youth clubs, or through family and friendship networks. In fact, parents' social networks supplied the majority of my interviewees' close Jewish friends.

Jewish friendships were of longer duration than German friendships. Indeed, over 60 percent of the Jews I interviewed reported knowing their closest Jewish friends for at least eleven years, and many Jews knew their closest Jewish friends for over twenty years. In contrast, friendships with Germans were much more recent. About half of all Jewish respondents had known their closest German friends for less than ten years, and very few respondents had known their closest German friends for over twenty years.

In *The Seven Day Circle*, Eviatar Zerubavel has argued that periods of time acquire specific cultural qualities by virtue of association with activities peculiar to them.[23] Thus, weekends in Western societies are experienced as special, extraordinary because they signify a break in the continuity of work, school, and routine undertakings. Weekends and "off-hours" are in a sense sacred, and are imbued with cultural codes and meanings that stand forever in contrast to the rest of the week. One's activities and contacts are suspended from the criteria that regulate ordinary everyday life. This would make friendships developed and sustained during the "peak" weekends qualitatively different from those friendships maintained during the "off-peak" work days. Following Zerubavel's conceptualization, my evidence indicates that Jews are more likely to spend "public" time with their German friends and reserve private time for their Jewish friends. Public time was limited to weekdays in public spaces such as school and after-school activities or work and work-related socializing. My interviewees spent weekends and holidays mostly with their families, relatives, and Jewish friends.

The net result of these structural circumstances was the establishment of two separate circles of friends – the German friends who were attached to the realm of school and work, and the Jewish friends who were attached to the realm of home, family, and *Gemeinde*. Thus, Jews could easily segregate their German friends from their Jewish friends. While most of the second-generation Jews I interviewed reported that their German friends knew their Jewish friends, and vice versa, a few respondents reported occasions when they deemed it necessary for the friendship circles not to mix. As Hermann, the physician remarked: "They don't have anything to say to each other. I wouldn't go out with them together." Eva expresses a similar sentiment: "I have Jewish circles and German circles. And I can mix the circles, but I'd rather not." At times maintaining two separate friendship networks becomes cumbersome. For example, some respondents held two separate parties for the same occasion on two separate evenings – one for their Jewish friends and one for their German friends. Herbert, the master's candidate in business administration describes the rationale behind such a tactic: "I can invite them together when I am inviting 10 people. But if I'm inviting 50 people or 30, then I wouldn't invite them together, because then we would have a Jewish circle and a German circle."

Finally, there is a structural distinction between Jewish friendship and German friendship networks. In the latter situation, the Jew resembled an independent satellite, within a universe of German friends. Therefore it was highly unlikely that the German friends of one respondent were friends or even acquainted with the German friends of another. The opposite was true for the Jewish friends. Since the community is so small, and every Jew tends to know every other Jew, one cannot avoid, even if one wanted to, running into other Jewish friends at parties or at other social gatherings. Therefore, the Jewish friends of one respondent tended to know of or be acquainted or friendly with the Jewish friends of another. There are many social occasions where Jewish circles intersect and Jewish networks overlap. The result is that Jewish friendship circles have a higher degree of visibility, and are more closely scrutinized by the community than the German friendship circles. The unanticipated consequence is that German friendship circles provide respondents with more opportunities for greater anonymity and freedom of movement – an often welcome retreat when my interviewees expressed the need to get out of the spotlight for a while.

Although more opportunities existed for Jews to cultivate contacts with Germans than with other Jews, nevertheless the majority of my interviewees reported that the majority of their friends, through different stages of life, have consistently been Jewish. Of the respondents in the sample, 40.7 have mostly Jewish friends, 28.2 have mostly German friends, and 27.3 percent believed they had equal numbers of Jewish and German friends. This finding is not much different from the results of studies regarding Jewish friendship patterns in the United States.[24]

Why is it that a plurality of Jews have mostly Jewish friends? Cultural preference patterns play a significant role in friendship development by influencing the attraction of Jews toward other Jews. That is, relationships with Jews are less complicated. Because Jews share with other Jews a common background, common worldview, and common life circumstances, they are more likely to strike immediate friendships together. Indeed, the friendship literature affirms that people more often choose friends who are similar to them in race, religion, social class, lifestyle, interests, values, opinions, and character traits.[25] Similarity leads to friendship development because it increases understanding and communication.[26] Celia, the pharmacist, explains:

When I meet a Jew, a bond is there. I can already start with the basic perception that we have things in common. I'm not sure I can do that with the non-Jew. That's truly the first moment. There is a greater basis of trust. It can change during the course of a conversation, but I can say that initially there is a difference. And it's not just because of the fascist past. But also because of a form of humor, common attitudes, similar family experiences – everything that deals with initial identification where I will say I am not a German, because I didn't grow up in a German home. And I don't have a German history. And that leads to the fact that one has a greater basic understanding among Jews.

There were friendships with both Jews and Germans that were significant and valuable, yet the data suggest that friendships with Germans were qualitatively different from friendships with Jews. These friendship patterns varied with the degree of intimacy and closeness of contact. The number of Jews who reported feeling closer to their Jewish friends (43.1 percent for same-sex friendship and 39.4 percent for opposite sex friendship) was more than triple the number of Jews who reported feeling closer to their German friends (12.1 percent for same-sex German friend and 13.6 percent for opposite-sex German friend). However, about a third of the respondents noticed no difference in their levels of closeness with their German and Jewish friends.

For those Jews who felt closer to their Jewish friends than their German friends, being Jewish and having the same family background related to the Holocaust accounted for such sentiments. Emil, the engineer, provides us with an explanation: "I certainly have close German friends, or at least as close as Jewish friends. But the contact to Jews is different. Even if they aren't close friends, the feelings toward them are close." Monika, whom we met at the beginning of Chapter 2, would agree: "Let's put it this way. We have a common past. And our parents know each other. And we have known each other since we were kids... There's something in common. In this respect, I feel closer to Jews."

This basic understanding and feeling of closeness that Jews feel with other Jews can also be seen through differences in Jewish–Jewish versus Jewish–German conversational themes. As ethnic similarity and feelings of closeness facilitate communication, I found that Jews communicated more effectively on certain topics with other Jews than with Germans, and that these exchanges were more satisfying. Jews perceived that other Jews understood better what was being communicated. In casual conversations with both Jewish and German friends, my interviewees tended to make presumptive attributions about differences in the thoughts, frames of reference, and interaction patterns of their friends. Jews communicate differently with other Jews; they use fewer words, take more things for granted, and are more likely to substitute shorthand, nicknames, and colloquial terms, as if sharing a secret language and universe. They anticipate a qualitative difference between Jewish-Jewish and Jewish–German friendship relationships. Martin, the graduate student in economics, offers a typical response: "You tell a joke, and Jews understand it immediately, whereas Germans do not." Like Martin, Amalie, the medical student, explains, "With the Jews you have to say a word and they've got it, while with the Germans you really have to say a whole sentence to make them understand."

Conversations between Jews and their Jewish friends differ from those they have with their German friends both in their themes and the intensities with which they are discussed. Not surprisingly, Jews talk somewhat more to their Jewish friends about Jewish themes than they do with their German friends: 80.3 percent of my interviewees talked with same-sex Jewish friends about anti-Semitism, while 60.6 percent discussed this topic with their German friends. Similarly, 78 percent discussed Middle East politics with their Jewish friends, compared to 62.1 with their German friends; 65.2 percent reported conversations about the Holocaust with their Jewish friends, in contrast to 54.5 percent with German friends; and 75.8 percent discussed Jewish–German relations with their Jewish friends, versus 60.6 percent with their German friends.

Jews characterize their conversations with their in-group friends as more emotional and as making them less fearful to show their sentiments. Specifically, conversations with Germans about the Holocaust are described as intellectual. With Germans, Jews exchanged facts, details, ideas, and information about names, dates, places, and policies. In contrast, discussions with Jewish friends about the Holocaust "go into depth," " are profound," or "reach a level of true understanding." Here "depth" is equated with reaching a heightened emotional state, a sense of empathy, compassion, affinity, harmony, and warmth.

Emotional exchanges with Jews about the Holocaust are experienced in several ways. Betty, the woman featured in the Prologue, gives one view:

When you talk with Germans, you talk about the facts. When you talk with Jews, you talk about feelings. About your parents... what happened to them. How pained they are. How sick they are... It's a conversation where you start to cry. I would never start to cry in front of a German. You don't talk about what happened. You know what happened, and he knows what happened. With Germans you have to talk about the fact of what happened. Because you have to know. You have to find a level to talk about. But with Jews you share the same level of understanding. It's more emotional.

For Norbert, the law student, the primary emotion that surfaces is anger: "It's strange. I talk more with my German friends about the Holocaust than with my Jewish friends. [With my Jewish friends] it's not possible to talk. It's just aggression. We just have to kill them all. And they [Jewish friends] spit on the floor that they should all be killed."

When communication with Germans about the Holocaust is difficult or compartmentalized, Jews feel frustration, a loss of affection, and a decreasing sense of security in the relationship. On the other hand, if the level of communication in Jewish–German interactions becomes more personal, more satisfactory, the relationship is likely to grow stronger.

Margret, the medical student featured at the beginning of Chapter 4, explains:

When the Holocaust film came out, I was living in Göttingen. My best [German] friend didn't want to watch the show, because there was a lot of criticism against it that it was American kitsch. So, when it started, she didn't watch it. And after the first part was shown, I phoned her up and told her to watch it. And then she phoned me and said, "Oh God." I had talked with her about it before, and she had known quite a lot about it. And she talked a lot with her mother about this time period. Her mother told her a lot, for a German, and about all of the people who disappeared. And we cried together. It was such a good experience for me that a non-Jew could cry over this. This brought us closer.

Jews talk somewhat more with their German friends of the same sex about love and personal relationships then they do with their Jewish friends: 43.9 percent of Jews in the sample discussed difficulties in love relationships with other Jewish friends, while 66.7 percent reported such discussions with their German friends. The same difference exists discussing personal problems: 37.9 percent discussed personal problems with Jewish friends, compared to 63.6 percent who confided in their German friends. Because Jewish circles are close-knit, one's secrets may not remain so for long. As outsiders, German friends are less likely to damage the reputation of their Jewish friends in the ethnic community. Oskar, the social science researcher, explains: "The Jewish people here form a clique. I have a more superficial relationship with them, because I know that things I tell them today might land somewhere else tomorrow."

To summarize, structural and cultural factors contribute in contradictory ways to the development of in-group and out-group friendships. The larger German population creates greater opportunities for Jews to develop interethnic friendships, while the small size of the Jewish community can undermine Jewish friendships by making Jews feel claustrophobic and too close to their Jewish friends. On the other hand, cultural factors – specifically similarities in background characteristics generated largely by the collective memory of the Holocaust – can lead to the qualitative differences in friendship patterns. Jews feel closer to their Jewish friends than German friends, and are more likely to forge more friendships with Jews than Germans.

Jewish–German role relationships

Some Jewish–German friendships and roles exist because the participants focus on their identities and the needs they can fulfill for each other. The members of the dyad create a mutual world that is characterized by a common culture and social organization – a division of labor, norms, power differences, communication channels, and the like. They construct a social reality where, according to Michal McCall, who has written extensively on the process of friendship, "the focus of involvement in relationships is not mutual activity, but the identity of its members."[27] McCall argues that all social relationships are shaped partly on the basis of personal knowledge and partly on the basis of role relationships. A relationship is personal insofar as it exists to provide role support for its members.

As noted earlier, Jews have difficulty in forging friendships with Germans. They are uncomfortable in revealing their Jewish identity. They determine which Germans to trust by reading how Germans deal with their own past, the past of their parents, anti-Semitism, philo-Semitism, contemporary racism, and related issues. Consequently, Jewish culture can shape the course of interpersonal relationships between Jews and Germans, as manifested in the types of role relationships that exist as Jews evaluate and experience these friendships. I have identified two sets of role relationships that Jews use to define themselves and Germans that are organized around the Holocaust in collective memory – "child of victim meets child of perpetrator" and "fighting parents' battles."

The extreme case: child of victim meets child of perpetrator

Friendship formation between a Jew and a German requires a down-playing of ethnic status. The Jew has evaluated the German based on personal characteristics, sees his or her friend as a non-typical German, and there is a clear path for a flourishing relationship. The idealized definition of friendship dictates that the ethnic attributes be secondary in importance to the unique qualities of the individuals. The Jew relates to a German friend on personal, individualistic terms. As friends they interact on a casual basis, discuss personal problems, exchange feelings of empathy, good laughs, and leisure-time activities. They engage in friendship assuming that both are presenting themselves sincerely. Friendships have a leveling influence: friends are required to treat each other as equals.[28]

Jews use fairly rigid cultural criteria for attributing friendship with Germans. The norms that regulate Jewish–German interactions limit the type of German whom Jews are likely to befriend. Jewish cultural values dictate that Jews should not befriend a child of Nazis nor a German who is anti-Semitic, philo-Semitic, or typical. One strategy that Jews employed to adhere to the cultural norm of avoiding children of Nazis was to find out in advance their German friends' parents' activities during the war. Oskar seeks such information as part of the filtering process in friendship formation:

It's more important to know [about parents' war whereabouts] for people who are not my friends. Because once I come to know the person and to trust him, I'm not really interested in what his parents did, because I go on face value. With the people whom I don't know, it gives me some hint in how to classify them – good ones or bad ones.

Other Jews, however, reported it appropriate to inquire into the war history of their friend's parents only in close relationships. As Simmel has pointed out, true friendships are established and strengthened as more intimate information is revealed.[29] A *Bekannter*, or acquaintance, is one with whom one might have friendly relations, but not a friendship. A *Freund*, on the other hand, is characterized by a deeper level of intimacy and personal involvement. The rights and obligations of a friendship legitimize and sanction those involved to inquire and speak about the war, the whereabouts of one's parents, the Holocaust and so on.

Still other interviewees stressed that once the friendship became close it was unnecessary to inquire about the German friend's family background – the friendship took precedence over any Jewish–German ideological conflict. Friendships, by definition, are voluntary and highly personal relationships, sanctioned to disregard prescribed institutional, organizational, or ethnic affiliations. As Gerald Suttles reminds us, "for those people who join in the friendship, it is regarded as an interstitial institution to bridge the chasm between groups, organizations, populations, and social categories."[30] For Jews, it was the German as person *qua* friend that mattered once the friendship was established, not the past actions, attitudes, or beliefs of the friend's parents.

Jews resolved conflicting allegiances to their ethnic background and to their friendship by compartmentalizing the friend from his or her family. As Ida, a thirty-eight-year-old Jewish woman who owns her own clothing boutique, put it, what her German friend's parents did is not an issue "because I don't seek contact with the parents." As noted in previous chapters, in personal relations with older Germans a taboo is observed on the subject of the war. This taboo can also serve a positive function, when one is invested in maintaining a friendship. Ida describes:

A: I have good friends, and there it's clear. There I don't ask because I don't even want to know.

Q: Why?

A: Out of fear. Fear that I will make something *kaputt*. Because I like the man or the woman. I don't want to know the entire family, whether they are Nazis or not. It doesn't interest me. But I believe I am afraid that something will break, that it will turn bad. And I also want to have good things for myself. Not that I will always ruin something because of this external factor – the history.

Once the friendship is formed, the Jew may be required to act out role obligations associated with this relationship. Close relationships develop their own set of moralities, their unique world views, as they are likely to take on a life of their own. A few Jews resent having the values of the larger Jewish community imposed upon their friendships, and empathize with their German friends regarding the burden of inheriting Germany's historical legacy. The Jew might refrain from asking the friend about his or her parents' war activities to avoid burdening the friend with the collective responsibility for the past. This was precisely the attitude of Anna, the physician:

I must honestly say that, with my friends, I don't have these thoughts. Because I am interested in the person as a person, and not in what her parents did. I cannot say that I repress it. But I say that one cannot hold a child responsible for what the parents might have done. With a friend of mine who is not Jewish, what is important to me is that she is honest. Then I don't know why I need to burden this person with this. Perhaps the person is herself burdened with this, when something like this exists.

Several respondents argued that, if they did inquire about their friend's parents' war histories, they would not get truthful answers since their German friends themselves did not know. Still others said that they already knew the answers; the past could not be changed, there was no reason to dwell on it. Some Jews felt that it was not up to them to confront their German friends, as Gertrud explains: "I thought somehow it's their business to get into contact with their past." However, when the German friend doesn't know, many agreed with Emil, the engineer, who revealed: "It makes me feel bad, because I think a child should know what his or her parents or grandparents did."

The most typical response reported was that Jews didn't ask or needn't ask, and that if it was found out it was because Germans told them "voluntarily" and "automatically." Yet, such information could also be disclosed inadvertently. This happened to Elisabeth, who found out her friend's father was in the SS:

Her sister told me. But she told me about something else, and in the course of this discussion she told me that her father was in jail. And I asked her why he was in jail. And she said he had a war violation and that he was put in jail because of that. She also knew that I was Jewish, but she didn't put two and two together. She didn't know that it was unusual or extraordinary for her father to go to jail.

While institutional safeguards work more or less effectively to restrict the growth of a friendship with a child of a bona-fide Nazi, such safeguards sometimes fail. As Elisabeth illustrates, the friendship had already been established when the disclosure of damaging information occurred. Such a disclosure can confound an already established friendship by challenging the character of the selves being presented. Interacting on an individual basis becomes untenable when questions of collective responsibility for Nazi atrocities emerge and the present becomes subordinated to the past. Jews may begin to define German friends in terms of the norms of the Jewish subculture. By doing so, Jews minimize their own autonomy in interpreting relationships.

Information discrediting their German friends pushes Jews to cling to their Jewish identity more vigorously than they would otherwise. Acknowledging discrediting information may also reinforce ethnic boundaries. During such situations a set of role relationships from the cultural repertoire can become activated. Jews can play the role of "child of victim" and can delegate to Germans the role of "child of perpetrator." The collective responsibility for the Holocaust is central to these roles: Jews assign to their German friends collective responsibility for the Nazi atrocities and attribute to themselves collective identification with the victims.

Elisabeth's German friend, prior to the disclosure of such morally contaminated information, had not given any signs of potential danger to the relationship. Recall, the friend's sister revealed the information, and had little concern over the safety of the relationship. The turmoil Elisabeth experienced was caused by the violation of friendship rules that call for honesty, intimacy, and disclosure. The damaging revelation made Elizabeth panic. Since the norm of avoiding morally contaminated Germans had been violated, and since no normative standards existed that specified how to proceed, she, like other Jews under similar circumstances, experienced anxiety and confusion:

Once I became friendly with a German woman, and we were friends for a couple of years, and then, somehow, I found out that her father was SS *Obersturmbannführer* in the Lublin ghetto, and he was in charge of deporting people to Majdanek.

That was a big crisis for me. You know, all my secret fears of confronting such a thing – being friendly with a German – suddenly became reality.

Elisabeth experienced the crisis as identity reinterpretation. However, she had still not resolved the question of whether it is legitimate to charge her friend, or young Germans in general, with the collective responsibility for the past. Yet, given her knowledge of the parents' war activities, the friend was recast in a more ominous light. Elisabeth was no longer confident of the role identity of her friend, and consequently, of her friend's moral status. Finally, Elisabeth grew suspicious, and began to wonder if her friend was as morally polluted as her parents: "Well, in the first moment it was absolutely impossible for me to differentiate between child and parents. They were sort of one item, so to speak. It was one thing, and it was very hard for me to distinguish the child, my friend, from her parents, as separate people, with separate identities, and separate ways of looking at the past."

Such scenarios produce emotional turmoil for most Jews because they call into question their loyalties toward parents and their loyalties toward their German friends. The dilemma is rooted in the belief system that befriending a child of a Nazi would on some level delegitimize the Holocaust experience. This goes against the norms and values rooted in Jewish culture, and threatens the basis by which Jews are socialized, and to which they generally adhere. Elisabeth explains:

It's very difficult to solve such a crisis in a personal way. To trust yourself that you don't lose your own identity, but that you stay what you are, and that you don't cheat anybody. And that you don't disrespect the history of your parents and what happened to them when you choose your way. That's very difficult. And that's only how people solve these problems. But to go through that is very dangerous. If you don't go through it, then you don't have any contact with non-Jews. And a lot of people here don't have any contact with non-Jews in the sense of having non-Jewish friends.

In sum, here was a danger of potential relationship breakage. To complicate matters, no clear norms had yet been established to minimize such dangers and overcome such a fracture. There was no plan or cultural response that could carefully guide Elisabeth out of her dilemma. Elisabeth and her German friend had to renegotiate, through trial and error, their relationship and role-identities.

By communicating openly about these issues, Jews and Germans can alleviate some of the hidden strains in a Jewish–German relationship and crises like Elisabeth's can be averted. This process can assist Jews to distinguish more clearly the autonomous identity of the friend from that of his or her parents. It can also function as a means for Jews to determine when and whom they should hold accountable for the atrocities committed under the National Socialist regime. This is exactly how Elisabeth and her friend handled the crisis:

Well, the friendship stayed a friendship, but I think only because we talked a lot about it, and we told each other what problems are involved in this issue. I think that was the precondition to stay on in this relationship, and to learn that she wasn't her father, and doesn't have the same personality and identity as her father. And that I could stay being friends with her, even though I was Jewish and my parents have a different history than her parents.

Several other interviewees expressed relief when the Holocaust could be discussed openly in their friendships. Rosanna, the medical student, explains:

And I tell you the truth. If they talk about it, I'm very glad, because I feel that they can talk so freely about it in front of me. Then they don't have a bad conscience about it, and they do not always feel ashamed of it. And it's a big relief in the whole relationship between Jews and non-Jews, and also between friends. Because it's a given fact. You cannot change it. They talk about it as a given fact. And I think it's correct. Because it is a given fact.

By renegotiating their role-identities in their friendships, and reestablishing the basis of the relationship on personal qualities instead of ethnic ones, the friends might adapt in such a way as to preserve the friendship. The Jew and German can reestablish the moral order on which the relationship was originally based, by reformulating their original bonds and identities as unique persons and equals, despite Jewish–German, victim–perpetrator identity threats. By doing so, the fragile morality of the relationship can survive the crisis. As Peter, the psychiatrist, aptly summed up, "There are obstacles a friendship can overcome if the friendship is very, very strong, so that the friendship is more important than the obstacles."

Fighting parents' battles

The actual war-time experience of their parents could induce Jews to try to fight the battles that their parents could not, which made relationships with Germans very complicated. One respondent explained: "You sometimes feel that you're overreacting to a lot of little things. And not reacting realistically, but fighting the fight that isn't your fight, but maybe your fantasy fight for your parents." A friendship with a German can be functional; it can provide Jews with a test of their own vulnerability as potential victims of Nazi persecution. For example, one respondent stated that, precisely because his parents were forced to flee Germany, he was determined never to leave: "I identify with the personal fate of my parents, which means having to live for years as a nervous refugee, away and apart from one another... It affects the way I behave toward Germans, in that I say I do not want to live as a refugee. This means that I made the decision to stay here."

Another woman uses encounters or relationships with Germans to test whether she will make the same mistakes that she perceives her parents did:

You always have your parents who went through that history. And of course your parents are really the conflict, not the society around you, and not the Germans or other Jews. Your parents, who went to concentration camps, and who weren't ideal parents in the sense that they fought for something or they were in the resistance. It is unpleasant to have victims as parents. You can't idealize parents whom you know weren't heroes. And then you start living your life with the idea that you would be much different than your parents. To me this wouldn't happen. I would fight. I would be organized. I wouldn't get into such a position – to be a victim and to be humiliated like my parents were. And then each contact with a German sort of gets into these dimensions of how you are now. Are you now different than your parents? Can you live up to your own ideals? And ideals mean actually not to make mistakes. And you don't know what is a mistake and what isn't a mistake. For people like my parents, each step was a mistake. You don't realize this as a child. As a child, you see the mistakes and you think that it was possible not to make mistakes. Whether to go to the ghetto. And whether to hide. And whom to trust. And whom not to trust. And how to survive in the camps. And which job to take. How to deal with the people you sleep with. You know every word. Everything you do is a decision. And it seems like the wrong decision. Otherwise, what happened wouldn't have happened... For a child's imagination, you don't want to make all the mistakes your parents did. And the moment you come into contact with a German, the fear of making mistakes, like being with the child of a murderer, is a tremendous mistake on that background. You don't know how to deal with it. Are you really different? Are you the hero your parents weren't?

Relationships or encounters with Germans can be used as an outlet for revenge. A few respondents mentioned being overly aggressive toward Germans. Many respondents were politically engaged and demonstrated against SS reunions, or distributed leaflets, fliers, or wrote letters to newspapers protesting against any form of anti-Semitism or racism.[31]

Germans can also benefit from friendships with Jews, some Jews suggested. An exchange can take place – the Jew can struggle with the past, while the German can overcome pent-up feelings of guilt. Peter, the psychiatrist, explains:

When a Jew is coming together with a German, there is something that is very, very difficult... It is kind of trying to get into contact, both sides trying to overcome their parents' deeds. For Germans, it's their anti-Semitic feelings, and also their deeds. Not to have so much guilt feelings to say that they act like their parents. And the Jews, for instance me, I think I do mostly the same thing, to show my parents and myself that you won't be killed the moment you come into contact with a German.

When a child of a victim confronts a child of a perpetrator, there is a refusal to relinquish the significance of the past, and to rely solely on personal criteria in defining a friendship. The role of fighting parents' battles provides further evidence of the subordination of everyday life to the past.

Conclusion

My data suggest that culture is central to explaining the character of interpersonal relationships between Jews and Germans. This is consequential because the American literature on friendship suggests that personality characteristics or physical attractiveness are pivotal factors in the development of a relationship. Traditional studies of friendship and interpersonal relationships have dealt primarily with factors that lead to attraction. This literature suggests that the attributes of attraction are often rooted primarily in psychological preferences. They are based on the fulfillment of interpersonal needs such as self-validation or on complementary personality attributes. In addition, friendships are influenced by structural factors such as close proximity, or by meeting instrumental goals such as status or other rewards resulting from interpersonal exchanges.

My data suggest that interpersonal friendships are not only rational, self-conscious activities occurring on the psychological or micro-level of interaction, but are strongly conditioned by cultural resources (expectations and beliefs) derived from particular social situations. Sociologists and anthropologists have been espousing for years the theory that different standards of beauty and attractiveness are culturally defined. However, little research has been conducted on the larger social processes that determine how groups define and rank each other, and by which people come to define what they consider to be attractive. It can be argued that affective responses toward relationship development are conditioned in the early internalizing of cultural norms and values considering what is attractive. For Jews in Germany, the meanings that Jews attach to themselves and Germans condition their interpretation and experience of Jewish–German friendships, and the collective memory of the Holocaust is the predominant cultural resource at their disposal for interpreting and defining their experience of themselves, of Germans, and of living in post-Holocaust Germany. Thus, social interactions such as friendship that under ordinary circumstances would be ethnically neutral become infused with ethnic overtones that shape the subsequent course of their development.

Two factors are central in the transition from acquaintance to friendship: an increasing sense of intimacy and the disclosure of information regarding an individual's identity. While the disclosure of identity is often viewed as the end result of increased intimacy, my data also suggest that a more nuanced approach must be taken to determine the role of identity disclosure and information exchange in the development of interethnic relationships. My interviewees often mentioned their difficulties in disclosing that they were Jewish based on their perceptions and expectations of negative reactions. Jews in Germany can disclose their identity to filter whom to befriend, to determine the level of intimacy, and to maintain some sense of control over the development of the friendship.

As a final note, I believe that a more textured approach regarding the special relationship between Jews and Germans can shed light on the process of readjustment. Readjustment must go beyond the public and official levels and must ultimately take place on the interpersonal level to be effective and meaningful. To my knowledge, no research exists on friendship formation between second-generation Jews and Germans in post-Holocaust Germany. It is my hope that this chapter and the following on Jewish–German sex, love, and intermarriage, will be a first step in contributing to a much neglected area in understanding the readjustment or lack thereof between Jews and Germans in their "special relationship."

6

Interethnic intimacy: the character of Jewish–German sex, love, and intermarriage

> Those who have the courage to love should have the courage to suffer.
> (Anthony Trollope, The Claverings, 1867)

The emotional tug-of-war

Rafael was born in 1949 at a military base in Northern Germany. When Rafael was three, his family moved to Frankfurt, and with the exception of attending a Swiss boarding school between the ages of fifteen and eighteen, Rafael has spent his entire life in Germany. Rafael first studied engineering, and then switched to complete a masters degree in psychology. He worked as a practicing psychologist for several years, but is now steadily employed in his father's real estate business.

Rafael's parents are from Poland and are Holocaust survivors. His father had false papers that identified him as a Pole, and spent part of the war years working for the Polish partisans in Cracow, helping Jews escape to Palestine and the United States. He was eventually caught, and transported to Auschwitz, but as a Polish partisan rather than a Jew. Rafael's mother was only eleven years old when the war broke out. As children, she and her sister were deported to Bergen-Belsen, and survived four years of internment. Both of Rafael's parents lost practically their whole families to the war.

Rafael says that his parents do not have German friends. They live in the invisible ghetto in Germany, and because of their Jewish friends, they feel strongly attached to their life in Germany. Although Rafael's parents were raised in religious homes, they did not want to raise Rafael religiously. Rafael was Bar-Mitzvahed, but no longer observes Jewish customs. He says he feels very Jewish, but does not know how to define it. "You know that you are different, and that you are Jewish, but you don't really know what it is," he explains.

Nevertheless, Rafael is a registered member of the Jewish *Gemeinde*, and has been active in many Jewish clubs. He was enrolled in the Jewish kindergarten, went to Sunday school, and was an active member of the Zionist Youth Group, the *Jugend Zentrum*, and the Jewish *Studenten Verband*. While his parents have little contact with Germans, and have tried to foster such behavior in Rafael, Rafael says he does not hold his parents' prejudices. For most of his life the majority of Rafael's friends have been German, and Rafael dates German women, even though it creates problems for him:

The most outstanding problem for young Jews here in Germany is that the parents don't want them to be good friends with Germans. Not with German girls, and not with German boys. But especially heterosexual relationships. They are an absolute crisis for Jewish families... When I started going out with that girl, and I started to make up my mind that I wanted to stay with that girl, my parents told me point-blank, "We don't want to see her. We don't want to have her in our home. Don't come here with her, and don't expect us to get together with you and that girl in any way." They started to work on separating us more and more. On the one side I had parents who said, "We don't want to know you anymore, you are not our son." On the other side I had this woman who said, "I want to be your wife. I don't want to run around with you just like this."

Rafael described a typical outcome when Jews become romantically involved with Germans: they face turmoil and crisis in their personal lives. The emotional tug-of-war is one of the most powerful and disorienting events, initiating for some Jews a process of reassessment and separation from their parents, friends, or the *Gemeinde*. Bipolarized notions regarding the purity of Jewishness and the evils of Germanness tended to disappear quickly when Jews discussed their German "significant other."

At the time of the interviews, about half of the respondents were involved in a serious intimate relationship, either married or living with a mate. Table 6.1 summarizes the marital status in the sample by gender. Among those respondents who were single, many were dating, and three were engaged. Three of the single respondents – two females and one male – were gay and dating partners of the same gender. Among those respondents who were married, two females and one male were on their second marriage.

While the majority of the Jews in the study made critical decisions about marriage that were aligned with the norms and values of Jewish

Table 6.1: *Frequency distribution of marital status by gender*

Marital Status	Male		Female		Total	
	Percent	Number	Percent	Number	Percent	Number
Single	41.9	18	27.5	11	34.9	29
Living together	9.3	4	5.0	2	7.2	6
Married	41.9	18	60.0	24	50.6	42
Divorced	7.0	3	7.5	3	7.2	6
Total	100.0	43	100.0	40	100.0	83

Table 6.2: *Frequency distribution of respondents' choice of mate by gender (respondents married or living together)*

Mate or Spouse	Male		Female	
	Percent	Number	Percent	Number
Jewish	45.5	10	92.3	24
German	27.2	6	7.7	2
Converted Jewish[a]	22.7	5	0.0	0
Other[b]	4.5	1	0.0	0
Total	100.0	22	100.0	26

[a] Converted Jewish refers to Germans who converted to Judaism.

[b] "Other" refers to mates who are neither German nor Jewish. The one case in my sample involved a Jewish man living with a non-Jewish Hungarian woman.

culture, their decisions about sex and love were more complicated. Typically Jews experienced new and unanticipated situations that persuaded them to behave in ways they could not have foreseen and that were contrary to their early socialization. Some Jews even made marital decisions that went against Jewish rules of endogamy. For instance, males tended to intermarry more than females.[1] Table 6.2 presents a breakdown of respondents' choice of mate by gender. About 50 percent of the males intermarried, of which 22.7 percent married German partners who converted to Judaism. Of the two Jewish women who were married to German men, both were on their second marriage. Their first marriages were with Jewish men, and ended in divorce.[2] In neither case did the German man convert to Judaism.

As the Holocaust in collective memory is at the core of Jewish culture in contemporary Germany, it shapes the moral perspectives of my respondents. This is not a passive process; each Jew by his or her actions is communicating and validating these moral evaluations. Jews who become intimate with Germans and those who intermarry represent alternatives to the traditional pattern of endogamy in Jewish culture worldwide. Their choices in mate selection have played, and will continue to play, a significant role in creating new alternatives and innovative approaches in defining Jewish–German relations. Their strategies and dilemmas can be understood, however, only in contrast to the strategies adopted by those Jews who have chosen to confine their intimate ties to the Jewish community. This chapter explores the choices, plans, and strategies adopted by my respondents in dating and mating. I examine the personal motives and social contexts that foster homogamy (marrying within the group) and exogamy (marrying outside of the group).[3] I also explore the factors that facilitate choosing Jewish partners, or contribute to choosing German partners, and the consequences of so doing.

The persistence of homogamy: institutional control and rules of endogamy

Almost all societies regulate their members' choices of mate. Jewish communities are no exception. Rules of endogamy severely restrict the pool of eligible mates. In most societies, social class, ethnicity, race, and religion are the most significant variables that circumscribe individual choice in marriage. For Jews in Germany, as well as Jews elsewhere, the social mandate is to marry other Jews.

Judaism assigns a major role to the institution of the family. Judaism does not proselytize. It is an ascriptive religion which relies on socialization and retention of its progeny rather than wholesale recruitment for its continuity as a group. As mentioned in Chapter 3, the home is the center of Jewish religious life and worship; it almost parallels the Synagogue in inculcating the essence of Judaism in its members. The sanctity and unity of the Jewish home rests on the presumption that both partners of the marital dyad are of the Jewish faith. Judaism does not recognize the legitimacy of a civil marriage: A Jew is properly married only when a rabbi has officiated the sacred ritual.

From its earliest history, Judaism has consistently regarded interfaith marriages unfavorably. Biblical injunctions against marriage with neighboring tribes were instituted to preserve Jewish identity and beliefs when Jews engaged in prolonged contact with other peoples. The basis for the historic taboo against interfaith marriage was that it would weaken or dissolve affiliation to the Jewish faith. Despite prohibitions, intermarriages were probably common in early Jewish history. Many patriarchs had Gentile wives, and Jews were allowed to marry Gentile women captured in battle, provided that the women shaved their heads, pared their fingernails, and mourned their parents for a full month.[4]

During Babylonian captivity (586–516 BC), the prophet Ezra noted that "the holy seed have mingled themselves with the people of those lands," and urged Jews to abandon their Gentile wives and children. During the first thousand years of the Christian era, Judaism and Christianity were not clearly distinguishable, so that intermarriages were frequent. They decreased in frequency following the Crusades, and in 1280 the rabbinical authorities reaffirmed the position of Ezra. These laws became codified in the Talmud and the Rabbinical Code. Intermarriage was prohibited, and declared punishable by banishment – the Judaic equivalent of excommunication.[5]

Jewish–German sexuality, love, and marriage today go beyond the rabbinical injunction against interfaith mixing. Intimacy between Jews and Germans takes on the additional character of interethnic relations. As we saw in the previous chapter, Jewish–German friendships are not ethnically neutral. Jewish–German intimacy is even more ethnically charged, as the metaphor of the Holocaust influences the perceived costs and benefits of crossing ethnic boundaries in search of sex, love, and marriage.

Jews in Germany try to limit intergroup relations in ways that have parallels in the caste system in India or other closed systems perpetuated by lifetime occupation, rules of endogamy, and cultural beliefs that foster separation and mandate avoidance of intimate contact with members of other groups. These taboos function more or less effectively to keep ethnic boundaries visible – to justify the status quo and maintain the moral purity and superiority of those defining the system. The pervasive belief is that amalgamation, the mixing of Jews and Germans, would result in the rapid deterioration of Jews as an ethnic group. Thus, there are strong normative prescriptions against dating, mating, and intermarriage.

I have identified eight factors that contribute to the deterrence of interethnic sex, love, and intermarriage: (1) etiquette rules in Jewish–German relationships; (2) lack of guidelines regulating the appropriate level of intimacy when breaking these etiquette rules; (3) opposition to a relationship by third parties; (4) the lack of social attraction of Jews toward Germans; (5) the prototype of German as murderer in Jewish ideology and its effect in deterring Jewish–German intimacy; (6) personal guilt from violating one's internalized norms concerning endogomy; (7) the perceived difficulties for intermarried couples in raising a family; and (8) difficulties in accepting a familial alliance with a German family. I will now examine each of these factors in turn.

The etiquette of Jewish–German love relationships

The etiquette of Jewish–German relations consists of rules that specify proper interethnic behavior. This etiquette should not be taken in the usual sense, because the rules, more often than not, require impolite rather than courteous behavior. This unwritten guide for behavior is deeply embedded within Jewish culture; it is prescribed informally as well as formally by the Jewish *Gemeinde*. The rules govern both the frequency of contact and the type of social relationships that Jews are allowed to develop with Germans.

The social rules vary by gender but the doctrine can be summarized as "thou shalt not become romantically involved with Germans." Deliberate socialization by my interviewees' parents attempted to increase or accentuate antagonisms between Jews and Germans, beyond the norms they had already internalized. This is precisely the experience of Claudia, the hearing specialist we first encountered in Chapter 2: "You are worked on for twenty years. 'The Germans are this and that. And don't bring a German boy home. Your father will have a heart attack.'" Similarly, Tomas, a computer consultant said: "My mother always tells me, 'If you get serious with a German, your father is going to kill himself.'" Kurt, the thirty-two-year-old attorney explains the consequences: "My parents said, 'Never marry a German girl, or we won't know you anymore. You will not be our son anymore if you do.'" Thus, second-generation Jews were undoubtedly threatened with fearful consequences for their family relations if they engaged in interethnic dating. Moreover, to marry a German, the antithesis of a Jew, was worse than dating interethnically.

The etiquette rules are designed to provide protection, they are geared toward minimizing the likelihood that Jews will leave the Jewish community through intermarriage. The rules are standard for all interethnic dating and mating relationships between Jews and Germans in Germany and can be summarized as follows:

1 Don't bring a German boyfriend or girlfriend home to meet your parents.
2 a. If you are a Jewish woman, don't date a German man.
  b. If you are a Jewish man, you can date German women, but don't become serious.
3 Never marry a German.

These rules contain a gender bias: Jewish men are allowed more freedom to interact with German women as long as the relationship remains non-serious. I will return to these issues later in the chapter.

Lack of guidelines regulating appropriate level of interethnic intimacy

The norms of the Jewish community in Germany forbid most interethnic intimate relations. Therefore, no guidelines exist to help second-generation Jews determine how to proceed if they do become involved with Germans. "Going one's own way," as one respondent described it, and becoming intimate with Germans, disrupts community life. It contradicts group values, threatens the traditional belief system, and risks blurring the boundaries that separate Jews from Germans. There is no collective support to guide such innovative behavior. Not only does the community actively hinder the establishment of a set of guidelines that would be useful to Jews involved in intimate relationships with Germans, but it also denies them access to sources of help. Jewish peers, friends, counselors and other experts are not readily available to openly discuss with second-generation Jews the intricacies of their affectionate and sexual relationships with Germans. To further a love relationship with a German, Jews had to fend for themselves, seek their own support systems, and use their private resources.

It should be noted that these structural factors – the absence of appropriate norms – interact with the Jewish cultural model of ethnicity. This model, as we have seen, is interpretive, a cultural lens through which relationships are anticipated, interpreted, and evaluated. This interaction is reflected clearly in the remark made by Monika, a second-generation Jew we first met in Chapter 2:

Since the Holocaust was a collective Jewish experience, I always had the feeling that there must be a collective answer to the Holocaust. There is sort of a need for a collective answer to this problem in order to feel you are in a framework of people with whom you share the reaction of the consequences of the Holocaust. And the moment you start having individual relationships [with Germans] you jump out of this collective answer. This is a very difficult thing to do. It's a very difficult thing to find your own personal way of dealing with personal relationships with Germans and still keep respect for yourself.

The absence of behavioral norms for interethnic intimacy, and pressures and expectations from parents, friends, and the *Gemeinde* to maintain Jewish ethnicity, provided important structural and cultural conditions that impeded interethnic intimacy. Thus, Judith, the ophthalmologist, had never dated a German man and had no interest in doing so. "I'm somehow afraid to go into non-Jewish society. Perhaps if I get to know a non-Jew, I'm scared that I'll have feelings. That's it." To marry a non-Jew is not even a question. "Because the religion is important for me. I want to keep kosher and hold Sabbath. And I couldn't do that with a non-Jewish man. You cannot learn that in one or two years with a rabbi, and then become Jewish. You cannot do that."

Thus, my respondents find it very difficult to navigate interethnic intimate relationships. How intimate to become is an issue Jews must work through by themselves on a case by case basis. Becoming too intimate with Germans could run the risk of moral contamination, and represents a marked deviation from accepted canons of appropriate relations. That is, breaking away from proscriptions against intimate contact with Germans means that Jews must break out of the mold of collective behavior. Indeed, in the romantic view of how relationships ought to be founded – on sympathy, compatibility, personality characteristics, and some notion of love regardless of race, religion, ethnicity, or the collective memory of the Holocaust – priority is placed on the significance of the individual over that of the group. Putting these beliefs into action, however, is another story. In the context of the perceived risks, the price of interethnic dating and mating appears unacceptably high to many.

Third-party influence

Third-party influence functions as a normative force that confines Jewish intimacy to be among group members, and thus contributes to group cohesiveness. That is, couples, whether interethnic or homogomous, do not live in a vacuum. The partners in an intimate dyad must recognize and handle the actual or potential reactions of parents, friends, and acquaintances to their liaison. It must be clear to others, and to themselves, that they are more or less appropriate for each other in terms of socially important characteristics.

While many Jews might have been attracted to German men and women, they were reluctant to confront the disputes they would have had with their parents, friends, and community if their relationship became too serious. Difficult and unhappy experiences with their parents over dating Germans had convinced many of my respondents that becoming serious with a German was too hazardous and too costly. Intermarriage was out of the question.

Parental rejection of the German partner was not simply a tragedy for the parent-child dyad, but it could also impact the relationships my respondents had with their German lovers. For example, Herbert, a divorced Jew, reflects in hindsight on how the lack of parental acceptance affected his German wife: "My wife always suffered because she was being rejected a little by my mother. And for her, actually, until the end [divorce], that was a major problem." David, whom we met in the Prologue, describes a similar reaction his parents had to his German girlfriend: "The problem was that she didn't understand why my parents had something against her. She was exactly as old as me. She would argue that she had nothing to do with the war... And she didn't understand why my parents never spoke to her." Thus, choosing a German partner seemed a shortsighted and irrational act. The threat of losing valued relationships with family and friends posed a powerful obstacle to the flourishing of interethnic love relationships. When an intimate relationship could only be developed at the expense of one's parents' alienation, many Jews chose to forgo temptations. Others who had already started a Jewish–German relationship broke it off.

Although third-party influence served as a countervailing mechanism that stabilized Jewish behavior, it was not a cost-free process socially or psychologically. Most interviewees drew heavily on this theme to articulate the problematic nature of growing up Jewish in post-Holocaust Germany. While external behavior and objective Jewish–German social arrangements might appear to be cordial and unproblematic to the casual observer, the internal turmoil of second-generation Jews should not be dismissed lightly. Jews in contemporary Germany find themselves in situations that are extremely challenging. The social climate within their subculture proscribes all intimate contact with Germans, yet Jews do not live in a physically cordoned-off ghetto. As human beings they are at times attracted to individuals who happen to be German, and they often fall in love, in spite of their better judgment. Nonetheless, fearful of the wrath of their parents and Jewish friends, most try hard not to commit the fateful mistake, or if it happens, to cut it short. They know that relationships with Germans can create long-range damage to their web of primary relationships and extended social networks.

The lack of social attraction

Jews who married other Jews, or were not interested in dating Germans, retained beliefs about Germans that legitimated their behavior. They were typically critical of Germans, did not find them attractive, and viewed dating Germans as a poor substitute for finding a Jewish mate. Their discourse on social attractiveness of Jews versus Germans is yet another example of the way the Jewish culture in Germany maintains ethnic identity. The endogamous Jews justify the position they have taken by arguing that Germans are not socially attractive to them. In a sense, this guarantees their own moral purity, by signaling their refusal to compromise on the importance of love as the basis for marriage. In other words, if romantic love is the necessary ingredient for marriage, these Jews did not find Germans attractive enough to date or to fall in love with. As Micha, a thirty-two-year-old businessman reveals, "I have never fallen in love with a German woman. I possibly could fall in love with a German woman. I think that once you're confronted with it properly, either it's there or not. You could fall in love with the devil, probably." Monika has similar feelings: "I had always said to myself that if I loved a German man, I would fight for him. But it's funny, I always seemed to find something in non-Jews that I didn't like."

Since similarity leads to attraction, Jews consider attractive the social world they share with fellow Jews, including characteristics and personality traits that define Jewishness. Jews and Germans are defined as binary opposites, and the awareness of these differences can dominate how one interprets and envisions a potential mate. This boundary maintenance is epitomized by Deborah, a political science graduate student who has never dated a German man. She says, "To fall in love with a German guy means such a difference of lives and lifestyles, that I don't think I could fall in love with a German guy." Suzanna, the physician, is more explicit. She says, "I find German men uninteresting. In Italy or in France, perhaps something else would have happened. I cannot judge it, and I think that perhaps it would have turned out differently. But I must say that I find the German women very pleasant, and I enjoy being friends with them very much."

Physical characteristics and personality factors were mentioned as unattractive. Several Jewish women found uncircumcised men unattractive. As one woman put it, "To sleep with a German is not just a moral question, but also an aesthetic one." Another woman echoed this view more explicitly: "I find it ugly, a non-circumcised man." A bisexual woman, who revealed her difficulty with men in general, said, "My problem was that I never fell in love with men. I had a long time where I really had difficulties with men who were not circumcised. It was a very intimate element." One Jewish woman who never had a sexual relationship with a German man, remembers her apprehension about seeing a non-circumcised man for the first time, "I thought I might go into shock or something. Especially if I saw it without first seeing pictures. I first saw pictures, and then I went with my husband to a sauna. I think I was 23, and it was the first time I saw men that weren't circumcised. I thought it looked very ugly." These in-group preferences interacted with powerful norms against interethnic intimacy to effectively impede interethnic attraction. Rosalyn, a mother of two who has been married to a Jewish man for nine years, reflects on her choices. "My generation had a different socialization process. We didn't have as much contact [with Germans] so the possibility to develop erotic feelings was not there. Our generation is more socialized by the postwar era. The borders, the moments of holding back, the fear of getting close was probably greater than any erotic attraction."

The prototype of German as murderer

The prototype of "German as murderer" is a symbol used by Jews who are committed to finding a Jewish spouse. It serves as a powerful deterrent device. For those committed to endogamy, their Jewish identity remains rooted in a strict binary opposition that maintains a clear separation between Jews and Germans. The association of German with murderer and Jew with victim becomes more vivid when one is confronted with the prospect of intermarriage, and traditional standards of being a good Jew and maintaining distance with Germans come into play.

While social attraction refers to attraction to members of a salient social group based upon typifications, personal attraction is idiosyncratic. One assesses the whole person as a unique self-contained biographical entity.[6] For endogamous Jews, group values were closely aligned with personal ones. Their own perceptions of Germans and the anticipated responses of their parents shaped their subsequent behavior. Their choices underscore the continuing force of the collective memory of the Holocaust. For these individuals, intimate relationships had little chance of success because the Holocaust hovered in the forefront of their consciousness. As Gertrud, the housewife, who dated German men before getting married explains: "Imagine marrying a man whose father killed your grandfather." Sarah, a psychiatrist, who is married to a Jewish man reflected on a previous relationship she had had with a German man, and her decision to find a Jewish partner:

I wanted to be together with a Jewish man. I could have married a Christian, but not a German. Ten years ago, before I met Emanuel [her Jewish husband], I already had the feeling with Peter [her German boyfriend], that there wouldn't be any future. And from that moment on, I said, "the next relationship should be a Jewish one." And from that time on, I also had the feeling that if I am going to be together with someone for a long time, it should be a Jewish person, because we have the background in common, and it will help in the relationship. Because marriage is difficult, and two people are so different, it will be one more point in common.

There was also a tendency to exaggerate the differences between marrying a German and marrying a non-Jew from another nationality on the basis of the collective memory of the Holocaust. Celia summed up a typical sentiment: "It's certainly easier to get involved in a relationship with a Frenchman than with a German ... because they are not so burdened down ... historically."

Guilt

Social attraction or its absence also serves a communicative or rhetorical function in delineating loyalties and punctuating solidarity.[7] Guilt can arise from violating one's own internalized norms concerning endogamy. It regulates the expression of one's tastes or ideology by facilitating self-examination regarding the consequences of one's actions. In this sense, guilt functions as an internalized policing agent, where respondents could rethink any marked deviations from accepted canons of good taste and morally appropriate behavior.

Many Jews internalized a moral conviction that their interethnic dating behavior was simply wrong. "I knew I was doing something that was forbidden," was a typical response I heard. Guilt can also arise when one thinks about the reactions of friends and family to a tabooed relationship. Self-blame or guilt for hurting their parents' feelings reduced respondents' inclination to develop serious interethnic relationships. As Peter, the psychiatrist reflects, "If you would do this [an interethnic relationship], it would create an extremely difficult conflict within the family. These Jewish young people avoid this, because the parents already suffered so much in concentration camps."

Tenaciously held notions of good children or good Jews reinforced this perception of the costs of an interethnic relationship, and many Jews concluded that interethnic relationships were not a good idea. Second-generation Jews know their place in the Holocaust hierarchy, and bringing a German date home upsets the moral conscienceness of their families and communities.

Emotional boundaries

Difficult and unhappy experiences with Germans had convinced some Jews that such relationships were too hazardous and too costly to risk, and that intermarriage was thus not an option. The rejection of the German partner was not simply because of a fear of social reprisal. Their own history with interethnic relationships had made it clear to them that a long-term commitment was simply not feasible. Jews realized that the emotional commitment and understanding necessary to form a marriage or long-term relationship were not there.

As sociologist Ira Reiss has observed, relationships that end up as love or marriage often start as mutual interest or generalized empathy.[8] They may begin by a casual interest in getting to know one another. If they continue, the partners explore their interests in one another by indulging in varying amounts of mutual self-disclosure. They reveal their interests, values, and tastes. They discuss their favorite books, movies, and the music they prefer. They reminisce on childhood experiences, reveal embarrassing events in their past, and tell each other their personal secrets. They share family histories, and slowly introduce to each other the cast of characters who occupy their lives. Mutual self disclosure builds familiarity and the foundation for a sense of trust. Emotional intimacy – revealing innermost thoughts and secrets – has been documented by psychologist Zick Rubin as one of the elements in love.[9]

The collective memory of the Holocaust rooted in Jewish culture was perceived by many respondents as a barrier that could not be crossed. When an interethnic couple came to the point of mutual self disclosure, the Holocaust erected an emotional barrier to intimacy. Respondents were unable to generate with their German partner the "we feeling" – solidarity, identification, and a true merging of fates that characterize romantic love. This outcome is not surprising given the dissimilarity in their identities, interests, and histories. In essence, whether intentional or not, Jews in Germany upheld the culturally appropriate response to their unique dilemma.

A Jewish physician who has been dating a German woman for several years offers an assessment of his difficulties in open communication with her. He keeps his innermost secrets to himself, and cannot discuss with her the plight of being Jewish in Germany:

Q: What problems do you have in your relationship with your girlfriend?
A: Of course my mother doesn't like her very much. That's one point. And she is sad about that.
Q: Do you live with her?
A: No. And also, I have a little bit of uncertainty. I don't know if I could really talk with her like I can talk with a Jewish girl. I don't know if I could talk with her like I talk with you. It's that you're Jewish, which makes speaking different. I am more open on this point about problems concerning Jews.

Both partners in a romantic dyad must introduce to the relationship not only their true selves, but also their immediate family and culture in order to build a sense of trust. As the Holocaust is an integral part of both Jewish and German cultures, and neither partner can be emotionally neutral to its memory, the dark shadows of the past can stand in the way of a meaningful relationship in the present. For example, Emil, the engineer, described the social distance he experiences with his German girlfriend: "It's just that certain situations occur where I feel there is a gap in our identities, or between our identities. And I wonder whether this gap can be closed." Similarly, Kathie, a writer, told me that the past can be understood as a barrier or wall to closeness:

A: Perhaps I am creating a myth that the problem is the history. Perhaps it's just a problem I have with men. That I always have power conflicts with men, or competition, or something that makes the relationship more difficult. Maybe if I went to Australia or America, then I can find out for sure.
Q: And with this German man you were with?
A: There was something between us. I don't know what it was, but there was always something that stood between us. Like a piece of ice that couldn't be broken. We spoke about it a lot. I believe that the more you speak about it, the more a wall builds and builds. It's funny, because you want to break it down when you speak about it, but instead you build one stone on top of the other and the wall gets higher. That's how I experienced it. And finally, it is so high that people separate.

Jews were unsure of how to overcome the emotional barriers they experienced, or whether the barriers could in fact be overcome, which became a source of emotional stress. The Holocaust in collective memory stood in the way of most solutions.

Raising a family

Another challenge intermarried couples face is how to raise their children. The ideals of child rearing that each person brings to a marriage are often key issues of marital negotiation. How to deal with a dual heritage, and which heritage will have precedence, are issues that all intermarried couples must settle. What would the new family's religious orientation be? How would the family be identified socially in the eyes of others? Would the Jewish spouse's religious and social identity prevail, or would the partner's ethnic category predominate?

Jews who were reluctant to intermarry specified their apprehensions regarding the raising of children and the religious orientation in which they would be schooled. Respondents discussed concerns not only about the child's religious orientation, but also his or her ethnic identity. Religion was assumed to be an ascribed status like age and race. Even though one can convert to Judaism, or leave the denomination, my interviewees were adamant about maintaining their Jewishness, even though the majority of them were not religious. For these Jews, if a relationship with a German were to proceed to intermarriage, it would be on their terms. This was particularly true for Jewish men dating German women. As Judaism follows a matrilineal system, the German woman would have to convert to Judaism for the children to be born and raised Jewish. Thus, a major rationale for opposing intermarriage was maintaining Jewish identity. Harry, the businessman reflects, "The woman isn't responsible; but I notice that we have a completely different mentality. Problems come up with marriage and children. How should you raise your child? The problems already start in kindergarten. Should the child go to a Jewish or non-Jewish kindergarten?"

If the family is a primary agent of cultural transmission, then intermarriage becomes a controversial issue. Intermarriage would threaten the transmission of cultural cohesion and the preservation of the Jewish culture. Several respondents adopted a negative attitude toward intermarriage for pragmatic reasons. For Viktor, for instance, intermarriage inevitably leads to discord and conflict because Jews and Germans are so different, and therefore should be avoided: "I think by raising a child, it [intermarriage] would be a big problem. Or when you are old, then she'll [German wife] say, 'You old Jew.' It could happen. I don't want to say that it will, but it could happen. And a Jew wouldn't say that, because she herself is Jewish."

The Jews' determination to have their children raised in their religion is reinforced by the fear that, lacking such training, their children might be engulfed by the majority culture. They reason that if a child's family environment is internally divided and both sets of spouses and grandparents exert equal pressure on the child to assume their orientation, the resolution may be influenced by the mainstream culture. In Germany, this culture is Christian, and, all else equal, the dominant culture may tip the scales, leading a large number of children of mixed parentage to become Christian.[10] As we will see later in this chapter, many intermarried Jews demanded that their partners convert to Judaism before they got married.

Some Jews formulated very specific plans regarding raising their children. Although they weren't religious, it was inconceivable to them to raise Christian children, and marrying a German created this possibility. They could not fathom the idea, and were unwilling to compromise. These Jews were against intermarriage because of the conflicts they envisaged during the family life-cycle. They were unwilling to yield their tradition in favor of the traditions of their German partners. They could not conceive of dual-family commitments, or a family life that fully reflected both heritages. It was more pragmatic to avoid situations that might jeopardize their sense of tribal loyalty.

My respondents believed that Jewish traditions should bless every rite of passage in an individual's life course and in a family's life-cycle. Jewish rituals should be enacted at one's marriage, at the circumcision of one's sons, at the Bar Mitzvah or Bat Mitzvah of one's children, even at one's funeral. They wished to celebrate Chanukah rather than Christmas, Passover instead of Easter. Some of these Jews felt a commitment to remain culturally different and socially separate and distinguishable from mainstream German society, even though, as we have seen in earlier chapters, they simultaneously wished to be equal participants, on their terms, in the wider society. They believed a family should have a shared universe of discourse about its heritage, and that this heritage should be a common one. Avoiding dating Germans, or certainly becoming seriously involved with Germans, was the most effective means of preventing a situation that could lead to further difficulties later in life.

Alliance with a German family: marrying into a family of Nazis?

The thought of having Germans as in-laws provoked an additional source of stress for many Jews I interviewed. Bringing a German into the purity of the Jewish family via marriage implies an equality of status, and a merging of ethnicities. The kinship bond represents a sacred institution that is being penetrated by potentially contaminating elements. Since in-laws are supposed to exchange cordial social relations and even provide emotional support, many Jews believed they would have difficulty performing these obligations. Jews find it problematic to accept German in-laws as members of the family. As one Jewish male explained, "I also notice that when one brings a girl home, one is not only bringing the girl home, but also some of her family." Jews take seriously the ideology of their culture. One Jewish woman who is married to a German man, said, "Let's say they [German in-laws] are very nice people. It's just that I could never say 'mamma' or 'dad' or something. I could never see them as my real family." Another respondent whose German wife has converted to Judaism echoes a similar concern; "There is still a problem to accept her [German girlfriend] parents as my relatives."

While meanings Jews imputed to the category of Germans are negotiable to a point, some are so fixed that they cannot be transformed. These meanings are not random. They are patterned within a social context that encourages their existence. Characterizations of Germans with whom one is friendly or intimate fall outside the mold of meanings aimed at anonymous Germans. Jews are able to date and become intimate with Germans only if they have transformed these Germans into "non-typical" ones. Nevertheless, Jews have problems in extending this definition to the German lover's immediate family.

While some Jews have crossed normative boundaries regarding interethnic dating and mating, many of these Jews continue to have difficulty accepting the consequences of their actions. They are particularly dismayed in social contexts where the characterization of Germans as typical is encouraged by the Jewish subculture. As one respondent put it, "It's impossible to imagine a wedding to take place where the relatives of my girlfriend would sit together with the relatives of my family." Elisabeth, who also dates German men, describes how the social context interacts with social beliefs about Germans and contributes to disconcerting feelings:

Problems aren't there at the beginning, because you have to first get to know the person. But once you enter their parents' home the problems begin. You might go to a birthday party, and there are others there who were on the front, and they are telling war stories. And automatically you are confronted. You cannot just plop yourself down and say that you are Jewish. That doesn't work. You can ask your boyfriend about it the next day, but it's not appropriate to bring it up in such a large social gathering. But that's the problem, when you go to a Christian boy's home.

This lack of closeness can be experienced by both Jewish and German in-laws:

Q: How do her [German girlfriend's] parents feel about you?
A: About me? I think they have a problem, but they cannot articulate it... For example, although we've known each other for 12 years already, it is a little strange. When they come to visit us, or we go visit them, we still say *"Sie"*[11] to each other. So, it's a very distant relationship.

The type of family one has married into, and where and what they were doing during the war, is a thought that continues to haunt second-generation Jews. As one respondent reflects, "It affects me to think about his [German husband's] parents, and to raise the question, what did they do in the war?" She describes the awkwardness she experienced when meeting his extended family:

I have to tell you one thing. When I got married to my [German] husband, I felt very strange about meeting his relatives. I knew his mother, who was a very lovely person. But when it came to meeting uncles and aunts, I had a very strange feeling. I didn't know how they would turn out... I was not worried that they would never accept me, because I was Jewish. It was different; it was the other way around. I was worried that I couldn't accept them, because of something they did or said.

She describes some difficult conversations she has had with her mother-in-law:

Well, my dear mother-in-law suffers a lot because during the Holocaust she had no milk for her kids. We've gotten to know each other, and to know our mutual anger. I towards her, because she thinks not having any milk for her kids is so terrible, and then she apologizes. She says, "I know your relatives experienced much worse, but it was terrible for me not to have any milk for my kids." We get along. She doesn't take offense, but I'm quite sure that somebody who met me for the first time with all my strange accusations could have taken offense.

Betty, a Jewish woman featured in the Prologue who married a German man, expressed her concerns and some contradictory voices that haunted her during an evening with her in-laws:

When I went with him [her German husband] to celebrate his brother's birthday, or the birthday of his mother, I saw all this family. I was sitting there, and I was saying, "What are you doing here, you must be crazy." When I saw how well organized everything was, that was enough for me. I started to have fantasies like this is the way they organized the killing of Jews or something like that.

If the actual German lover was "off the hook" for the past, the lover's family was still suspect. Jews obliquely blame the prospective in-laws for the crimes of the past. They position the lover as responsible for the difficulties that would emerge in their relationship, by positioning his or her parents as responsible for creating the situation that allowed the Holocaust to take place, and subsequently creating the complications in their present relationship. Very few Jews can afford to ignore contradictory voices ringing in their minds concerning the families of their German lovers. As Joshua put it, "I would always have this thought that her parents could have participated, or didn't do anything to prevent it." Since the binary opposition of Jew and German is well entrenched in Jewish culture, Jews who engage in interethnic dating and meet the spouse's parents and extended family bring to the forefront the dialectical drama of ethnicity versus resistance. Their deviant behavior and the contradictions they try to resolve in their lives become serious threats to their ethnic allegiance.

The prospect of meeting the lover's parents forced some Jews to reconsider the seriousness of their interethnic relationship. They found themselves caught between their desires for love and happiness on the one hand, and self-definition and ethnic solidarity on the other. One respondent describes a romantic relationship he had with a German woman, and his reaction, several years later, when he found out that her father had been active in the SS.

I had a girlfriend. She was a journalist. I knew that something wasn't in order with her parents. Her parents were divorced. She saw her father now and then, but never spoke about him. She spoke about her mother a lot. We met a few years later on a ship, and we got together again, and she told me how awful her family background was for her, because her father was in the SS, and not just an SS man, he was also in the camps. And I never saw her again. I was in Paris a few times, and I never visited her, and I know that when she was in Frankfurt a few times she didn't try to contact me. That symbolized the entire relationship. It was a disappointment. I hear from her, and she hears from me, but we don't get together anymore. She knew this would happen. It had occurred to me that such an incident could happen with other friends, but this was the first time it happened. I never heard of this happening to anyone, but from the beginning I was also afraid that this could happen. That is, what would happen if... We didn't split up because of this, but for other reasons. I went to Israel. It was always a fear I had with German girls, but I only found out what had happened with her years later. It had the effect that I didn't want to marry a German woman.

Crossing ethnic boundaries: the persistence of interethnic intimacy

In spite of forces regulating Jewish dating and mating behavior, most of the second-generation Jews with whom I spoke have had German lovers. About 95 percent of the males and 80 percent of the females have dated Germans. It was not only chance circumstances and individual personalities that determined the choices these Jews made. Their choices reflected the force of socially structured opportunities and cultural constraints, and their active attempts to make sense of and respond to these factors. Having described so far some of the factors that contribute to maintaining endogamy, I now examine six factors that contribute to interethnic sex, love, and intermarriage: (1) limited opportunity structures; (2) the incest taboo and the lack of personal attraction toward Jews; (3) the forbidden fruit syndrome and a special erotic attraction toward Germans; (4) interethnic intimacy as rebellion against parents and the *Gemeinde*; (5) interethnic dating that allows a Jew to have casual sex without obligation; and (6) the perception that etiquette rules violate a sense of democratic individualism. I shall examine each of these factors in turn.

Limited opportunity structures

Sociologist Peter Blau and others have investigated structural factors in intermarriage in contemporary populations.[12] One basic finding is that the smaller the group, the greater the rate of outmarriage. For Jews in Germany, the opportunities to meet Jews in one's immediate environment are limited. There are many more Germans one can choose from. However, what was most frustrating to my respondents was the very narrow pool of eligibles in their areas of residence. The *Gemeinde* in most cases was so small that it could not provide an adequate supply of candidates to match requirements for age, educational level, class background, lifestyle, interests, let alone for idiosyncratic likes, dislikes and physical attractions. It is not surprising that many of my interviewees felt compelled to cross ethnic boundaries and date Germans. Structural constraints, notably limited choice of partners, often overcame the cultural preference rules of ethnic endogamy.

Having been born and raised Jewish in Germany is often viewed with regret. Intimate knowledge of the consequences of limited Jewish marital prospects can be frightening. As much as they might want to marry another Jew, often they feel that finding such a partner in Germany is an impossibility. For those who are wholeheartedly and earnestly looking for Jewish mates, the search is exasperating and anxiety provoking. Respondents complained about how few would-be Jewish romantic partners they were meeting. "I don't want to speak for others, but to find a Jewish partner here, I think it is certainly a problem," says one. Living in Germany seriously compromised the overall opportunity structures for finding a Jewish partner. "From the number of Jews here, that's a problem. I want to marry a Jewish girl, but living in Germany, that's a problem... I'd say that's the biggest problem of living in Germany at the moment," says one respondent. The narrow pool of eligibles created tremendous hurdles for those seeking a Jewish spouse:

The choices are not so great. You cannot compare it with America, where really so many Jews live. Here you have very little choice. You grow up with these people. You know them from childhood. That means, to meet someone whom you haven't known for 20 years rarely happens. And then you marry someone who you played with in the sandbox in kindergarten. It's truly a Jewish ghetto.

Obviously, the larger the number of Jews in the community, the larger is the pool of prospective marriage candidates, and the lower the rate of intermarriage. Given their lack of acceptable alternatives, Jews believed that they would have a better chance finding a Jewish partner if they didn't live in Germany. The limited choices in finding a Jewish partner were particularly trying for Jews in their thirties, those who were more religiously devout, and Jews who lived in smaller *Gemeinden*. Jews in their thirties who are determined to find a Jewish mate face increasing obstacles in securing their goals. As the mean age at marriage is the mid-twenties, Jews who enter their thirties find the eligible pool of Jews smaller and smaller as each year goes by. One Jewish physician in his thirties described the predicament:

Until I was twenty, all of my girlfriends were Jewish. From then on, German. It's not because I don't know any Jewish women in Frankfurt that I like. I don't know, the girls my age that I grew up with, they've gotten married. And now I am mostly with non-Jews. I meet a lot of Jews, but I have a few close friends who are Jewish. When I am going out to a pub, I'm with Germans. As it happens, it's mostly Germans. The Jewish girls I know are mostly kind of JAPs [Jewish American Princess]. It's not a conscious choice: I'd prefer to marry a Jewish girl.

This problem was particularly acute in the mid-1980s for Jewish women in their late thirties, who were born right after the war. "There just aren't many Jewish men around of a decent age," is how one respondent summed it up. They suffer from what demographers call "the marriage squeeze." These Jewish women typically searched for Jewish men of their age or slightly older. But because few Jews were born during the Second World War, or because Jewish children were the first to be killed and deported, there are few men in this cohort. Moreover, by the mid-1980s, most of them were married. Elisabeth, whom we met in Chapter 2, describes the dilemma. "You know, a lot of men my age, my generation, who were born either after the war or during the war, that's a generation that doesn't exist in Germany. You have no Jewish people of that generation. Of course, almost no Jew was born during the war in Europe."

The situation is even more desperate for an orthodox Jew such as Leah, whom we met in Chapter 3. She told me that one reason she went to London for college was to be in a larger orthodox community. In London she met her husband and they both subsequently returned to Germany. She recalls her youth in Germany,

I did not go out with boys. That's what happened to me. I stayed home. I had no choice. I wasn't even allowed to go out with Jewish boys, because they wouldn't keep the Sabbath. So I was held back by both, non-Jewish and Jewish boys. A religious girl does not go out with any boy, especially a non-Jewish one, or a non-religious boy. That was a great problem... There were about three or four orthodox Jewish boys my age when I was growing up.

This structural constraint makes the lives of Jews in Germany very dependent on Jewish networks. The *Gemeinden* try to take effective action to create opportunities for young Jews to meet and to socialize. Many Jews actively participated in Jewish seminars and retreats that brought together Jews from other *Gemeinden* and European countries. But as the following respondent describes, this is not an adequate solution, because other *Gemeinden* are just as small: "In Cologne it was very limited. There were only about 1,500 Jews. Maybe twenty people my age. I went out with all the Jewish girls. All three of them. All the Jewish girls in Cologne."

Although seminars sponsored by Jewish organizations are important meeting grounds for second-generation Jews in Germany and throughout Europe, and are quite popular, wanting a Jewish partner, and even placing oneself in situations to meet Jews, does not guarantee success. In spite of the growing Jewish networks throughout Europe, respondents felt that their choices remained limited. Sarah, for instance, who ended up meeting an American Jew in Germany, recalls her struggles at meeting a Jewish man. "I went to Italy to try to catch an Italian husband. An Italian–Jewish one. And then I went to England to do the same. But America was always too far for my imagination, because I always felt very close to my parents, and I had to be with them, so it didn't work out." Part of the reluctance to travel to distant countries in search of eligible Jews can be related to the risks of having to settle there.

Many Jews in the study accepted pieces of prevailing Jewish culture, and tried to live out the script as best they could. They put themselves through a lot of agony to improve their chances of finding a Jewish mate: they traveled to other countries, went to Jewish-sponsored events, and exploited Jewish networks to the best of their abilities. Their attempts, however, were not always successful. While cultural norms and values are organized against interethnic intimacy, the limited structural opportunities prevailed. The choices that remained were often to marry a German or not to marry at all.

The reversal of status patterns: the attraction to the German over the Jew

The search for a Jewish partner with whom to have a romantic relationship was sometimes met with ambivalence. The chemistry between Jews as romantic partners can be complicated: for some, such relationships are "too familiar" to be romantic, for others they can come very close to violating the "incest taboo."

In *Children of the Kibbutz*, sociologist Melford Spiro reports that children raised in the same children's house on an Israeli Kibbutz feel toward one another as brother and sister and never have sexual relations or marry each other.[13] This analogy is appropriate for some second-generation Jews living in Frankfurt. Their behavior was strongly affected by the way in which Jewish relations were interpreted within their peer subculture. In order to comprehend the logic of this disincentive, it is useful to realize that among some Jews whose families lost most of their relatives during the war, or who have few relatives left living in Germany, their Jewish friendship circle has become a substitute or surrogate extended family.

These Jews mostly have known each other since childhood. They feel as if they had grown up together as part of the same family. In any case they were members of the same tribe, the "invisible ghetto." Several Jewish women mobilized the metaphor of family to describe the lack of attraction they felt toward Jewish men. One Jewish woman said: "Actually, for me, Jewish men are in the dimension of loving your brother or your father. It's too much family." Another Jewish respondent echoes her sentiment: "You're looking for a boyfriend, and you feel close like brother and sister."

Familiarity as a characteristic that impedes physical attraction is another disincentive toward dating Jews. Jews often sought out one another's company, but not necessarily in terms of future romantic partners. Jewish friends tended to function as a support group helping each other surmount the difficulties of living in Germany. Such familiarity and the family metaphor hamper the probability of later developing an attraction based on igniting the slow-burning flame of passion. Indeed, several respondents referred to having sexual relations with other Jews in the *Gemeinde* as breaking the "incest taboo." This disinterest in Jewish men was epitomized by Rachel, a dentist:

> Although you don't know each other, you don't really have to meet. You meet in a Jewish setting, and it's too familiar to be romantic. It isn't romantic. That's what's wrong with it. Whereas the German is the total stranger....With the Jew, it's like *déjà vu*. Everything that he says and everything that you say is something you've heard all your life.

Monika also provides testimony that long-term familiarity impedes the likelihood of sparking romantic interests:

Q: Why don't the Jewish women have much to do with the Jewish men here?

A: With Jewish men? Oh, the whole society here is very complicated. For me, now that I am alone, it's a catastrophe. I don't see a future here. The Jewish men who are now our age and aren't married yet, oh, they all have problems with themselves... Most of them were already married and are divorced like me, and have something wrong with them somehow. And I've already known many of them for several years. If one is good friends, and then if it's in the air that we spend the night together, we might sleep together, but that isn't a relationship.

Given the lack of opportunities to meet eligible Jews, an alternative myth was developed among some Jews I interviewed. They suggested that a special erotic attraction exists between Jews and Germans. Several Jewish men said they preferred to date "blond, blue-eyed women" or "Aryan-looking women." On the other hand, Jewish women said they were more attracted to German men because they were less familiar and therefore more mysterious. This is how Pnina felt toward German men in general:

It's much easier to have sexual relationships with a non-Jewish man than with a Jewish man. I think it's connected with this whole family, marriage, children business and with the closeness that goes into the dimension of incest things. A non-Jewish man is much more disconnected. In a personal sense, he's really a stranger... In this sense, it's much easier to have sexual relationships with a non-Jewish man.

More generally, Jews pointed out that Germans were particularly sexually attracted to them. This perception held true for Jewish women as well as Jewish men. They believed that the erotic attraction toward the Jew stems from Jewish typifications of warmth and sensuality. As Esther, the law student describes, "I'm different than German women. And that's what the German men tell me... The experiences they've had with German women were not as erotic and not as good for them as it was with an Israeli woman or Jewish woman." Anna, the physician agrees: "I think German men think that Jewish women are somewhat special. Something exotic. Just like they would say that they would like to have a black, or an Italian, and a Jew. Something exotic, or something different." Amalie, the medical student, does not have a special attraction toward German men, yet believes that German men find Jewish women particularly attractive.

It doesn't hold for me that I would say I find German men especially erotically attractive. I know, that in certain circles, for German men, Jewish women are somewhat racy, something attractive, on the level of White Americans with Black women, or something like that. I know this, and I have heard this often, but not for Jewish girls with German men. That I've never heard, only for German men with Jewish girls.

Given the value put on scarcity and the context of the collective memory of the Holocaust, a perception exists that Jews are prime sexual commodities in Germany. Jews believed that they were perceived as being novel and exotic both sexually and emotionally. Being circumcised was perceived as a sexual asset. Tom, the computer consultant, affirms this. He says,

Because of the hygiene, I've had many women tell me that they were very happy... Many want to sleep with Jews because they are told by other women who have slept with a Jew that it was really nice. It is a curiosity for a German woman to sleep with a Jew... It always happens that women like to sleep with circumcised men. It looks very pretty and hygienic. They find it nice. It's a positive experience.

There was a recognition among my respondents that once a German woman experienced a Jewish man, she would continue to be sexually attracted to Jewish men. Oskar, the social science researcher provides us with an illustration of this perception: "If a German girl is together with a Jewish guy, they are always attracted to Jewish men again. I found that to be very often true. Even when I was together with my girlfriend, she had previously been with one or two other Jewish guys."

Rebellion

The decision to reject Germans and thus only date and marry Jews was often experienced as a sentence imposed from without, a sort of punishment that prevented the attainment of adulthood and independence. As circumstances converged to make marrying a German difficult, some Jews questioned the validity of the norms and customs, and rebelled against them. In a few cases, respondents suggested that intermarriage was a result of a revolt against their parents and the community. For instance, when parental interference threatened to undermine their love relationship with a German, as well as their perceived personal happiness, some became defiant. They took the decision to break off contact with their parents. They were more likely to blame parental intolerance for their interethnic relationships than to hold themselves responsible.

Some respondents became involved with Germans as a means to exert their own independence. "The only way to be on my own – against my parents – to be myself, was to have a German boyfriend," is how one respondent put it. These Jews were especially likely to encounter a strenuous opposition to their choice of mate, and such opposition was an incentive to continue with the relationship. Several respondents mentioned that they think they might not have broken the rules and married non-Jews if the rules hadn't been so strict and the pressure to enforce them hadn't been so great. As Philip, a thirty-eight-year-old physician married to a German woman put it: "I think I married out of spite. Out of my own right. I wanted to make my own decisions."

Like their counterparts who married Jews, these Jews developed orientations toward intermarriage that were closely tied to their parents' feelings and preferences. Their decision to accept Germans as potential mates was not made in isolation. Rather, marrying a German was judged as totally unacceptable and threatening in the context of Jewish culture, Jewish identity, and the collective memory of the Holocaust. These Jews shifted a large share of responsibility for deciding to marry a German onto their parents. The fact that their parents decided to remain in Germany rather than emigrating elsewhere was judged as inappropriate and dangerous in the context of creating an uncertain and tempting situation for their children. They argued that raising children in Germany and trying to maintain Jewish endogamy was a short-sighted and poorly executed decision on the part of their parents. A Jewish woman married to a German man, explains, "Maybe sometimes I think that this is my way of getting along with it [living in Germany] – to marry a non-Jew. You know, to make my own protest, and to show to myself, and to them all, that this is the result of what you are doing here." The anger toward one's parents is sometimes mingled with a sense of righteous indignation. This incites the Jewish respondent to act against the parents' wishes. These respondents discredited the behavior of their parents. One respondent noted that his own parents, as well as those of his German girlfriend, were against the marriage: "I think if her parents hadn't made a fuss, and my parents hadn't made a fuss, then maybe we wouldn't have stayed together. I think we both stayed together as a protest toward our parents. Look, we also loved each other a lot. But I think this also played a role." The irony is that the very people who oppose the relationship often help to galvanize the couple. That is not to say that a Jewish–German couple would have broken up without parental opposition, but that the style of opposition used by the parents which treats the interethnic couple as children often encourages a resistance or rebellion by young adults who view themselves as autonomous actors. The opposition may constitute a challenge for the young dyad; like the Romeo and Juliet saga, it catapults the lovers to test and prove their love and commitment for one another. Like forbidden fruit, the relationship becomes more desirable, an end in itself.

Casual sex without obligations

Jews who wish to have casual sexual relationships without being involved in any social obligations often date Germans. When Jews meet Germans, they do not necessarily know each other's families, nor do they have mutual friends. They do not meet one another as a part of a web of social interrelations. Their social nexus is minimal, and their relations can be as casual as they wish with a minimum of social ties and obligations.

Jews, on the other hand, meet other Jews as members of a tightly connected web of social relations. Due to the small community size, they often know each other's families and have mutual friends. Therefore, their private life becomes penetrable and open to public scrutiny. In the interest of social reputations "one had to be careful with Jewish girls," says Samuel, the attorney we met in the Prologue.

While Jews could have more anonymity in their dating relationships with Germans, they could simultaneously downplay the seriousness of these relationships. In contrast, while dating other Jews, many interviewees perceived that the community at large stood watch over their romantic pursuits. Martin, the graduate student in economics explains:

A: It's impossible to avoid the fact that you are together with a Jewish person. Everybody would know.
Q: And what about dating a Jewish woman from Munich?
A: It's the same.

Second-generation Jews recognize the social messages conveyed by dating another Jew. They must manage public appearances with extreme self-consciousness. Both the Jewish man and the woman can become public personae. Intense community surveillance may bring about undue pressure on a fragile or burgeoning relationship, making it more likely to fail. A relationship with a Jew is interpreted more seriously by the community than it actually might be. Consequently, it is taken more seriously by those involved. Jews do not date other Jews casually. Jews sensed a tendency for others to view their relationship as friendship, when they were actually acquaintances, or as a couple, when they were actually only friends. In fact, I personally had the experience of being asked if I and a young man with whom I had been seen on several occasions were a couple. Tomas, the computer consultant, had a similar experience. He reports, "When you were with a Jewish girl three times, you were already marked as a couple. That was the negative side of this closed community. If you dared to have a sexual relationship with a Jewish girl, it could have meant marriage."

Being watched by everyone in the community, or having the community know one's business can be embarrassing if one's love is unrequited. This is how Oskar, the social science researcher experienced it:

I mean, I'm not going out with Jewish women at the moment at all. But when I did in the past, the rest of the community knew about it. That does not make me any less prepared to go out with them. It becomes a bit more embarrassing when you chase them and don't get them, and everybody knows about it. What does have an inhibiting effect is that when you woo somebody, and you're unsuccessful, the sense of defeat is rather higher, because it is shared by the rest of the community.

The forces that deter one from dating Jews had a number of consequences. To begin with, casual sexual relationships are much easier across ethnic lines. The anonymity gained in crossing over to the German world, and the lack of pressure from or surveillance by family, friends, and community creates a situation conducive to sexual liaisons. Norbert, the law student describes how he lost his virginity: "Of course I've gone out with German girls. You never start out with a Jewish girl. Otherwise, you'd be married the next day in a hick town like Frankfurt with a small Jewish community." It is easier for Jewish men to have casual sexual relations with German women because the consequences are not as severe. In dating German women, Jewish men are less likely to be held accountable for their sexual behavior. These relationships take place out of the spotlight, where Jews are less concerned about public respectability. If the woman becomes pregnant, a man does not have to marry her. There was a tendency to "sow one's wild-oats" across ethnic lines. In fact, 85 percent of the men in the study lost their virginity with German women. The evidence clearly shows that the double standard of morality continues to operate in this community, a legacy from the old patriarchal Jewish culture.

Patterns of behavior are shaped not only by the values that are important in society, but also by the cultural messages that are diffused community-wide. There exists a powerful set of cultural norms designed to limit and direct sexuality into socially productive channels. The social control of sexual impulses is accomplished through rules that specify who can legitimately have sexual intercourse with whom, and who can marry whom. My interviews clearly indicated that a gender bias exists in relations toward German lovers. There is a two-fold double standard of morality. First, Jewish males have more freedom than Jewish females to have sexual relationships in general. Second, this freedom is especially pronounced when Jewish men are dating German women.

The evidence suggests that Jewish males are more likely than Jewish females to exploit their German lovers sexually. Jewish men might sexually exploit German women as a way to gain status, or to reaffirm their relatively higher status position at the expense of a German, viewed as lower on identity hierarchies. Judith, the ophthalmologist, attributes the double standard to Jewish socialization:

There's a Jewish saying, *Schickse hin, Schickse her, Schickse zu mir...* I think that for many it holds true. Many travel around in German society, but do want to marry a Jew. But I think now there are many mixed marriages. And from many men whom one would never have thought. Where they were raised traditionally, and many were in Jewish society and organizations. And where one thought that they place a lot of emphasis on the Jewish tradition. And then they marry a German... A few also say that many parents tell their boys, much less so than their girls, that they should learn with a *Schickse*, but be more careful with a Jewish girl. With girls, less so, because parents are more strict with the girls.

There are also parents who are indifferent, and let their children have their freedom. That also exists. But for the majority I think that the girls are handled more strictly.

The thrill of sexual conquest often blurs the better judgment of young Jewish men. They come to realize that acting with integrity is a strategy to use with Jews, but not necessarily with Germans. Obviously the stakes are higher within the community. I asked Larry, "Did you have relationships with German women?" "It was only on a sexual level," he replied. "German girls who you can forget. I would never marry a non-Jewish girl." One respondent used the double sexual standard as a way of getting back at Germans. In other words, he slept with German girls to fight his parents' battles:

I don't have these moral strings. Sometimes I get back at them. Sometimes I think when I am with German girls, "Ach, if Hitler could have seen that." It was a private joke with myself. When I'm with a German girl, I think, what's a Jewish guy who has a background like this, doing with a German girl like this?

In other words, sexual relations with Jewish women must be carefully managed and rationally calculated. The double standard was a functional alternative for channeling casual sexual behavior; it maintained the purity and good reputation of Jewish women within the community. While respondents generally acknowledged the existence of this double standard, many denied that it was true for them. Emil, the engineer, says:

You had to be more careful with Jewish girls. These relationships were more serious because you lived in a smaller circle. You knew the parents. You knew where she came from. With a German girl, it was totally easy and loose. I was never interested in having such an intensive relationship with a German girl, that the opportunity for marriage might develop. With the Jewish girls, the danger was that marriage could happen. Whereas with the Jews, you'd have to marry them under the circumstances [pregnancy]... With the Jewish girls, there was pressure from the *Gemeinde* and you were already a couple. With the German girls it was accepted that you were too young to marry. With the Jews, it was treated more seriously.

Several respondents suggested that the double standard of morality did not necessarily end with marriage, among them Sarah, the psychiatrist:

Q: Is there a double standard here in Germany?

A: Yes, it is true. And the terrible thing is that we know many Jewish families, Jews of our age, that after the woman had children, they started having such terrible marital problems. I think it results from this fact that the boys have been socialized with this idea, "You sleep with a German, and you marry a Jew." And as soon as their Jewish wife is a mother, and not their lover, they start having affairs with German women.

Q: And what about the women?

A: I don't know. They are more discreet. It's certainly not true for me.

The acknowledgment of the double standard concerned many Jews that the community at large was not accountable for the behaviors of its members. If Jews are to be the embodiment of humanity and a force for human betterment, their sexual behavior does not always confirm the impressions of themselves that they are trying to project. There is much disagreement within the community about the dignity of the double standard of morality. This is particularly relevant because Jews prided themselves on being fair and on treating others with a sense of worth and respect. But aside from these controversies, the pressures against seeking casual sex without obligation with other Jews were offset by the availability of consummating casual sex with Germans.

Romantic notions of love and the perceived violation of democratic individualism

In spite of social forces promoting endogamy, some respondents believed that their chances for a happy, successful marriage were based on finding partners with whom they were in love. They had accepted the individualistic ethos of the West, which posits that marriage is based on social and personal compatibility. While respondents retained a strong interest in meeting, falling in love with, and marrying other Jews, they were guided by romantic notions of love. Romantic love is believed to be blind to racial, ethnic, religious, and Jewish–German concerns. "Love is like a passion," Stendhal has written. "It comes and goes without the will having any part of the process."[14]

The acceptance of an individualistic ethos contradicts demands made by parents, or the community at large. By this standard, one should not marry somebody who is Jewish if one does not love that person. It is preferable to have a loving marriage with a German. Those who advocate such principles tend to criticize rules of endogamy, and resent parents and the community for enforcing supposedly love-less marriages.

Second-generation Jews in Germany are supposed to keep their romantic feelings in check, and not place themselves in situations where temptations can arise. These proscriptions can cause social problems for Jews, as Gertrud, the housewife, explains:

They bring you here, you grow up here, and then there is a boundary, a border, where you are afraid of going into a discotheque. When you work, it could happen that you meet someone. And the evaluation wouldn't be how the person is as a person, but whether they are Jewish or non-Jewish. This is something that is very problematic.

The themes of romantic love and democratic individualism occupy an important place in the culture of second-generation Jews in Germany. Democratic individualism is defined here by the notion that anything one does is voluntary, a matter of personal choice. The rules of etiquette regarding proper and improper interethnic behavior limits the freedom built into the ethnic roles Jews are supposed to play. The restriction to date only other Jews is seen by some interviewees as an arbitrary and peripheral part of a cultural system based on outworn notions of "perpetrator" versus "victim" or "us" versus "them." It is seen as a nuisance, as total loyalty to a culture that does not take into account that Jews may wish to have lives and relationships beyond the community. Several Jews expressed a sense of violation of their individual rights. They felt cheated by their inability to choose with whom they might have a relationship, because they argued that they were in no position to control with whom they were going to fall in love. These sentiments are clearly reflected in comments made by Avital, the school teacher:

You are pushed into the Jewish environment. You are not given any chance to slide out of this, because as you grow older, you feel the anxiousness about getting to know somebody not Jewish. And it could count as a serious relationship... Not to have a free choice at this time really cuts your liberty enormously... And if you are a thinking person, you ask yourself "Why is he better?" or "Why is he worse – the non-Jewish guy, or the Jewish guy who goes out with a non-Jewish girl?" You are constantly in a position to evaluate things, and I think at this age, this is a very strong burden to carry.

Mechanisms of social control: mobilizing forces to prevent a Jewish–German relationship

The collective memory of the Holocaust and the situational context of Jews living in Germany have produced conditions that are conducive to the establishment of social dislike. The rules of etiquette established in interethnic relations were generally regarded by my respondents as valid. There was much consensus regarding which behaviors should not be carried out. "To marry a German was practically ruled out from the very beginning," is how one respondent summed up the predicament. The etiquette rules are designed to prevent behavior that is likely to encourage conflict or cause disruption in the respondent's relationship to Jewish family, friends, and community. Respondents were well aware that breaking these rules could damage these relationships, or at least demand some repair.

Given the high probability of meeting other Germans in the course of everyday life, and given the likelihood that such meetings could develop into intimate relationships, a set of countervailing norms exists to prevent anew the improper mixtures. Elements of the collective memory of the Holocaust are mobilized more vigorously by second-generation Jews to maintain ethnic identity and continuity, particularly when they are confronted with interethnic dating and mating. This concerted effort to regain a sense of equilibrium about Jews and their proper place within German society is motivated by the recognition of the realities of change, struggle, and confusion as inherent tendencies of social groups.

The postwar period in which my respondents came of age was marked by a reorganization and restructuring of prior Nazi ethnic roles and ideologies. At this time, the cultural interpretation of romantic relations between Jews and Germans in Germany placed Jewish men and women on a pedestal. In contrast, German men and women were not considered appropriate partners for second-generation Jews. They were perceived as social inferiors. The anger and frustration that respondents expressed regarding growing up in Germany, and being restricted to only Jewish mates, attests to the turbulence of these years. There was a sense among my respondents that something was amiss. The supposed serenity of the marriage market within the Jewish community was a mask. The inherent difficulties can be discerned by the way in which Jewish–German relationships were interpreted by the second-generation Jews I interviewed, and by the social control mechanisms that were put into place to encourage in-group dating and mating.

Gossip and the overvisibility of social life

Through surveillance techniques the Jewish community exerts social control over its members. There is a plethora of social knowledge that circulates about any Jew's past misdeeds, and this affects the reputation of that person, his or her normative status. The high social visibility of Jewish networks and the high intensity of social bonds, combined with the low geographic mobility of German society in general, increase exponentially the amount of information that Jews acquire about one another. Since such knowledge is in the public domain, there is great need to preserve one's reputation. Deviants are sanctioned by being labeled moral offenders. Jews typically know about the affairs of other Jews, and social opinion does matter. In such settings, Jews demonstrate their worth and integrity to their fellow Jews by refusing to tolerate mistreatment. As Avital, the school teacher, remembers, "I think there was just one intermarriage [when she was growing up]... And everyone knew it. And everyone commented on it, and said 'Beware, look at them.'" She continues:

When you live in a city like Frankfurt with a Jewish community that's not too large, that comprises about four or five thousand people, you are very closely watched by all the others in the community. You don't have just your mother to guard you. But you are guarded by all the others in the community... You have many, many other people who watch [your] every step. That's one of the reasons why you could just not intermarry. So, you just married people who were not suited, but they were Jewish. And there were many divorces of people who married in my age.

Because Jews tend to move within tightly knit networks – "strong ties" in the words of some sociologists – they tend to develop intense antipathies against Germans as well as close bonds of relations amongst themselves. They are not as divided as the general population in their interests and commitments, and are less distracted from their conflicts. They have a great opportunity to accumulate grudges, and their cohesive networks are able to collect, store, collate, and disseminate damaging information efficiently.

Much of the effective control comes directly from one's parents. They can impose punitive sanctions on their children to voice a protest against what they perceive as "improper behavior." For second-generation Jews who lived at home, or were still financially dependent on their parents, material deprivation became one form by which parents sanctioned their children. In several cases, parents cut off their allowance, threatened to disinherit them, or refused to give them the funds they requested. The parents had greater leverage when their children were younger, less financially independent, and lived under their roof. Once respondents became financially independent, material deprivation became less effective as a means of social control.

Another response that parents used to show their disapproval of their child's German lover was avoidance. By suspending normal interactions between themselves and their child, and particularly between themselves and their child's German lover, they were able to symbolically reaffirm the moral order. This tactic was also useful in avoiding further conflicts and confrontations. David's parents used avoidance when it became known that he was romantically involved with a German woman. "I had major problems with my parents," he reveals. "For my father, it came to be that we didn't speak with one another for several years. For four years. I was 16 to 21. I got less money, and then no pocket money."

I also heard a rumor about a Jewish family who sat shiva (Jewish mourning ritual) when their son married a German woman.[15] For many Jews, however, the avoidance was frequently exercised in a modified form. That is, while their parents did not avoid my respondents, they did avoid interacting with the German boyfriends and girlfriends my respondents were dating. This type of parental avoidance can continue on a routine basis, as Joshua, the psychiatrist, discovered when he married his German wife:

Q: Did you have problems in your marital relationship because you were marrying a German woman?

A: I don't believe so. There was a very big problem that's related, but that wasn't a problem with my wife and me, but a problem between my wife and my parents. My parents boycotted this marriage. My parents didn't come to the wedding. It went so far that even when my son was born – and it was more my mother who stood behind this than my father – my mother didn't even want to get to know him. When the kid was two months old, I brought the kid with me and I said, "Here is your grandson." And we spoke about it. My father was different. He was happy that he was a grandfather. But he had to hide this in front of his wife. My mother argued that my wife wasn't Jewish and because of this, she was against the marriage. But I believe this was a displaced argument. She was actually envious that another woman took away her son. And then she had a reason to be against the marriage. She had already presented it very strongly, and surely it was already mentioned in many of your interviews, that almost all Jews from the generation of my parents that I know here in Frankfurt put an exceptionally high value on the fact that their children should marry Jewish.

Q: Did you lose contact with your parents?

A: No, I didn't lose contact with my parents, but I lived in a divided world. On the one hand, I lived here together with my wife, and I regularly visited my parents without my wife, and the situation at home would practically not be spoken about. My mother acted as if my wife didn't exist. You cannot even look at all of this from a normal point of view. My mother's behavior led to her depression a few months later, and she was sick psychologically. She extended this so far that when her brother visited from America she said that I just left town for a few days, and that's why I wasn't at home, in order to keep it a secret from the entire family that I had married. Nobody knew that I had moved out of the home, and that I had married. My cousin, the brother of John, he somehow found out, and called me, and said, "I have no idea at all what is going on in your life." It was really already absurd, I must say. She tried to completely hide this, and since I scarcely had contact with other Jews, I was seldom in the situation to participate in this. I was simply away, and my mother tried to keep it a secret.

Q: How do you feel about this story?

A: I feel bad. It upset me very much then, and still upsets me now. I can understand the reason for this up to a certain point, but I find it horrible, the radical consequences to which this behavior was driven. For me, an entirely crass example is a conversation my mother had with an acquaintance, which was long before I married this woman. And they spoke about how in another family the son was also friendly with a German girl, and the parents wanted to break off their contact, and forbade the youth to marry that girl. And then the kid attempted suicide. And they didn't speak about this to say how awful it was that it drove this kid to suicide, but the point in this conversation was that it was better that a Jew commit suicide than marry a non-Jew. And, I find this attitude horrible. I cannot understand it, and it makes me really angry.

Jews in Germany have not abandoned attempts to combat intermarriage. They do not accept intermarriage as a foregone conclusion, and the community at large at times shows great remorse when its members marry Germans. Besides parental avoidance, the community can collectively engage in some degree of suspension of normal interaction. Because friendship networks tend to be closely knit, Jews can exercise avoidance collectively, that is, ostracism. When several people avoid a person at the same time, it is usually the product of collective action, the action of groups of friends or acquaintances, and resentment might even be voiced about those who continue to associate with the offender. Betty, the woman featured in the Prologue, experienced ostracism when she married her German husband. Even her parents were shunned because they were viewed as deficient in their socialization duties.

When I married him [German man], a lot of people didn't say hello to me anymore, which is offensive... I know they were bad mouthing us. I think it's more difficult for my parents than for me. Because I don't care. I have my work. And what makes me cry is that I'm afraid. And this is another reason why I think we are really going to move to America, my husband and I. Because I am afraid that my child will feel it. Because this community won't change. Not in another hundred years. And as I want to educate him as a Jew, I don't want him to be hurt by people.

With the large number of intermarriages among Jews in Germany in recent years, the community is being forced to face the unpalatable fact that intermarriage will continue to flourish so long as so few Jews remain in Germany. While attitudes toward intermarriage in the United States are becoming more lenient, particularly among Reformed and even Conservative congregations, for Jews in Germany who are on the whole religiously secular, attitudes against Jewish–German intermarriage remain severe and uncompromising.

Strategies to manage potential conflict with parents, the community, and oneself

Throughout world Jewry, similar sources of irritation lie at the heart of a great many family conflicts. When a child commits a dramatic offense against the family, conflict is almost inevitable. At issue are questions of interpersonal respect and obligation, the tension between respect toward one's heritage and the right to individual autonomy. Jews have developed several strategies to maintain their intimate relationships with Germans and simultaneously limit the conflict they would have with their parents and the community at large.

Keeping Jewish–German dates a secret

An easy way that second-generation Jews could avoid conflict with their families was to keep their relationships with Germans a secret. This was quite common among Jews I spoke with, such as Elisabeth, who said: "I kept it a secret, and I always had to come up with stories of where I went and what I did."

Some Jewish interviewees told their parents that they only went out in groups. Others lied to friends and family about their involvements. For instance, Sarah told her mother that her German boyfriend was actually Jewish. She explains,

Most of my boyfriends were German. I didn't have that many problems because either I had very, very, very, short relationships with them, like one day to a week, or when they were longer, I told them that my parents can only accept a Jew. I asked them if it was okay that they say they are Jewish. So I made them Jewish. I think my father knew what was going on, because he always left the room when my boyfriend and I were talking. But my mother didn't know... One boyfriend that I was very serious with had a very close relationship with my mother. In fact, when my mother would come to Wizo she would say, "Sarah has such a nice boyfriend, but you wouldn't believe that he is Jewish. He looks like a goy, with blond hair and blue eyes." She had a lot of close contact with him, and he liked her too.

Samuel, who was featured in the Prologue says: "I made a point for German girls not to call me at home. Not because we were Jews, but because I didn't want my parents to put their long Jewish noses into my affairs, which they always do, until this day." Richard knows that to keep his personal life secret, he must not appear in Jewish company with his German girlfriends: "When I was with the German girls, I wouldn't go to that many places where Jews were. There are cafes and parties where one cannot bring a German girl. It is forbidden. With Jews, it's okay. My close Jewish friends would know who I was dating, but not acquaintances."

Viktor, the mathematician, experienced tremendous conflict with his parents when he dated a German woman at one point in his life, but learned to routinely withhold information from them about his personal life:

Q: Have your parents known about your German girlfriends?
A: Oh, this is a difficult question. Of course they've known. We've had some rather nasty scenes because of that. Oh, quarrels, lots of them...
Q: Did your parents' reaction affect your relationship?
A: Oh, yes, it killed it. You know, because they were rather offensive. To me, certainly, and to her, not eye-to-eye, but talking too much to different people, and things like that. They did every possible thing that they could to kill the thing, and they succeeded.
Q: How did your parents antagonize the relationship?
A: You know, you have a quarrel. Everybody has quarrels, right? The way things work when you have quarrels, is that all sorts of poison bubbles come up, and this may be one of them. This certainly entered it. My parents did a lot of talking to different people. I don't know how much slander they spread, and I'd rather not know.
Q: To whom?
A: To other Jews in the community who apparently had contacts with the

parents of that particular girl. It was all a very unfortunate affair, and they did plenty of yelling at me. My father would even threaten to disinherit me if I married her. It was a fairly emotional affair with my parents. Anyway, she heard this after a while, and it put her off eventually. You know, these things never work on their own. It put her off when things were not going okay anyway. And when she hears things like that, it certainly doesn't help.

Q: Did she want to end the relationship?

A: Well, this is very difficult to say. It depends on what stage of the relationship we're talking about... It varies, at some stages I wanted to end it, and at some stages she wanted to end it. It just varied. In the end we split.

Q: Did this relationship have an effect on your future relationships with German women?

A: Yes, my parents never knew about them anymore. No, seriously, they never knew a single thing anymore. They sometimes complain and say, "We never know a thing about your private life," and then I keep quiet. I very much feel like saying, "Does it surprise you? It shouldn't." That's the effect it has had.

Q: What if you fall in love with a German woman?

A: Then I fall in love and enjoy it.

Q: Are you interested in getting married and settling down?

A: I don't know. To me, getting married and settling down, should it come to it, I'm not walking away from it. On the other hand, I'm not walking around the street shopping to get married.

Q: Is it important for you to marry Jewish?

A: As I said before, that has a lot to do with how much I want to avoid getting into trouble with my parents. I want to avoid trouble with my parents.

Q: Will it affect your choice of mate?

A: I don't know. It's never come that far. I don't think I've known anybody recently that I've thought I should marry... I'm not going around, like some people I know who travel to Israel to pick a bride. I don't particularly feel like doing that. On the other hand, I'm not that confirmed a bachelor that I would say "never." What happens, happens.

Self-control

Human beings are assumed to be responsible for their actions. In order to maintain a sense of morality, second-generation Jews must be in control of their inner feelings because affection could develop with Germans under certain conditions. It should be noted, however, that public displays of emotion are acceptable, so long as the relationships did not appear to be serious.

Some Jews, male and female, consider it a moral virtue to be emotionally restrained, and Jews fear the consequences of emotional attachment. Self-control was exercised to its maximum to create emotional barriers. Feelings were controlled and kept in check as a defense against relationships getting out of hand. As Juliane, the secretary, says regarding a former German boyfriend: "I could not even let my feelings go so strongly, that I could imagine to want to or be able to marry him." A consensus emerged from about half the Jews who dated Germans that emotional control was a viable and legitimate strategy. The legitimacy of this strategy was not judged in terms of its means, rather the outcome. If marriage is the outcome of love, one could date Germans, so long as one did not fall in love. For these Jews, emotions could be controlled, turned on or off like a faucet. Monika had this to say: "I couldn't allow myself to feel what came to my head, because I always thought, 'This is not a Jew,' and I wouldn't marry him."

Because of their parents, because of growing up Jewish in post-Holocaust Germany, because of the meanings inherent in maintaining Jewish ethnicity, falling in love with a German is perceived as an emotionally inappropriate response – one that is out of keeping with Jewish norms and customs. It would be a moral failing to allow oneself to fall in love with a German. Martin, whom we met in Chapter 4, reflects on these constraints. He says, "I never fell in love with a German girl. I think an iron-clad safety lock is put on that... With my family background, I couldn't do that to my parents." A self-imposed barrier is intentionally constructed to avoid falling in love. Martin describes how he must coordinate his emotions to correspond with the normative guide for external appropriateness of Jewish–German intimacy:

I discovered that I have had many relationships with girls in the last few years which are not emotional. We are together, but it's not a big love affair. It probably has something to do with the girls, too. But it probably has something to do with the fact that deep down inside you know you are not going to marry that girl. So you build up something like a barrier. This is not the only reason, because it also depends on the girl. But this is a reason. And I find it true for other Jews, too. That you build up some kind of a barrier, which you probably have in front of every woman. But you build it up because of that special situation. Because you think about marriage, and that it would get into problems. And you want to avoid all of that. There is something in that... It's probably not just the girl, but the fact that she's German that causes the big barrier.

These emotional barriers have costs. They affect one's relationship with the German lover. Whether intentional or not, they signal a moral message regarding where the relationship stands, and its possible future. At some point, Jews' motivations and long-range goals become clear, both to themselves and their lovers. In the words of one respondent,

Of course I had problems. I had thoughts that I couldn't so freely experience. When you don't think you have a future with the person, the relationship breaks up. It's that simple. It's hopeless because you can't go further... And I believe that a love between two people should have no restrictions, regardless of what happens. But not already from the onset that you know that this "yes" and that "no." It should be a free relationship.

The following Jewish man sums up the Jewish dilemma: "Ninety percent of the time you're with non-Jews. There are two possibilities: one is to be emotionally crippled and to castrate yourself and have no emotional relationship to non-Jews. And, two, is to have it."

Jews who did not believe in controlling their emotions, did not deem it proper to exploit Germans sexually or to place obstacles in the path of their emotional development. They did not practice the double standard and many in this group viewed it as a social problem deserving public criticism. They were bitter toward Jews who practiced such strategies, claiming that it was morally wrong. Some viewed Germans from a universalistic humanist philosophy, as one respondent put it, "I don't think the double standard is right, because everyone has feelings. It's wrong because you have to treat a person as a person." David, who was featured in the Prologue would have agreed. He said, "I think that if I started a relationship with a woman, if I slept with a woman, there was always a potential for an intense relationship regardless of her being German or not." Rachel felt the same way. She said, "No, I always fell in love with Germans."

Other Jews would not practice the double standard if it meant putting Jews on a pedestal, or treating Jews as untouchables for casual relationships. "I also sleep with Jewish women," says one respondent. "Did you feel this double standard?" I asked another respondent. "No, not at all. It wasn't a theme for me, that I would say, 'Avoid Jewish women because they are potential marriage partners.' When a nice, sweet woman was there, who was intelligent and pleasant, then why not?"

This more relaxed attitude toward having sexual relationships with Jews was more prevalent amongst younger Jews.[16] The point was not so much that Jews and Germans were no longer viewed differently, but rather that sexual mores were changing, and with birth control widely available, sexual intercourse with Jews did not take on the same risks, and need not imply a greater emotional commitment toward marriage. "The double standard doesn't exist anymore. Now everyone sleeps with everyone," explained one respondent. "When I sleep with somebody now, then it doesn't have any special meaning, because I'm not thinking about marriage," said another.

Formal and informal conversion

When relationships with Germans become emotional and serious, and marriage becomes an issue, problems arise.[17] Monika summed up the dilemma: "Being in love is never a problem. Everything that comes after that is the problem." If marriage becomes a possibility, conversion is the most common strategy Jews have developed to deal with Jewish–German relationships. In other words, they transform a discordant relationship into a religiously homogeneous relationship. My data revealed that more Jewish males than females marry Germans. Studies of the Jewish community in the United States have documented similar patterns. They have also noted that in recent years the rate of intermarriage among Jewish women is rapidly approaching that of Jewish men. Among my respondents, however, it was not common for Jewish women to marry German men. As mentioned earlier, I was only able to locate two Jewish women in the second generation who had married German men. In both cases, neither German partner converted to Judaism. Furthermore, it was not important for either woman in these mixed marriages that her husband convert. One reason might be that because the Jewish heritage is matrilineal, there is less pressure on the husband to convert; their children will be recognized as Jews anyway. Both women expressed how unpleasant it would be for their husbands to convert, given that as adults they would have to be circumcised. One of these women married a famous scholar, and said that because her husband was a celebrity she was suddenly invited to numerous weddings, Bar Mitzvahs, funerals, brisses, and other parties hosted by Jews. The other woman felt that since her husband was German, he had "celebrity status" with some members of the community:

You know what is so strange. There are some people who won't say hello to me. And I have more respect for them than for some people who think that I did something very outstanding. They think it's very chic. And they would like to have me as a friend, just like people like to have a socialist as a friend. To show him off at a party as something very special. This is more offensive, I think.

While Jewish men marry outside their ethnic group to a greater degree than Jewish women, they also bring into their families a far greater number of converts. As one respondent remarked, "They [Jewish men] want their Jewish women, but meet a non-Jew, and they make her into a Jew." One rumor I heard was that if their German girlfriends had not converted, the Jewish men might not have married them.

When formal conversion of the German partner did not take place, a sort of informal conversion was done in the minds of the Jews: the German lover was redefined by using personal attributes rather than cultural categories. For instance, as mentioned in the previous chapter regarding Germans whom Jews befriend, German lovers were also viewed as not typical Germans. This is reflected clearly in Elisabeth's description of her German boyfriend: "He's very international. He would never cook a German meal with sauerkraut or wurst. He would always cook a French or Italian meal. He has more sympathy for non-German cultures than German cultures." German lovers were also portrayed as more Jewish than Jews. This is how Betty, the woman featured in the Prologue, describes her German husband: "He's not very German in his ways. As I told you, that they are very cold. So, he's much more Jewish than most of the other people I know who are Jewish. He's already speaking Yiddish to my father." One Jewish woman mentioned her delight at being able to mentally transform the physical features of her German boyfriend, making him appear more Jewish. She says, "He's not circumcised, but he looks like he's circumcised, because when he was five the skin was too tight, and he had to have some of it removed. So he looks like he's circumcised! There are really tricks!"

Such redefinition reduces the dissimilarity between the Jew and German. By making the German more socially attractive, it also makes the Jews' deviant behavior somewhat less serious. Such efforts to secure equal moral status for Jews and their German lovers, however, does not resolve the problem of ethnic status asymmetry. For instance, experience has shown that even if German spouses convert, nagging doubts frequently remain in the eyes of the community regarding the authenticity of this person's newly adopted Jewish identity. Moreover, one should remember that only the German lover's status has been redefined and elevated, not Germans as an ethnic category. Unless the underlying symbolic meanings associated with Jew and German are redefined, ethnic segregation and asymmetry will remain.

Reevaluation and other strategies

There are several occasions where an individual's behavior is not governed by the norms of the group to which one belongs, even though one might be affirmatively oriented toward the group itself. I came across a few cases where Jews unequivocally feel that intermarriage was a betrayal of their group, that it jeopardized their cultural integrity or disgraced them culturally. For Jews who did pursue interethnic relationships, and were reluctant to give them up, we shall see that three additional strategies made their choices less costly. These strategies were: (1) long-term living together and by-passing procreation; (2) dissociating the German lover from the history of the country; and (3) accepting the responsibility and consequences of their actions.

A few Jews got around the issue of intermarriage by postponing the decision indefinitely, and living with their German lover in a common-law relationship. Under these conditions, bringing children into the world was avoided. This strategy was not cost-free. Indeed, a respondent who has been living with his German girlfriend for over twelve years told me that the most basic problem for him was the continuation of a Jewish family: "Somehow the deep-rooted goal for Jews, and also for me, sentimentally, is to continue Judaism." He explains his dilemma,

We live together, but this is not a Jewish family... And somehow this disturbs me a little bit... I'm thinking more often about whether I'm really living my life the right way. There are some very deep-rooted Jewish moments or elements in my life, deep-rooted wishes that are not fulfilled that way. And then I always have to think about whether it is really good to have those wishes and not to satisfy them. Or I wonder whether this is really a rational way to handle those feelings. Is it something that I've been educated to do? So what? Does it really have to disturb me that I have these Jewish sentiments?... The outcome is a high degree of reflection.

Reevaluation was another coping strategy. While Jews have not given up their typifications of Germans, nor released Germany from its collective guilt, the disassociation of the country's past from the individual in question enables successful friendships and love relationships to develop. In other words, the particular German was not viewed as a representative of his or her country's past. One respondent sums up the whole message as she describes how her mother reassured her before she was about to marry a German man:

Actually, my mother behaved in a very superior way. She told me, "Is this the man you think is the right one?" And I said, "Yes. I think so." So she said, "So what. Are you marrying his country's past? Are you marrying his family? You're marrying him." Really, I admired her. It wasn't much conflict. But I believed it could be a conflict. I really expected a conflict.

In her search for a way to combine personal happiness with ethnicity, this woman who intermarried changed her beliefs about the nature of her German partner and his country's past. To her surprise, her own ideas and those of her mother's were more malleable than the relatively intransigent ideologies of the community. Their emerging beliefs contrasted sharply with the views and behavioral patterns of others in the *Gemeinde* more committed to ethnicity. They also represent a break from views they held in the past. To ease the dilemma of marrying a German, this respondent and her mother rejected the traditional views they held, and challenged the widely espoused notion that Germans were murderers and that Jews should maintain distance from them. This process offered an escape from an otherwise unsolvable dilemma, but it also required a difficult break from past assumptions and cultural messages. Bereft of viable cultural alternatives, ideological change became the path of least resistance. Caught between pressures to give up love due to ethnicity, this Jewish woman and her mother surrendered traditional beliefs that the community had lived by and passed on to them.

Finally, some Jews have accepted responsibility for their actions. This is the last strategy developed by Jews who have pursued interethnic relationships. Betty explains:

I was very sad and I was crying about it. And I feel how bad he [husband] feels at this moment. And he can't change it. Because if I married him, okay, it's also my fault. I should have not married him. And I think that I'm not allowed – and this is something that my father told me – I'm not allowed to make him feel bad, because, first of all, what happened cannot be changed. And I had two choices – to say, "Okay I'm not able to marry a German," or, to say, "Yes, I am able, so I did it." And, I say, "Okay, now that you did it, you cannot fault him for anything." And, I think that it's true.

These Jews were caught in a dilemma of putting their own needs before those of their parents and culture. They created strategies to minimize the burden of their choices, yet they suffered in other ways. In some sense they tried to correct their behavior of being intimately involved with Germans by untangling awkwardly established norms, meanings, and values, and within this framework establishing more personally appropriate Jewish–German expectations and modes of action. While they did not want to turn against their own kind, they paid

a price in different ways of going against community norms while
maintaining a sense of ethnic group membership.

Conclusion

Research findings about social relationships are important because, as
Eric Klinger found, relationships serve as a focal point around which
many people orient their lives. Indeed, Klinger argues that people focus
on social relationships more than anything else because they believe it is
relationships that make their lives meaningful.[18] In Chapter 5 I explored
the criteria for friendship formation amongst Jews and between Jews and
Germans, and analyzed the character of Jewish–German friendships.
Marriage is a much more serious matter. For most people throughout
human history, marriage has been less a personal affair than a familial
and societal obligation. Kinship ties, the oldest institutional system in
human societies, provided the most basic integrative force in preindus-
trial societies. The kin-group provided for the physical, political, economic, educational, religious, and psychic needs of all of its members.

In industrial societies, marriage has become more personal. Happiness
and self-fulfillment are important goals. Research has shown that people
who report having satisfactory marriages are also more likely to report
higher levels of well-being in other areas of their lives.[19]

Intermarriage lies at the heart of the study of intergroup relations.
Intermarriage has been conceptualized both as a measure of assimilation
and an agent producing it. According to Peter Blau, Carolyn Beeker, and
Kevin Fitzpatrick, "high rates of intermarriage are considered to be
indicative of social integration, because they reveal that intimate and
profound relations between members of different groups and strata are –
more or less – socially acceptable."[20]

My findings question the significance of intermarriage as a process and
correlate of assimilation among Jews in Germany, particularly the degree
to which intermarriage is supposed to produce ethnic assimilation. While
intermarriage does provide some information regarding crossovers, as
Fredrik Barth reminds us in *Ethnic Groups and Boundaries*, ethnic
boundaries can still remain intact, regardless of the extent of crossovers.
That is, while it is generally understood that acculturation and structural
assimilation (e.g., with respect to education and occupation) can occur
without extensive intermarriage, it is rarely questioned whether intermarriage can occur without assimilation. Intermarriage is generally recognized as an indicator of assimilation, but my findings suggest that Jewish
ethnicity can be persistently viable in the face of intermarriage. Macro-

structural explanations of assimilation and intermarriage neglect cultural explanations, particularly ideologies that frame an individual's actions. This suggests that despite a long and illustrious research tradition focusing on structural processes of intermarriage, there needs to be more focus on cultural processes, the frame of reference through which groups interpret their experience. Much can yet be learned about interethnic intimacy through the use of in-depth interviewing, and comparative analyses of more diverse settings.

Rather than studying the norm in social science, I suggest that attention be devoted to studying outlier populations. Here new insights into interpersonal relationships can be generated. While intermarriage does take place at a dramatic level for Jews in Germany, strong ideological factors rooted in Jewish culture, the collective memory of the Holocaust, are embedded in cherished normative behavior. Guilt, problems, and awareness of potential difficulties give testimony to the significance and internalization of the value orientations of Jews, even if their behavior might not necessarily be consistent with the values that they hold. The major criticism I can level against structuralist theories is that behavior cannot be taken at face-value for assimilation, particularly ethnic behavior, and by doing so, one masks the values that might actually be held by the group. Values and the manner in which individuals live with those values are two different things. Human beings are contradictory animals, and are expert at creating coping mechanisms and a variety of strategies to accommodate their behavior. Only through a cultural analysis, and by illuminating the cultural codes that structure beliefs, can we begin to shed light on this more-nuanced approach and analyze more effectively the state of Jewish–German relations in contemporary Germany.

7

Theoretical implications and future research

We wanted to leave Auschwitz, but Auschwitz will never leave us.
(A survivor)[1]

We live in a post-Holocaust time, in which fragments of a broken past present us with enduring questions about the human condition and how to come to terms with our memory, responsibility, faith, and hope. I have used the lens of sociology to explore how the collective memory of the Holocaust continues to live on in the minds of the people I interviewed. More generally, by focusing on collective memory, I have tried to uncover something of all culture. By describing identity, I have tried to reveal something of all of us. And, by demonstrating how collective memory can play a crucial role in shaping identity, I have tried to show how people attribute meaning to symbols as they create ethnic boundaries to define themselves and their group.

The concerns of Jews in Germany are common ones for Jews throughout the world, as they must find strategies for responding to the challenges of modernity and constructing new forms of Jewish ethnicity in the context of modern secular society. A number of specific issues arise.

How should Jews deal with members of other ethnic groups? How close to such persons should one become? What is the proper place in Jewish culture for a history of oppression? How does one define what it means to be a Jew in secular society? What are the appropriate identities for Jews and non-Jews? What is the appropriate balance between being rooted in the past, living in the present, and envisioning a future? How does a Jewish community in the Diaspora provide for the social and spiritual needs of its members in today's modern world, in the face of declining religious affiliation, observance, and education, and a rise in intermarriage?

Theoretical implications

Rethinking Jewish and ethnic identity

As mentioned in Chapter 1, ethnic groups have traditionally been defined on the basis of racial and cultural characteristics. Visible differences in skin color, body size, facial features, hair texture, and so on have been used to delineate group membership. Language, beliefs, values, and norms as well as material and non-material products of culture like arts, crafts, and rituals have also served to distinguish "us" from "them." Sociologists who study race and ethnic relations have been outsiders calculating a group's cohesiveness and probability of survival, and have generally relied on *a priori* categories such as rates of birth, death, and intermarriage, normative and symbolic behaviors, and other statistics collected in surveys on the prevalence of ethnic symbols. They have rarely bothered to ask group members how they define themselves as part of a distinctive cultural entity.

The nature and complexity of the Jewish experience is obscured if we conceptualize it as a more or less homogeneous phenomenon, divisible only in gross differences of religiosity, Holocaust experience, social class, education, political preference, nationality, and the like. Such variables do not address what it means to be Jewish in the modern secular world, and can distort our understanding of people's attachments and identity.

In contemporary Germany, as in many Diaspora communities throughout the world, Jews are increasingly moving away from religious sources of meaning or norms. Nonetheless, Jews in Germany have created a distinctively Jewish world within a secular society. In spite of widespread variations in political orientation, biography, education, life-style, generation, personality, and life experience, the second-generation Jews I interviewed are unquestionably *Jewish*. They are Jewish because they create and maintain transcendent meaning systems, and adhere to the code of behavior, norms, and values that hold sway in the Jewish community. The distinction of being Jewish flows from the collective memory of the Holocaust. Jews in Germany define their Jewishness in terms of moral traits that distinguish them from others. The culture they share informs how they interact with other Jews and Germans. In the course of interethnic contact, valuing their distinctiveness is at the core of their identity, the source of their ethnic survival.

The dichotomies that Jews draw between themselves and Germans create the boundaries that separate them physically, symbolically, and morally. Differences between Jews and Germans are infused in Jewish culture and institutionalized in the practices and patterns of everyday Jewish life. Jews cling to these cultural definitions because they have an interest in preserving their identity: their sense of self, their security, and their dignity are all tied to these particular boundary distinctions.

Ethnic identity is indeed as much a cognitive process as it is a behavioral manifestation. That is, we come to understand what Jewishness is, or more to the point, what it means, through the way Jews describe it, and set it in relationship to non-Jews. Something can be evaluated and invested with meaning only when it is placed somewhere in a mental universe – when it is understood to be like one thing and not like another. As Durkheim argued, sociology is about the classification of social facts. An act or phenomenon makes sense once it is placed into an existing taxonomic grid through which the vastness and complexity of reality is organized and reduced to manageable terms. Incomprehensibility or confusion occur when something is encountered which cannot be, or has not yet been, assigned a place in the intelligible universe. The terms we have available for describing new entities, and the meanings and connotations of already existing ones, will influence the way we regard the newly named entities.

I have attempted to identify various patterns of social life and identity construction that I found across my sample. I have focused on meanings – linguistic categories that make up respondents' views of reality and with which they understand their own and other's actions. It is important to note that meanings can vary in terms of the breadth or range of situations to which they apply. On the broadest level, they are often ideologies or world-views, yet they can be more discrete and limited in range, such as those referring to particular aspects of a person's life or activities. In this sense, I have focused on how Jews define for themselves their lives in Germany.[2]

Focusing on the process of distinction places culture and social meaning at the core of ethnic identity construction. The focus on meaning applies not only to descriptions of events and objects, but also, and more central to my point, to evaluations. One routinely makes such evaluations on the basis of personality, established relationships, culturally available patterns of thought, generally accepted linguistic conventions, or past experience. And when people are called upon to legitimize their thoughts or actions, they usually refer to immediate perceptions and socio-cultural expectations.

In this study I have attempted to capture a slice of life – the meanings inherent in second-generation Jewish culture in contemporary Germany. All too often, sociologists assume that ethnicity is defined in a uniform manner, and neglect the range of definitions within an ethnic group. This study questioned that assumption and demonstrated that ethnic identity is best conceptualized as an aggregate of collected meanings. Its meanings emerge in specific social contexts, and are created and recreated through human interaction. Meanings are not inherent in reality, but are endowed to it by human beings. Because life's situations are constantly changing, new and often novel meanings are generated to cope with new contingencies. Future research would be more fruitful if it incorporated a cultural approach that focused on the variety of collective meanings that emerge as ethnic identity is constructed and maintained.

Collective memory as an arena of distinction upon which Jewish identity is based

This study also showed how the repertoire of meanings that distinguish Jew from German solidifies a sense of Jewish community. Focusing on meanings, however, begs the question of what these meanings are based on. In other words, what are the variables that account for the construction of ethnic boundaries?

In this book I have followed in the footsteps of Max Weber, who argued that ethnic groups are socially constructed, and of subjectivists like Fredrik Barth, who focused on the significance of boundaries in their construction. While I agree with Barth that boundaries define ethnic groups, I disagree with his view that the analysis of ethnicity should not emphasize the "cultural stuff" that the boundaries enclose. The "cultural stuff" – the traits that Jews mobilize to create internally generated boundaries – contains the dynamics of the process of boundary construction. Moreover, I am not certain that the criteria that get mobilized to construct the boundaries are objective criteria, such as group behavior. Groups can create subjective criteria – myths, ancestral heroes, or typifications – about themselves and others, which become factors that they mobilize to create ethnic distinctions.

Yet subjective expressions of ethnicity are also grounded in time and place. Memories change over time, and so do our recollections of them. While Jews in Israel, the United States, South America, other European countries, and elsewhere may share some of the meanings of German or Jew that my respondents demonstrated, they might also have other cultural resources at their disposal that they draw upon for generating ethnic boundaries. The process is similar, but the criteria mobilized might be based on other factors particular to their social, historical, and geographical circumstances: the meaning of being Jewish might be different in different parts of the world. The availability of these options actually increases the range of people who might become involved in Jewish life and opens opportunities for involvement to people who might well remain unrecognized, if the only option of being Jewish is defined as practicing Jewish ritual or other types of traditional Jewish normative behavior.

The large majority of sociological studies of race and ethnicity have ignored collective memory as a significant factor in defining ethnic identity. Similarly, the sociological literature on Jewish experience rarely looks at the memory of the Holocaust as a central analytical category in the analysis of Jewish identity and Jewish-Gentile relations. Nevertheless, we know that ethnic behavior, like all behavior, is shaped by memory, and the growth of collective memory as an analytical tool in the last decade has highlighted how memory informs social experience. Yet to show concretely how memory impacts identity roles, privileges, images, and friendship and love relations – as this book has attempted to do for the case of second-generation Jews in Germany – is unprecedented in the literature. For example, several chapters of Y. Michal Bodemann's recent edited volume, *Jews, Germans, Memory*, suggest how Holocaust memory formed the background of Jewish life in Germany at the institutional level, but do not show specifically how it affected Jewish images of themselves, of Germans, and ultimately, of Jewish–German interpersonal relationships. Moreover, Herbert Sallen and Alphons Silbermann's large-scale but non-representative survey of Jewish self-images in Germany predefined what identity looks like through the use of *a priori* sample questions, and failed to include Holocaust memory as a criterion. Since these scholars did not conduct personal interviews with second-generation Jews, the differences in my findings and theirs about the importance of collective Holocaust memory in forming Jewish identity and Jewish–German relationships could reflect differential access to data.

Historians Michael Wolffsohn and Dan Diner report the decline of the quality of Jewish experience in Germany and focus on the malaise felt by Jews who live there. Wolffsohn warns that the fixation on the Holocaust is a process of historicizing and de-Judaizing Judaism, because the content of Judaism is not based on religion, but rather on the traumatic experience of organized genocide.[3] Dan Diner echoes his sentiments: "There is a particular danger for Jews living in Germany that they might become prisoners of earlier experiences particularly because the past is so close to them."[4] Despite the concerns of Diner and Wolffsohn, my findings suggest that the Holocaust in collective memory has been instrumentalized by Jews as a major strategy for community survival: the collective memory of the Holocaust is a resource that in some respects has served Jews in Germany well. My findings suggest that, more than the symbolism of the state of Israel, it has been the social cement that has held together this particular community.

The larger debate about secularization – the question of whether religion will inevitably decrease in influence in modern societies – has been a core concern for debates on the future of modern Jewry. Some scholars project a religious revitalization in Germany. While there are certainly more Jewish bodies in Germany, and some evidence of grass-roots religious pluralism, I am cautious about predicting a religious revival for Jews in Germany or elsewhere. Nevertheless, I show that a lack of religious behavior does not necessarily weaken Jews' commitment to their Jewish community. This is not to say that Holocaust memory is the only source of ethnic identity for Jews in Germany, or that it can maintain ethnic distinctiveness for the indefinite future. Indeed, in the wake of religious decline, it is important for Jews in Germany and elsewhere to find alternative resources for Jewish identity.

Jewish identity and Jewish–German relationships

The nature of Jewish identity is significant because it frames interaction between Jews and the wider German society. That is, people are not only aware of their own culture, as opposed to that of the host society, but they also attribute some value to each, both positive or negative. This value is determined in part by comparing their own culture with the culture of their host society. The collective labels that Jews use to distinguish themselves from Germans can be interpreted as comments about their own culture, as well as about German society.

On a more concrete level, this study has illustrated that strong cultural norms exist to guide Jewish–German interpersonal behavior, particularly on the level of love and friendship. These norms are established to maintain the proper social distance between Jews and Germans, according to Jewish community values. Of course, group norms are not always adhered to by individuals in real-life relationships. I have shown how a number of Jews manage to cross over ethnic boundaries to form friendships and love relationships, taking advantage of opportunities presented to them. Even though individuals criss-cross communal boundaries, the boundaries remain. The cultural resource that makes up a boundary may change over time, but some sort of boundary remains that is visible to in-group members.

Milton Gordon and Peter Blau, among others, treat intermarriage as an outcome of social structure: it occurs when there is a high degree of social and cultural integration or assimilation between two groups. For example, Blau, Schwartz, and Blum write that intermarriage occurs when "cultural values discouraging intermarriage are not sufficient to nullify structural influences encouraging it."[5] Moreover, a structural approach would assume that Jews who intermarry have lost specifically "Jewish traits" or values – the endogamous attitudes of their group and their prejudices against the out-group – at least enough to permit them to treat a member of the out-group as an object of affection. However, the intermarriage profile of second-generation Jews in Germany cannot be explained by a structural framework. In this book, I have shown how Jews can still identify strongly as Jews, even though they might not act like Jews, and may have little knowledge of things Jewish. They might outwardly appear to be assimilated to a casual observer, yet a closer look reveals that they still maintain a strong sense of in-group membership. Most macrostructural studies of assimilation use aggregate data that do not identify contextual factors which may negate or modify structural forces of assimilation. By focusing on cultural beliefs and ideologies, and the various coping mechanisms that individuals employ when crossing over ethnic boundaries, we can see the need for caution in equating behavior such as intermarriage, which might outwardly appear to be assimilative, with genuine integration.

Conceptualizing Jewishness in terms of normative patterns of behavior, and making assumptions about how Jews who intermarry feel, obscures the complexity of the situation. Indeed, ethnic ideology is a very powerful determinant of Jewish–German relations. The fear of upsetting family, friends, and the community at large affects the way that Jews perceive social opportunities. Their fears stem from past experience and their anticipation of similar problems. Most Jewish men and women are deeply committed to strong community ties, and are integrated into family networks that monitor behavior. However, Jews are also secure about their Jewishness and their Jewish identity. For those who cross boundaries, in most instances, their behavior is not internalized as a real threat to their Jewishness.

Some social scientists have suggested that intermarriage is a form of seeking status, a way to escape from the burdens of Jewishness.[6] My findings suggest that a Jew in Germany does not marry a German to escape the social liabilities of being Jewish. On the contrary, Jewish–German intermarriage often creates heavy personal and social burdens for second-generation Jews in Germany. Many Jewish leaders, both formal and informal, are married to German spouses, and the postwar *Gemeinden* were reestablished by those who were the most marginal members of the pre-war *Gemeinden*. Nevertheless, these factors do not legitimize intermarriage within Jewish culture in Germany. Instead, Jews who intermarry are questioned regarding their reputation and the legitimacy of their actions. Most second-generation Jews believe that the collective memory of the Holocaust matters, and they wish to remain within the fold, even if they might not always behave that way.

There has been a tradition in sociology that argues that conflict can have positive social functions: it can strengthen group consciousness and increase solidarity. Yet conflicts can exist not only at the material level, but also at the ideological level. Ideology, in the strictly Marxian sense, defines values and worldviews primarily in terms of the manner in which these beliefs legitimize existing social and material relations. But what if there is no need to mobilize or separate based on material interests? Why, then, do groups still do so?

Sociological determinists argue that the character of ethnicity is conditioned only by political or economic forces, and view culture as an epiphenomenon, a by-product of this process. The Jews in Germany are a case to the contrary: they are economically and politically privileged. It is not the material conditions that propel Jews to remember the collective memory of the Holocaust. Rather, the collective memory of the Holocaust furthers the actions of Jews in creating and defining themselves as a separate ethnic entity. Jews mobilize ethnic distinctions around a cultural motif – to keep alive the memory of the Holocaust.

Future research

The recognition of the changing historical situation in the aftermath of German reunification, and the advent of large numbers of Russian *émigrés*, gives a sense of some urgency for Jews to search for new institutional patterns. Time will tell what form Jewish experience will take. Will it become more religiously based? Will it be similar to the pre-war Jewish–German symbiosis? To what extent will it rely on the collective memory of the Holocaust? Will a completely new configuration based on fragments of diverse cultural patterns emerge?

The minute amount of scholarly research on Jews in contemporary Germany has been conducted primarily by historians or German studies scholars, who have focused on traditional Jewish culture, the reconstruction of the communities, or other forms of more traditional Jewish behavior. Rather than conducting extensive in-depth interviews to gain an inside view of Jewish experience, their research has relied on historical or literary sources, documenting the Jewish experience from the outside. The few exceptions to this rule – such as Robin Ostow's *Jüdisches Leben in der DDR* (Jewish Life in the GDR) or John Borneman and Jeffrey Peck's *Sojourners: the Return of German Jews and the Question of Identity* – have used very small samples, and focused on Jews in East Germany, and not primarily on the memory of the Holocaust or the second generation.

This book was about a particular group of people, Jews who were born and raised in Germany after the Second World War. It is not a book about Jewish intellectuals, Jewish leaders, recent Russian immigrants, or Israelis or American Jews living in Germany. It does not intend to grasp every type of Jewish experience in contemporary Germany. On the contrary, I chose to study second-generation Jews who were born right after a period of severe intergroup conflict, because they are especially well situated to illuminate the contours of Jewish–German relations and the difficulties in forging readjustment. These Jews came of age during a period of rapid social change when new developments and life patterns differed from the past ones in important ways. My emphasis was on what their lives were like, and the cultural codes that were at the core of their social world. There has not yet been any comprehensive sociological study that has relied on a data base of so many in-depth interviews of second-generation Jews in Germany, or has focused on how the memory of the Holocaust affects everyday interactions between Jews and Germans. Thus, I have shown a heretofore unexamined dimension of Jewish experience in Germany, by demonstrating the salience of the past in the mental images of how Jews view themselves and Germans, and how these images affect their social and political integration into German society.

Further analysis is also warranted on the salience of ethnic boundaries over time. Recall that the bulk of my interviews were conducted in the mid-1980s. Thus, I provide a "snap-shot" rather than a moving picture, and it will be important to monitor changes in Jewish identity over time. A longitudinal or time series study might capture changes in the relevance of the collective memory of the Holocaust over time on my respondents or on the third generation. A focus on sets of groups that share members might be profitable. For example, new Russian immigrants, Israelis living in Germany, Jews who have immigrated into Germany within the past ten years, and so on, could be surveyed in order to capture their social world, the basis upon which they draw their ethnic boundaries, and to analyze the extent to which their worlds and concerns overlap with those of the second generation examined in this study.

It will also be important to continue to monitor the perceptions of Jews in Germany, as Germany struggles with defining its own national identity. In the aftermath of reunification and in the course of debates about immigration, citizenship, and calls for a multiethnic society, the social landscape of Germany has changed and may well continue to change in the coming years. It will be important to study how institutional and structural transformations, and changes in social policy, affect ethnic mobilization and boundary maintenance for Jews and other groups like Turks, Yugoslavs, Greeks, Gypsies, Eastern European refugees, and the like, who are commonly defined as the "other" by the host society.

Finally, my study is of a particular social world, of a group of people whose host society had subjected their predecessors to genocide. It might be profitable to explore the social worlds of other groups who share similar experiences, to gain insight into the relevance of collective memory for their identity and relations with their host society. Such a project might allow for inferences to be made regarding the point at which genocide or conflict in collective memory becomes a salient feature of ethnic distinctiveness, and what other influences make the ethnic package solidify. We also need to explore the rigidity or fluidity of ethnic boundaries, and the effectiveness of gatekeepers versus reformers regarding the production of boundary work.

If we wish to understand Jewish–German relations, or, in particular, readjustment, we cannot remain at the level of social policy, public discourse, or institutional analysis, for all of our answers. We must also take a view from below, and see how readjustment plays out on the interpersonal level. By exploring group identities, and the meanings that make up these identities, the difficulties in readjustment become clearer. As I have shown, group identities can be rooted in collective memories that oppose readjustment, and groups may go to extremes to maintain and defend these definitions.

People choose what they wish to remember, and certainly what they want to forget. The Holocaust commands a special chapter in Jewish history. Jews remember with reverence and pain the loved ones they lost, the communities that were destroyed, the cultural traditions that were erased. Germans must also struggle to confront this catastrophe and to find its appropriate place within German history and their national heritage. For better or worse, the Holocaust is the common experience that unites Jews and Germans today, while it simultaneously stands in the way of their readjustment. By focusing our attention on the collective memories that Jews carry in their heads, and the impact these memories have for their identity and interpersonal relations, we can begin to understand the complexity of interethnic relations, and the processes that encourage readjustment, or make it unattainable. In the end, it is up to Jews and Germans to reflect the meaning of their Holocaust memories for their own identity and for Jewish–German relations. While I doubt they will find a common memory, perhaps they can each learn more about themselves and one another in light of their own remembered past.

Appendix:

Methodology

I began collecting data for this study in 1984, when I lived in Germany for one calendar year to witness Jewish life through the changing of the seasons. I have returned in subsequent years to collect additional data, and most recently in 1994, to reinterview a subsample of my original responses to see if and how their lives have changed after German reunification. In 1984 I formally interviewed eighty-three respondents, mostly Jews who were born and raised in Frankfurt.[1] An equal distribution of males and females was sought; the final sample ultimately included forty-three males and forty females. An attempt was made to interview as many Jews as possible in intermarriages who fit the age and residence criteria, as one goal of the study was to explore Jewish–German love relationships. I drew a stratified sample so as to include roughly equal numbers of respondents whose parents were survivors of concentrations camps, in hiding, or living relatively protected lives in Germany throughout the war, and those parents who spent the war years in exile. I was careful to include in the sample Jews whose parents were of German origin, as well as those from Eastern Europe and elsewhere.

I chose Frankfurt as the site of the study, because at that time it had the largest Jewish community in Germany proper (excluding West Berlin which was Allied occupied and held a special status), and I had heard that its youth were politically diverse.[2] In addition, Frankfurt has had a strong Jewish presence and tradition, and typifies Jewish community life in contemporary Germany.[3] I thought Frankfurt would provide an interesting and informed picture of the difficulties that young Jewish people experience today in their readjustment with Germans.

The sample was initially limited to Jews between the ages of twenty-five and thirty-nine. I chose the age of twenty-five as a minimum cut-off point to ensure selecting participants who were old enough to emigrate, to seriously consider emigrating, or who faced significant career, family and life decisions. The age of thirty-nine was the natural ceiling at that time, as May 8, 1945, marked the end of the war in Europe.

Due to the sensitivity of the topic, respondents were selected for the study through networking techniques, commonly known as "snowballing." Initial contact was made by telephone a few days to a week before the interview was scheduled. It soon became known that an American sociologist from Columbia University was in the field. This facilitated access to respondents, as a number of respondents I telephoned told me that they had heard of the study, were expecting my call, and were interested in participating.

In order to reduce possible bias from snowballing, 50 percent of the universe was interviewed.[4] Through community records I was able to search and tally the number, ages, and dates of arrival of all Jews registered in the Frankfurt Jewish community. I intended initially to interview only second-generation Jews who were born and raised in Frankfurt. However I found that only fifty-seven Jews between the ages of twenty-five and thirty-nine, who were born and raised in Frankfurt, were still in residence there.[5] I had to modify my sampling scheme to draw a larger sample. I decided to interview Jews who met the following two criteria: (1) they had arrived in Frankfurt by the age of ten (predominantly from other Jewish communities in Germany), and (2) they had resided in Frankfurt for at least twenty years. This increased the universe to 187 respondents. To reduce the duplication of information, I then eliminated siblings and spouses, which reduced the universe to 160. I sampled from this modified universe, and also included several cases that did not fit the above two criteria. These included Jews who were born and raised in Frankfurt, but who were not currently registered as Jews with the authorities.[6]

Most respondents were open to participation. In fact, two Jews who did not fit the participant criteria approached me and asked if they could be included in the study. I was fortunate to meet with only five refusals.

I interviewed each respondent using a semi-structured interview schedule.[7] Most of the questions in the interview were open-ended, and I followed standard questionnaire construction and techniques to limit possible interviewing and questionnaire bias. For example, I refrained from giving any personal information about myself until the interview was over. Furthermore, during the course of the interviews I used probing techniques and also repeated some questions to check for reliability in responses.

I conducted the majority of the interviews in German, unless the respondent wished to speak English. The interviews were tape-recorded and averaged two to three hours. Sixty-two of the interviews were carried out in private settings at the home of the respondent. Eight were conducted at my residence in Frankfurt, three at my office at the Goethe University, and ten at the work place or office of the respondent.

When I first began the interviews, I heard, again and again, two major areas of problems that Jews experienced in their relationship with Germans. These problems were expressed as difficulties in defining their Jewish identity, and as difficulties in their interpersonal relationships with Germans. These problem areas, as well as coping mechanisms – the strategies that Jews developed to come to terms with these problems – provided me with a point of departure for the focus of the study.

I also administered a written questionnaire documenting background characteristics of the study sample. The questionnaire was mailed to respondents several months after the interview, and the response rate was over 80 percent.

Ethnographic techniques were also employed at every relevant occasion.[8] I went to almost all formal community events during my stay in Frankfurt, and was invited to many informal ones – weddings, funerals, parties, and coffee-breaks. By doing so, I was exposed to the public and private world of my respondents. My participation in the life of the community provided me with the opportunity to check the reliability of the data I had gained through the personal interviews. I was able to gain an overall picture of Jewish life in Germany and its difficulties, thereby complementing data provided by the interviews, newspaper accounts, documents, and the written questionnaire. Moreover, I visited every major research institute and Jewish community throughout Germany, where I gathered and reviewed secondary literature and documents.

The interviews yielded approximately 200 tapes with over 300 hours of recorded data. After leaving the research site and returning to the United States, I translated and transcribed the interviews, which averaged about thirty-five typed pages. The first step in the analysis entailed coding the information in the interview along general themes. About twenty such themes emerged from the interviews. Some of the most consistent ones were identity problems, boundaries and barriers to contact, anti-Semitism, and coping strategies. The text of each interview was cut up, and the data sorted and filed into a thematic folder. The interviews were coded, so that if necessary each data slice could be retraced to the original interview. This also provided a checking system when analyzing the data, to insure that sociological generalizations were not based on data slices from only a few select interviews. The next step in the analysis entailed sifting through each major-theme folder, discovering and categorizing sub-themes and filing them into new folders. The end result was a set of folders within folders.

Within each sub-theme, I focused on units of the social setting – patterns and relationships along various "thinking units." The units included meanings, practices, episodes, encounters, roles, relationships, groups, and lifestyles. I took a piece of data, identified its unit, and then proceeded to ask questions about these units. The following questions were most commonly asked, but varied depending upon their appropriateness to the data-slice. (1) What type of unit is this? (2) What is its structure? (3) How frequently does it occur? (4) What are its causes? (5) What are its processes? (6) What are its consequences? and (7) What are people's strategies?[9]

A general design was constructed depicting the relationship between various themes, units, and data items. When a pattern became apparent, a check was made throughout the entire data set to determine whether the pattern was frequent or unique. If the pattern occurred consistently across various types of situations it was considered frequent. If the pattern occurred only in specific situations or under certain circumstances it was considered unique. An outline was drawn indicating the main argument and findings, and the report was written.

Quotations are used extensively throughout this book. The rationale is to show the story rather than to tell it. The quotations selected were those that most succinctly and vividly depict the point being made. However, because of the personal nature of the information, and the promise that it would be kept confidential, I do not use the names or any identifying characteristics of any respondent. In some cases, to make clear the meaning of the quote, it has been necessary to add or delete a word, phrase, or sentence. Added words or phrases are enclosed in brackets and deletions are indicated by ellipses. The term "most" is used to describe issues or situations typical of the Jewish experience in general, based on my sample. In many instances actual percentages are used indicating the level of reported experience.

I have tried to write this monograph for both sociologists and a general audience. I hope to present as clear a picture as possible of the means by which a group of people define and experience their existence. Empirical reality, however, is a complicated phenomenon; it does not flow neatly along any one direct path and cannot always be organized along clean and neat categories. I was asked, for example, why I did not write about categories of people. The simple answer is that I checked initially to see if responses varied in such a way as to be organized according to particular categories of people, and, to put it simply, they did not. For example, while I thought that children of concentration camp survivors would differ systematically in their attitudes toward Germany and Germans from children whose parents were not incarcerated, I was surprised to find that they did not. While I initially anticipated that children whose parents were born and raised in Germany would differ significantly in their responses and attitudes toward Germans from children of Eastern European background, I was surprised, again, to find that they did not. While, of course, there was variation within responses, that variation did not fall neatly along categories enabling me to classify types of second-generation Jews. What I have done, then, is to organize the data according to themes that demonstrate a general argument, while simultaneously indicating the extent of variation and diversity of responses within each theme.

This book has several limitations. To begin with, I am only dealing with Jewish perceptions, and thus, can only fill in one part of the readjustment puzzle. I believe additional research is warranted to approach this topic from the German perspective, with in-depth interviews with the postwar generation of Germans, or perhaps even with children of perpetrators of the Holocaust. Also, my study deals with the perceptions of Jews toward Germans. While Jews revealed to me interethnic personal accounts of their relations with Germans, observing and studying how they actually behave in personal interethnic interactions is another issue. Furthermore, my data deal specifically with second-generation Jews. As time passes, it will be important to document the perceptions and attitudes of the third generation of both Jews and Germans regarding their interethnic relations.

Twelve years have passed since I began conducting the interviews for this book. This manuscript was first a doctoral dissertation, and then rewritten into this book. I was disappointed with the race and ethnicity literature in my field, and struggled long and hard to find a fit for my work. Preexisting theories about assimilation and acculturation abounded, but there was nothing in the literature to even hint at interethnic readjustment after the Holocaust. The small literature on Jews in Germany was historical, descriptive, or journalistic, or consisted of edited volumes lacking overarching theoretical frameworks, and empirical pieces suffering from small and non-random sampling. Instead of massaging my data to come up with a confirmation of some preexisting sociological theory, I persevered to generate an original argument about ethnicity and collective memory that captured what I had discovered. I am creating theory inductively, not testing it.

In the interim, many changes have emerged in Germany, and its Jewish population has increased due to an influx of Russian immigrants. Although I returned to Germany in 1994 to chart some of those changes, and to revisit a sample of my interviewees, I have updated information, but have left the interview data and ages of the people as they were in 1984. I felt it was important to capture where they were in their lives at that point in time.

Finally, by focusing on Jews before unification, we can see very clearly the impact of the Holocaust on their identity, their everyday lives, and their relations with Germans. Yet, even with the lapse of time, the principle ideas developed in this book continue to be confirmed. Primarily, that the past is still present, and very much present in the lives of Jews who were born and raised in Germany after the Holocaust.

Notes

Setting the stage: the Jewish community of Frankfurt and the voices of its members

1 Each resident in Germany is obliged to register with German authorities. This entails completing an information card for which one entry is religion. The 5,715 persons refers to the total number of Jews registered as such in 1996.

2 *Gemeinden* are historically established forms of Jewish communal organization in Germany dating back to the first quarter of the nineteenth century.

3 In 1946 the US military government ordered the city of Frankfurt to erect a memorial plaque on the northern wall of the cemetery to recall the destruction of the Börneplatz Synagogue.

4 A Mikvah is a ceremonial Jewish bath.

5 In 1985 the city began excavating the land to construct a new administrative headquarters of Frankfurt's municipal gas company. In the course of excavation the ruins of nineteen houses and two Mikvahs dating from 1462 were unearthed. The discoveries raised questions about whether the original plans for the gas company should be altered to preserve the historic site. The Frankfurt Jewish community was divided. Prior to construction, its leaders had demanded that a memorial be built on the site. However, they also gave permission for the construction to proceed. Once the foundation was excavated, the community tried to reopen the matter. When the city administration conceded only the symbolic preservation of a small part of the remains, Jewish representatives did not press their case. The younger generation of Jews began a protest, and along with other Jewish and German opponents of construction, who formed the "Save the Börneplatz Action Group," occupied the construction site for five days, blocking further work, until they were removed by police. The matter became a hotly debated public issue and a compromise was reached and some of the ruins were preserved in the museum, which opened in October, 1992. For an outline of the controversy, see *Stationen des Vergessens – Der Börneplatz-Konflikt* (Frankfurt: Jüdisches Museum, 1992).

6 The *Gemeinde* center was bombed in 1990, and had a history of bomb threats for years.

7 To make aliyah means to immigrate to Israel and become an Israeli citizen.

1 Holocaust memory and Jewish identity

1 We may want to ask why ethnic groups exist at all. What purpose do they serve for those members who adhere to them? Debates within the sociological literature on race and ethnic relations indicate that there may be two answers to this question. Experts disagree on whether primordial factors are more significant than instrumental factors in the mobilization of ethnic groups. The primordial approach argues that individuals group together along ethnic lines because of a fundamental psychological need to experience a sense of affinity or peoplehood with others with whom they supposedly share a common origin. Instrumental theorists focus on the conscious efforts of ethnic leaders to manipulate ethnic symbols in order to obtain access to social, political, or material resources.

2 These theories emerged as a response to growing criticism of the models of adaptation, which lacked an emphasis on economic stratification and power issues. For a good overview of these approaches see Mario Barrera, *Race and Class in the Southwest* (Notre Dame and London: University of Notre Dame Press, 1979), pp. 174–219.

3 Assimilation, which comes from the Latin *assimulare* (to make similar) refers to the extent to which an ethnic group gives up its distinctive cultural traits and conforms to the dominant preexisting core culture, leaving the dominant culture essentially unchanged. Assimilationist studies measure the extent of absorption of an ethnic group into the host society. Full assimilation requires extensive social ties with members of the host society at work and during leisure time, and exogamy. Amalgamation, another form of adaptation, refers to the mutual modification and mixing of ethnic and core populations, resulting in a combined or hybrid population, often described as a "melting pot." Finally, models of accommodation or the phenomenon of "ethnogenesis" describe the persistence of ethnic cultural distinctiveness in spite of economic or political integration of the ethnic group in the host society. This type of accommodation is better known as cultural pluralism. This does not mean that the ethnic culture remains intact. On the contrary, through ethnogenesis a new ethnic culture emerges, one that has creatively adapted to the social, economic, and political conditions of the host society.

4 This argument was first made by Herbert Gans in "Symbolic Ethnicity: The Future of Ethnic Groups and Cultures in America," *Ethnic and Racial Studies* 2 (1979), pp. 1–20. According to Gans ethnicity does not altogether disappear with the advent of modernization, but it is no longer a dynamic determinant of social behavior.

5 These models fail to confront their assumptions about ethnicity, and fail to see

the complexity of ethnic identity, as a particular identity may be pluralistic – expressed differently by different members within a society, or by ethnic groups in different societies around the world. Ethnicity is more fluid and complex than implied by theories that see it as being primarily about domination and power.

6 The underlying assumption is that people similarly located in social structure would behave in similar ways, such behavior including perception and meaning. Ethnicity is thus viewed as monolithic, measured in terms of the manifestation of ethnic symbols, objective cultural criteria such as the expression of language, customs, specialty foods, newspapers, organizations, rituals, and the like, that surface or descend according to structural and economic conditions.

7 The sample was stratified to include equal numbers of Jews whose parents were (1) of German or Eastern European origin, and (2) among those who were Holocaust survivors, or who had survived the war in hiding, or who were in exile and returned to Germany after the war. The sample also included an equal number of males and females.

8 Barth's argument is part of a larger debate about how ethnic groups are constituted, and what elements go into their construction. At one end are "objectivist" arguments that see ethnic groups in terms of objective cultural characteristics such as common ancestry, distinctive language, religion, or customs that enable groups to form a sense of "peoplehood" or community among their members. A classic example is the definition of "ethnic group" given by Melvin M. Tumin in Julius Gould and William L. Kolb (eds.), *Dictionary of the Social Sciences* (New York: The Free Press, 1964), p. 243. He defines an ethnic group as "a social group which, within a larger cultural and social system, claims or is accorded special status in terms of a complex of traits (ethnic traits) which it exhibits or is believed to exhibit." At the other end are "subjectivist" arguments, such as those of Fredrik Barth in, *Ethnic Groups and Boundaries* (Boston: Little, Brown, and Co., 1969). See also, the work of Michael T. Hannan, "The Dynamics of Ethnic Boundaries in Modern States," in John Meyer and Michael Hannan (eds.), *National Development and the World System* (Chicago: The University of Chicago Press, 1979), pp. 253–275, which emphasizes the subjective boundaries that groups themselves draw to distinguish themselves from others. In the middle of this continuum are "compositivist" arguments that encompass aspects of both objective and subjective definitions.

9 See Emile Durkheim and Marcel Maus, *Primitive Classification,* trans. Rodney Needham (Chicago: University of Chicago Press, 1963).

10 Pierre Bourdieu, *Distinction*, trans. Richard Nice (Cambridge, Mass.: Harvard University Press, 1984 [1979]).

11 Anthony Giddens, *The Constitution of Society: Outline of the Theory of Structuration* (Berkeley: University of California Press, 1984).

12 For an early statement on trauma, see Freud, "Introductory Lectures" and

"Beyond the Pleasure Principle," in *The Standard Edition of the Complete Works of Sigmund Freud*, 24 vols., translated from the German under the general editorship of James Strachey (London: Hogarth Press and The Institute of Psycho-Analysis, 1953–74).

13 Plato articulated two senses of memory – one being the powers of memory or retention, and the other the powers of recollection or recall. Building upon Plato's discussions, Aristotle argued that memory is a consequence of stamping individual perceptions onto a receiving surface, and that recollection is based on the process of association by continuity, contrast, and similarity. Within this tradition, memory is conceptualized as a system of storage and retrieval mechanisms, or as mental habits resulting from actions of reinforcement and frequency of occurrence. The history of the study of memory has for the most part been a quest for the discovery of mind-brain codes, or mental faculties, that store and retrieve information. For a good overview, see, for example, Marion Perlmutter, "Research on Memory and its Development: Past, Present and Future," in Franz E. Weinert and Marion Perlmutter (eds.), *Memory Development: Universal Changes and Individual Differences* (New Jersey: Lawrence Erlbaum Associates, 1988), pp. 353–354.

14 Symptoms include chronic anxiety, fear of renewed persecution, depression, recurring nightmares, psychosomatic disorders, an inability to experience pleasure, social withdrawal, fatigue, hypochondria, an inability to concentrate, irritability, a hostile and mistrustful attitude toward the world, a profound alteration of personal identity, and in many cases, hallucinations and depersonalization. There is a wealth of literature on the long-term effects of the Holocaust on actual survivors and their children. For works on the effects on survivors see, for example, Leo Eitinger, *Concentration Camp Survivors in Norway and Israel* (Norway: Oslo University Press, 1964) and *Psychological and Medical Effects of Concentration Camps* (Haifa: Haifa University Press, 1980); and Harry Krystal and W. G. Niederland, *Psychic Traumatization: After Effects on Individuals and Communities* (Boston: Little, Brown, and Co., 1972); D. Carmil and R. S. Carel, "Emotional Distress and Satisfaction in Life Among Holocaust Survivors," *Psychological Medicine* 16 (February 1986), pp. 141–149; and Martin Wangh, "On Obstacles to the Working Through of the Nazi Holocaust Experience and on the Consequences of Failing to Do So," *Israel Journal of Psychiatry and Related Sciences* 20 (1983), 147–154.

15 See, in particular, Harvey Barocas and Carol Barocas, "Wounds of the Fathers: The Next Generation of Holocaust Victims," in *International Review of Psycholanalysis* 6 (1979), pp. 331–341. For the effects of the Holocaust on children of survivors, see, for example, Gertrud Hardtmann, *Spuren der Verfolgung: Seelische Auswirkungen des Holocaust auf die Opfer und Ihre Kinder* (Gerlingen: Bleicher Verlag, 1992); M. S. Bergmann and M. E. Jucovy (eds.), *Generations of the Holocaust* (New York: Columbia University Press, 1982); Eva Fogelman and B. Savran, "Therapeutic Groups for Children of

Survivors," *International Journal of Group Psychotherapy* 29 (1979), pp. 211–235. For the effects of the Holocaust on children of survivors who live in Germany, see Kurt Grünberg, *"Folgen nationalsozialistischer Verfolgung bei jüdischen Nachkommen Überlebender in der Bundesrepublik Deutschland,"* *Psyche* 41 (1987), pp. 492–507.

16 See, in particular, George Herbert Mead, "The Nature of the Past," in John Coss (ed.), *Essays in Honor of John Dewey* (New York: Henry Holt, 1929), pp. 235–242; George Herbert Mead, *The Philosophy of the Present* (Chicago: Open Court Publishing Co., 1932); George Herbert Mead, *The Philosophy of the Act* (Chicago: University of Chicago Press, 1938). For discussions of Mead's notion of time, see, for example, Elizabeth Ramsden Eames, "Mead's Concept of Time," in Walter Robert Corti (ed.), *The Philosophy of George Herbert Mead* (Winterthur, Switzerland: Archive für Genertische Philosophie, 1973), pp. 59–81; Harold N. Lee, "Mead's Doctrine of the Past," in *Tulane Studies in Philosophy* 12 (1963), pp. 52–75; David R. Maines, Noreen M. Sugrue, and Michael A. Katovich, "The Sociological Import of G. H. Mead's Theory of the Past," *American Sociological Review* 48 (April 1983), pp. 161–173; and, Alfred Toness, "A Notion of the Problems of the Past – With Special Reference to George Herbert Mead," *Journal of Philosophy* 24 (1932), pp. 599–606.

17 Eric Hobsbawm and Terence Ranger (eds.), *The Invention of Tradition* (New York: Cambridge University Press, 1983).

18 Because Holocaust experiences were diverse, rather than speaking about "collective memory" *per se*, a more accurate term might be, in the words of James E. Young, "collected memory," the many discrete memories that are gathered together and assigned meaning socially. See, James E. Young, *The Texture of Memory* (New Haven: Yale University Press, 1993), preface. I will continue to employ the term collective memory because the main issue I am dealing with is how these memories function for the construction of Jewish ethnic identity, and for Jews' interpersonal relationships with Germans.

19 What follows is an adaptation of an excellent discussion of factors contributing to the survival of artistic reputations. See Gladys Engel Lang and Kurt Lang, "Recognition and Renown: The Survival of Artistic Reputation," *American Journal of Sociology* 94 (July, 1988), pp. 79–109.

20 Hannah Arendt, *Eichmann in Jerusalem* (Harmondsworth: Penguin, 1964); Art Spiegelman, *Maus: A Survivor's Tale* (New York: Panthean, 1986); Anne Frank, *The Diary of Anne Frank* (London: Valentine, Mitchell, 1953); Jerzy Kosinski, *The Painted Bird* (New York: Modern Library, 1965). For example, the media play an important role in the reporting or recording of events. They affect the manner in which one remembers the Holocaust, because what is conveyed to the public as news can never replicate the event as experienced by the individual actually present at the scene. In turn, personal recollections of the Holocaust based on direct experience can also act as a means to verify

inaccuracies in the media and in the reporting and recording of the Holocaust in print or on film.

21 For an interesting discussion of how different nations deal with Holocaust memorials, see Young, *The Texture of Memory*.

22 For an excellent discussion on the nature of Jewish memory see Yosef Hayim Yerushalmi, *Zakhor* (Seattle: University of Washington Press, 1982).

23 Primo Levi, *Survival in Auschwitz*, trans. Stuart Woolf (1959; New York: Collier Books, 1986).

24 Elie Wiesel and Phillipe de Saint-Cheron, *Evil and Exile*, trans. Jon Rothschild (Notre Dame: University of Notre Dame Press, 1990), p. 15.

25 Halbwachs defines collective memory is an image of the past bounded by a social context. The importance of social context is obvious, as we remember our childhood in the context of a family, our neighborhood within the context of a local community, our career within the context of our place of employment. Maurice Halbwachs, *The Collective Memory* (New York: Harper and Row, 1980).

26 See, Charles Meier, *The Unmasterable Past* (Cambridge, Mass.: Harvard University Press, 1988).

27 Saul Friedlander, *When Memory Comes* (New York: Noonday Press, 1979), pp. 144–145.

28 See, Jean Paul Sartre, *Anti-Semite and Jew* (1948; New York: Schocken Books, 1970), and Schmuel N. Eisenstadt, "Philip Gillon, Who is a Jew?," quoted in the *Jerusalem Post*, Feb. 2, 1970, p. 7.

29 Much of this literature focuses on Jewish community life in the United States. See, for example, Steven Cohen, *American Assimilation or Jewish Revival* (Bloomington and Indianapolis: Indiana University Press, 1988); Arnold Dashefsky and Howard Shapiro, *Ethnic Identification Among American Jews* (Lantham: University Press of America, 1993); and Sidney Goldstein and Calvin Goldscheider, *Jewish Americans* (Englewood Cliffs, NJ: Prentice-Hall, 1968).

30 See, in particular, Donald Feldstein, *The American Jewish Community in the 21st Century: A Projection* (New York: American Jewish Congress, 1984); Arthur Hertzberg, *Being Jewish in America* (New York: Schocken Books, 1979) and "Assimilation: Can the Jews Survive Their Encounter With America," *Hadassah Magazine* 65 (August-September, 1983); B. Farber and L. Gordon, "Accounting for Jewish Intermarriage: An Assessment of National and Community Studies," in *Contemporary Jewry* 6 (Spring/Summer, 1982), pp. 47–75; and, U. O. Schmelz, "Jewish Survival: The Demographic Factors," in *American Jewish Year Book* 83 (1983), pp. 141–187.

31 See, for example, Charles Silberman, *A Certain People: American Jews and their Life Today* (New York: Summit Books, 1985) and "The Jewish Community in Change: Challenge to Professional Practice," *Journal of Jewish Communal Service* 58 (Fall 1981), pp. 4–11; Calvin Goldscheider, "Demography and American Jewish Survival" in M. Himmelfarb and V. Baras

(eds.), *Zero Population Growth: For Whom?* (Westport, Conn.: Greenwood Press, 1978), pp. 119–147; Calvin Goldscheider, "The Demography of Jewish Americans: Research Findings, Issues, and Challenges," in M. Sklare (ed.), *Understanding American Jewry* (New Brunswick, New Jersey: Transaction Books, 1982); Calvin Goldscheider, *Jewish Continuity and Change: Emergent Patterns in America* (Bloomington: Indiana University Press, 1986); Calvin Goldscheider, *The American Jewish Community: Social Science Research and Policy Implications* (Atlanta, Ga.: Scholars Press, 1986); and Calvin Goldscheider and Alan Zuckerman, *The Transformation of the Jews* (Chicago: The University of Chicago Press, 1984).

32 In 1880, for example, Moritz Lazarus, the cofounder of the *Völkerpsychologie* and of the *Hochschule für die Wissenschaft des Judentums*, published a pamphlet entitled *Was heißt National* (What does the nation mean)? Lazarus wrote that the nation could not be described solely in objective terms, but was dependent on subjective factors, particularly the emotional attachment of individuals or groups. Jews' attachment to Germany as a fatherland was straightforward. Lazarus wrote, "We are Germans, nothing but German, when we talk about the concept of nationality we belong to only one nation, the German one."

33 See, for example, Adolf Diamant, *Durch Freitod aus dem Leben geschiedene Frankfurter Juden 1938–43* (Frankfurt: Steinmann & Labuhn, 1983).

34 In general, three types of camps existed: transition camps, slave labor camps, and concentration camps. The first concentration camps were established in early 1933, primarily for political prisoners. In the wake of the Final Solution, death camps were established, either as separate institutions or as part of already existing concentration camps.

35 For more information on the reconstruction of the Jewish communities in Germany see Lynn Rapaport, "The Cultural and Material Reconstruction of the Jewish Communities in the Federal Republic of Germany," *Jewish Social Studies* 49, No. 2, Spring 1987.

36 *American Jewish Yearbook* 1946, p. 404.

37 *American Jewish Yearbook* 1946, pp. 314–315.

38 The Nuremberg Laws stipulated the following: (1) "racial" Jews included all persons with at least three racially Jewish grandparents; (2) first degree *Mischlinge* (mixed-marriage offspring) included all persons with two racially Jewish grandparents; and (3) second degree *Mischlinge* were all persons with one racially Jewish grandparent.

39 Other Jews in mixed marriages with either no children or children raised as Jews were Gestapo-designated "non-privileged" intermarrieds who were also relatively exempt from severe social and economic restrictions.

40 Harry Maor, "Über den Wiederaufbau der jüdischen Gemeinden in Deutschland seit 1945," Ph.D. thesis, University of Mainz (1961), p. 2.

41 The Jewish population in Frankfurt increased further to 4,055 by 1964 and to 4,886 by 1980.

42 Institute for Jewish Affairs of the World Jewish Congress, *West German Federal Legislature* (New York: Institute of Jewish Affairs, 1956), p. 20, and Muhler, p. 46.

43 The 1952 Slansky trial in Prague, the 1953 "Doctor's Plot" in the Soviet Union, and the development of a progressively anti-Jewish attitude in the Eastern bloc countries affected Jewish community life in East Germany and initiated a wave of Jewish migration in the 1950s, predominantly from East Germany to West Germany. Following the Slansky trial, similar persecutions and accusations took place in Romania, Hungary, the Soviet Union, and East Germany.

44 For example, the Council for the Protection of the Rights and Interests of Jews from Germany headquartered in New York City argued that "no Jew who escaped from Germany ought to be held by legal means or by any moral or material pressures to return, and no former citizen of Germany ought ever again to acquire German nationality except by his own wish." Furthermore, one Zionist writer stated that "there was talk of a Cherem [a historic Jewish ban and curse] to be directed against the land of Hitler, but also against all Jews who might think of settling in Germany" (Norbert Muhlen, *The Survivors: A Report on the Jews in Germany Today* (New York: Cromwell, 1962), p. 12).

45 As of January 1, 1996, 46,111 Russian immigrants have come to Germany, but not all of them are Jewish. There are family members who are not Jewish. About 22,000 Russian Jews have become members of the Jewish communities in Germany.

46 Membership also terminates due to death, change of residence to another municipality, or by a two-thirds community vote when a person impedes and/ or obstructs the pursuit of community goals.

47 Today almost 70 percent of all Jews in Germany live in six major communities, all in large metropolitan urban centers – Berlin (9,840), Frankfurt (5,715), Munich (4,168), Dusseldorf (3,586), Hamburg (2,851) and Cologne (2,167). The remaining Jewish population is spread across 500 localities, affiliated with only 59 Jewish communities, mostly situated in larger cities.

48 In the early 1970s, Heinrich Böll, the Nobel prize winning novelist, protested the Church tax by refusing to pay and refusing to relinquish his Church membership. The Roman Catholic Church pressed charges and won, thus compelling the author to pay back taxes or resign his Church membership.

49 As quoted in Marion Kaplan, "What is Religion among Jews in Contemporary Germany?" in Sander Gilman and Karen Remmler (eds.), *Reemerging Jewish Culture in Germany* (New York: New York University Press, 1994), p. 89.

50 For more information, see Edward Hartrich, *The Fourth and Richest Reich* (New York: Macmillan Publishing Co., 1980); Constantine Fitz Gibbon, *Denazification* (New York: W. W. Norton and Company, Inc., 1969); and Rapaport, "Cultural and Material Reconstruction."

51 Literature confronting the Nazi crimes against the Jews was not abundant until the late 1950s. There were a handful of articles and documents in specialized reviews, and several autobiographies treating some startling accounts of a few extreme cases. While a small literary elite began to deal with the Nazi era, they left the extermination of the Jews untouched. See, for example, Jean-Paul Bier, "The Holocaust, West Germany and Strategies of Oblivion 1947–1979," *New German Critique* 19 (Winter 1980), pp. 9–29.

52 Alexander Mitscherlich and Margarete Mitscherlich, *Die Unfähigkeit zu trauern* (Munich: A. Piper Verlag, 1967).

53 Hajo Funke, "Einige persönliche Notizen," in *Deutsche, Linke, Juden, Ästhetik und Kommunikation* 51 (1983), p. 91.

54 For instance, British historian David Irving argued that Hitler had no knowledge of the Final Solution (*Hitler's War 1942–1945*, London: Hodder and Stoughton, 1977). Although Irving's thesis was subjected to criticism by historians and journalists, in Germany it became a national bestseller. Hellmut Diwald's *Geschichte der Deutschen* claimed that the extermination camps did not exist in Germany, but neglected to point out that they were built in Poland. Diwald argued that the deportations of Jews during the war were due to the need for labor in armaments factories, and claimed that the ovens built in Birkenau were used to control a typhoid epidemic and that the gas chambers in Dachau were "test models" that were never used. When confronted with criticisms, Diwald suggested that when documents became available to the public his position would be borne out.

55 Some notable exceptions include Peter Lilienthal's *David*, Volker Schlöndorff's *The Tin Drum*, Rainer Werner Fassbinder's *Lili Marleen*, and Hans Jürgen Syberberg's *Hitler, a Film from Germany*. For a good analysis, see Saul Friedlander, *Reflections of Nazism: An Essay on Kitsch and Death* (New York, 1984).

56 Doris Kuschner, "*Die jüdische Minderheit in der Bundesrepublik Deutschland,*" Ph.D. Thesis, University of Cologne (1977), pp. 78–106.

57 The *Zentralrat* announced that Silberman's estimations were exaggerated, stating that 98 percent of the German voting population cast their ballots for democratic parties. Rather than confronting the German state and its educational institutions for an inadequate fostering of tolerant attitudes, the *Zentralrat* questioned the validity of Silberman's study. They argued that his methodology was controversial and his results invalid.

58 In the introduction Broder asks: "How representative are the outspoken views of the Zentralrat? How is it that they have a monopoly on the Jewish voice? Why is it that the pro-Filbinger explanation of Werner Nachmann cannot be discussed in the newspaper *Allgemeine Jüdische Wochenzeitung?* Isn't there more to say about Jewish life in the Federal Republic of Germany than what the Zentralrat officially broadcasts?", Henryk N. Broder and Michael Lang, *Fremd in eigenen Land* (Frankfurt: Fischer Taschenbuch Verlag Gmbtl.).

59 Similar groups emerged in Austria and Switzerland. These critical Jews in

German speaking countries form a network that meets biannually to discuss Jewish issues.

60 The controversy began in 1985 with an essay by Ernest Nolte, followed by another in 1986, which argued that Nazi barbarism was not unique and was in fact a defensive response to the genocidal domestic policies of the Soviet Union during the 1920s and 1930s. Nazism and the war, Nolte stated, were a "justified reaction" to the "Asiatic deeds of the Soviets. As for the horrors of the Final Solution, they were prefigured by the atrocities of the Soviet Gulag, which provided a model for Hitler. To oversimplify Nolte's position only slightly, neither the war nor the Final Solution could be attributed solely to the Nazis. The debate focused on the uniqueness of the Final Solution and its centrality to German national identity.

61 The Supreme Court of the Federal Republic of Germany has ruled anti-Semitism unconstitutional, and calling another person "a Jew" in a derogatory manner is a constitutional violation.

62 See, for example, EMNID Institute, *Zum Problem des Antisemitismus in der Bundesrepublik. Bielefeld: 1954;* and Herbert A. Sallen, *Zum Antisemitismus in der Bundesrepublik Deutschland* (Frankfurt: Fischer Verlag GmbH, 1980). See also Alphons Silbermann, *Sind Wir Antisemiten?* (Cologne: Verlag Wissenschaft und Politik, 1982) and Badi Panahi, *Vorurteile* (Frankfurt: Fischer Verlag GmbH., 1980).

63 As quoted in Michael Wolffsohn, "Without Identity and Future? German Jews between Diaspora and Israel," unpublished paper, p. 10.

2 Living in the land of the murderers? How Jews who live in Germany view Germans

1 Maurice Halbwachs, *On Collective Memory*, trans. Lewis A. Coser (Chicago: University of Chicago Press, 1992); George Herbert Mead, "The Nature of the Past," in John Coss (ed.), *Essays in Honor of John Dewey* (New York: Henry Holt, 1929), pp. 235–242.

2 Max Weber, *Economy and Society*, ed. Guenther Roth and Claus Wittich (Berkeley: Univeristy of California Press, 1978).

3 Victor Turner, *The Ritual Process* (New York: Aldine Publishing Co., 1969), p. 3.

4 Emile Durkheim, *The Elementary Forms of the Religious Life*, trans. Joseph Swain (London: Allen and Unwin, 1915; reprint ed. New York and London: The Free Press, 1954), pp. 14–15.

5 Bubis made these remarks in a question-and-answer period following a public presentation at the American Institute for Contemporary German Studies at Johns Hopkins (February 1994) in which he was asked about the rise of neo-Nazis and skinheads and their destabilizing impact on Germany's democracy.

6 Robert N. Bellah et al., *Habits of the Heart* (Berkeley: University of California Press, 1985).

7 Robert Brislin, *Cross-Cultural Encounters* (New York: Pergamon Press, 1981), pp. 51–52.

8 Max Horkheimer, "Foreword" in Theodore Adorno, Else Frenkel-Brunswik, Daniel J. Levinson, and R. Nevitt Sanford, *The Authoritarian Personality* (New York and London: W. W. Norton and Co., 1982), p. vii.

9 Adorno, *The Authoritarian Personality*, p. 157.

10 Lucy Dawidowicz, *The War Against the Jews 1933–1945* (New York: Bantam Books, 1975).

11 Daniel Goldhagen, *Hitler's Willing Executionaries* (New York: Alfred Knopf, 1996).

12 Stanley Milgram, *Obedience to Authority* (New York: Harper and Row, 1974).

13 Philip Zimbardo, Craig Haney, and W. Curtis Banks, "A Pirandellian Prison," in Edward Krupat (ed.) *Psychology is Social* (Greenview, Ill.: Schott, Foresman and Company, 1975), pp. 246–253.

14 Brislin, *Cross-Cultural Encounters*, p. 93.

15 Public opinion polls have supported Sylvia's perceptions of philo-Semitism during the Israeli-Arab 1967 war, and concluded that German public opinion favored Israel as opposed to the Arabs. For example, Friedemann Buttner examined the attitudes of the German media and public toward Israel at the time, and concluded that the German public completely identified with and supported Israel as opposed to the Arabs. See, Friedemann Buttner, "German Perceptions of the Middle East Conflict: Images and Identifications during the 1967 War," *Journal of Palestinian Studies* 6, n. 2 (Winter, 1977), pp. 66–81.

16 Gordon Allport, *The Nature of Prejudice* (Reading, Mass.: Addison-Wesley, 1954).

17 Such views are not far-fetched. Public opinion polls have documented strong ethnocentric prejudices currently directed against foreign guest workers such as Turks. Sociologist Fredrick Weil, for instance, argues that Germany is no different from other Western democracies in its tendency to seek a scapegoat during periods of social or economic crises. See Frederick Weil, "The Imperfectly Mastered Past: Anti-Semitism in West Germany Since the Holocaust," *New German Critique* 20 (Spring-Summer, 1980), pp. 135–153.

18 Robert K. Merton, *Social Theory and Social Structure* (New York: The Free Press, 1968).

19 Ferdinand de Saussure, "Signs and Language," *Course in General Linguistics* (New York: McGraw-Hill, 1964), as quoted in Jeffrey C. Alexander and Steven Seidman (eds.), *Culture and Society* (Cambridge: Cambridge University Press, 1990), p. 55.

20 For a brief introductory overview of the manner in which language is applied in the analysis of cultures, see, for example, Abraham Rosman and Paula Rubel, *The Tapestry of Culture* (New York: Random House, 1985), pp. 23–32; Robert B. Taylor, *Cultural Ways* (Boston: Allyn and Bacon, 1976), pp.

82–96; see also, for an overview and examples, Johnetta B. Cole (ed.), *Anthropology for the Eighties* (New York: The Free Press, 1982), pp. 65–104.

21 Comparative and historical linguistics tries to determine how language changes through time and geographical diversity. Lexicon statistics or glotto-chronology, a controversial technique used by some linguists, attempts to determine whether vocabulary and grammatical changes occur at constant rates in order to determine the point in time when similar languages detached from one another.

22 For the development of the concept of "speech community" see, for example, John J. Gumperz, "Speech Variation and the Study of Indian Civilization" in Dell Hymes (ed.), *Language in Culture and Society* (New York: Harper and Row, 1964) pp. 416–423; and John J. Gumperz, "Linguistic and Social Interaction in Two Communities," in John J. Gumperz and Dell Hymes (eds.), "The Ethnography of Communications," *American Anthropologist* 66 (December 1964), pp. 137–153.

23 Note the differences between white, Latino, Asian, Jewish, and "Black English," or a working-class Brooklyn accent and a speaker from Boston's upper-crust Beacon Hill, and, of course, as Deborah Tanner articulated in her best seller, *You Just Don't Understand*, there are gender differences in dialogue and linguistic style.

24 Anselm Strauss, *Mirrors and Masks: The Search for Identity* (Glencoe, Ill: The Free Press, 1959), p. 160.

25 Joseph Vendryes, *Language* (New York: Alfred Knopf, 1925), p. 249, as quoted in Strauss, *Mirrors and Masks*, 1959, p. 160.

26 See Suzanne J. Kessler and Wendy McKenna, *Gender: An Ethnomethodological Approach* (New York: Wiley, 1978), pp. 1–20.

27 Friedrich Nietzsche, "On Truth and Falsity in Their Ultramoral Sense" [1873] in Oscar Levy (ed.), *The Complete Works of Friedrich Nietzsche*, trans. Maximilian A. Magge (New York: Gordon 1974), quoted in Howard Eilberg-Schwartz, *The Savage in Judaism* (Bloomington and Indianapolis: Indiana University Press, 1990), p. 115.

28 Erving Goffman, *The Presentation of Self in Everyday Life* (New York: Doubleday, 1959), p. 1.

29 As quoted in Goffman, *The Presentation of Self*, p. 3.

30 Erving Goffman, *Stigma* (Englewood Cliffs, NJ: Prentice Hall, 1964), p. 4.

31 For a good example of this strategy, see Nancy J. Herman, "Return to Sender: Reintegrative Stigma-Management Strategies of Ex-Psychiatric Patients, *Journal of Contemporary Ethnography* 22 (October, 1993), pp. 295–330.

32 The public lecture was given on November 10, 1993, at the American Institute for Contemporary German Studies, at the Johns Hopkins University in Washington, DC.

33 As quoted in Detlev Claussen, "In the House of the Hangman," in Anson Rabinbach and Jack Zipes (eds.), *Germans and Jews Since the Holocaust* (New York: Holmes and Meier: 1986), p. 50.

34 Franz Steiner, *Taboo* (Harmondsworth: Penguin Books Ltd., 1956), pp. 20–21.
35 Goffman, *Stigma,* pp. 4–5.
36 Mary Douglas, *Purity and Danger* (Harmondsworth: Penguin Books, 1966).
37 Murray S. Davis, *Intimate Relations* (New York: Free Press, 1973), p. 4.
38 George J. McCall and J. L. Simmons, *Identities and Interactions*, rev. ed. (New York and London: The Free Press, 1966), p. 104.

3 Here in Germany I am a Jew: identity images and the criteria for group membership

1 Georg Simmel, *Conflict and the Web of Group Affiliations*, trans. Kurt H. Wolff (New York: The Free Press, 1955).
2 These social scientists espoused "melting pot" theories that were described in Chapter 1.
3 Louis Wirth, *The Ghetto* (Chicago: The University of Chicago Press, 1928).
4 Gustav Landauer, "Jewishness is an Inalienable Spiritual Sensibility," in Mendes-Flohr and Reinharz, *The Jew in the Modern World*, p. 240; Jean-Paul Sartre, *Anti-Semite and Jew* (New York: Schocken Books, 1970 [1948]); Schmuel N. Eisenstadt, "Philip Gillion, Who is a Jew," *Jerusalem Post*, Feb. 2, 1970, p. 7.
5 As quoted in Daniel Bell, "Jewishness As Memory," in Mendes-Flohr and Reinharz, *The Jew in the Modern World*, p. 242.
6 See, in particular, Dashefsky and M. Shapiro, *Ethnic Identification*, pp. 1–9. Harold Himmelfarb points out that most early studies of Jewish life in Diaspora communities were of Jewish identity, and that later studies have been more of Jewish identification. This is due to historical circumstances, early studies were concerned with integration, and later studies with survival. Also, there has been a disciplinary shift in studying Jewish life: in former times it was primarily conducted by psychologists, more recently by sociologists and political scientists. For a good overview of these studies, see Harold S. Himmelfarb, "Research on American Jewish Identity and Identification: Progress, Pitfalls, and Prospects," in Marshall Sklare (ed.), *Understanding American Jewry* (New Brunswick and London: Transaction Books, 1982), pp. 56–95. For an overview of the sociological perspective on Jews see, for example, Jack Nusan Porter (ed.), *The Sociology of American Jews: A Critical Anthology* (Washington, DC: University Press of America, 1980). For an interesting look at American Jewry from an anthropological perspective, see Walter P. Zenner (ed.), *Persistence and Flexibility* (Albany: State University of New York Press, 1988).
7 Council of Jewish Federations, *Highlights of the CJF 1990 National Jewish Population Survey* (New York: CJF Publication, 1991) p. 28.
8 Durkheim, *Elementary Forms of the Religious Life.*
9 Marshall Sklare and Joseph Greenblum, *Jewish Identity on the Suburban Frontier*, 2nd ed. (Chicago: University of Chicago Press, 1979,) p. 46.

10 Statistisches Bundesamt, 1995.

11 Rosh Hashonah is the Jewish New Year. It falls on the first of the lunar month Tishri, which usually occurs in September. The ten days from Rosh Hashonah until Yom Kippur are known as the "Ten Days of Repentance." In these ten days, the most solemn of the year, all of the world is judged by God. These ten days end on Yom Kippur, the Day of Atonement, on which the fate of each human being is decided for the coming year. On Yom Kippur Jews are suppose to serve God as if they were angels, not mortals, and refrain from eating and drinking, their sole task being to praise God.

12 See Goldstein and Goldscheider, *Jewish American*; Morris Axelrod, Floyd J. Fowler Jr., and Arnold Gurin, *A Community Survey for Long Range Planning: A Study of the Jewish Population of Greater Boston* (Boston: Combined Jewish Philanthropies, 1967); Floyd J. Fowler, Jr., *1975 Community Survey: A Study of the Jewish Population of Greater Boston* (Boston: Combined Jewish Philanthropies of Greater Boston, 1977); Harold S. Himmelfarb, "Patterns of Assimilation-Identification among American Jews," *Ethnicity* 6 (September 1979), pp. 249–267.

13 Sklare, *Jewish Identity*, p. 49.

14 I listed a number of religious ritual practices, and asked respondents to check the number of practices that they adhered to regularly, and the number of practices that were adhered to regularly in their home when they were growing up and in their parents' home when their mother and father were about their age. I also posed questions regarding how often they and their parents attended synagogue, and how often their parents attended synagogue before the Second World War.

15 Chanukah is the eight-day holiday commemorating the destruction of the Second Temple and of the victory of the Jewish Maccabees over the Syrians.

16 Two other trends are apparent regarding religious observance in the Jewish community in Frankfurt. First, among the first generation, traditional ritual practice (such as frequent worship, dietary law observance, and Sabbath candle lighting) was less frequent after the Second World War. This was also true of synagogue attendance. Before the war, 15 percent of fathers attended synagogue on a daily basis, whereas today the percentage has fallen to only 7.6 percent; 32 percent of respondents' fathers attended synagogue on a weekly basis prior to the war, but only 20 percent do so today. The decrease in regular synagogue attendance has been displaced by an increase in High Holiday worship. Prior to the Second World War, about 45 percent of respondents' fathers were High Holiday worshippers, whereas today nearly three-quarters (74.2 percent) are. The same patterns prevail for respondents' mothers. Second, and similar to patterns documented in the United States and elsewhere, cohort differences between Jews exist. To maintain consistency, I asked respondents to describe which of the previously mentioned observances were practiced more or less regularly in their home when their parents were about the respondents' present age. The older cohorts were more

observant than the younger ones, as illustrated in a decline in the performance of traditional rituals.

17 Pnina Nave Levinson, "Religiöse Richtungen und Entwicklungen in den Gemeinden," in Micha Brumlik, Doron Kiesel, Cilly Kugelmann, and Julius Schoeps (eds.), *Jüdisches Leben in Deutschland seit 1945* (Frankfurt: Athenäum Verlag GmbH, 1988), p. 141.

18 Levinson argues that Geneva, for example, in the past twenty years has developed a liberal religious community that has its own *Gemeinde* center. In Zurich, the *Gemeinde* has a liberal character (and it even publishes its own newspaper entitled *Luchot* and the same is true of Holland. Luxembourg's Jewish community, she remarks, offers activities for liberal Jews, though the Rabbi there is conservative. See Levinson, "Religiöse Richtungen," p. 144.

19 As quoted in Levinson, "Religiöse Richtungen," p. 141.

20 Landauer, "Jewishness Is an Inalienable Spiritual Sensibility," p. 241.

21 Dashefsky and Shapiro, *Ethnic Identification*, p. 116.

22 Rabbi Morris N. Kertzer, *What is a Jew?* (New York: Macmillan Publishing Co., 1953), p. 103.

23 Durkheim, *The Elementary Forms of Religious Life*, p. 62.

24 Daniel Bell, "Jewishness As Memory," in Mendes-Flohr and Reinharz, *The Jew in the Modern World* (eds.), p. 242. A *Minyan* is a quorum of ten males traditionally required for public worship. *Yizkor* is the memorial prayer recited on certain holidays, particularly Yom Kippur.

25 It has been argued that *Roots* (Garden City, NY: Doubleday, 1976) has had a similar impact on African American society in the United States, by demonstrating the process of historical search, and the tracing of family history. For an excellent article on this linkage, see Tamara Hareven, "The Search for Generational Memory," in David K. Dunaway and Willa K. Baum (eds.), *Oral History* (Nashville, Tennessee: American Association for State and Local History, 1984), pp. 284–263.

26 As quoted in Victor Turner, *Dramas, Fields and Metaphors* (Ithaca and London: Cornell University Press, 1974), p. 45.

27 This point will be explored further in Chapter 4.

28 Purim commemorates the deliverance from extermination of the Jews of the Persian Empire during the reign of Xerxes I (485–465 BCE). In the book of Esther, the story is told of Haman, Xerxes's chief minister, who engineers a plot to annihilate the Persian Jews. With the consent of King Xerxes, he sets the date of their doom by lot. The King's wife Esther, a Jewess, intercedes and as a result the King authorizes the Jews to defend themselves. On their fated day of doom, the Jews rout their enemies. Today Jews celebrate this victory and call it Purim – the festival of lots – alluding to the lots Hanan had drawn.

29 A spring festival commemorating the Exodus of the children of Israel from bondage in Egypt, it is observed for seven days by reform Jews and the state of Israel, and for eight days by Jews in the Diaspora. It is the first of three Pilgrim festivals, "the festival of Freedom," and the Hebrew word "pesah"

(meaning Passover) refers to the "passing over" of the houses of the Children of Israel during one of the ten plagues – the plague of the first born (see Exodus 12:13). The seder ritual is the highlight of the festival – a festive banquet on the first night with the recitation of the Hagadah, the account of Egyptian bondage, the exodus from Egypt, and thanksgiving for redemption.

30 The *Gemeinde's* social services division is staffed with one social worker, three nurses, and a part-time secretary. Close to 4,000 home visits to nearly 200 families are carried out annually. Services range from helping disabled and elderly people in walking and bathing, to shopping for them, reading to them, doing their laundry, preparing meals, and administering medicine. For Passover, approximately 160 families were given matzos, matzo meal, wine, money and other goods necessary to prepare a seder. For Rosh Hashonah approximately 150 families were helped in a similar manner. The social services division supports nearly 110 families monthly – financially and otherwise.

31 A kosher butcher shop also exists in Frankfurt, but it has no official *Gemeinde* affiliation. The kosher restaurant is open daily to Jews and non-Jews, with special rates for Jewish students, family parties, and kiddishim. The Jewish cemetery, however, is exclusive – non-Jews and Jews not registered with the *Gemeinde* cannot be buried there.

32 In its formative years, the agency handled mostly children with so-called neurotic symptoms such as asthma, bed-wetting, stuttering, eating and sleeping disorders, or nail-biting. In more recent years, however, there has been an increase in the number of children with more serious behavioral disorders such as interaction disorders, aggressive personalities, low frustration tolerance, and disorientation. There has also been an increase in the number of families applying for this service.

33 Emile Durkheim, *Moral Education: A Study in the Theory and Application of the Sociology of Education* (1925; New York: The Free Press, 1961), p. 240.

34 Kai Erikson, *Everything in its Path* (New York: Touchstone, 1976), p. 80.

35 Kurt H. Wolff, editor and translator, *The Sociology of Georg Simmel* (New York: The Free Press, 1950).

36 According to historian Paula Hyman, some small Jewish communities (approximately 50,000 members) have been viewed by historians as being culturally significant in their host society. See, Paula Hyman, "The Jewish Family: Looking for a Useable Past," *Congress Monthly* (October 1975).

37 Claude Fischer, *To Dwell Among Friends: Personal Networks in Town and City* (Chicago: University of Chicago Press, 1982).

38 Everett V. Stonequest, *The Marginal Man* (New York: Charles Scribner's Sons, 1937). See also Robert E. Park, "Human Migration and the Marginal Man," *American Journal of Sociology* 33 (1928), pp. 881–893.

39 Esther Dischereit, *Jöemis Tisch: Eine jüdische Geschichte* (Frankfurt: Suhrkamp Verlag, 1988), p. 23.

40 See Kurt Lewin, *Resolving Social Conflicts* (New York: Harper, 1948). See

also Simmel, *Conflict and the Web of Group Affiliation*, and Lewis Coser, *The Functions of Social Conflict* (New York: Free Press, 1964).

41 Lea Fleischmann, *Dies ist nicht mein Land* (Hamburg: Hoffman und Campe Verlag, 1980), p. 25.

42 Goffman, *Stigma*, p. 3.

43 Jean Amery, "On the Necessity and Impossibility of Being a Jew," in Rabinbach and Zipes, (eds.), *Germans and Jews*, pp. 83–84.

44 Dischereit, *Jöemis Tisch*, p. 23.

45 Dan Diner, "Fragments of an Uncompleted Journey," in Rabinbach and Zipes (eds.), *Germans and Jews*, p. 127.

4 I have German citizenship but I wouldn't call myself a German: ethnic group loyalty and the lack of national affiliation

1 During Passover Jews are supposed to abstain from eating leavened products.

2 The Bar Mitzvah is a rite of passage symbolizing the transition from childhood to adulthood for males in the Jewish religion, at or after the age of thirteen.

3 Richard F. Nyrop, *Federal Republic of Germany* (Washington, DC: Library of Congress, 1982), p. 247.

4 The extent and manner in which groups relate to the modern nation-state impacts its stability, political legitimacy, cohesiveness, and ultimately its continuity as a vital political entity.

5 Within an ethnically heterogeneous nation, the nature of one's attachment to an ethnic group, and to the nation of which one is a citizen, has been a topic of debate for scholars of ethnicity and nationalism. In the 1960s and 1970s, debates and theories on nationalism viewed nations and nationhood as the result of the process of modernization. Drawing on the classic work of Karl Deutsch, *Nationalism and Social Communication* (Cambridge, Mass.: MIT Press, 1953), the arguments focused on the development of nations due to economic transformation. Contemporary scholars maintain that nationalism is a recent phenomenon – a social construction, emphasizing the elements of invention, imagined communities, and social engineering. See, for example, Benedict Anderson, *Imagined Communities* (London: Verso, 1983) and Anthony Cohen, *The Symbolic Construction of Community* (London and New York: Tavistock, 1985).

6 Herbert C. Kelman, "Patterns of Personal Involvement in the National System: A Social-Psychological Analysis of Political Legitimacy," in James Rosenau (ed.), *International Politics and Foreign Policy* (New York and London: Free Press, 1969), p. 278.

7 Carlton J. H. Hayes, "Contributions of Herder to the Doctrine of Nationalism," *American Historical Review* 32, 4 (July 1927), 719–736; Sidney Bolkosky, *The Distorted Image* (New York: Elsevier, 1975), p. 63.

8 See Joyce Marie Mushaben, *Identity Without a Hinterland? Continuity and Change in National Consciousness in the German Democratic Republic, 1949–1989* (Washington, DC: American Institute for Contemporary German Studies, Research Report No. 3, July 1993), pp. 27–29.

9 Leonard W. Doob, *Patriotism and Nationalism* (New Haven and London: Yale University Press, 1964), pp. 26–27.

10 Ibid., p. 24.

11 Ibid.

12 Ibid. p. 65.

13 Johannes Kirschweng, "Heimat," in *Reimmichls Volkskalender* (Bozen: Athesia, 1953), p. 54, as quoted in Doob, *Patriotism and Nationalism*, p. 66.

14 See Mushaben, *Identity Without a Hinterland?*, pp. 27–29.

15 Ibid.

16 Doris Kuschner, *Die jüdische Minderheit in der Bundesrepublik Deutschland*, pp. 123–129.

17 Anson Rabinbach, "Introduction" in Rabinbach and Zipes (eds.), *Germans and Jews*, p.18.

18 Kelman, "Patterns of Personal Involvement," p. 280.

19 The Royal Institute of International Affairs, *Nationalism* (London and Edinburgh: Frank Cass and Co., Ltd., 1963), pp. xviii–xix.

20 Bolkosky, *The Distorted Image*, 48–49.

21 Prior to the First World War, *völkische* ideas had been rejected by Jewish assimilationists in favor of more liberal values. After the First World War, however, *völkische* ideas had their influence on many younger Jews who wished to be accepted as Germans and to deepen their Jewish-German identity.

22 George Mosse, *Germans and Jews* (Detroit: Wayne State University Press, 1987), p. 79.

23 Ibid.

24 Michael Wolffsohn, "Without Identity and Future, German Jews Between Diaspora and Israel," unpublished paper, p. 2. Shorter version published in *Die Zeit*, May 27, 1983.

25 Kuschner, *Die jüdische Minderheit in der Bundesrepublik Deutschland*, pp. 136–137.

26 See, Micha Brumlik, *"Zur Identität der zweiten Generation deutscher Juden nach der Shoah in der Bundesrepublik,"* in *Jüdisches Leben in Deutschland seit 1945* (Frankfurt: Athenäum Verlag GmbH, 1988), pp. 172–76.

27 For a good review of recent books on modern German Jewry, see Shulamit Magnus, "German Jewish History," *Modern Judaism* 11 (February 1991).

28 Anderson, *Imagined Communities*, p. 15.

29 Michèle Lamont, *Money, Morals and Manners* (Chicago: Chicago University Press); see also, for example, Fredrik Barth, *Ethnic Groups and Boundaries* (Boston: Little Brown & Co., 1969).

30 See Ignatz Bubis, *Ich bin ein deutscher Staatsbürger jüdischen Glaubens: Ein*

Autobiographisches Gespräch mit Edith Kohn (Cologne: Verlag Kiepenheuer & Witsch, 1993).

31 Robert K. Merton, *Sociological Ambivalence* (New York: The Free Press, 1976), p. 6.

32 See Dan Diner, "Negative Symbiose," *Babylon* 1 (Frankfurt: Verlag Neue Kritik, 1986).

33 As quoted in Bolkosky, *The Distorted Image*, p. 188.

34 Cohen, *The Symbolic Construction of Community*, p. 21.

35 Ibid.

36 Rafael Seligmann, *Rubinsteins Versteigerung* (Frankfurt: Eichborn, 1989), p. 54.

37 See Kuschner, *Die jüdische Minderheit in der Bundesrepublik Deutschland*.

38 *American Jewish Yearbook*, 1968, p. 488.

39 Martin Löw-Beer, "Von Nirgendwo nach Israel und zurück: Zum Wandel des Öffentlichkeitsverständnisses einiger jüdischer Jugendzeitschriften in den letzten dreissig Jahren," *Babylon* 9 (Frankfurt: Verlag Neue Kritik, Nov. 1991) pp. 47–77.

40 I must mention, however, that neither Bodemann nor Löw-Beer sample randomly, nor review all *Gemeindeblätter* or newsletters. Therefore their conclusions should be taken cautiously. See Y. Michal Bodemann, "Staat und Ethnizität: Der Aufbau der jüdischen Gemeinden im Kalten Krieg," in Brumlik et al., *Jüdisches Leben in Deutschland seit 1945*, pp. 49–69.

41 Walter W. Jacob Oppenheimer, *Jüdische Jugend in Deutschland* (Munich: Bronner and Daentler KG, 1967), p. 67.

42 *Frankfurter jüdisches Gemeindeblatt*, 1982, nos. 1–4.

43 See Julius Schoeps, *Leiden an Deutschland* (Munich: R. Piper GmbH & Co., 1990), pp. 103–106.

44 See Diner, "Negative Symbiose."

45 Slang for a German Jew.

46 Bolkosky, *The Distorted Image*, p. 12.

47 All second-generation respondents spoke fluent German – most without an accent. In fact, one reason they claimed to have more contact with Germans than their parents was precisely that they were fluent. They did not feel constrained by language barriers.

48 *Webster's New Twentieth Century Dictionary*, 2nd ed., s.v. "citizenship, patriotism."

49 In trying to assess political apathy and disaffiliation, we often think of why only some citizens exercise certain political acts that all citizens are formally empowered to exercise. However, some forms of participation have structural or legal restrictions peculiar to a particular country that may make it difficult to compare with a socially induced lack of motivation. According to Giuseppe Di Palma, voting is one such activity. See Giuseppe Di Palma, *Apathy and Participation* (New York and London: The Free Press, 1970), pp. 32–44.

50 Richard E. Dawson, Kenneth Prewitt, and Karen S. Dawson, *Political*

Socialization (Boston and Toronto: Little, Brown and Co., 1966), pp. 14–32. See also, David Easton, *A Framework for Political Analysis* (Englewood Cliffs, NJ: Prentice-Hall, 1965); and David Eastman, *A Systems Analysis of Political Life* (New York: Wiley, 1965).

51 Kelman, "Patterns of Personal Involvement," p. 280.
52 Ibid.

5 My friends are not typical Germans: the character of Jewish–German friendships

1 For a good introduction to this perspective, see Howard Eilberg-Schwartz (ed.), *People of the Body* (Albany: SUNY Press, 1992).
2 Ashley Montagu, *Man's Most Dangerous Myth: The Fallacy of Race* (1942; London: Oxford University Press, 1974), p. 353.
3 Sander Gilman, *The Jewish Body* (New York: Routledge, 1991), p. 203.
4 Oskar Panizza, "The Operated Jew," as quoted in Gilman, *The Jewish Body*, p. 203.
5 Ibid., p. 205.
6 Harold R. Isaacs, *Idols of the Tribe: Group Identity and Political Change* (New York: Harper & Row, 1975).
7 Mary Waters, *Ethnic Options* (Berkeley: University of California Press, 1990).
8 For empirical studies that have attempted to debunk this myth, see Raphael Patai and Jennifer Patai Wing, *The Myth of the Jewish Race* (New York: Charles Scribner's Sons, 1975); Karl Kautsky, *Are the Jews a Race* (Westport, CT: Greenwood Press, 1926); and Maurice Fishberg, *The Jews: A Study in Race and Environment* (London: The Walter Scott Publishing Co., 1911).
9 The opposite was also true. A few respondents believed that they were not identifiable as Jews, because they had so-called Aryan features. They said things like, "I don't look Jewish because I'm blond."
10 Stuart Schoenfeld, "Integration into the Group and Sacred Uniqueness: An Analysis of Adult Bat Mitzvah," in Walter Zenner (ed.), *Persistence and Flexibility: Anthropological Perspectives on the American Jewish Experience* (Albany: SUNY Press, 1988), p. 129.
11 A Star of David is the six-pointed star symbolizing Judaism. *Chai* is the Hebrew word for life, which is often worn as a charm on a necklace. A *mezuzah* is a rectangular piece of parchment with biblical inscriptions, which is rolled up and inserted in a wooden or metal case, and affixed to the upper part of the righthand door post. A charm depicting a *mezuzah* is often worn on a necklace or bracelet.
12 Stanford Lyman and William Douglas, "Ethnicity: Strategies of Collective and Individual Impression Management," *Social Research* 40 (1963), p. 358.
13 Indeed, anthropologists Leonard Plotnicov and Myrna Silverman have documented how Jews in the United States intentionally and unintentionally signal their common ethnicity to each other to enhance the basis of their

relationship. Leonard Plotnicov and Myrna Silverman, "Jewish Ethnic Signalling: Social Bonding in Contemporary American Society," *Ethnology* 18, no. 4 (October, 1978), pp. 407–23.

14 EMNID Institute, "Current German Attitudes Toward Jews and Other Minorities: A Survey of Public Opinion" unpublished paper (New York: American Jewish Committee, 1994).

15 For example, in *Money, Morals, and Manners*, Michèle Lamont has pointed out the loose-boundedness of American society in comparison to French society.

16 Teru L. Morton and Mary Ann Douglas, "Growth of Relationships," in Steve Duck and Robin Gilmour (eds.) *Personal Relationships 2: Developing Personal Relationships* (London: Academic Press, 1981), p. 14.

17 Ibid., p. 25.

18 Valerian J. Derlega and Janusz Grzelak, "Appropriateness of Self-Disclosure," in Gordon Chelune (ed.) *Self Disclosure* (San Francisco: Jossey-Bass, 1979).

19 Kurt Lewin, *Resolving Social Conflicts* (New York: Harper & Brothers, 1948), p. 20.

20 John M. Reisman, *Anatomy of Friendship* (New York: Irvington Publishers, 1979), p. 2.

21 This is also a difficult issue for young Germans. For an interesting personal account of a German struggling with this issue, see Hajo Funke, "Einige persönliche Notizen," in *Deutsche, Linke, Juden, Ästhetik und Kommunikation* 51, June 1983.

22 *Statistisches Jahrbuch deutscher Gemeinden* (Cologne Deutscher Städtetag, 1985).

23 Eviatar Zerubavel, *The Seven Day Circle* (New York: The Free Press, 1985).

24 See, for example, Benjamin B. Ringer, *The Edge of Friendliness* (New York, Basic Books, 1967); or, more recently, William L. Yancey et al., "The Structure of Pluralism: We're all Italian Around Here, Aren't We?" *Ethnic and Racial Studies* 8 (1985), 94–116; Steven Martin Cohen, *Interethnic Marriage and Friendship* (New York: Arno Press, 1980), p. 95.

25 See C. N. Winslow, "A Study of the Extent of Agreement Between Friends' Opinions and their Ability to Estimate the Opinions of Each Other," *Journal of Social Psychology* 8 (1937), pp. 433–442; C. B. Broderick, "Predicting Friendship Behavior: A Study of Friendship Selection and Maintenance in a College Population," Ph.D. thesis, Cornell University (1956); D. Byrne, G. L. Clore, Jr., and P. Worchel, "Effects of Economic Similarity–Dissimilarity on Interpersonal Attraction," *Journal of Personality and Social Psychology* 16 (1966), 220–224; N. Miller, D. T. Campbell, H. Twedt, and E. J. O'Connell, "Similarity, Contrast, and Complementarity in Friendship Choice," *Journal of Personality and Social Psychology* 3 (1966), 3–12.

26 Steven W. Duck, *Personal Relationships and Personal Constructs: A Study of*

Friendship Formation (London: John Wiley & Sons, 1973). See, also, Graham Allen, *Friendship: Developing a Sociological Perspective* (Boulder, Col.: Westview Press, 1989); P. J. Runkel, "Cognitive Similarity in Facilitating Communication," *Sociometry* 19 (1956), pp. 178–191; H. C. Triandis, "Cognitive Complexity and Interpersonal Communication in Industry," *Journal of Applied Psychology* 43 (1959), pp. 321–326; and R. J. Menges, "Student-Instructor Cognitive Compatability in the Large Lecture Class," *Journal of Personality* 37 (1969), 444–459.

27 Michal McCall, "Boundary Rules in Relationships and Encounters," in George McCall et al. (ed.), *Social Relationships* (Chicago: Aldine Publishing Co., 1970), p. 41.

28 Gerald Suttles, "Friendship as a Social Institution," in George McCall et al. (eds.), *Social Relationships*, p. 97.

29 See Georg Simmel, "The Isolated Individual and the Dyad," in Kurt H. Wolff, (trans.), ed. and, *The Sociology of Georg Simmel* (New York: The Free Press, 1950).

30 Suttles, "Friendship as a Social Institution," p. 97.

31 A more benign way of fighting back was to be a "moral savior." A few respondents mentioned choosing careers in specific professions, such as education and psychotherapy, because it allowed them an avenue to try to "reform" the Germans. Others mentioned their political activities, such as participating in demonstrations or political clubs, as a means to try to reform or enlighten the Germans about the situation of Jews, other minorities, or other social issues in general.

6 Interethnic intimacy: the character of Jewish–German sex, love and intermarriage

1 Historically, Jewish men have intermarried at a rate about twice that of Jewish women (Steven Cohen, *Interethnic Marriage and Friendship* [New York: Arno Press, 1980], p. 122).

2 Regarding male respondents who had been divorced, two were previously married to German women and one to a Jewish woman. Among female respondents who had been divorced, two were previously married to Jewish men and one to a German.

3 William Goode defines homogamy as "marriage between people of similar traits." See William Goode, *The Family,* 2nd ed. (Englewood Cliffs, NJ: Prentice Hall, 1982).

4 As quoted in Milton Barron, *People Who Intermarry* (Syracuse: Syracuse University Press, 1946), p. 23.

5 Ibid.

6 Michael Hogg, *The Social Psychology of Cohesiveness* (New York: New York University Press, 1992), p. 100.

7 Ibid., p. 104.

8 Ira Reiss, *The Family System in America* (New York: Holt, Rinehart, and Winston, 1971).

9 As cited in John D. Cunningham and John K. Antill, "Love in Developing Romantic Relationships," in Steve Duck and Robin Gilmore (eds.), *Personal Relationships* 2 (London: Academic Press, 1981), p. 40.

10 John Mayer makes this point in *Jewish-Gentile Courtships* (New York: The Free Press, 1961). It is an adaptation of the "breakage" effect prompted by a study of voting behavior. It was found that when individuals are politically divided, yet live in a community that is Republican, the surrounding environment will cause a large proportion of residents to vote Republican. See Bernard R. Berelson, Paul F. Lazarsfeld, and William N. McPhee, *Voting* (Chicago: University of Chicago Press, 1954), pp. 98–101.

11 By *Sie*, the respondent is referring to the formal personal pronoun, which is used in the German language to signify respect. It is commonly used when conversing with strangers and acquaintances.

12 See Peter Blau, Terry Blum, and Joseph Schwartz, "Heterogeneity and Intermarriage," in *American Sociological Review* 47, no. 1 (February, 1982), 45–62; and Peter Blau and Joseph E. Schwartz, *Crosscutting Social Circles: Testing a Marcrostructural Theory of Intergroup Relations* (Orlando, Flor.: Academic Press, 1984).

13 Melford E. Spiro, *Children of the Kibbutz* (New York: Schocken Books, 1969); for a systematic investigation supporting this finding, see, Joseph Shepher, "Mate Selection Among Second Generation Kibbutz Adolescents and Adults," *Archives of Sexual Behavior* 1 (1971), pp. 293–307. See also Yonina Talmon, "Mate Selection in Collective Settlements," *American Sociological Review* 29, 4 (August 1964), 491–508.

14 In Marie Henri-Beyle, *On Love* (New York: Liveright Publishing Co, 1927), p. 16.

15 Cases like this obviously occur in Jewish communities in the United States and elsewhere. However, as mentioned earlier, there is a distinction in Germany between marrying a non-Jew and marrying a German, with a sliding scale of social disapproval.

16 The classical preconception that holding a double sexual standard would vary by social class, education, and political orientation did not hold in this case.

17 See John Mayer's interesting US study of the difficulties experienced in Jewish-Gentile courtships, *Jewish-Gentile Courtships* The difficulties here, however, are more extreme considering the backdrop of the Holocaust.

18 See Eric Klinger, *Meaning and Void: Inner Experience and the Incentives in People's Lives* (Minneapolis: University of Minnesota Press, 1977).

19 Ibid.

20 Peter Blau, Carolyn Beeker, and Kevin Fitzpatrick, "Intersecting Social Affiliations and Intermarriage," *Social Forces* 62 (1984), pp. 585–606.

7 Theoretical implications and future research

1 This statement was made by a survivor of Auschwitz at a ceremony there to commemorate the fiftieth anniversary of its liberation by the Soviet Red Army.
2 Notable exceptions include the work of Anthony Cohen and others in Anthony Cohen (ed.), *Symbolising Boundaries: Identity and Diversity in British Cultures* (Manchester, United Kingdom: Manchester University Press, 1986) and Anthony Cohen (ed.), *Belonging: Identity and Social Organisation in British Rural Cultures* (Manchester: Manchester University Press, 1982).
3 Michael Wolffsohn, "Globalentschädigung für Israel und die Juden?" in Ludolf Herbst and Constantine Goschler (eds.), *Wiedergutmachung in der Bundesrepublik Deutschland*, in *Schriftenreihe der Vierteljahreshefte für Zeitgeschichte* (Munich, 1989), pp. 161–190.
4 Diner, "Fragments of an Uncompleted Journey," p. 134.
5 Peter Blau, Terry Blum, and Joseph Schwartz, "Heterogeneity and Intermarriage," *American Sociological Review* 47, 1 (February, 1982), 48.
6 Sklare, *Jewish Identity*, p. 48.

Appendix

1 Five of the interviews were conducted in New York as part of a pre-study, where I located Jews who were born and raised in Germany and were currently living in or visiting New York.
2 At the time of the study there were approximately 30,000 Jews registered in the Jewish communities throughout West Germany. According to the *Zentralrat*, close to 70 percent of all Jews live in six major Jewish communities, all of which are in large metropolitan urban centers: Berlin (6,506), Frankfurt (4,808), Munich (3,949), Dusseldorf (2,859), Hamburg (1,415) and Cologne (1,276). As a point of reference, census figures for 1984 show the total population for those cities as follows: Berlin, 1,851,800; Frankfurt, 604,600; Hamburg 1,600,300; Cologne, 932,400; Dusseldorf, 570,700; and Munich, 1,277,000. Statistisches Bundesamt, *Statistiches Jahrbuch* (Stuttgart: W. Kohlhammer GmbH, 1985).
3 See, for example, Paul Arnsberg, *Die Geschichte der Frankfurter Juden*, vols. 1–3 (Darmstadt: Eduard Röther Verlag, 1983), and Paul Arnsberg, *Neunhundert Jahre FFM 1074–1974* (Wiesbaden: Joseph Knecht Gesamtherstellung, 1974).
4 Susan Welch notes that "the amount of bias appears to be inversely related to the proportion of the target population interviewed." See Susan Welch, "Sampling by Referral in a Dispersed Population," *Public Opinion Quarterly* 39 (Summer 1975), 238. See also, Patrick Biernacki and Dan Waldorf, "Snowball Sampling," *Sociological Methods & Research* 10 (November 1981), 141–163.
5 After the war there were mass migrations in all directions – back home in

search of missing relatives, to rehabilitation centers, and the like. Jewish community life did not stabilize in West Germany until the late 1950s. For additional information see Lynn Rapaport, "The Cultural and Material Reconstruction of the Jewish Communities in the Federal Republic of Germany," pp. 137–154.

6 These cases are mostly Jews who do not wish to be registered with the community because they do not want to pay the mandatory Church tax in Germany. I doubt there are many such unregistered persons who have lived in Frankfurt since birth, because Jews were classified as "victims of fascism" after the war, and those who registered with the Jewish communities were entitled to special privileges and rations. For additional information, see Rapaport, "The Cultural and Material Reconstruction."

7 See, for example, Raymond Gordon, *Interviewing Strategy, Techniques and Tactics* (Homewood, Ill: The Dorsey Press, 1969); and Stephen Richardson, Barbara S. Dowrenwend, and D. Klein, *Interviewing, Its Forms and Functions* (New York: Basic Books, Inc., 1965).

8 For a delightful personal discussion of these techniques see in particular the Introduction in Bronislaw Malinowski, *Argonauts of the Western Pacific* (New York: E. P. Dutton and Co., 1961); or Hortense Powdermaker, *Stranger and Friend: The Way of an Anthropologist* (New York: W. W. Norton and Co., 1966).

9 For more discussion of this technique, see John and Lyn Lofland, *Analyzing Social Settings* (Belmont: Wadsworth Publishing Company, 1971); Leonard Schatzman and Anselm L. Strauss, *Field Research* (Englewood Cliffs, NJ: Prentice-Hall, 1973); and Barney Glaser and Anselm Strauss, *Discovery of Grounded Theory: Strategies for Qualitative Research* (Chicago: Aldine Publishing Co., 1967).

Select bibliography

Adorno, Theodore W., Else Frenkel-Brunswik, Daniel J. Levinson and R. Nevitt Sanford. *The Authoritarian Personality*. New York: W. W. Norton and Co., 1969.

Alexander, Jeffrey C., ed. *Durkheimian Sociology: Cultural Studies*. Cambridge: Cambridge University Press, 1988.

Alexander, Jeffrey C., and Steven Seidman, eds. *Culture and Society*. Cambridge: Cambridge University Press, 1990.

Allport, Gordon. *The Nature of Prejudice*. Reading, Mass: Addison-Wesley, 1954.

American Jewish Committee. *The Jews in Nazi Germany*. New York: Howard Fertig, Inc., 1935.

American Jewish Committee. *The Jewish Communities of Nazi-Occupied Europe*. New York: Howard Fertig, Inc., 1944.

American Jewish Yearbook. 1945–85. Philadelphia: The Jewish Publication Society of America.

Arendt, Hannah. *The Origins of Totalitarianism*. Cleveland: The World Publishing Company, 1958.

Eichmann in Jerusalem. Harmondsworth: Penguin, 1964.

Arnsberg, Paul. "Der Aufbau der jüdischen Nachkriegsgemeinde Frankfurt am Main," in *Israel und Wir, by Keren Hajessod Jahrbuch der jüdischen Gemeinschaft in Deutschland*. Frankfurt: Verlag des Keren Hajessod, 1966.

Die jüdischen Gemeinden in Hessen. Vols. 1–2. Frankfurt: Frankfurter Societäts-Druckerei GmbH, 1971.

Neunhundert Jahre FFM 1074–1974. Wiesbaden: Joseph Knecht Gesamtherstellung, 1974.

Die Geschichte der Frankfurter Juden. Vols. 1–3. Darmstadt: Eduard Roether Verlag, 1983.

Ashkenasi, Abraham. *Modern German Nationalism.* Cambridge, Mass: Schenkman Publishing Company, 1976.

Axelrod, Morris, Floyd J. Fowler, Jr., and Arnold Gurin. *A Community Survey for Long Range Planning: A Study of the Jewish Population of Greater Boston.* Boston: Combined Jewish Philanthropies, 1967.

Balfour, Michael. *West Germany: A Contemporary History.* London: Croom Helm Ltd., 1982.

Barocas, Harvey, and Carol Barocas. "Wounds of the Fathers: The Next Generation of Holocaust Victims." *International Review of Psychoanalysis* 6 (1979), 331–341.

Bar-On, Dan. *Legacy of Silence: Encounters with Children of the Third Reich.* Cambridge, Mass.: Harvard University Press, 1989.

    "Children of Perpetrators of the Holocaust: Working Through One's Own Moral Self." *Psychiatry* 53 (1990), 229–245.

Barrera, Mario. *Race and Class in the Southwest.* Notre Dame and London: University of Notre Dame Press, 1979.

Barron, Milton L. *People Who Intermarry.* New York: Syracuse University Press, 1946.

Barth, Fredrik. *Ethnic Groups and Boundaries.* Boston: Little, Brown and Co., 1969.

Bauer, Yehuda. *A History of the Holocaust.* New York: Franklin Watts, 1982.

Becker, Howard S., ed. *Social Relationships.* Chicago: Aldine Publishing Co., 1970.

Becker, Kurt E., et al., eds. *Juden in Deutschland 1983: Integriert Oder Diskriminiert?* Landau/Pfalz: Pfaelzische Verlagsanstalt GmbH, 1983.

Bellah, Robert, et. al. *Habits of the Heart: Individualism and Commitment in American Life.* Berkeley: University of California Press, 1985.

Bendix, Reinhard. "Tradition and Modernity Reconsidered." *Comparative Studies in History and Society* 9 (1967), 292–346.

Benz, Wolfgang, ed. *Rechtsextremismus in der Bundesrepublik: Voraussetzungen, Zusammenhänge, Wirkungen.* Frankfurt: Fischer Verlag, 1980.

    Zwischen Antisemitismus und Philosemitismus: Juden in der Bundesrepublik. Berlin: Metropol Verlag, 1991.

    Jahrbuch für Antisemitismusforschung 3. Frankfurt: Campus Verlag, 1992.

Berelson, Bernard R., Paul F. Lazarsfeld, and William N. McPhee. *Voting.* Chicago: University of Chicago Press, 1954.

Berger, Peter L., and Thomas Luckmann. *The Social Construction of Reality*. New York: Anchor Books, 1967.

Berghe, Pierre L. van. *Race and Racism: A Comparative Perspective*. 2nd ed. New York: Wiley, 1978.

Bergmann, M. S., and M. E. Jucovy, eds. *Generations of the Holocaust*. New York: Columbia University Press, 1982.

Bergmann, Werner. *Antisemitismus in der Bundesrepublik Deutschland: Ergebnisse der empirischen Forschung von 1946–1989*. Opladen: Leske und Budrich, 1991.

Bergmann, Werner and Erb Rainer. *Antisemitismus in der Politischer Kultur Nach 1945*. Opladen: Westdeutscher Verlag, 1990.

Bettelheim, Bruno. *The Informed Heart*. New York: The Free Press, 1971.

Bettelheim, Bruno, and Morris Janowitz. *The Dynamics of Prejudice*. New York: Harper and Brothers, 1950.

Beuf, Ann. *Red Children in White America*. Philadelphia: University of Pennsylvania Press, 1977.

Beyle, Marie-Henri. *On Love*. New York: Liveright Publishing Corp., 1927.

Bier, Jean-Paul. "The Holocaust, West Germany and Strategies of Oblivion." *New German Critique* 19 (1980) 9–29.

Biernacki, Patrick and Dan Waldorf. "Snowball Sampling." *Sociological Methods & Research* 10, 1981.

Blau, Bruno. *The Jewish Population of Germany 1939–45*. New York: Conference on Jewish Relations, 1950.

Blau, Peter, Carolyn Beeker, and Kevin Fitzpatrick. "Intersecting Social Affiliations and Intermarriage." *Social Forces* 62 (1984).

Board of Deputies of British Jews. *The Jews in Europe: Their Post-War Situation*. Anglo-American Committee of Inquiry by the Board of Deputies of British Jews, 1946.

Bodemann, Y. Michal, ed. *Jews, Germans, Memory*. Ann Arbor: University of Michigan Press, 1996.

Bogt, Bernhard. "Chronik jüdischen Lebens in Deutschland." Bundeszentrale für politische Bildung. *Deutsche Juden–Juden in Deutschland*. Bonn: Bonner Universität-Buchdruckerei, 1991.

Bolkosky, Sidney M. *The Distorted Image: German-Jewish Perceptions of Germans and Germany, 1918–1935*. New York: Elsevier Press, 1975.

Bolles, Edmund. *Remembering and Forgetting*. New York: Walker and Company, 1988.

Bonacich, Edna and John Modell. *The Economic Basis of Ethnic Solidarity*. Berkeley, Calif.: University of California Press, 1980.

Borneman, John and Jeffrey Peck. *Sojourners*. Lincoln: University of Nebraska Press, 1995.

Bossman, Dieter. *Was ich über Adolf Hitler gehört habe*, Frankfurt: Fischer Verlag, 1977.

Bourdieu, Pierre. *Distinction*. Trans. Richard Nice. Cambridge, Ma.: Harvard University Press, 1984.

  Language and Symbolic Power. Cambridge, MA: Harvard University Press, 1991.

Brain, Robert. *Friends and Lovers*. New York: Basic Books, 1976.

Brenner, Michael. *Nach dem Holocaust*. Munich: C. H. Beck Verlag, 1995.

Brislin, Robert. *Cross-Cultural Encounters*. New York: Pergamon Press, 1981.

Broder, Henryk M., "Leiden an Deutschland; Deutsche Juden und Deutsche." *Der Spiegel*. *Spiegel-Spezial* 2 (1992), 18–29.

Broder, Henryk M. and Michael Lang, eds. *Fremd im eigenen Land: Juden in der Bundesrepublik*. Frankfurt: Fischer Taschenbuch Verlag GmbH., 1979.

Broderick, C. B. "Predicting Friendship Behavior: A Study of Friendship Selection and Maintenance in a College Population." Ph.D. diss., Cornell University, 1956.

Brumlik, Micha. "Zur Identität der zweiten Generation deutscher Juden nach der Shoah in der Bundesrepublik." *Jüdisches Leben in Deutschland seit 1945*. Frankfurt: Athenäum Verlag GmbH., 1988.

Bubis, Ignatz. *Ich bin ein deutscher Staatsbürger jüdischen Glaubens: Ein autobiographisches Gespräch mit Edith Kohn*. Cologne: Kiepenheuer & Witsch, 1993.

Bullock, Alan. *Hitler: A Study in Tyranny*. New York: Harper and Row, 1962.

Bundeszentrale für Politische Bildung, Deutsche Juden – Juden in Deutschland. Bonn: Bundeszentrale, 1991.

Burgauer, Erica. *Zwischen Erinnerung und Verdrängung – Juden in Deutschland nach 1945*. Hamburg: Rowohlt Taschenbuch Verlag, 1993.

Buttner, Friedemann. "German Perceptions of the Middle East Conflict: Images and Identifications during the 1967 War." *Journal of Palestinian Studies* 6 (1977), 66–81.

Byrne, D., G. L. Clore, Jr. and P. Worchel. "Effects of Economic Similarity-Dissimilarity on Interpersonal Attraction." *Journal of Personality and Social Psychology* 16 (1966), 220–224.

Carey, Jane Perry Clark. *The Role of Uprooted People in European Recovery*. Washington, DC: National Planning Association, 1948.

Carmil, D., and R. S. Carel. "Emotional Distress and Satisfaction in Life among Holocaust Survivors." *Psychological Medicine* 16 (1986), 141–149.

Cohen, Anthony. *The Symbolic Construction of Community*. London and New York: Tavistock Publications, 1985.

Cohen, Steven. *Interethnic Marriage and Friendship*. New York: Arno Press, 1980.

American Modernity and Jewish Identity. New York: Tavistock Publications, 1983.

American Assimilation or Jewish Revival. Bloomington, IN: Indiana University Press, 1988.

Cohn, Michael. *The Jews in Germany, 1945–1993*. Westport, CO: Praeger, 1994.

Cole, Johnnetta B., ed. *Anthropology for the Eighties*. New York: The Free Press, 1982.

Coles, Robert. *Children of Crisis*. New York: Dell Publishing Co., Inc., 1964.

Conference on Jewish Material Claims Against Germany, Inc. *Twenty Years Later 1952–72*. New York, 1972.

Conference on Jewish Material Claims Against Germany, Inc. *Ten Years of German Indemnification*. New York, Nehemiah Robinson, 1964.

Corti, Walter Robert, ed. *The Philosophy of George Herbert Mead*. Amriswiler, Switzerland: Amriswiler Bucherei, 1973.

Coss, John, ed. *Essays in Honor of John Dewey*. New York: Henry Holt, 1929.

Council of Jewish Federations. *Highlights of the CJF 1990 National Jewish Population Survey*. New York: CJF Publication, 1991.

Craig, Gordon. *The Germans*. New York: G. P. Putnam's Sons, 1982.

Dahrendorf, Ralf. *Society and Democracy in Germany*. New York: Doubleday and Co., 1967.

Dashefsky, Arnold and Howard Shapiro. *Ethnic Identification Among American Jews*. Lantham: University Press of America, 1993.

Davis, Murray S. *Intimate Relations*. New York: Free Press, 1973.

Dawidowicz, Lucy. *The War Against the Jews 1933–1945*. New York: Holt, Rinehart and Winston, 1975.

Dawson, Richard E., Kenneth Prewitt, and Karen S. Dawson. *Political Socialization*. Boston and Toronto: Little, Brown and Co., 1966.

Della Pergola, Sergio and Nitza Genuth. *Jewish Education Attained in Diaspora Communities: Data for 1970s*. Jerusalem: Hebrew University, The Institute of Contemporary Jewry, 1984.

Derlega, Valerian J., and Janusz Grzelak. "Appropriateness of Self-Disclosure," in G. J. Chelune, ed. *Self Disclosure*. San Francisco: Jossey-Bass, 1979.

Deutsch, Andre. *The Jewish Communities of the World*. New York: World Jewish Congress, 1971.

Diamont, Adolf. *Geschändete jüdische Friedhöfe in Deutschland 1945–1980*. Frankfurt: Selbstverlag, 1982
Durch Freitod aus dem Leben geschiedene Frankfurter Juden 1938–43. Frankfurt: Steinmann & Labuhn, 1983.

Dicker, Herman. *Creativity, Holocaust, Reconstruction*. New York: Sepher-Hermon Press, Inc., 1984.

Di Palma, Giuseppe. *Apathy and Participation*. New York: The Free Press, 1970.

Diner, Dan. "Negative Symbiose." *Babylon* 1 (1986), 9–20.

Dischereit, Esther. *Jöemis Tisch: Eine jüdische Geschichte*. Frankfurt: Suhrkamp Verlag, 1988.

Doob, Leonard W. *Patriotism and Nationalism*. New Haven: Yale University Press, 1964.

Douglas, Mary. *Purity and Danger*. Middlesex, England: Penguin Books, 1966.

Duck, Steven W. *Personal Relationships and Personal Constructs: A Study of Friendship Formation*. London: John Wiley & Sons, 1973.

Duck, Steven and Robin Gilmore, eds. *Personal Relationships 2*. London: Academic Press, 1981.

Dudek, Peter, ed. *Hakenkreuz und Judenwitz, Antifaschistische Jugendarbeit in der Schule*. Bensheim: päd. extra Buchverlag, 1980.

Durkheim, Emile. *The Elementary Forms of the Religious Life*. Trans. Joseph Ward Swain. 2nd rev. ed. New York: The Free Press, 1965 [1915].
Moral Education: A Study in the Theory and Application of the Sociology of Education. Trans. E. K. Wilson and H. Schnurer. New York: The Free Press, 1961 [1925].

Durkheim, Emile and Marcel Maus. *Primitive Classification*. Trans. Rodney Needham. Chicago: University of Chicago Press, 1963.

Eastman, David. *A Systems Analysis of Political Life*. New York: Wiley, 1965.

Easton, David. *A Framework for Political Analysis*. Englewood Cliffs, NJ: Prentice-Hall, 1965.

Edinger, Lewis J. *West German Politics*. New York: Columbia University Press, 1986.

Eilberg-Schwartz, Howard. *The Savage in Judaism*. Bloomington, IN: Indiana University Press, 1990.

Eilberg-Schwartz, Howard, ed. *People of the Body*. Albany: SUNY Press, 1992.

Eisenstadt, Schmuel N. "Philip Gillon, Who is a Jew?" *Jerusalem Post*, February 2, 1970.

Eitinger, Leo. *Concentration Camp Survivors in Norway and Israel*. London: Allen and Unwin, 1964.

Psychological and Medical Effects of Concentration Camps. Haifa: Haifa University Press, 1980.

Eitzen, Stanley D. *In Conflict and Order*. Boston: Allyn and Bacon, 1988.

Elazar, Daniel J. *Jewish Communities in Frontier Societies: Argentina, Australia, and South Africa*. New York: Holmes and Meier, 1983.

Elazar, Daniel J., et al. *The Jewish Communities of Scandinavia: Sweden, Denmark, Norway, and Finland*. Lantham: University Press of America, 1983.

Elazar, Daniel J., et al. *The Balkan Jewish Communities: Yugoslavia, Bulgaria, Greece and Turkey*. Lantham: University Press of America, 1984.

Eliach, Yaffe, ed. *Hasidic Tales of the Holocaust*. New York: Oxford University Press, 1982.

EMNID Institute. *Zum Problem des Antisemitismus in der Bundesrepublik*. Bielefeld, 1954.

Current German Attitudes Toward Jews and Other Minorities: A Survey of Public Opinion. New York: American Jewish Committee, 1994.

Engelmann, Bernt. *Germany Without Jews*. New York: Bantam Books, 1984.

Epstein, Helen. *Children of the Holocaust*. New York: G. P. Putnam's Sons, 1979.

Erikson, Kai. *Everything in its Path*. New York: Touchstone, 1976.

Fackenheim, Emil. *God's Presence in History*. New York: Harper Torchbook, 1972.

Farber, B., and L. Gordon. "Accounting for Jewish Intermarriage: An Assessment of National and Community Studies." *Contemporary Jewry* 6 (1982), 47–75.

Federal Ministry of Interior. *Verfassungsschutzbericht 1983*. Bonn, 1984.

Feinberg, Anat. *Wiedergutmachung im Programm: Jüdisches Schicksal im deutschen Nachkriegsdrama*. Cologne: Prometh, 1988.

Feldman, Lily Gardner. *The Special Relationship Between West Germany and Israel*. Boston: Allen & Unwin, 1984.

"Comment," in *German Unification and the Question of Antisemitism.* ed. Frank Stern. New York: American Jewish Committee, 1993.

Feldstein, Donald. *The American Jewish Community in the 21st Century: A Projection.* New York: American Jewish Congress, 1984.

Fentress, James and Chris Wickham. *Social Memory.* Cambridge, Mass.: Basil Blackwell Publishers, 1992.

Fischer, Claude. *To Dwell Among Friends: Personal Networks in Town and City.* Chicago: University of Chicago Press, 1982.

Fishberg, Maurice. *The Jews: A Study in Race and Environment.* London: The Walter Scott Publishing Co., 1911.

Fishman, Joshua A., ed. *Readings in the Sociology of Language.* The Hague: The Netherlands: Mouton & Company, 1968.

Fleischmann, Lea. *Dies ist nicht mein Land. Eine Jüdin verläßt Deutschland.* Hamburg: Hoffman und Campe Verlag, 1980.

Fogelman, Eva and B. Savran. "Therapeutic Groups for Children of Survivors." *International Journal of Group Psychotherapy* 29 (1979), 211–235.

Fowler, Floyd J., Jr. *1975 Community Survey: A Study of the Jewish Population of Greater Boston.* Boston: Combined Jewish Philanthropies of Greater Boston, 1977.

Francis, Emerich K. *Interethnic Relations: An Essay in Sociological Theory.* New York: Elsevier Scientific Publishing Co., Inc., 1976.

Frank, Anne. *The Diary of Anne Frank,* London: Vallentine, Mitchell, 1953.

Frankfurter jüdisches Gemeindeblatt 1980–94.

Frenkel-Brunswik, Else, Daniel J. Levinson, and R. Nevitt Sanford. *The Authoritarian Personality.* New York and London: W. W. Norton and Co., 1982.

Freud, Sigmund. "Introductory Lectures" and "Beyond the Pleasure Principle," in James Strachey and Anna Freud, eds., *The Standard Edition of the Complete Works of Sigmund Freud,* 24 vols. London: Hogarth Press and The Institute of Psycho-Analysis, 1953–74.

Friedlander, Saul. *When Memory Comes.* New York: Noonday Press, 1979.

Frisch, Michael. "American History and the Structures of Collective Memory: A Modest Exercise in Empirical Iconography." *Journal of American History* 75 (1989), 1130–1155.

Funke, Hajo. "Einige persönliche Notizen." *Deutsche, Linke, Juden. Ästhetik und Kommunikation* 51 (1983), 90–93.

Gans, Herbert J. *The Urban Villagers: Group and Class in the Life of Italian Americans.* New York: The Free Press, 1962.

The Levittowners: Ways of Life and Politics in a New Suburban Community. New York: Pantheon Books, 1967.

"Symbolic Ethnicity: The Future of Ethnic Groups and Cultures in America." *Ethnic and Racial Studies* 2 (1979), 1–20.

Ganther, Heinz. *Die Juden in Deutschland, Ein Almanach.* Hamburg: Gala Verlag, 1953.

Gershon, Karen. *Postscript.* London: Trinity Press, 1969.

Gibbon, Constantine Fitz. *Denazification.* New York: W. W. Norton and Company, Inc., 1969.

Giddens, Anthony. *The Constitution of Society: Outline of the Theory of Structuration.* Berkeley: University of California Press, 1984.

Gilman, Sander. *Jewish Self-Hatred.* Baltimore: The Johns Hopkins University Press, 1986.

The Jew's Body. New York: Routledge, 1991.

Gilman, Sander and Karen Remmler, eds. *Reemerging Jewish Culture in Germany.* New York: New York University Press, 1994.

Ginzel, Günther, ed. *Antisemitismus: Erscheinungsformen der Judenfeindschaft gestern und heute.* Cologne: Verlag Wissenschaft und Politik, 1991.

Glaser, Barney and Anselm L. Strauss. *Status Passage.* Chicago: Aldine Atherton, 1971.

The Discovery of Grounded Theory. Chicago: Aldine Publishing Co., 1973.

Glazer, Nathan, and Daniel P. Moynihan. *Beyond the Melting Pot: The Negroes, Jews, Italians, and Irish of New York City.* Cambridge, Mass.: MIT Press, 1963.

Glazer, Nathan, and Daniel P. Moynihan, eds. *Ethnicity: Theory and Experience.* Cambridge, Mass.: Harvard University Press, 1975.

Goffman, Erving. *The Presentation of Self in Everyday Life.* New York: Doubleday and Company, 1959.

Encounters. Indianapolis: Bobbs-Merrill Co., Inc., 1961.

Behavior in Public Places. New York: The Free Press, 1963.

Stigma: Notes on the Management of Spoiled Identity. Englewood Cliffs, NJ: Prentice-Hall, Inc., 1963.

Relations in Public. New York: Harper and Row, 1971.

Goldscheider, Calvin. "Demography and American Jewish Survival," in M. Himmelfarb and V. Baras, eds. *Zero Population Growth: For Whom?* Westport, Conn.: Greenwood Press, 1978.

"Demography of Jewish Americans: Research Findings, Issues, and Challenges," in Marshall Sklare, ed. *Understanding American Jewry.* New Brunswick, NJ: Transaction Books, 1982.

The American Jewish Community: Social Science Research and Policy Implications. Atlanta, Georgia: Scholars Press, 1986.

American Jewish Fertility. Atlanta, Georgia: Scholars Press, 1986.

Jewish Continuity and Change: Emergent Patterns in America. Bloomington, IN: Indiana University Press, 1986.

Goldscheider, Calvin, and Alan Zuckerman. *The Transformation of the Jews.* Chicago: University of Chicago Press, 1984.

Goldstein, Sidney, and Calvin Goldscheider. *Jewish American: Three Generations in a Jewish Community.* Englewood Cliffs, NJ: Prentice-Hall, 1968.

Gordon, Milton M. *Assimilation in American Life: The Role of Race, Religion, and National Origins.* New York: Oxford University Press, 1964.

"Toward a General Theory of Racial and Ethnic Group Relations," in Nathan Glazer and Daniel P. Moynihan, eds. *Ethnicity: Theory and Practice.* Cambridge, Mass.: Harvard University Press, 1975.

Gordon, Raymond L. *Interviewing: Strategy, Techniques and Tactics.* Illinois: The Dorsey Press, 1975.

Gordon, Suzanne. *Lonely in America.* New York: Simon and Schuster, 1976.

Gorschenek, Günter and Stephan Reimers, eds. *Offene Wunden – Brennende Fragen: Juden in Deutschland von 1938 bis heute.* Frankfurt: Verlag Josef Knecht, 1989.

Gould, Julius, and William L. Kolb, eds. *Dictionary of the Social Sciences.* New York: The Free Press, 1964.

Gottlieb, Roger S. ed. *Thinking the Unthinkable: The Meanings of the Holocaust.* New York: Paulist Press, 1990.

Gottschalk, Max, and Abraham G. Duker. *Jews in the Post-War World.* New York: Dryden Press, 1944.

Gress, Franz and Hans J. Gerd. *Rechtsextremismus in der Bundesrepublik nach 1960.* Munich: PDI-Sonderheft, 1982.

Grosser, Alfred. *Germany in Our Time.* New York: Praeger Publishers, 1971.

Grossman, Kurt R. *The Jewish DP Problem.* New York: World Jewish Congress, 1951.

Grünberg, Kurt. "Folgen nationalsozialistischer Verfolgung bei Kinder von überlebenden Juden in der BRD." Masters' thesis, University of Marburg, 1983.

"Folgen nationalsozialistischer Verfolgung bei jüdischen Nachkommen Überlebender in der Bundesrepublik Deutschland." *Psyche* 41 (1987), 492–507.

Gumperz, John J. "Speech Variation and the Study of Indian Civiliza- tion." in Dell Hymes, ed., *Language in Culture and Society*. New York: Harper and Row, 1964.

Gusfield, Joseph. "Tradition and Modernity: Misplaced Polarities in the Study of Social Change." *American Journal of Sociology* 72 (1968), 351–362.

Halbwachs, Maurice. *The Collective Memory*. New York: Harper and Row, 1980.

Halperin, Irving. *Here I Am: A Jew In Today's Germany*. Philadelphia: The Westminster Press, 1966.

Handlin, Oscar. *The Uprooted*. Boston: Little, Brown and Co., 1951.

Hannan, Michael T. "The Dynamics of Ethnic Boundaries in Modern States," in H. Meyer and M. Hannan, eds. *National Development and the World System*. Chicago: The University of Chicago Press, 1979.

Hapgood, Hutchins. *The Spirit of the Ghetto*. New York: Schocken Books, 1966.

Hardtmann, Gertrud. *Spuren der Verfolgung: Seelische Auswirkungen des Holocaust auf die Opfer und ihre Kinder*. Gerlingen: Bleicher Verlag, 1992.

Hareven, Tamara. "The Search for Generational Memory," in David Dunaway and Willa Baum, eds. *Oral History*. Nashville, Tenn.: American Association for State and Local History, 1984.

Harrison, Earl J. *The Plight of the Displaced Jew in Europe*. Report to President Truman, 1945.

Hartrich, Edward. *The Fourth and Richest Reich*. New York: Macmillan Publishing Co., Inc., 1980.

Hass, Aaron. *In the Shadow of the Holocaust*. Ithaca: Cornell, 1990.

Hayes, Peter, ed. *Lessons and Legacies: The Meaning of the Holocaust in a Changing World*. Evanston, Ill.: Northwestern University Press, 1991.

Henry, Francis. *Victims and Neighbors*. South Hadley, Mass.: Bergin and Garvey Publishers, Inc., 1984.

Herbst, Ludolf. ed. *Westdeutschland und die Wiedergutmachung*. Munich: Oldenbourg Verlag, 1988.

Herman, Nancy J. "Return to Sender: Reintegrative Stigma-Manage- ment Strategies of Ex-Psychiatric Patients." *Journal of Contem- porary Ethnography* 22 (1993), 295–330.

Hermand, Jost. "Juden in der Kultur der Weimarer Republik." *Juden in der Weimarer Republik*. Stuttgart: Burg Verlag, 1986.

Hertzberg, Arthur. *Being Jewish in America*. New York: Schocken, 1979.

"Assimilation: Can the Jews Survive Their Encounter With America." *Hadassah Magazine* 65 (1983).

Judaism. New York: Simon and Schuster, 1991.

Hessisches Institut für Lehrerfortbildung. *Spuren des Faschismus in Frankfurt.* Frankfurt: Institut für Lehrerfortbildung, 1984.

Heuberger, Georg. "Judentum ohne Heimat." *Emuna Horizonte.* Cologne: Emuna-Verlags-Verein, 1970.

Hilberg, Raul. *Documents of Destruction.* Chicago: Quadrangle Books, 1971.

The Destruction of the European Jews. New York: Holmes and Meier, 1985.

Perpetrators, Victims, Bystanders: The Jewish Catastrophe 1933–1945. New York: Harper Collins, 1992.

Himmelfarb, Harold S. "Patterns of Assimilation–Identification among American Jews." *Ethnicity* 6 (1979), 249–267.

"Research on American Jewish Identity and Identification: Progress, Pitfalls, and Prospects," in Marshall Sklare, ed. *Understanding American Jewry.* New Brunswick and London: Transaction Books, 1982.

Hiscocks, Richard. *Democracy in Western Europe.* London: Oxford University Press, 1957.

Hobsbawm, Eric and Terence Ranger, eds. *The Invention of Tradition.* New York: Cambridge University Press, 1983.

Hogg, Michael. 1992. *The Social Psychology of Cohesiveness.* New York: New York University Press.

Humphreys, Laud. *Tearoom Trade: Impersonal Sex in Public Places.* Chicago: Aldine Publishing Company, 1975.

Hunter, Albert. *Symbolic Communities: The Persistence and Change of Chicago's Local Communities.* Chicago: The University of Chicago Press, 1974.

Hyman, Paula. "The Jewish Family: Looking for a Useable Past." *Congress Monthly* 42 (1975), 10–15.

Institute of Jewish Affairs of the World Jewish Congress. *West German Federal Legislature.* New York: Institute of Jewish Affairs, 1956.

European Jewry Ten Years After the War. New York: Institute of Jewish Affairs, 1956.

Isaacs, Harold. "Basic Group Identity: The Idols of the Tribe." *Ethnicity* 1 (1974), 15–41.

Idols of the Tribe: Group Identity and Political Change. New York: Harper and Row, 1975

Jacobmeyer, Wolfgang. "Jüdische Überlebende als 'Displaced Persons.' " *Geschichte und Gesellschaft* 9 (1983), 421–452.

Jasper, Willi, Bernhard Vogt, and Astrid Wirz. *Das Deutschlandbild jüdischer Einwanderer aus der GUS*. Duisberg/Potsdam, Herausgegeben von Prof. Dr. Julius H. Schoeps, 1993.

Jewish Central Information Office. *Jews in Europe Today: Two Reports by Jewish Relief Workers in Germany*. London: Jewish Central Information Office, 1945.

Jüdische Gemeinde Frankfurt am Main. *Frankfurter Jüdisches Gemeindeblatt*. Frankfurt: S. Alter Verlag, 1980–84.

Kagan, Saul, and Ernest H. Weismann. *Report on the Operations of the Jewish Restitution Successor Organization 1947–72*. JRSO, 1972.

Kanter, Rosabeth. *Men and Women of the Corporation*. New York: Basic Books, 1977.

Kapralik, C. I. *Reclaiming the Nazi Loot: The History of the Work of the Jewish Trust Corporation for Germany*. London: Sidnew Press Ltd., Bedford, 1962.

Katcher, Leo. *Post-Mortem: The Jews in Germany Today*. New York: Delacorte Press, 1961.

Kaufmann. Uri, ed. *Jüdisches Leben heute in Deutschland*. Bonn: Inter Nationes, 1993.

Kautsky, Karl. *Are the Jews a Race*. Westport, Conn.: Greenwood Press, 1926.

Kelley, Harold H, et al. *Close Relationships*. New York: W. H. Freeman and Company, 1983.

Kelman, Herbert C. *International Politics and Foreign Policy*. Edited by James Rosenau. New York and London: Free Press, 1969.

Keren Heyesod United Israel Appeal. *Israel und wir.* Frankfurt: Mendel Karger-Karin Verlag, 1966.

Kertzer, Rabbi Morris N. *What is a Jew?*. New York: Collier Books, Macmillan Publishing Company, 1993.

Kessler, Suzanne J., and Wendy McKenna. *Gender: An Ethnomethodological Approach*. New York: Wiley, 1978.

Keval, Susanna. "Jüdische Identität in der Bundesrepublik Deutschland am Beispiel autobiographischer Literatur." Master's thesis, Goethe Universität Frankfurt, 1983.

Kirschweng, Johannes. "Heimat." *Reimmichls Volkskalender*. Bozen: Athesia, 1953.

Kommission zur Erforschung der Geschichte der Frankfurter Juden.

Dokumente zur Geschichte der Frankfurter Juden 1933–1945. Frankfurt: Verlag Waldemar Kramer, 1945.

Kornblum, William. *Blue Collar Community.* Chicago: The University of Chicago Press, 1974.

Kosinski, Jerzy. *The Painted Bird.* New York: Modern Library, 1965.

Kranzler, David. *The Jewish Refugee Community of Shanghai 1938–45.* London: The Eastern Press, 1972.

Krejci, Jaroslav. *Social Structure in Divided Germany.* New York: St. Martin's Press, 1976.

Kropat, Wolf Arno. "Jüdische Gemeinden, Wiedergutmachung, Rechtsradikalismus, und Antisemitismus nach 1945," in *900 Jahre Geschichte der Juden in Hessen.* Wiesbaden: hrsg. v. d. Kommission für die Geschichte der Juden in Hessen, 1983.

Krystal. Henry, ed. *Massive Psychic Trauma.* New York: International Universities Press, 1968.

Krystal, Henry, and William G. Niederland. *Psychic Traumatization: After Effects on Individuals and Communities.* Boston: Little, Brown, and Co., 1972.

Kuschner, Doris. "Die jüdische Minderheit in der Bundesrepublik Deutschland." Ph.D. diss., University of Cologne, 1977.

Lang, Gladys E., and Kurt Lang. "Recognition and Renown: The Survival of Artistic Reputation." *American Journal of Sociology* 94 (1988), 79–109.

Langer, Lawrence. *The Holocaust and the Literary Imagination.* New Haven and London: Yale University Press, 1975.

Holocaust Testimonies. New Haven: Yale University Press, 1991.

Lazarsfeld, Paul F., and Robert Merton. "Friendship as a Social Process," in M. Berger, ed., *Freedom and Control in Modern Society.* New York: Octagon, 1954.

Lazerwitz, Bernard. "Current Jewish Intermarriages in the United States." *Papers in Jewish Demography 1977.* Jerusalem, Hebrew University: Institute of Contemporary Jewry, 1980.

Lee, Harold N. "Mead's Doctrine of the Past." *Tulane Studies in Philosophy 12* (1963).

Lenski, Gerhard E. *Power and Privilege.* New York: McGraw-Hill, 1966.

Levi, Primo. *The Drowned and the Saved.* New York: Summit Books, 1986.

Survival in Auschwitz. Trans. Stuart Woolf. New York: Collier Books, 1986 [1959].

Lewin, Kurt. *Resolving Social Conflicts.* New York: Harper, 1948.

Lieberson, Stanley, and Mary Waters. *From Many Strands.* New York: Russell Sage Foundation, 1988.

Liebow, Elliot. *Tally's Corner: A Study of Negro Streetcorner Men.* Boston: Little, Brown and Co., 1967.

Lifton, Robert J. *Nazi Doctors.* New York: Basic Books, 1987.

Lofland, John and Lyn Lofland. *Analyzing Social Settings.* Belmont: Wadsworth Publishing Company, 1971.

Lyman, Stanford M., and William A. Douglas. "Ethnicity: Strategies of Collective and Individual Impression Management." *Social Research* 40 (1973), 344–365.

Lynd, Robert, and Marrel Lynd. *Middletown: A Study in Contemporary American Culture.* New York: Harcourt, Brace and World, 1967.

Magnus, Shulamit. "German Jewish History." *Modern Judaism* 11 (1991).

Maines, David R., Noreen M. Sugrue, and Michael A. Katovich. "The Sociological Import of G. H. Mead's Theory of the Past." *American Sociological Review* 48 (1983), 161–173.

Malinowski, Bronislaw. *Argonauts of the Western Pacific.* New York: E. P. Dutton and Co., Inc., 1961.

Maor, Harry. "Über den Wiederaufbau der jüdischen Gemeinden in Deutschland seit 1945." Ph.D. diss., University of Mainz, 1961.

Margolin, Nathan. "East German Jews Don't Say Goodbye; They Silently Vanish to the West." *Look* 17 (1953), 73–74.

Mattenklott, Gert. *Über Juden in Deutschland.* Frankfurt: Jüdischer Verlag, 1993.

Mayer, John E. *Jewish–Gentile Courtship.* New York: The Free Press, 1961.

Mayhew, Leon. "Ascription in Modern Societies." *Sociological Inquiry* 38 (1968), 105–120.

McCall, George J., Michal M. McCall, Norman K. Denzin, Gerald D. Suttles, Suzanne B. Kurth. *Social Relationships.* Chicago: Aldine Publishing Co., 1970.

McCall, George J., and Simmons, J. L. *Identities and Interactions.* rev. ed. New York and London: The Free Press, 1966.

Issues in Participant Observation: A Text and Reader. Mass: Addison-Wesley, 1969.

McClaskey, Beryl R. *The History of U.S. Policy and Program in the Field of Religious Affairs Under the Office of the U.S.* High Commissioner for Germany. Office of US High Commissioner for Germany, Project No. 104, 1951.

McHugh, Peter. *Defining the Situation*. New York: The Bobbs-Merrill Company, Inc., 1968.

Mead, George Herbert. "The Nature of the Past," in John Coss, ed. *Essays in Honor of John Dewey*. New York: Henry Holt, 1929, 235–242.

The Philosophy of the Present. Chicago: Open Court Publishing Co., 1932.

The Philosophy of the Act. Chicago: University of Chicago Press, 1938.

Mead, Margaret. *Coming of Age in Samoa*. New York: William Morrow and Co., Inc., 1928.

Culture and Commitment. New York: Doubleday and Co., Inc., 1970.

Meier, Charles. *The Unmasterable Past*. Cambridge, Mass.: Harvard University Press, 1988.

Meinecke, Friedrich. *Weltbürgertum und Nationalstaat*. Munich: R. Oldenbourg, 1908.

Mendes-Flohr, Paul R., and Jehuda Reinharz, eds. *The Jew in the Modern World*. New York: Oxford University Press, 1980.

Menges, R. J. "Student–Instructor Cognitive Compatibility in the Large Lecture Class." *Journal of Personality* 37 (1969), 444–459.

Merton, Robert K. *Social Theory and Social Structure*. New York: The Free Press, 1968.

Sociological Ambivalence. New York: The Free Press, 1976.

Merton, Robert K. and Patricia Kendell. "The Focused Interview" *American Journal of Sociology* 51 (1946), 541–557.

Meyer, Alwin. *Unsere Stunde wird kommen*. Bornheim-Meron: Lamuv-Verlag, 1980.

Middleton, David, and Derek Edwards. *Collective Remembering*. London: Sage Publications, 1990.

Milgram, Stanley. *Obedience to Authority*. New York: Harper and Row, 1974.

Miller, Alice. *Das Drama der begabten Kinder*. Frankfurt: Suhrkamp Verlag, 1973.

Am Anfang war Erziehung. Frankfurt: Suhrkamp Verlag, 1980.

Du sollst nichts merken. Frankfurt: Suhrkamp Verlag, 1981.

Miller, N., D. T. Campbell, H. Twedt and E. J. O'Connell. "Similarity, Contrast, and Complementarity in Friendship Choice." *Journal of Personality and Social Psychology* 3 (1966), 3–12.

Mills, C. Wright. *The Sociological Imagination*. New York: Oxford University Press, 1959.

Mitscherlich, Margarete. *Erinnerungsarbeit: Zur Psychoanalyse der Unfähigkeit zu Trauern.* Frankfurt: Fischer Verlag, 1987.

Mitscherlich, Alexander, and Margarete Mitscherlich. *Die Unfähigkeit zu Trauern.* Munich: R. Piper. Verlag, 1967.

Montagu, Ashley. *Man's Most Dangerous Myth: The Fallacy of Race.* London: Oxford University Press, 1974 [1942].

Mosse, George. *Germans and Jews.* Detroit: Wayne State University, 1987.

Moritz, Klaus and Ernst Noam. *NS-Verbrecher vor Gericht 1945–55.* Dokumente aus hessischen Justizakten, Wiesbaden. Schriften der Kommission für die Geschichte der Juden in Hessen II, 1978.

Mourant, Arthur. E., et al. *The Genetics of the Jews.* Oxford: Clarendon Press, 1978.

Muhlen, Norbert. *The Survivors: A Report on the Jews in Germany Today.* New York: Cromwell, 1962.

Mushaben, Joyce Marie. *Identity Without a Hinterland? Continuity and Change in National Consciousness in the German Democratic Republic, 1949–1989.* Washington DC, American Institute for Contemporary German Studies, Research Report No. 3, 1993.

Nachama, Andreas, and Julius Schoeps. *Aufbau nach dem Untergang: Deutsch-Jüdische Geschichte nach 1945.* Berlin: Argon Verlag, 1992.

"Special Issue Germans and Jews." *New German Critique* 19 (1980).

"Special Issue on the German-Jewish Controversy." *New German Critique* 38 (1986).

"Special Issue on the Historikerstreit." *New German Critique* 44 (1988).

Niederland, William C. "Psychiatric Disorders among Persecution Victims: A Contribution to the Understanding of Concentration Camp Pathology and Its After Effects." *Journal of Nervous and Mental Diseases* 139 (1964), 458–474.

Nietzsche, Friedrich, "On Truth and Falsity in their Ultramoral Sense." *The Complete Works of Frederick Nietzsche.* Ed. Oscar Levy. Trans. Maximilian A. Magge. New York: Gordon, 1974 [1873].

Niewyk, Donald L. *The Jews in Weimar Germany.* Baton Rouge: Louisiana University Press, 1981.

Nyrop, Richard F. *Federal Republic of Germany.* Washington DC: Library of Congress, 1982.

Olzak, Susan, and Joanne Nagel. *Competitive Ethnic Relations.* Orlando, Florida: Academic Press, 1986.

Oppenheimer, Walter W. Jacob. *Jüdische Jugend in Deutschland.* Munich: Bronner and Daentler KG, 1967.

Ostow, Robin. *Jüdisches Leben in der DDR*. Frankfurt: Athenäum Verlag, 1988.

Packard, Vance. *A Nation of Strangers*. New York: Pocket Books, 1972.

Panahi, Badi. *Vorurteile*. Frankfurt: S. Fischer Verlag GmbH., 1980.

Park, Robert E. "Human Migration and the Marginal Man." *American Journal of Sociology* 33 (1928).

Patai, Raphael and Jennifer Patai Wing. *The Myth of the Jewish Race*. New York: Charles Scribner's Sons, 1975.

Pierson, Ruth. "German Jewish Identity in the Weimar Republic." Ph.D. diss., Yale University, 1970.

Pinson, Koppel S. "Der Antisemitismus der Nachkriegszeit," in Heinz Ganther, ed., *Die Juden in Deutschland*, Hamburg: Gala Verlag, 1953.

Plotnicov, Leonard, and Myrna Silverman. "Jewish Ethnic Signalling: Social Bonding in Contemporary American Society." *Ethnology* 17 (1978).

Porter, Jack Nusan. ed. *The Sociology of American Jews: A Critical Anthology*. Washington, DC: University Press of America, 1980.

Portes, Alejandro, "The Rise of Ethnicity: Determinants of Ethnic Perceptions among Cuban Exiles in Miami." *American Sociological Review* 49 (1984), 383–397.

Portes, Alejandro, and Robert L. Bach. *Latin Journey*. Berkeley, Calif.: University of California Press, 1985.

Powdermaker, Hortense. *Stranger and Friend: The Way of an Anthropologist*. New York: W. W. Norton and Co., 1966.

Rabinbach, Anson, and Jack Zipes, eds. *Germans and Jews Since the Holocaust: The Changing Situation in West Germany*. New York: Holmes and Meier, 1986.

Rapaport, Lynn. "The Cultural and Material Reconstruction of the Jewish Communities in the Federal Republic of Germany." *Jewish Social Studies* 49 (1987), 137–154.

Raphael, Ernest R. *Vital Statistics of the Jewish Population in the US Zone of Germany for the Year 1948*. American Joint Distribution Committee, 1948.

Reisman, John M. *Anatomy of Friendship*. New York: Irvington Publishers, 1979.

Reiss, Ira. *The Family System in America*. New York: Holt, Rinehart, and Winston, Inc., 1971.

Reitlinger, Gerald. The *Final Solution: The Attempt to Exterminate the Jews of Europe, 1939–1945*. New York: Yoseloff, 1968.

Rich, Harvey. *The Governance of the Jewish Community of Calgary*.

Jerusalem: Center for Jewish Community Studies of the Jerusalem Center for Public Affairs, Canadian Jewish Community Reports, 1974.

Richardson, Stephen, Barbara S. Dowrenwend, and D. Klein. *Interviewing, Its Forms and Functions*. New York: Basic Books, Inc., 1965.

Richarz, Monika. *Jüdisches Leben in Deutschland*. Stuttgart: Deutsche Verlags-Anstalt, 1982.

Richarz, Monika. "Jews in Today's Germanies." *Leo Baeck Institute Yearbook*, 1985.

Riesman, David. *The Lonely Crowd*. New Haven: Yale University Press, 1950.

Ringer, Benjamin B. *The Edge of Friendliness*. New York: Basic Books, 1967.

Rosen, Gladys, ed. *Jewish Life in America*. New York: Ktav, 1978.

Rosen, Klaus Henning. "Vorurteil im Verborgenen – Zum Antisemitismus in der Bundesrepublik Deutschland," in Herbert Strauss and Norbert Kempe, eds. *Antisemitismus: Von der Judenfeindschaft zum Holocaust*. Bonn: Bundeszentrale für Politische Bildung, 1984.

Rosman, Abraham, and Paula Rubel. *The Tapestry of Culture*. New York: Random House, 1985.

Roth, John K., and Michael Berenbaum, eds. *Holocaust: Religious and Philosophical Implications*. New York: Praeger, 1991.

Roth, Jürgen. *Z. B. Frankfurt: Die Zerstörung einer Stadt*. Munich: C. Bertelsmann Verlag, 1975.

Royal Institute of International Affairs. *Nationalism*. London and Edinburgh: Frank Cass and Co., Ltd., 1963.

Runge, Irene. *Vom Kommen und Bleiben: Osteuropäische jüdische Einwanderer in Berlin*. Berlin: Die Ausländerbeauftragte des Senats, 1992.

Runkel, Philip J. "Cognitive Similarity in Facilitating Communication." *Sociometry* 19 (1956), 178–191.

Sachar, Howard Morley. *The Course of Modern Jewish History*. New York: Dell Publishing Co., 1958.

Sagi, Nana. *German Reparations: A History of the Negotiations*. Jerusalem: The Magnes Press, Hebrew University, 1980.

Sallen, Herbert A. *Zum Antisemitismus in der Bundesrepublik Deutschland*. Frankfurt: Fischer Verlag GmbH., 1980.

Sartre, Jean Paul. *Anti-Semite and Jew*. New York: Schocken Books, 1970 [1948].

Saussure, Ferdinand. "Signs and Language," in *Course in General Linguistics*. New York: McGraw-Hill, 1964 [1915].

Schatzman, Leonard and Anselm Strauss. *Field Research: Strategies for a Natural Sociology*. Englewood Cliffs, NJ: Prentice-Hall, Inc., 1973.

Schermerhorn, Richard A. *Comparative Ethnic Relations*. New York: Random House, 1970.

Schmelz, U. O. "Jewish Survival: The Demographic Factors." *American Jewish Year Book* 83 (1983), 141–187.

Schneider, Richard Chaim. *Zwischen welten: Ein jüdisches Leben im heutigen Deutschland*. Munich: Kindler Verlag, 1994.

Schoeps, Julius. *Leiden an Deutschland*. Munich: R. Piper GmbH & Co., 1990.

Scholem, Gershom. *On Jews and Judaism in Crisis*. New York: Schocken Books, 1976.

Schooler, Carmi. "Serfdom's Legacy: An Ethnic Continuum." *American Journal of Sociology* 81 (1976), 1265–1286.

Schudson, Michael. "The Present in the Past versus the Past in the Present." *Communication* 11 (1989), 105–113.

Schutz, Alfred. *The Phenomenology of the Social World*. Evanston, IL: Northwestern University Press, 1967.

Schwartz, Barry. "The Social Context of Commemoration: A Study in Collective Memory." *Social Forces* 61 (1982), 374–402.

Schwartz, Barry, Yael Zerubavel, and Bernice M. Barnett. "The Recovery of Masada: A Study in Collective Memory." *The Sociological Quarterly* 27 (1986), 147–164.

Segalman, Ralph. "Jewish Identity Scales: A Report." *Jewish Social Studies* 29 (1967).

Sellenthin, Hans G. *Jüdisches Gemeindehaus Berlin 1959*. Berlin: Jüdisches Gemeindehaus, 1959.

Shapiro, Howard M. *Ethnic Identification Among American Jews*. Lanham, Maryland: University Press of America, 1993.

Shepher, Joseph. "Mate Selection Among Second Generation Kibbutz Adolescents and Adults." *Archives of Sexual Behavior* 1 (1971).

Shibutani, Tamotsu, and Kian M. Kwan. *Ethnic Stratification*. New York: Macmillan, 1965.

Shils, Edward. "Primordial, Personal, Sacred, and Civic Ties." *British Journal of Sociology* 8 (1957), 130–145.

Sichrovsky, Peter. *Wir wissen nicht was morgen wird, wir wissen wohl was gestern war*. Cologne: Verlag Kiepenheuer and Witsch, 1985.

   Schuldig geboren: Kinder aus Nazifamilien. Cologne: Verlag Kiepenheuer & Witsch, 1987.

Sievers, Leo. *Juden in Deutschland.* Hamburg: Stern-Magazin im Verlag, 1978.

Silbermann, Alphons. "Die Schwierigkeit in Deutschland Jude zu Sein." *Tribune* 3 (1964), 1276–1283.

Sind wir Antisemiten? Cologne: Verlag Wissenschaft und Politik, 1982.

Silbermann, Alphons, and Herbert Sallen. *Juden in Westdeutschland: Selbstbild und Fremdbild einer Minorität.* Cologne: Verlag Wissenschaft und Politik, 1992.

Silbermann, Alphons, and Julius Schoeps. *Antisemitismus nach dem Holocaust.* Cologne: Verlag Wissenschaft und Politik, 1986.

Silberman, Charles. "The Jewish Community in Change: Challenge to Professional Practice." *Journal of Jewish Communal Service* 58 (1981), 4–11.

Silberman, Charles. *A Certain People: American Jews and their Life Today.* New York: Summit Books, 1985.

Simmel, George. *Conflict and the Web of Group Affiliations.* Trans. K. H. Wolff and R. Bendix. New York: The Free Press, 1955.

Sklare, Marshall and Greenblum, Joseph. *Jewish Identity Marshalln the Suburban Frontier.* 2d ed. Chicago: University of Chicago Press, 1979.

Speer, Albert. *Erinnerungen.* Frankfurt: Ullstein, 1969.

Spiegelman, Art. *Maus: A Survivor's Tale.* New York: Panthean, 1986.

Spiro, Melford. *Children of the Kibbutz.* Cambridge, Mass.: Harvard University Press. New York: Schocken Books, 1969 [1958].

Stack, Carol B. *All Our Kin.* New York: Harper and Row, 1974.

Statistisches Bundesamt. *Statistisches Jahrbuch 1984.* Stuttgart: W. Kohlhammer GmbH, 1984.

Statistisches Jahrbuch 1985. Stuttgart: W. Kohlhammer GmbH., 1985.

Statistisches Jahrbuch 1986. Stuttgart: W. Kohlhammer GmbH., 1986.

Statistisches Jahrbuch deutscher Gemeinden. Cologne: Deutscher Städtetag, 1985.

Steiner, Franz. *Taboo.* Harmondsworth: Penguin, 1956.

Stern, Frank. *Am Anfang war Auschwitz, Antisemitismus und Philosemitismus in Deutschen Nachkrieg.* Gerlingen: Bleicher, 1991.

Stern, Susan. *Speaking Out.* Chicago: Atlantic-Brücke, 1995.

Stonequest, Everett V. *The Marginal Man.* New York: Charles Scribner's Sons, 1937.

Strauss, Anselm. *Mirrors and Masks: The Search for Identity.* Glencoe, Ill.: The Free Press, 1959.

Strauss, Herbert A., ed. *Der Antisemitismus der Gegenwart*. Frankfurt: Campus Verlag, 1990.

Sturtevant, William C. "Studies in Ethnoscience." *American Anthropologist* 66 (1964).

Sumner, William Graham. *Folkways*. New York: Dover Publications, Inc., 1906.

Suttles, Gerald D. *The Social Order of the Slum: Ethnicity and Territory in the Inner City*. Chicago: The University of Chicago Press, 1968.

The Social Construction of Communities. Chicago: The University of Chicago Press, 1972.

Tauber, Kurt P.. *Beyond Eagle and Swastika Vol. I and II: German Nationalism Since 1945*. Middleton, Conn.: Wesleyan University Press, 1967.

Taylor, Robert B. *Cultural Ways*. Boston: Allyn and Bacon, 1976.

Thompson, Jerry. "Jews, Zionism, and Israel: The Story of Jews in the German Democratic Republic Since 1945." Ph.D. diss., Washington State University, 1977.

Toness, Alfred. "A Notion of the Problems of the Past – With Special Reference to George Herbert Mead." *Journal of Philosophy* 24 (1932), 599–606.

Trepp, Leo. *A History of the Jewish People*. New York: Behrman House, Inc., 1962.

Triandis, H. C. "Cognitive Complexity and Interpersonal Communication in Industry." *Journal of Applied Psychology* 43 (1959), 321–326.

Turner, Victor. *The Ritual Process*. New York: Aldine Publishing Co., 1969.

Dramas, Fields and Metaphors. Ithaca and London: Cornell University Press, 1974.

Van Damm, Hendrik George. "Die Juden in Deutschland nach 1945." in *Das Judentum: Schicksal, Wesen und Gegenwart*. Wiesbaden: Böhm, Franz und Walter Dirks, 1965.

Vendryes, Joseph. *Language*. New York: Alfred Knopf, 1925.

Vidich, Arthur J., and Joseph Bensman. *Small Town in Mass Society: Class, Power and Religion in a Rural Community*. Princeton, NJ: Princeton University Press, 1968.

Vos, George de, and L. Romanucci-Ross, eds. *Ethnic Identity: Cultural Continuities and Change*. Palo Alto: Mayfield Publishing, 1975.

Wangh, Martin. "On Obstacles to the Working Through of the Nazi Holocaust Experience and on the Consequences of Failing To Do So." *Israel Journal of Psychiatry and Related Sciences* 20 (1983), 147–154.

Warhaftig, Zorach. *Uprooted: Jewish Refugees and Displaced Persons After Liberation*. New York: International Press, 1946.

Waters, Mary. *Ethnic Options*. Berkeley, CA: University of California Press, 1990.

Weber, Max. *Economy and Society*. Ed. Guenther Roth and Claus Wittich. Berkeley: University of California Press, 1978.

Weil, Frederick. "The Imperfectly Mastered Past: Anti-Semitism in West Germany Since the Holocaust." *New German Critique* 20 (1980), 135–153.

Welch, Susan. "Sampling by Referral in a Dispersed Population." *Public Opinion Quarterly* 39 (1975), 237–245.

Wertsch, James. "Collective Memory: Issues from a Sociohistorical Perspective." *The Quarterly Newsletter of the Laboratory of Comparative Human Cognition* 9 (1987), 19–22.

Wetzel, Juliane. *Jüdisches Leben in München 1945–51: Durchgangsstation oder Wiederaufbau?* Munich: Uni-Druck, MBM Band 135, 1987.

Whyte, William Foote. *Streetcorner Society: The Social Structure of an Italian Slum*. Chicago: The University of Chicago Press, 1955.

Wiesel, Elie, and Phillipe de Saint-Cheron. *Evil and Exile*. Trans. Jon Rothschild. Notre Dame: University of Notre Dame Press, 1990.

Wild, Martin Trevor. *West Germany*. Totowa, New Jersey: Barnes and Noble Books, 1980.

Wilder-Okladek, F. *The Return Movement of Jews to Austria After the Second World War*. The Hague: Martinus Nijoff Press, 1969.

Winslow, C. N. "A Study of the Extent of Agreement Between Friends' Opinions and their Ability to Estimate the Opinions of Each Other." *Journal of Social Psychology* 8 (1937), 433–442.

Wippermann, Wolfgang. *Das Leben in Frankfurt zur NS-Zeit*. Frankfurt: Verlag Dr. Waldemar Kramer HG., 1986.

Wirth, Louis. *The Ghetto*. Chicago: The University of Chicago Press, 1928.

Wolf, Christa. *Patterns of Childhood* (formerly *A Model Childhood*). Trans. Ursele Molinaro and Hedwig Rappolt. New York: Farrar, Strauss and Giroux. [Originally *Kindheitmuster*. Berlin and Weimar: Aufbau-Verlag, 1976], 1980.

Wolf, H. E. "Sozialpsychologische Untersuchung der Vorurteile gegen 'Neger' und 'Juden' bei Ober-und Volksschülern." *Kölner Zeitschrift für Soziologie und Sozialpsychologie* 4 (1959), 651–665.

Wolff, Kurt W. *The Sociology of Georg Simmel*. New York: The Free Press, 1950.

Wolffsohn, Michael. *Ewige Schuld?: 40 Jahre Deutsch-Jüdisch-Israelische Beziehungen*. Munich: Piper Verlag, 1988.

Yahil, Leni. *The Holocaust*. New York and Oxford: Oxford University Press, 1990.

Yancey, William L. et al. "The Structure of Pluralism: We're all Italian around here, aren't We?" *Ethnic and Racial Studies* 8 (1985), 94–116.

Yerushalmi, Yosef Hayim. *Zakhor*. Seattle: University of Washington Press, 1982.

Young, James E. *The Texture of Memory*. New Haven and London: Yale University Press, 1993.

Zborowski, Mark, and Elizabeth Herzog. *Life is With People*. New York: Schocken Books, 1952.

Zenner, Walter P., ed. *Persistence and Flexibility*. Albany: State University of New York Press, 1988.

Zerubavel, Eviatar. *The Fine Line*. New York: The Free Press, 1991.

Zimbardo, Philip, Craig Haney, and W. Curtis Banks. "A Pirandellian Prison," in *Psychology is Social,* ed. Edward Krupat. Greenview, Ill.: Schott, Foresman and Co., 1975.

Index

Adorno, Theodore 49, 50, 52, 61, 73
age
  of the German population 80
  of the Jewish population 189
  and marriage prospects 225–226
aggression, in Germans 52, 53–54
Ahren, Yizhak 93
Allport, Gordon 58–59
Amery, Jean 120–121
Anderson, Benedict 143
anti-Semitism 63, 161, 194
  and the German personality 51, 54
  Jewish characterization of German
    57–59, 62, 81
  Jewish experiences of 177–178
  Jewish reaction to 42, 165, 175
  in postwar Germany 36–38
  and Zionism 148
anti-Zionism 58
assimilation 14–15, 139–140
  ethnic group 85–86
  and German Jews between the wars 142
  and Jewish identity 25
  and tokenism 113
  and Zionism 151
asylum seekers, in Germany 36
authoritarian personality traits 45, 49–52,
  55

Barth, Fredrik 16, 95, 125, 250, 255
Basic Law (Germany) 45–46, 128
Beeker, Carolyn 250
Bell, Daniel 101
Bellah, Robert 46
binary opposition
  and Holocaust metaphors 66
  of Jew and German 45, 118–119, 141
  of victims and perpetrators 145

Blau, Peter 14, 224, 250, 258
Bodemann, Y. Michal 150, 256
Bolkosky, Sidney N. 86, 137
  The Distorted Image 102
Borneman, John 260
Bossmann, Dieter 33
Bourdieu, Pierre 17
Brislin, Robert 55
Broder, Henryk 34, 38, 132
Brumlik, Micha 142
Buber, Martin 86
Bubis, Ignatz 45, 94, 144, 151

Carlebach, Julius 30
Chanukah 91
children
  attitude of Germans to 61–62
  of intermarriages 219–220
  see also schoolchildren
Christianity, Jews converted to (prewar) 28
citizenship (German) 138, 144
  and commitment to the nation-state
    160–161
  and the German passport 153
civic ties 154
Cohen, Anthony 147
collective behavior, in Germany 46–47
collective consciousness, and Judaism as a
  tradition 95–100
collective memory of the Holocaust *see*
  Holocaust
collective representations, cultural
  typifications as 80
collective war responsibility, and Jewish-
  German friendships 185
communitas, and Jewish identity 104
community *see* Jewish *Gemeinde*
  (community)

community leaders, second-generation Jews
    as 34
concentration camps, Theresienstadt 28
conflict management strategies, and Jewish-
    German love relationships 241–250
conformity, in German society 47
cultural analysis 251
cultural boundaries, between Jews and
    Germans 110–112
cultural dimension of Jewish identity 105
cultural forces
    and barriers to contact 162–164
    and friendship 162–164
cultural heritage, and family history
    100–101
cultural organization, of the Jewish
    Gemeinde (community) 106–112
culture
    German 154–156
    and personality 49
Czaplicka, John 71

Dawidowicz, Lucy 53
democratic society, Jewish view of
    Germany as a 45–49
Derlega, Valerian 179
Diaspora, German Jews as a nation in 151
dietary habits, and Jewish identity 91
Diner, Dan 121, 145, 151, 256
Dischereit, Esther 116, 121
discrimination 14, 177
displaced persons (DPs) 28, 29
Doob, Leonard 131–132
double standard, of sexual morality
    233–235, 245–246
Douglas, Mary 17, 68, 75
Douglas, William A. 173
Durkheim, Emile 17, 43, 89, 99, 109, 110,
    254

Eastern Europe, Jews from 28, 29
education 111, 170
Eisenstadt, Schmuel N. 25, 86
elections, Jews voting in 129, 160
emigration
    of displaced persons (DPs) 28
    expectations of Jews 130–131, 163
    of Jews to Israel 28, 131, 150
    see also immigrants
emotional control, and Jewish-German love
    relationships 243–246
Enlightenment values, and German culture
    138, 143, 155
Erikson, Kai 111–112
ethnic boundaries 85
    further research on 260–261

and intermarriage/love relationships 209,
    224–236, 250
and Jewish identity 104–105, 253–254, 255
and Jewish moral values 98
and objective cultural features 140–141,
    152
ethnic group identification 113
ethnic identity 253–255
    see also identity; Jewish identity
ethnicity 14–19, 24–27
European Jews 142
European-Jewish mentality 84

Fackenheim, Emil 87
families
    and intermarriage 219–224
    Jewish community as extended family
        227–228
family history 100–101
Fassbinder, Rainer W. 35
Fest, Joachim 33
Filbinger, Hans 34
Fischer, Claude 112
Fitzpatrick, Kevin 250
Fleischmann, Lea 34, 118–119, 133
foreigners in Germany 36–37, 59, 138
Frankfurt 1–12
    Fritz-Bauer Institute 94
    Jewish *Gemeinde* (community) 2–4, 38,
        90–91, 107, 108
    and Israel 149–150
    Jüdische Gruppe (Jewish Group) 34–35
    population 2, 30
        Jewish 27, 28–29, 189
    preservation of Jewish ghetto 36
    reestablishment of the Jewish community
        28–30
    Westend Synagogue 2–3, 90
Friedlander, Saul, *When Memory Comes*
    23–24
friendships 84, 184–204, 257
    American compared with German
        concept of 184
    and "children of Nazis" 196–201
    and conversations 193–195
    and cultural preference patterns 192–193
    fighting parents' battles 201–203
    frequencies 188–195
    Jewish-German role relationships
        195–203
    Jewish and German networks 191–192
    Jewish networks 189–190
    and reciprocity 187
    and similarity of values 186–187
    and trust 187–188
    and "typical Germans" 186, 187

Funke, Hajo 32

Gemeinde see Jewish *Gemeinde* (community)
Gemeinschaft (community) relationships
109–110
gender
choice of mate by 207–208
and conversion to Judaism 246–247
and marital status 207
see also men; women
German
as a polluting category 54–62
symbolic meanings of the term 43–45
German Jews 128, 138–143
between the wars 142
German language 156
German mentality, and the Eastern
European mentality 84
German national identity 23
German nationalism 151
German society
Jewish adaptation to, and the Jewish
community 108
visibility of Jews in 113–115
German-Jewish identity 27
Germans
alternative meanings of 45–54
attitude to Jews 37–38
authoritarian personality traits 45, 49–52
characterizations by Jews
as anti-Semites 57–59, 62
and Jewish-German friendships
185–186
as Nazis/murderers 55–57, 62, 63, 66,
72, 79, 81, 157
as "typical Germans" 57, 59–62, 141
as xenophobic 57, 59, 62
disclosure of Jewishness to 171–178
as in-laws 220–224
Jewish attitudes towards 39–82
selective perceptions 80–82
social perception and appraisal 66–68
and Jewish identity 95, 96, 110–111
Jewish interactions with 117–118
and Jewish moral values 98–99
Jewish sexual attraction towards 228–230
Jews able to "pass" as 181–182
moral status of 40, 44–45, 49, 119–120,
141
war whereabouts of older 68–79
see also "typical Germans"
Germany
Basic Law 45–46, 128
and the concept of *Heimat* (homeland)
131–136
as a democratic society 45–49

denazification 30–32, 38, 46
Jewish identity in 104–105
numbers of Jews in 30
postwar anti-Semitism 36–38
residential permanency in 158–159
"ghetto thinking" 85
Giddens, Anthony 18
Gilman, Sander, *Jewish Self-Hatred* 115
Goethe, Johann Wolfgang von 155
Goffman, Erving 19, 66–67, 70, 75, 120,
154, 170
Gordon, Milton 14, 258
group affiliation, and Jewish identity 85–87
group boundaries
obscuring of 143–147
symbolic construction and embellishment
of 147–159
Grzelak, Janusz 179
guestworkers
and German citizenship 138
and the "xenophobic German" 59
guilt
and Jewish-German love relationships
216–217
and the Holocaust 101
war guilt 32

Halbwachs, Maurice 23, 42
Haley, Alex, *Roots* 101
health care professionals 74–75, 76–78
Heidelberg, Academy for Jewish Studies 94
Heimat (homeland), Jewish longing for 130,
131–136
Herder, Johann 131
Hitler, Adolf 32–33
holidays, Jewish 90, 91, 106–107, 220
Holocaust
collective memory of the 18, 19–24, 27,
38, 161, 252, 259, 261–262
effect on present-day lives 40–43
and ethnic distinctions 259
and intermarriage 230
and Jewish identity 100–122, 123–124,
255–257
and Jewish perceptions of Germans 80,
81
and Jewish perceptions of being
German 144–145
and Jewish-German relationships
164–165, 215–216, 217–219
and lack of religious devotion 92–93
and the moral status of Germans 40, 67
commemoration 21, 22, 71
and the concept of *Heimat* 132
cooperation of German society in the
46–47

Jewish-German exchanges 194–195
metaphors 65–66, 150–151
    and Jewish-German friendships 188
    and revealing Jewish identity 176
    taboos on Germans and Jews discussing
        68–79
Horkheimer, Max 3, 49–50

identification, and Jewish identity 89
identity
    German national identity 23
    markers of Jewishness 165–171
    positioning 146–147
    redefinition 156–159
    see also Jewish identity; national
        identity
imagined community 143
immigrants
    postwar return of Jews to Germany
        28–29
    see also emigration
"incest taboo" 227, 228
individualism
    in German society 46–47
    and national consciousness in Germany
        171
    and romantic notions of love 235–236
interethnic relations, understanding 14–19
intermarriage *see* marriage
invisible ghetto 4, 205, 227
Iran, postwar Jews in Germany from 29
Israel
    and the Academy for Jewish studies
        Heidelberg 94
    attitudes of second-generation Jews to
        134
    children raised in Kibbutz 227
    immigration of Jews to 28, 131, 150
    German attitudes to 32, 58
    Jewish financial support for 149
    Jewish identification with 32, 139, 140
    as a symbol of Jewish nationhood
        148–151
    version of the Holocaust 22
Israeli mentality 84
Israeli–Palestinian conflict 35
Italians, compared with Germans 61

Jenniger, Phillip 36
Jew–German, as a binary cultural code
        18–19
Jewish culture, and social perception and
        appraisal of Germans 68
Jewish *Gemeinde* (community)
    in Frankfurt 2–4, 38, 90–91, 107, 108,
        148–150

    and Jewish-German love relationships
        206, 210, 211, 226, 232
    interactions with Germans 117–118
    and intermarriage 259
    and Israel 148, 149–151
    and Jewish identity 123
    and lack of religious devotion 93–94
    membership 30
    as a parallel society 134
    and religious institutions 89–91, 105,
        106
    social services 108–109
    sponsored events 117
Jewish identity 24–27, 83–124
    consequences of disclosure 171–178
    and cultural boundaries 110–112
    and dress 166–167, 168–169
    and Jewish-German relationships
        257–259
    and group boundaries 143–159
    and the Holocaust in collective memory
        100–122, 123–124, 255–257
    and intermarriage 219
    and Jew as the Other 103–105
    markers of 165–171
    names 168
    negative associations of 114–116
    physical appearance of Jews 165,
        166–168
    and religion 87–91, 122
    rethinking 253–255
    as self-ascribed 85–87
    self-disclosure of 179–180
    and sense of peoplehood 95–97, 136–143
    and socializing 170–171
    as stigmatized 120–122, 124, 173, 177
    symbols of 170
    and synagogue attendance 90, 91
    and the work-place 171
"Jewish mentality" 84–85
Jewish moral values 97–100
Judaism
    meaning of, and Jewish identity 84–94
    as a tradition 95–100
justice, and Jewish values 99

Kanter, Rosabeth 113, 115
Kelman, Herbert 133, 137, 160
Keren Hayesot (Magbit) 149
Kertzer, Morris N. 99
Kessler, Suzanne 64–65
Klinger, Eric 250
Kohl, Helmut 80
Kuschner, Doris 33, 133, 142, 149

Landauer, Gustav 86, 96

landscape, and the concept of *Volk* 137–138
Lang, Michael 34, 132
language
 as collective behavior 63–64
 of metaphors 65–66
 "special language" 64
 and the symbolic construction of group
  boundaries 147
Left (German), and anti-Zionism 58
Levi, Primo, *Survival in Auschwitz* 22–23
Levinson, Pnina Nave 93–94
Lewin, Kurt 118, 184
liberalism, and German values 137
Lifton, Robert, *Nazi Doctors* 55
love relationships 205–251, 257
 casual sex 231–235
 conflict management strategies 241–250
 and crossing ethnic boundaries 224–236
 and democratic individualism 235–236
 emotional boundaries 217–219
 etiquette of 210–211, 236–237
 and guilt 216–217
 keeping secret 241–243
 and lack of social attraction to Germans
  214–215
 living together 248
 and long-term familiarity between Jews
  227–230
 and rebellion 230–231
 and self-control 243–246
 social control mechanisms over 236–241
 third-party influence on 212–214
 see also marriage
Löw-Beer, Martin 150
Luxemburg, Rosa 137
Lyman, Stanford M. 173

McCall, Michal 196
McKenna, Wendy 64–65
marital status 207
marriage
 and crossing ethnic boundaries 224–236
 homogamy 208–224
 intermarriage 9–10, 11, 207–209,
  250–251, 258–259
 and alliance with a German family
  220–224
 and conversion to Judaism 219, 220,
  246, 247
 and limited opportunity structures
  224–227
 and parental avoidance 238–241
 and raising a family 219–220
 rates 30, 207–208
 and rebellion 230–231
 and reevaluation 248–250

social control mechanisms over
  236–241
 and the Jewish faith 208–209
 and romantic notions of love 235–236
 see also love relationships
Mauss, Marcel 17
Mead, George Herbert 21
media, and collective memory of the
  Holocaust 21–22
Meinecke, Frederich 171
melting pot theories 86
memory *see* Holocaust, collective memory
men
 German, and Jewish women 228–229
 Jewish, and German women 229–230
 see also gender; women
Merton, Robert K. 60, 145
metaphors *see* Holocaust, metaphors
methodology 263–268
Middle Ages, Jews in Frankfurt 2
Middle East 194
military service, Jewish attitudes to 129–130
mind and heart, separation of 154–156
Mitscherlich, Alexander and Margarete 32
moral community, and Jewish identity
  96–97, 119
moral status
 of Germans 40, 44–45, 49, 119–120, 141
 of Jews and German lovers 247
moral values, Jewish 97–100
Moses-Mendelsohn Centre for European
  Jewry, Potsdam 94
Mosse, George 137
murderers
 Germans perceived as 56–57, 62, 63, 66,
  79, 81, 157
 and Jewish-German love relationships
  215–216
Mushaben, Joyce 131, 132
myths, and cultural identity 20

Nachmann, Werner 34
names, Jewish 168
nation-state, Jewish attitude to German
  133
national identity
 German 23
 Jewish 96
National Socialist ideology
 and the concept of *Volk* 138
 and the German personality 49, 51, 53
 and Jewish identity 103, 104, 119, 120
 and the physical appearance of Jews 166
national symbols, German, Jewish attitudes
  to 135
Nazi war criminals, prosecution of 31, 32

Nazis
    Germans perceived as 54–57, 62, 63, 66,
        72, 79
    see also National Socialist ideology
Nazism, denazification of Germany 30–32
neo-Nazis 32, 36, 54–55
    concealing Jewish identity from 183
Nietzsche, Friedrich 65

Old Testament values
    and German culture 155
    and Judaism 98–99
older Germans
    war whereabouts of 68–79, 196–201
    see also parents (of Germans)
older Jews
    attitudes to Germany 133
    see also parents (of second-generation
        Jews)
Ostow, Robin 260
Other, Jew as the 103–105

Panizza, Oskar 166
parents (of Germans)
    and Jewish-German friendships 197–201
    and Jewish-German intermarriage
        220–224
    and war guilt 32
parents (of second-generation Jews)
    attitudes to Germans 5, 7, 126, 164
    and disclosing Jewish identity 182–183
    fighting parents' battles 201–203
    and Jewish-German love relationships
        206, 210, 213, 231, 249
    and Germans as murderers 56–57
    and Jewish identity 100, 101
    and lack of religious devotion 92–93
    relationships with children 7, 8, 11
    sanctioning of children, and
        intermarriage 238–241
    strategies to manage conflict with
        241–250
    survival experiences 8–9, 16, 39, 83–84,
        125–126, 162, 205
passport, variable meaning of the 152–154
Peck, Jeffrey 260
peoplehood, Jewish sense of 95–97,
        136–143, 150
personality traits, in Germans 45, 47, 49–54
philo-Semitism 58–59, 62, 63, 127
    Jewish experiences of 177–178
    Jewish reactions to 165
physical characteristics
    and Jewish-German love relationships
        214–215
    of Jews 165, 166–168

Plato 20
political culture 130, 161
political integration 129, 159–161
pollution beliefs
    and Jewish characterizations of Germans
        43–45, 49, 54–62, 85, 107
    and Jewish perceptions of being German
        144–145, 155
    and moral values 68
power, ethnicity as 14
prejudice, and discrimination 177
preventive deception, by older Germans 71
primordial ties 154
professional relationships, between Jews
    and older Germans 74–75
public/private dichotomy, and the
    demarcation of ethnic boundaries
        154–156
purity/impurity
    and cultural distinctions 17, 18
    see also pollution beliefs

Rabinbach, Anson 134
racism
    and the German authoritarian
        personality 51
    see also anti-Semitism
Ranger, Terence 21
rebellion, intermarriage as 230–231
Reiss, Ira 217
religion
    and Jewish identity 87–94, 122, 257
        lack of devotion 92–94
        rituals in the home 91
    observance of religious holidays 90, 91,
        106–107, 220
    synagogue attendance 90, 91, 106
religious education in Germany 111, 170
right-wing extremist groups 36–37
role relationships (Jewish-German) 195–203
Rosh Hashonah 90, 107
Rubin, Zick, 217
Russian immigrants in Germany 29, 30
    and Jewish identity 94

sacramentalism, Jewish 89, 91
sacred and profane spheres, in Jewish
    culture 85
Sallen, Herbert 159–160, 256
Sartre, Jean-Paul 25, 86, 129
Saussure, Ferdinand de 63–64
Schneider, Richard Chaim 115, 133
Schoeps, Julius 151
schoolchildren
    experiences of Jewish 172
    Jewish-German friendships 190

schoolchildren (*cont.*)
knowledge of Hitler and the Third Reich 33
Second World War
collective responsibility for, and Jewish-German friendships 185
and Jewish population in Frankfurt 27–28
reconstructing Jewish life after 28–30
war guilt 32
whereabouts of older Germans 68–79
and Jewish-German friendships 196–201
secularization 257
self-control, and Jewish-German love relationships 243–246
self-transformation, by older Germans 71
Seligmann, Rafael 148
sexual morality, double standard of 233–235, 245–246
sexual relationships
between Jews 245–246
between Jews and Germans 228–230
casual sex 231–235
Shapiro, Harold M. 89, 97
shiva (Jewish mourning ritual) 121–122, 239
Silbermann, Alphons 34, 159–160, 256
Simmel, Georg 112, 197
The Web of Group Affiliations 85
Sklare, Marshall 89, 91
social networks 178, 238
social services, and the Jewish *Gemeinde* (community) 108–109
socializing, and Jewish identity 170–171
sociological ambivalence 145
Soviet Union, postwar Jews in Germany from 29
"speech community" 147
Jews as a 64
Speer, Albert 32
Spiro, Melford, *Children of the Kibbutz* 227
status, and Jewish identity 165
Steiner, Franz 74
Stonequest, Everett 115
structural boundaries, and Jewish identity 114–115
structural dimension of Jewish identity 105
structuralist approaches to ethnicity 14, 15, 19, 251
"survivors guilt" 151
Suttles, Gerald 197
symbolic community, ethnicity as 16–17
symbols, ethnic, and Jewish identity 25
symbolic meanings, of the term "German" 43–45
synagogue attendance 90, 91, 106
Szajak, Stefan 29–30, 38, 90

Szobel, Rabbi 90

Third Reich, compared with the Federal Republic of Germany 45
Thomas, William I. 42, 67
tokenism 112–114, 116
transformationalism, and Jewish identity 25, 26
Trotsky, Leon 137
Turner, Victor 43, 78, 104, 119
"typical Germans"
and Jewish-German friendships 186, 187
and intermarriage 221, 247
Jewish characterization of 57, 59–62, 141
negative responses to Jewishness 179
rationally motivated behaviour of 62–63

United States
and the Academy for Jewish Studies Heidelberg 94
Americans and friendship 184
immigration of Jews to 28
German Jews in 5, 6
and the Holocaust in collective memory 123
Jewish identity 89, 97, 139
mobility in society 178
universities 31

values, Jewish 97–100
Vendryes, Joseph 64
visibility of Jewishness 165–171
Volk
concept of 137–138, 142
redefined by Jews 157–158
voting 129, 160

war guilt, and Jewish perception of Germans 81
Wasserman, Jakob 146
Waters, Mary, *Ethnic Options* 167
Weber, Max 42–43, 255
Wiesel, Elie 22, 23
Wirth, Louis, *The Ghetto* 85
WIZO (Women's International Zionist Organization) 149
Wolffsohn, Michael 139, 256
women
German, and Jewish men 229–235
intermarriage of Jewish 246–247
Jewish
and German men 228–229
marriage prospects of 225–227
see also gender; men
work-place, and Jewish identity 171
Wyler, Bea 94

xenophobic German
as emotionally driven 63
Jewish characterization of 57, 59, 62

Yom Kippur 90, 91, 107
young people
and the concept of *Volk* 138
and the Jewish *Gemeinde* (community) 109
and Zionism 150

Zentralrat 30, 33, 34, 94, 133

Zerubavel, Eviatar 128
The Seven Day Circle 190–191
Zimbardo, Philip 55
Zionism 140, 149, 151
and anti-Semitism 148
and German Jews between the wars
142
Zionistic Youth Group 131
ZJD (*Zionistische Jugend Deutschlands*)
150
Znaniecki, Florian 104